STREET ATLAS

North Hampshire

PHILIP'S

First edition published 1994
First colour edition published 1998 by

Ordnance Survey®   and   George Philip Ltd
Romsey Road   an imprint of Reed Consumer Books Ltd
Maybush   Michelin House, 81 Fulham Road,
Southampton   London SW3 6RB
SO16 4GU   and Auckland and Melbourne

ISBN 0-540-07473-X (pocket edition)

Printed and bound in Spain by Cayfosa

Digital Data

The exceptionally high-quality mapping
found in this book is available as digital
data in TIFF format, which is easily
convertible to other bit-mapped (raster)
image formats.

The index is also available in digital
form as a standard database table. It
contains all the details found in the
printed index together with the National
Grid reference for the map square in
which each entry is named and feature
codes for places of interest in eight
categories such as education and
health.

For further information and to discuss
your requirements, please contact the
Ordnance Survey Solutions Centre on
01703 792929.

(22a)	**Motorway** (with junction number)
	Primary route (dual carriageway and single)
	A road (dual carriageway and single)
	B road (dual carriageway and single)
	Minor road (dual carriageway and single)
	Other minor road
– – –	**Road under construction**
	Pedestrianised area
	Railway
	Tramway, miniature railway
	Rural track, private road or narrow road in urban area
	Gate or obstruction to traffic (restrictions may not apply at all times or to all vehicles)
– – – – –	**Path, bridleway, byway open to all traffic, road used as a public path**
	The representation in this atlas of a road, track or path is no evidence of the existence of a right of way
48 / **106**	**Adjoining page indicators**

⇌	**British Rail station**
⊖	**Underground station**
D	**Docklands Light Railway station**
🚂	**Private railway station**
⬤	**Bus, coach station**
◆	**Ambulance station**
◆	**Coastguard station**
◆	**Fire station**
◆	**Police station**
✚	**Accident and Emergency entrance to hospital**
H	**Hospital**
+	**Church, place of worship**
i	**Information centre** (open all year)
P	**Parking**
PO	**Post Office**
Prim Sch	**Important buildings, schools, colleges, universities and hospitals**
– ∙ – ∙ –	**County and unitary authority boundaries**
River Medway	**Water name**
	Stream
	River or canal (minor and major)
	Water
	Tidal water
	Woods
	Houses
House	**Non-Roman antiquity**
VILLA	**Roman antiquity**

Acad	**Academy**	Mon	**Monument**
Cemy	**Cemetery**	Mus	**Museum**
C Ctr	**Civic Centre**	Obsy	**Observatory**
CH	**Club House**	Pal	**Royal Palace**
Coll	**College**	PH	**Public House**
Ent	**Enterprise**	Recn Gd	**Recreation Ground**
Ex H	**Exhibition Hall**	Resr	**Reservoir**
Ind Est	**Industrial Estate**	Ret Pk	**Retail Park**
Inst	**Institute**	Sch	**School**
Ct	**Law Court**	Sh Ctr	**Shopping Centre**
L Ctr	**Leisure Centre**	Sta	**Station**
LC	**Level Crossing**	TH	**Town Hall/House**
Liby	**Library**	Trad Est	**Trading Estate**
Mkt	**Market**	Univ	**University**
Meml	**Memorial**	YH	**Youth Hostel**

■ The dark grey border on the inside edge of some pages indicates that the mapping does not continue onto the adjacent page

■ The small numbers around the edges of the maps identify the 1 kilometre National Grid lines

The scale of the maps is 3.92 cm to 1 km
(2½ inches to 1 mile)

0	¼	½	¾	1 mile
0	250m	500m	750m	1 kilometre

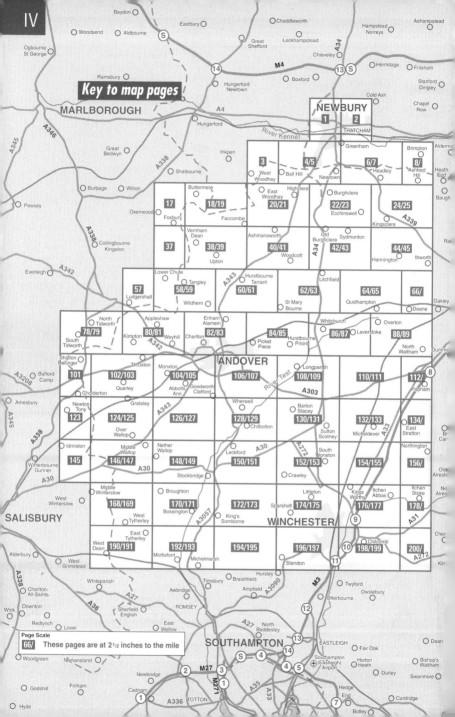

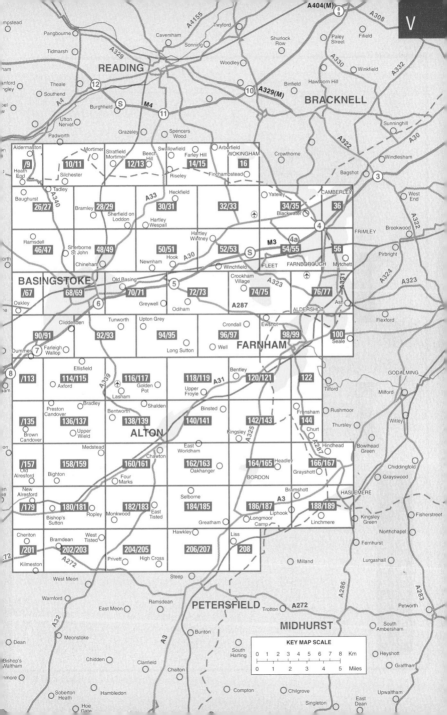

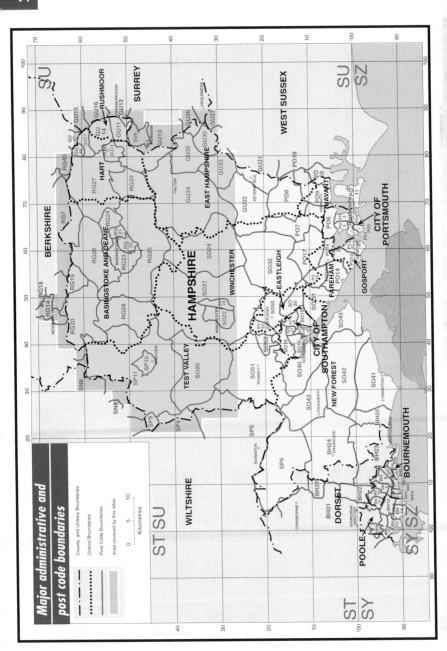

Major administrative and post code boundaries

County and Unitary Boundaries

District Boundaries

Post Code Boundaries

Area covered by this atlas

0   5   10
Kilometres

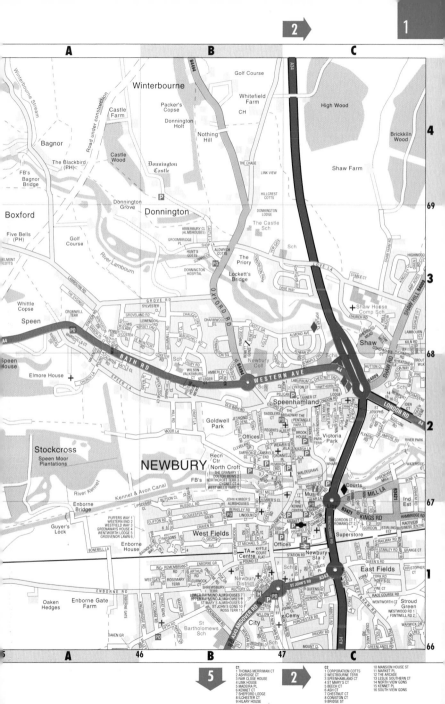

A   B   C

Winterbourne

Golf Course

Packer's
Copse

Whitefield
Farm
CH

High Wood

Castle
Farm

Donnington
Holt

Brickkiln
Wood

4

Bagnor

Nothing
Hill

The Blackbird
(PH)

Castle
Wood

Donnington
Castle

Shaw Farm

FB's
Bagnor
Bridge

P
Donnington
Grove

Donnington

69

Boxford

Five Bells
(PH)

Golf
Course

ABBERBURY CL
(ALMSHOUSES)

The Castle
Sch

DONNINGTON
LODGE

BELMONT
COTTS

River Lambourn

HUNT'S
COTTS

ALDWYCH
CLO

The Priory

Lockett's
Bridge

Sch

3

Whittle
Green

DONNINGTON
HOSPITAL

Shaw House
Comp Sch

STABLE CT

HIGHWOOD

Speen

Sch

Shaw

68

Speen
House

Elmore House

Newbury
Coll

Schs

WESTERN AVE

Speenhamland

LONDON RD

2

Stockcross

Speen Moor
Plantations

Goldwell
Park

Offices

Victoria
Park

RIVER PARK RD

River Kennet

NEWBURY

Recn
Ctr
North Croft

FB's

Kennet & Avon Canal

Courts

Mus

MILL LA

Ind
Est

67

Enborne
Bridge

Guyer's
Lock

West Fields

Offices

Superstore

Newbury
Sta

Kings Rd

RACEVIEW
BUSINESS CENTRE

1

Enborne Gate
Farm

Enborne
House

TA
Centre

Newbury
District

H P

St John's
City

St
Bartholomews
Sch

Cemy

East Fields

Stroud
Green

Oaken
Hedges

ENBORNE RD

66

5   A   46   B   47   C

Ct
1 THOMAS MERRIMAN CT
2 ASHRIDGE CT
3 FAIR CLOSE HOUSE
4 LINK HOUSE
5 MADEIRA PL
6 KENNET CT
7 SHEFORD LODGE
8 ILCHESTER CT
9 HILARY HOUSE

Ct
1 CORPORATION COTTS
2 WESTBOURNE TERR
3 SPEENHAMLAND CT
4 ST MARY'S CT
5 BEECH CT
6 ASH CT
7 CHESTNUT CT
8 CONISTON CT
9 BRIDGE ST

10 MANSION HOUSE ST
11 MARKET PL
12 THE ARCADE
13 LESLIE SOUTHERN CT
14 NORTH VIEW GDNS
15 KENNET PL
16 SOUTH VIEW GDNS

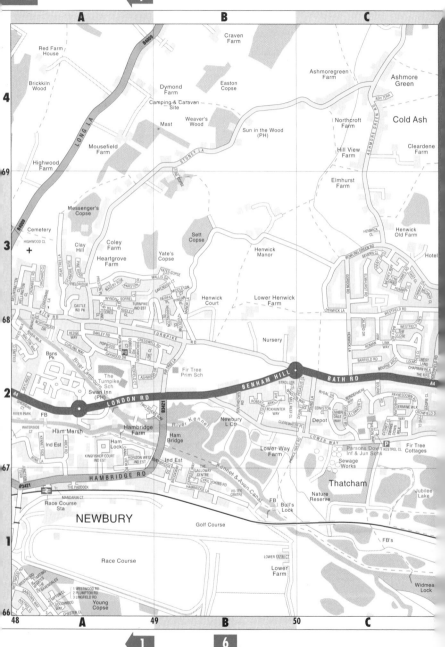

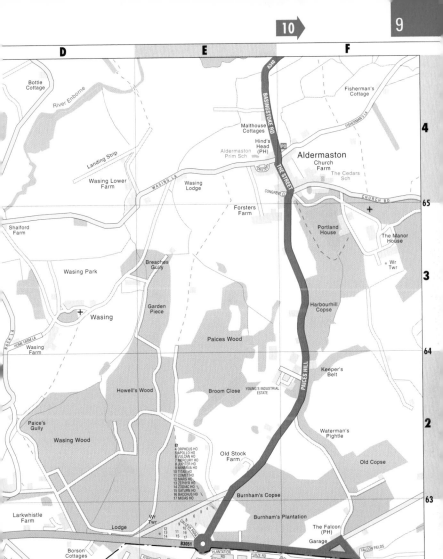

A B C

4

Aqua Vitae Copse

Upper Church Farm

Upper Lodge Farm

The Old Rectory

Ufton Park

Brent's Gully

Padworth

Padworth Gully

Springhill Farm

Wrays Farm

The Croft

SILVER LA

RECTORY RD

MAY'S LA

RAMPTING LA

65

SPRING LA

CHURCH RD

Hatch Farm House

The Round Oak (PH)

BLOCK COTTS

The Birches

Court Farm

Padworth Common

RECTORY HILL

RAGHILL

Raghill Farm

3

Aldermaston Park

Black Pightle

Old Warren

Burnt Common

Budd's Firs

HILL LA

WELSHMAN'S RD

64

Little Heath

VALENTINE WOOD IND EST

Fox Hill

2

Decoy Pond

Alders Slade

Benyon's Inclosure

Pond Farm

CHAPEL LANE

SOKE RD

Aldermaston Soke

Hungry Hill

Park Farm

Upper Moor's Gully

63

SPRINGFIELD LA

Soke Pig Farm

Catthaw Lands Copse

White House Farm

Catthawlands Farm

1

PELICAN RD

WAKEFORD CL

SILCHESTER RD

KINGS RD

Tadley Court

SPENDER CL

HOLLY GR

WAKEFORD CL

KNOLLYS RD

SCHOOL LA

Silchester CE Prim Sch

Mus

STACEY'S IND EST

PH

SPRINGFIELD RD

ESSEX CL

Silchester

Calleva Arms (PH)

Tadley Common

CHURCH RD

VALLEY WAY

THOMAS GATE

Pamber Heath

Silchester Common

BROADWAY

PAMBER RD

WESTLYN RD

LASTLYN RD

THE GLEN

LITTLE LONDON RD

ROMANS FIELD

BLAKES LA

CONGLANDS

ARNEWOOD AVE

HEATH RD

BURNEY BIT

WHISTLER LA

ROMANS RD

BRAMLEY RD

2

60 A 61 B 62 C

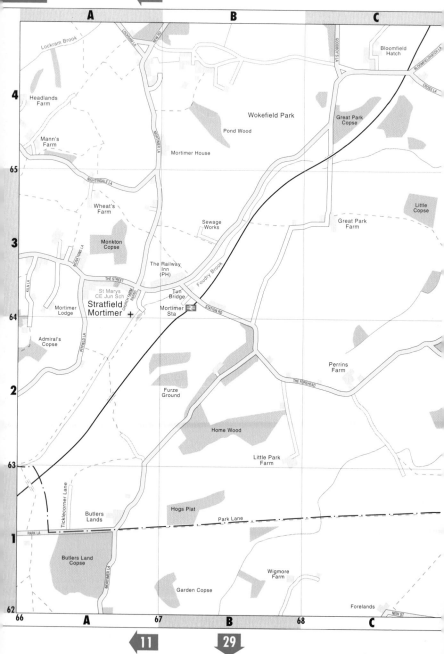

Lockram Brook

Bloomfield
Hatch

Headlands
Farm

Wokefield Park

Great Park
Copse

Mann's
Farm

Pond Wood

Mortimer House

Little
Copse

Wheat's
Farm

Great Park
Farm

Monkton
Copse

Sewage
Works

The Railway
Inn
(PH)

Foudry Brook

St Marys
CE Jun Sch

Tun
Bridge

Stratfield
Mortimer

Mortimer
Sta

Mortimer
Lodge

Admiral's
Copse

Perrins
Farm

Furze
Ground

THE FOREHEAD

Home Wood

Little Park
Farm

Ticklecorner Lane

Butlers
Lands

Hogs Plat

Park Lane

PARK LA

Butlers Land
Copse

Wigmore
Farm

Garden Copse

Forelands

NEW ST

Clappers Farm
Missels Bridge
Brook Farm
Reid's Bridge
Foudry Brook
Crosslane Farm
CROSS LA
BEECH HILL RD
Woodcock Lane
Beech Hill Coverts
Wood Lane
White House Farm
May's Hill
Caravan Site
Loddon Court Farm
Shinfield
BASINGSTOKE RD
B3349
Lamb's Lane Prim Sch
BACK LA
Lamb's Farm
LAMB'S LA

4
65

Home Farm
Trunkwell Farm
Trunkwell House
+
WOOD LA
VACK HILL RD
PARK VIEW
Beech Hill
Old Elm Tree (PH)
Beech Hill House
Priory Copse
Priory Farm
Meat
The Priory
Priory Farm
Loddon Court
BARGE LA
SPRING LA
THEOBALDS HILL
King's Bridge
Handpost Farm
Goddard's Farm
BASINGSTOKE RD
B3349

3
64

River Loddon
Cannon Bridge
TROWE'S LA
BROAD HWY
Stanford End Farm
BARGE LA
Great Hills Farm
Chequers
Stanford End
Newbarn House
New Barn Farm
BULL LA
Highgrove Copse
SPRING LA
Taylor's Lane
Collins Copse
St Leger's Copse
BULL LA

2
63

Fair Cross
Home Farm
CHEQUER LA
Lake Pond
Stanfordend Bridge
Stratfield Saye Park
Stone Bridge
WELSH LA
Park Corner Farm
Top Hill Copse
BASINGSTOKE RD
A33
B3349

1
62

Lower Tumbling Bay

River Loddon

Sheepbridge Court Farm

Great Wood

Swallowfield Park

Kilnclose Pond

Sheep Bridge

BUTTS LA

Tanner's Farm

Wokingham La

SWALLOWFIELD RD

New Plantation

Great Copse

RG'S HILL

COPSE RD

Wyvols Court

Cuckoo Pen

George & Dragon (PH)

SWALLOWFIELD RD

BASINGSTOKE RD

THE STREET

VILLA PL

HOLLYBUSH LA

RISES RD

PH

P

THE STREET

Swallowfield

THE NAYLORS

BROOKSIDE BSNS CTR

CHURCH RD

Salter's Bridge (FB)

Rowe's Farm

RUNGLER'S HILL

Raggett's La

Clarkes Farm

CHARLTON LA

TROWE'S LA

Blackwater River

Cemetery

NUTBEAN LA

Fir Grove

Chill Hill

Dacre Farm

WHITE'S LA

The Boathatter

B3349

Springalls Farm

Yew Tree Farm

Riseley Farm

PART LA

Wheelers Farm

Sandpit Farm

FORD LA

Wheeler's Copse

Glasspool Farm

Bottom Farm House

BASINGSTOKE RD

BULL LA

LODDON LA

Riseley Gorse Farm

Riseley

HALPIN HO

Walnut Tree Farm

BENGALS LA

SCHOOL RD

SCHOOL LA

Thatcher's or Little Ford

WELL HOUSE LA

CHAPEL LA

BUSTE WAY

B3349

ODIHAM RD

P

Mus

Ham's Wood

River Whitewater

Cordery's Farm

Pound Copse

Birchen Copse

Camp Site

Riseley Mill

Bramshill Plantation

FORD LA

Wellington Country Park

Mill Wood

Hall's Farm

B3349

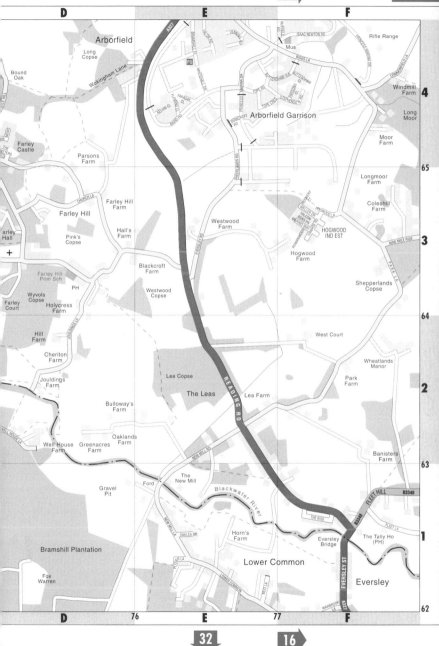

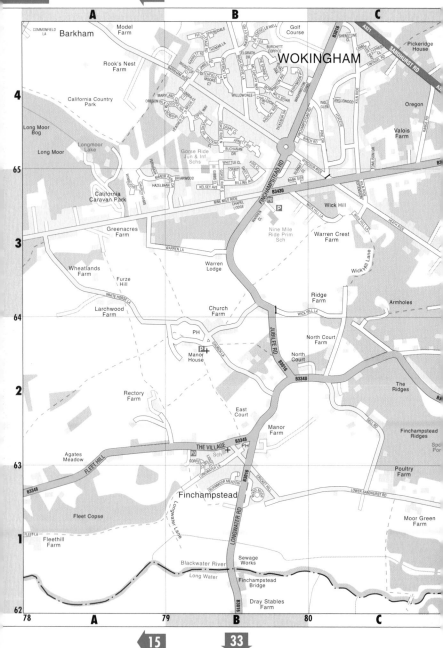

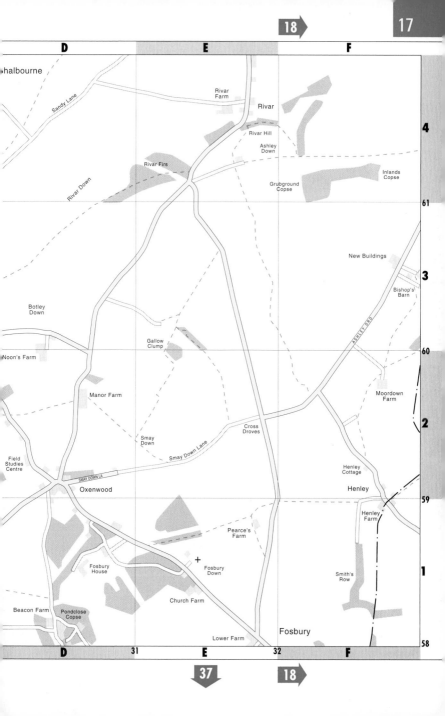

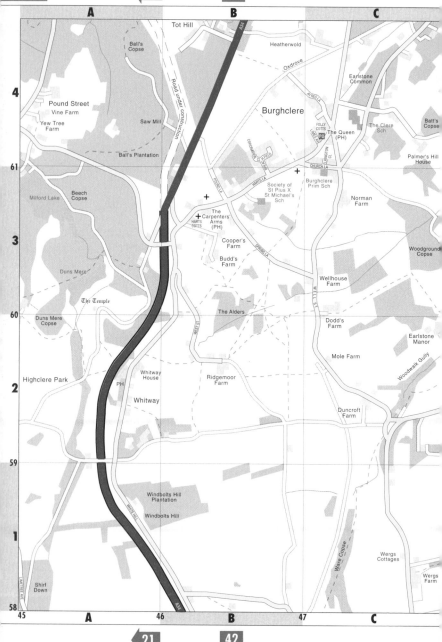

Tot Hill

Heatherwold

Oxdrove

Earlstone
Common

Burghclere

The Queen
(PH)

The Clere
Sch

Batt's
Copse

Pound Street

Vine Farm

Yew Tree
Farm

Saw Mill

FOLLY
COTTS

Palmer's Hill
House

Ball's Plantation

Society of
St Pius X
St Michael's
Sch

Burghclere
Prim Sch

Milford Lake

Beech
Copse

The Carpenters'
Arms
(PH)

Norman
Farm

Woodground
Copse

HARTS
COTTS

Cooper's
Farm

Budd's
Farm

Wellhouse
Farm

Duns Mere

The Temple

The Alders

Dodd's
Farm

Earlstone
Manor

Duns Mere
Copse

Mole Farm

Woodwalk Gully

Highclere Park

PH

Whitway
House

Ridgemoor
Farm

Whitway

Duncroft
Farm

Windbolts Hill
Plantation

Windbolts Hill

Wergs
Cottages

Wergs
Farm

Shirf
Down

Road under construction

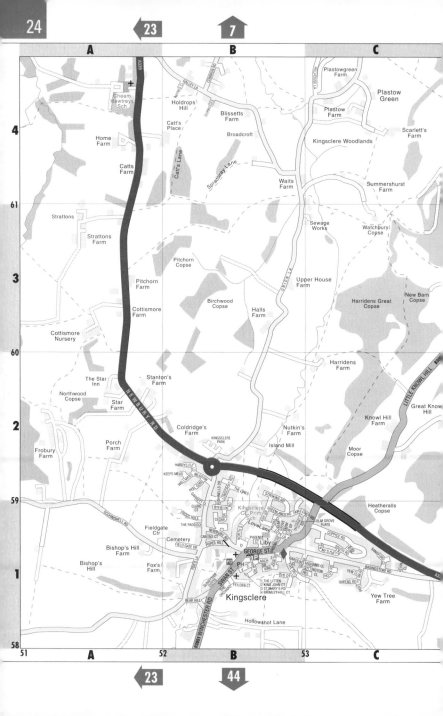

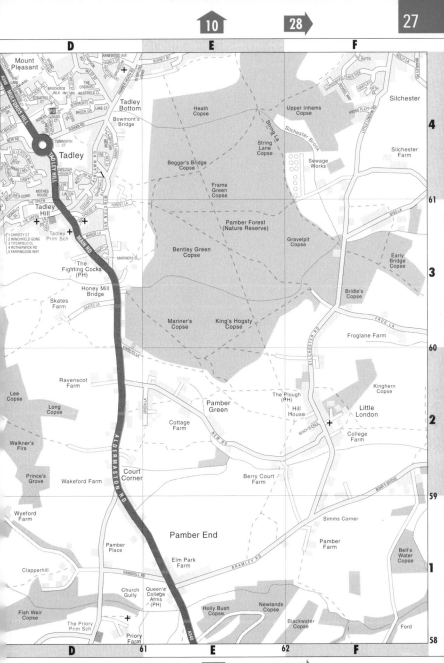

27
11

A **B** **C**

Greenlands Farm
Dicker's Copse
Dicker's Farm

North Copse

Haskers Farm

Great Scrub Copse

Ford

Brickledon's Farm

Church Lane Farm

Clapper's Farm

4

Brook Farm
Pound Farm

Lower Farm

Three Ashes

BRAMLEY RD

Park Copse

CHURCH LA

CLAPPERS FARM RD

61

Silchester

Halls Farm

3

Haines Farm

Davnage Copse

Withy Copse

Barefoot House

AYN LA

Latchmere Green

Latchmere Green Farm

FROG LA

60

Holly Cross Farm

HOLLY CROSS

Latchmore Farm

Bramley Frith Wood

MANCHESTER LA

MOAT CL

BRAMLEY CE Prim Sch

Bramley

2

Bramley Corner Farm

Stock's Farm

PH

LC

PO

BRAMLEY LA

Bramley Corner

Bramley Sta
P

IBBS MEADOW

Boar's Bridge

Park Gate Farm

SILCHESTER RD

Middle Farm

THE STREET

Church Farm

CHURCH LANE

THE STABLES

59

Tudor Farm

Middle Lodge

The Honey Farm

Street Farm

King's Copse

Park Copse

1

Beaurepaire Park

Beaurepaire Mill Bridge

Lock's Bridge

TYFE RD

GERMANS LA

Bow Brook

Beaurepaire House

Watford Copse

58

63 **A** **64** **B** **65** **C**

27
48

Parson's Farm

Dollery's Farm

Lavell's Farm

LAVELL'S LA

THE SPRINGS

The Four Horse Shoes (PH)

GREEN LA

West End Green

New Inn (PH)

NINE ST

Stratfield Saye

Herriot's Farm

4

MORTIMER LA

FAIR OAK LA

King's Farm

61

Purdue's Farm

Ives Farm

Fair Oak Green

3

STRATFIELD SAYE RD

Southend Farm

Heywood's Farm

OLIVER'S LA

Pizzie Green

60

Oliver's Farm

FOLLY LA

Ladyland Copse

Tubbs Copse

MILL LA

+

Folly Farm

River Loddon

The Fishery

2

POTTERS LA

Lillymill Farm

Bramley Green

Green Farm

Newhouse Farm

59

A33

LANE END

HERRIDGE CL 1
THORNTON CL 2
BARTLETT CL 3
ILUNGWORTH CL 4
THE LIMES 5
DEERFIELD CT 6
ST MARY'S CT 7

Sherfield Rd

CLIFTON RD

FORGE

BRAMLEY GREEN RD

CAMPBELL

CAMPBELL

DONALDS

ST BARBARA'S

WOODLAND DR

THE MEWS

HARTLEY LA

Flood's Farm

1

BRAMLEY RD

GERMAN RD

OFFICERS ROW

BULLSDOWN RD

LC LC

Sewage Works

THE CHESTNUTS

NORTHFIELD

LONGBRIDGE RD

Long Bridge

Longbridge Mill

Hartley Wood Common

Bow Bridge

Sherfield Green

BULLSDOWN CL

CARPENTERS

WILLOW RD

WILLOW LA

HOLLY LA

GREENWAY

BRAMLEY RD

MILL LA

WESTON

PLOUGH RD

A33

Sherfield on Loddon

Sherfield Farm

Bull's Down Copse

P

58

A
B
C

Bramshill
Plantation

St Neot's
Sch

Warbrook
(Con Ctr)

EVERSLE

Warren
Farm

4

Yalden's
Farm

Church
Farm

61

Refuse
Tip

Moor Place
Farm

Heath
Warren

Cudbury Clump

3

Peatmoor
Copse

60

The Welsh Drive

Bramshill Park

Warren Heath

2

Bramshill House
(Police Coll)

Sir Richard's Drive

Deer Park   Long
Water

High Bridge

Birch
Bottom

Sand &
Gravel P

59

Chalwin's
Copse

Hazeley
Heath

Crabtree Copse

1

Crabtree
Lodge

Hulford's Copse

Warren Hill Plantation

Purdies Farm

Warren Hill
Farm

STAR HILL

Star
Hill

Hatts
Cottage

Hazeley
Heath

SPRINGWELL LA

HULFORDS LA

58

75

A

76

B

77

C

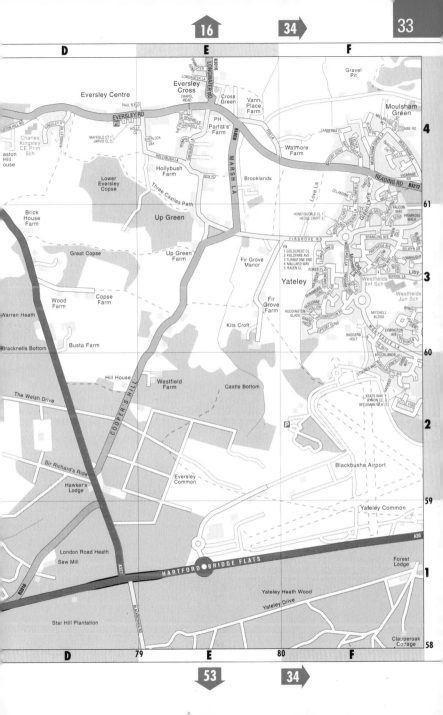

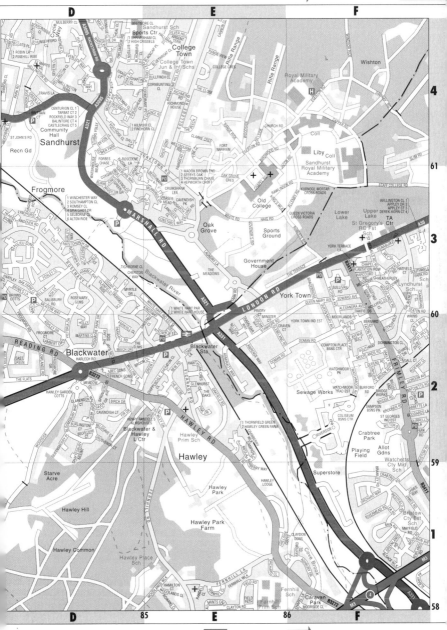

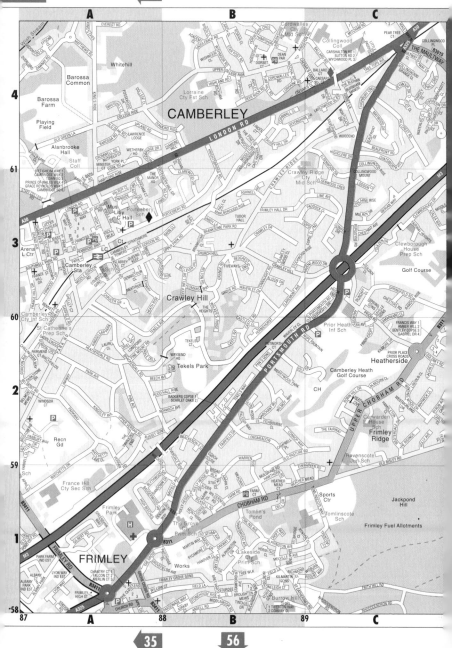

D

E

F

4

Maccombe
Bottom

Bulpit's
Copse

Bushy
Leaze

Round
Hill

Tummer
Copse

Saw
Mill

TIDBALL LA

Newfield
Copse

East Down

Coneygre
Copse

Hollygres
Plantation

Oakhill Wood

57

Fosbury
Farm

The Slay

Haydown Hill

Knolls Down
Fosbury

3

Warren
Cottages

Hippenscombe

Hippenscombe Bottom

Conholt Bottom

CONHOLT HILL

56

2

Cleves
Copse

Little Down

Chute Causeway

Conholt
Farm

Middle
Conholt
Farm

55

Conholt
House

New Barn

DUMMER LA

Breach Lane

Mafeking
Clump

Conholt Park

1

Bottomhalves
Copse

HEDGEHOG LA

Main Place
Row

Hampshire
Gate

Cathanger
Wood

54

50

D

31

E

32

F

D
E
F

4

57

3

56

2

55

1

54

Manor Farm

Netherton

Green Lane

Test Way

Heaven Hill

Rymer's Barn

Faccombe Wood

Wilster Copse

Sawyers Wood

Netherton Bottom

Netherton Hanging Copse

Day's Copse

Clinchorn Farm

Test Way

Cockley's Copse

Parsonage Farm

Upton

River Swift

Soper's Farm

Ambley Farm

The Warren

Ambley Wood

Ford

Upton Valley

DRANE LANE 5 YARD

Fairway

Ppg Sta

Spring Row

Test Way

A343

A

B

C

4

57

3

56

2

55

1

54

PH

Robins
Croft
Copse

Privet Copse

Manor
Farm

Woodhay
Poor

The Isle

The Plough
(PH)

Ashmansworth

Bartlett's
Down

HIGHFIELD

London Lane

Spencefield
Copse

Steeles
Farm

PO

Hall Lane

Codley
Copse

Hipple La

Kimmer Farm

Alexander
Farm

Church
Farm

The
Bushes

Lower
Manor
Farm

Faccombe Wood

Sidley
Wood

Ten
Acre
Brow

Sidley
Bottom

Doyley
Manor

DOILEY HILL

P

Lye
Copses

Doyley Manor
Farm

Esseborne
Manor
(Hotel)

Lye
Farm

Doiley Hill
Farm

Doiley
Wood

DOILEY BOTTOM

Splatts
Copse

Sladen
Green
Farm

Lo
Co

A343

Lower
Doiley
Farm

Sladen
Green

D   **E**   **F**

Ox Drove

Old
Lodge
Ray
Piece

Sidown Hill

Sidown Glades

4

Keepers
Cottage

Three Legs
House
Charters
Farm

Grotto
Copse

Highclere
Stud

Redhill
Plantation

Field
House

57

Crux Easton
Farm

Bigg's
Copse

Wayfarer's Wlk

Mopper's
Barn

Rabbit
Warren

Sidown
Range

Manor
House

3

Crux
Easton

Upper
Woodcott
Down

The
Kennels

Crux Easton
House

56

Beech
Hanger
Copse

Hook Copse

2

Charlie's
Wood

Hook
Farm

55

Hall
Cottage

Easton Park
Wood

Woodcott

Lower
Woodcott
Farm

Upper
Woodcott
Farm

1

Danegrove
Copse

Woodcott
House

Highfield
House

Paul's
Copse

Stubb's
Copse

Suggeaston
Copse

54

D   43   **E**   44   **F**

RED HILL

A343

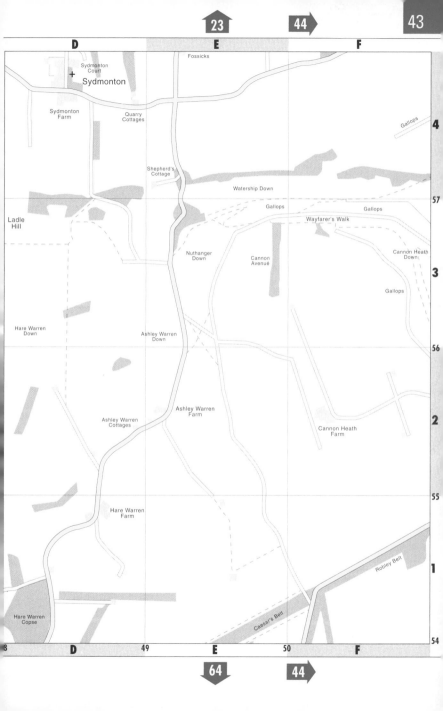

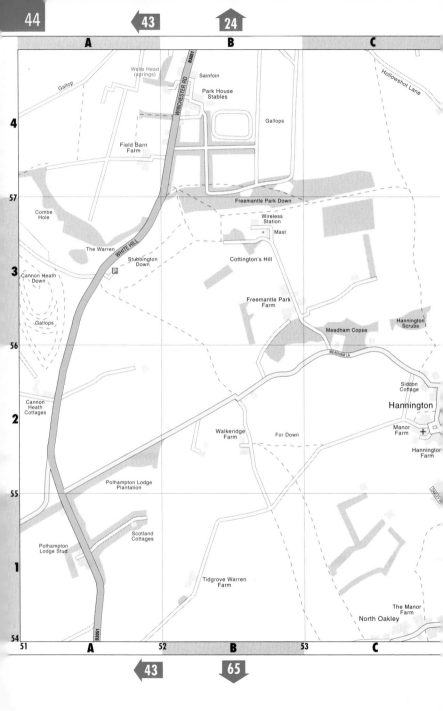

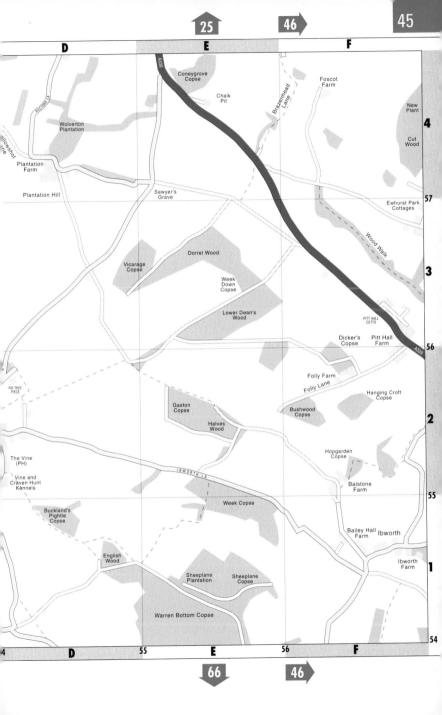

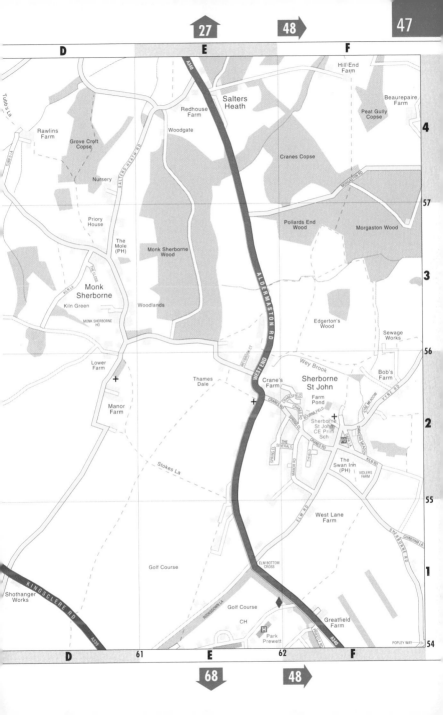

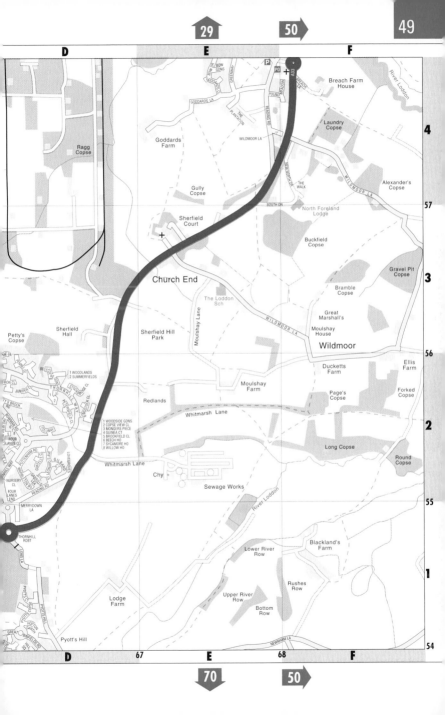

A   B   C

4

Topford
Cottage

Webb's
Hill

Kilnclose
Copse

Hall's Lane

Peter's
Copse

Webb's
Copse

Lower Home
Copse

Cooper's
Farm

Poplars
Farm

Upper Home
Copse

Allen Mo

ROTHERWICK LA

Hays
Farm

Allenmoor Lane

Mill
Farm

Cooper's
Copse

The Fox
(PH)

Lyde Green
Farm

57

Lance Levy
Farm

Lyde
Green

Black We

WILL LA

Wedman's
Farm

FROG LA

Winnells
Copse

WEDMAN'S
PL

LAMPARDS CL

3

Soperslip
Copse

Rooks
Farm

Rotherwick

River Loddon

Lyde River

Summerstead
Farm

Tim's
Copse

Whitewater
CE Prim Sch

THE STREET

The Coach
and Horses
(PH)

Wildmoor
Farm

The Old
Rectory

56

The Old
House

Sewage
Works

Runten's
Farm

2

Club
House

Golf
Course

North Runten's
Copse

Cedar
Clump

Tylney
House

Tylney
Park

Home
Farm

55

Tynley
Hall

Shir
Co

College
Copse

Beehive
Farm

Outdoor
Education
Centre

Hill
Copse

College
Copse

Compfield
Copse

1

Hale
Farm

BROWN
CROFT

Deanlands
Farm

Newnham

PRINTERS
CASTLE

TYRELL LA

RIDGE LA

BOWLING
GREEN DR

NEWNHAM LA

Newnham
Green
Farm

PH

Owen's
Farm

Lyde Mill

Webb's
Copse

BLUEHAVEN
WLK

54

69   70   71

A   B   C

A **B** **C**

B3011

Hazeley
Heath

Sewage
Works

HULFORDS
LA

The Hartford
Bridge
(PH)

Hartfordbridg

CALTHORPE
HOS

Hazeley
Bottom

Works

Hazeley
House

Hares
Farm

Hartford
Bridge

ELETHAM LA

4

Inholmes
Court

The Old
Manor House

River Hart

BRACKNELLA

HAREBELL GDNS 1
WALPOLE GDNS 2
DAIRY WALK 3
BELGRAVE MEWS 4
OAKLEY PL 5

Golf Course

A30 STH MIL

James's
Farm

SPRINGFIELD AVE
HEATHER GR

CAMPION
WAY

HAYWARDEN
PL

CH

HARTLEY
MEWS

57

WEST GREEN RD

HAWLEY

HAZELEY

HARTFORD
CT

Causeway
Farm

The
Dutch House

BRACKLEY AVE

MEADOW LA

HIGH ST

WALBURTON
HO

Hartley
Wintney

West
Lodge

3

LONDON RD

HOLMWOOD
TERR

Greenfields
Jun Sch

Oakwood
Inf Sch

The Grey
House Sch

FLEET RD

Hartley Grange
Farm

GRANGE LA

OAKLANDS
PADDOCK CT

CLAYTON

Phoenix
Green

Fouracres
House

CEDAR
TERR

ST MARY'S
WARREN

A

56

THACKHAM'S LA

The
Croft

The
Shepherds Cottage

Wintney
Court

Phoenix
Green

B3016

Church House
Farm

Three Castles Path

Sergeants
Copse

Wallme
Cops

2

A30

Ashley

Taplin's
Farm

Wintney
Farm

River Hart

Nursery

Mabs
Copse

Winchfield
House

55

Winchfield
Lodge

NEW HENFIELD

Shapley Heath
Copse

OLD POTBRIDGE RD

Winchfield

Woody's
(PH)

Cranford's
Farm

Vale
Farm

SHAPLEY
HILL

P
Winchfield
Sta.

SEAUCLERK GN

1

Beggar's
Corner

ODIHAM RD

Furzy Moor

Hurst
Farm

Winchfield
Hurst

Tossell
Wood

HURST

54

Bottom
Copse

B3016

BAGWELL LA

M3

75   **76**   **77**

A **B** **C**

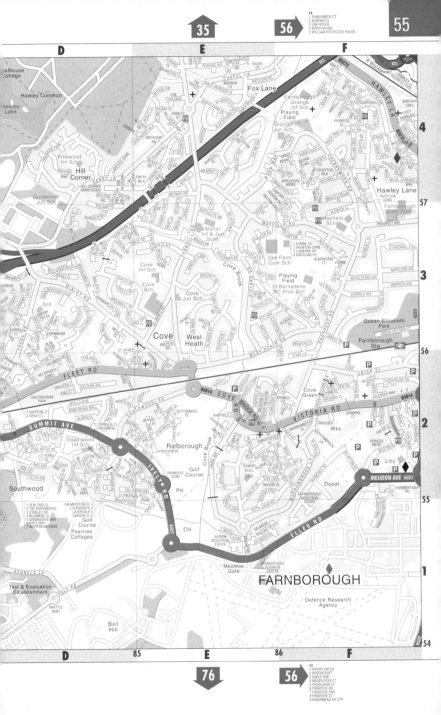

4   **57**   **3**   **56**   **2**   **55**   **1**   **54**

A   **B**   **C**

Frimley Business Pk
Frimley Sta
Factory
Frimley CE Fst & Mid Sch
Sandringham Inf Sch
Loen
The Grange
St Cross
Richmond Hill
Buckland Cl
Farnborough Gate Ret Pk
Cemetery
Rec Gnd
Frimley Green
Prospect Ave
Farnborough Green
Green Croft Special Sch
Gloucester Cl
Grenville Gdns
Cross Farm Cty Fst Sch
Wharfenden Lake
Frimley Lib
Farnborough North Sta
Farnborough Hill (Girls Public Sch)
Highgate La
North Farnborough Int Sch
Highgate
Farnborough Street
Water Works
The Kings Head (PH)
Frimley Lodge
Guildford Rd
Aqueduct
Cheswycks Prep Sch
The Old Mill
Jubilee Hall Rd
Church Path
Coleford Bridges
Blackwater River
Four Winds
Abbey La
St Peter's CE Jun Sch
Rectory Rd
St Patrick's RC Prim Sch
Montacute
Brookwood
Mytchett Cty Fst Sch
Basingstoke Canal
Picnic Area
Farnborough Park
Coleford Farm
Mytchett
Rowkes Drift
Rosewood
Vine House
Playing Field
Basingstoke Canal Ctr
Waverley Rd
Cleveden
Pirbright Rd
Linsford Bsns Pk
Linsford Farm
Salisbury Terr
Wimborne Gdns
Virginia Gdns
South Farnborough
Farnborough Golf of Tech
King George's Field
South Farnborough Jun Sch
Caravan Park
Jubilee Rd
Potters (PH)
Mytchett Place
North Gate Rd
Boundary Rd
Gainsborough Rd
Chalfont Dr
Fernhill
Albert Rd
Chatfield Rd
Farley
Cambridge Rd
Grove
Fellows Rd
Pegasus
Whites Rd
Hazel Rd
Glenmount
Rushmoor Ind Est
Reading
South St
Caravan Site
Mytchett Lake
Salesian Coll
Yeovil
Grove Farm
Keog
Barra
Playing Field
Oak Tree Cl 1
The Beeches 2
Cordelia Gdns 3
Stratford Rd
Warwick
Meadow La

87   88   89

A1
1 CAMBRIDGE CT
2 BARTON CT
3 DENBY CT
4 REDE CT
5 NEELEM CT
6 KASHMIR CT
7 BULLER CT
8 WYKEHAM HO
9 ALEXANDRA CT
10 WETHERBY GDNS
11 SOMERSET CT

A B C

Standen
House

BROADWAY

FOSBURY RD.

Cathanger
Wood

Young's
Copse

DUNGENESS RD.

MALTHOUSE LA.

Chute
Standen

Standen
Farm

Chute
Cadley

Home
Farm

NEW
BLOGS

Clarke's Lane

4

WOODLAND LA.

Collis
Farm

The Hatchet
(PH) +

Chessams
Copse

FOSBURY LA.

Lower
Chute

53

Tangley
Bottom

The
Cricketers Arms
(PH)

Home F
Dair

Tang

Jolly's
Farm

Great Lodge
Copse

Little
Pill

Home
Farm

Forest
House

Tangley
House

Man
Far

3

Coldridge Ride

Little Lodge
Copse

Cadley Bottom

Tangley
Park

CLARKE'S LA.

Long Bottom

+

MEADEN RD.

CHURCH HILL

52

Poultry
Houses

Chute Lodge
Farm

Big
Wood

Sexton's
Heath

LODGE LA.

ORCHARD
COTTS

**Chute
Forest**

Cooper's
Acre

2

Longbottom
Farm

Chute
Lodge

Pollards
Farm

Redhouse
Farm

ROUNDWAY LA.

Roundaway
Farm

51

Mankhorn
Round

Appleshaw
Round

Soper's Bottom

1

Mankhorn
Cottage

South
Lodge

BIVERHAM DRO.

INN HOUSE

Soper's
Barn

Poultry
House

50

30 A 31 B 32 C

D E F

4

Tangley
Clumps

Sheep
Down

. Mast

LUCKE'S DRO

Dowlands
Farm

Whistler's
Farm

Poultry
Farm

Pill Heath
Farm

53

HOLT LA

Eastend
Farm

HUNGERFORD LA

Tangley
Farm

Pill Heath

Dales
Wood

3

Blagden
Copse

Fox
Plantation

Stanchels

Blagden House

52

The Fox Inn
(PH)

Dines
Farm

Hungerford Lane

Dines
Copse

2

White Hill

51

Peaks
Copse

Hatherden
Manor

Wildhern

THE AVENUE

WILDHERN

Plough
Farm

Roundaway
Copse

LITTLE
HATHERDEN

1

LANCASHIRE
COTTS

Hatherden CE
Prim Sch

Hatherden

Hatherden
House

THE CLOSE

HUNGERFORD LA

HATCHET LA

HATHERDEN

P

Goddards
Farm

The
Hamster
(PH)

Hatherden
Farm

Pachington
Farm

CHARLTON
DOWN

Pigeon House
Farm

50

3 D 34 E 35 F

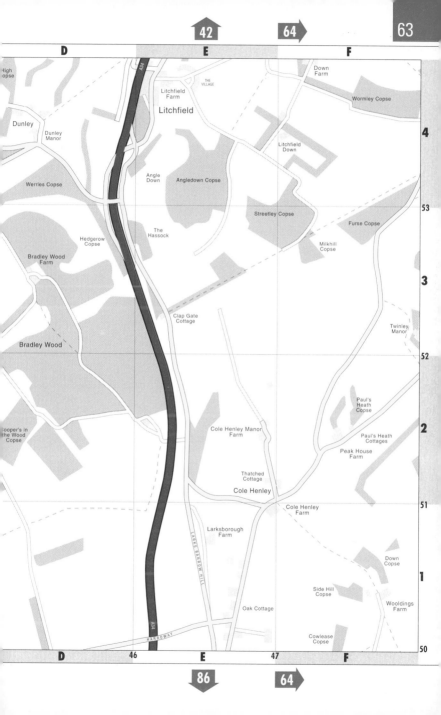

D
E
F

Down Farm

Litchfield Farm

THE VILLAGE

Wormley Copse

High Copse

Dunley

Dunley Manor

Litchfield

Litchfield Down

4

Werries Copse

Angle Down

Angledown Copse

Streetley Copse

Furse Copse

53

Hedgerow Copse

The Hassock

Milkhill Copse

Bradley Wood Farm

3

Clap Gate Cottage

Twinley Manor

Bradley Wood

52

Cooper's in the Wood Copse

Paul's Heath Copse

Cole Henley Manor Farm

Paul's Heath Cottages

2

Peak House Farm

Thatched Cottage

Cole Henley

51

Cole Henley Farm

Larksborough Farm

LARKSBOROUGH HILL

Down Copse

1

Side Hill Copse

Oak Cottage

Wooldings Farm

A34

Cowlease Copse

HARROWAY

50

D
46
E
47
F

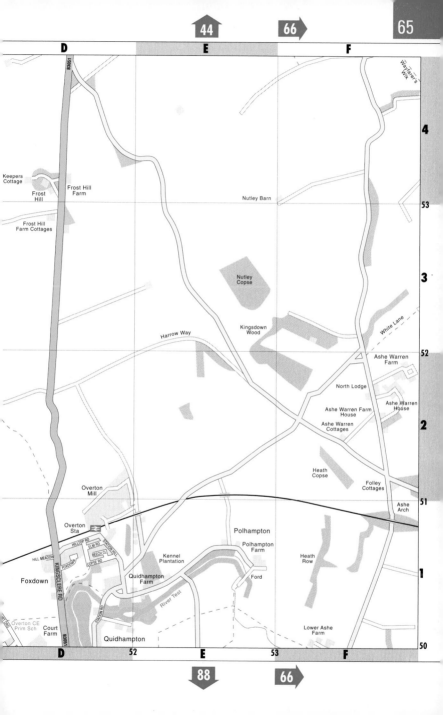

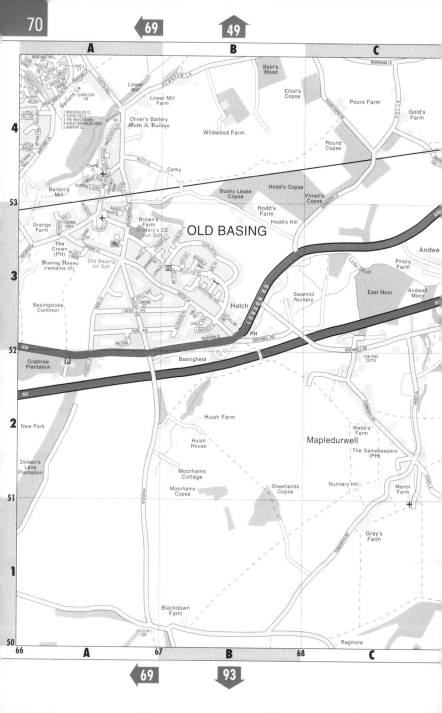

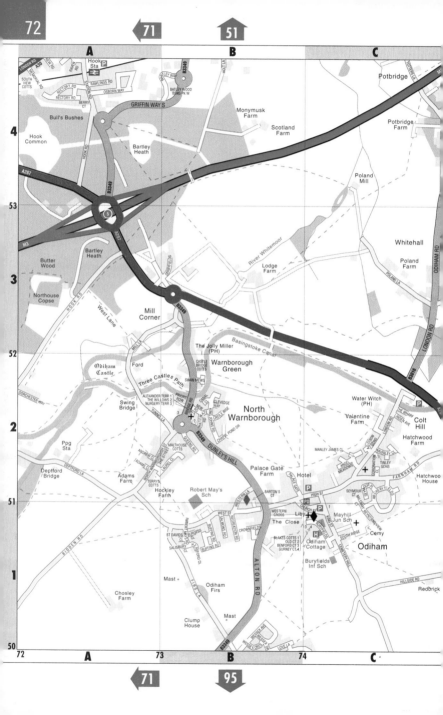

A B C

4

53

3

52

2

51

1

50

Hungerford Farm
Gunner's Copse
Burnbake Copse
Chatter Alley
Pilcot Farm
Norman's Green
Dogmersfield
Dogmersfield CE Prim Sch
Pilcot
Pilcot Bridge
PH
Brook Meadow Farm
Daegmarsfield Farm
Peatmoor Copse
Ormersfield Farm
Whitlow Alders
Cunningham's Row
Coxmoor Wood
Coxmoor Farm
Coxmoor Wood
El Sub Sta
Oakes Copse
Bowenhurst Farm
Mill Lane
Bowenhurst Lane
Golf Course
Triggs

Hitches Farm
Calthorpe Park Sec Sch
Hart L Ctr
Jack Reid's Copse
Sewage Works
PRIORY CL 1
SHALDON WAY 2
COPSE END 3
THE CROFT
All Saints CE Jun Sch
Tavistock Inf Sch
MEADOW WLK
LARMER CL
NETHERHOUSE CT
Netherhouse Copse
CROSSWAYS
HILLSIDE CL
Brook Hill
The Black Horse (PH)
Crookham Village
PO
THE STREET
MALTHOUSE BRIDGE COTTS
Grove Farm
STROUD LA
The Chequers (PH)
Bridge House
Chequers Bridge
CRONDALL RD
Hancock's Farm
MOVEHOURST
Two Ponds
Falkner's Copse
Fusney Copse
Zebon Copse
Community Ctr
Poulter's Bridge
Velmead Farm
Redfield Rows
Redfields Rows
Redfields
Redfields Cottage Farm
BLUE PRYOR
WATERY LA
Downsland House
The Horns (PH)
A287
FARNHAM RD
A287

Calthorpe Park
GURKHA SQ
READING RD S
A323
HEATHFIELD CT
BADGERS
Court Moor Sch
LINKWAY PARK
BROOM ACRES
Grange Estate
Crookham CE Inf Sch
WOODLAND CT 1
HOUSE PLAT CL 2
HORNES FIELD CT 3
NICOTIANA CT 4
LANGLEY CL 5
CHRISTCHURCH CL 6
CONSTANTIUS
Garden Ctr
Stables
Stillers Farm
Blackmoor Copse
Dares Farm
Goddards Farm
Seymour Farm
DARE'S LA
DARE'S CNR

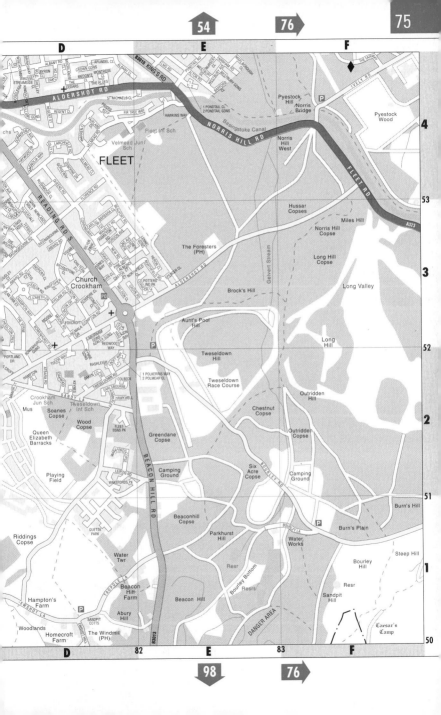

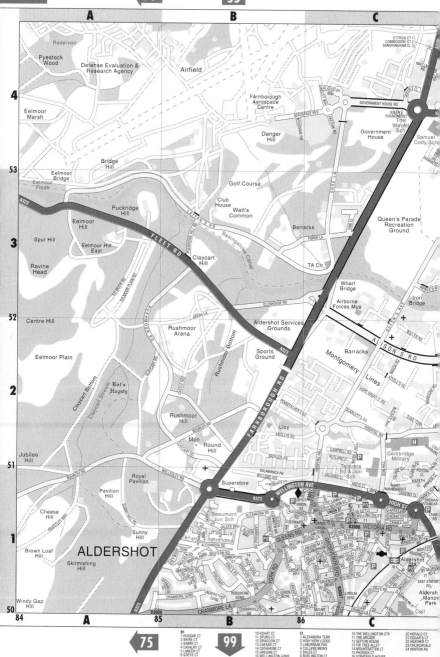

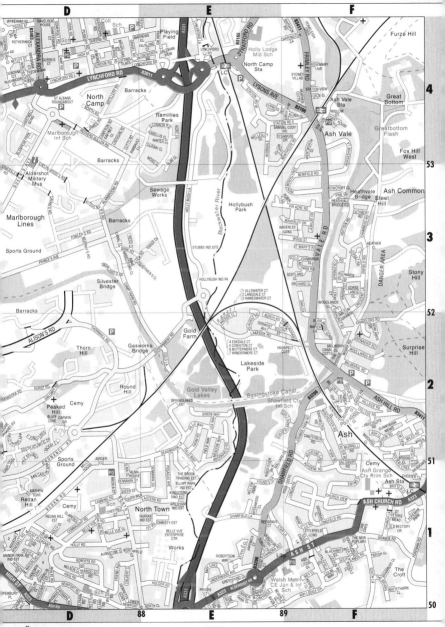

D1
1 REDAN GDNS
2 AMBER CT
3 POUND RD
4 WINDMILL CT
5 SUNNY VIEW CL
6 BEMBRIDGE CT
7 RYDE CT

79
57

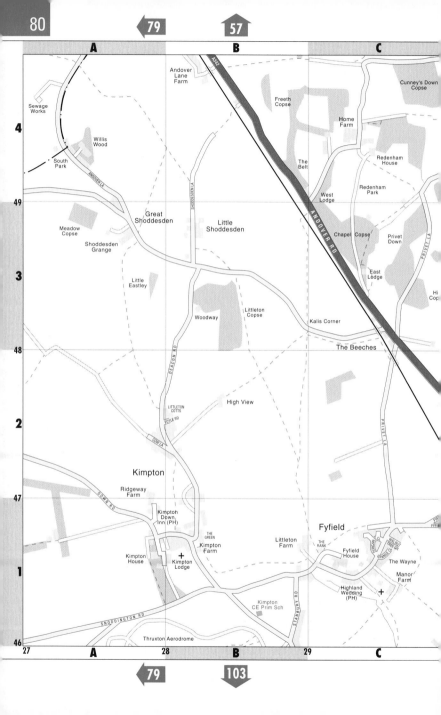

A   B   C

Sewage Works

Andover Lane Farm

Freeth Copse

Cunney's Down Copse

Home Farm

Willis Wood

The Belt

Redenham House

South Park

West Lodge

Redenham Park

Great Shoddesden

Little Shoddesden

Chapel Copse

Privet Down

Meadow Copse

East Lodge

Shoddesden Grange

Hi Cop

Little Eastley

Littleton Copse

Woodway

Kalis Corner

The Beeches

PRIVET LA

DEACON RD

LITTLETON COTTS

High View

EASTLE RD

DOWN LA

Kimpton

Ridgeway Farm

Kimpton Down Inn (PH)

THE GREEN

Fyfield

Littleton Farm

THE RANK

Fyfield House

The Wayne

DOWN RD

Kimpton House

Kimpton Lodge

Kimpton Farm

Manor Farm

Highland Wedding (PH)

Kimpton CE Prim Sch

STANBURY RD

SNODDINGTON RD

Thruxton Aerodrome

27   A   28   B   29   C

79
103

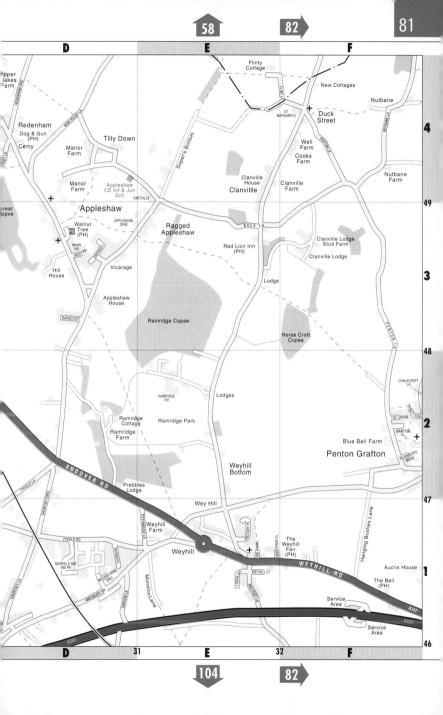

D E F

4

49

3

48

2

47

1

46

Upper Enham

RIDGES VIEW
PH

Mount Pleasant Farm

Ridges Copse

Home Farm

MACCALLUM RD

DUNNILEA

Little London

STOKE RD

Factory

KINGS RD

MALTHOUSE LA

Postgrove Copse

Woodhouse Farm

Smanell & Enham CE Prim Sch

Enham Alamein

TURNHILL CT

POPLE CL

KNIGHTSBRIDGE RD

CHAPEL

TOBRUK CL

ARUNDEL

Woodhouse

Pound View

British Oak (PH)

Smannell

Bilgrove Copse

NEWBURY RD

KINGSDOWN LA

Ashley Copse

SMANNELL RD

Finkley House

Knights Enham

BIRCH LA

Finkley Manor Farm

FINKLEY RD

Manor Farm

GARRARD WY

DANEFELD

East Anton

Eastanton Farm

Eastanton Manor Farm

Romano Way Prim Sch

WHEELERS

CRICKETERS WY

TURIN

CLAUDIUS CL

GENOA CT

GENOA CT

TURIN

Knights Enham Jun Sch

TINTAGEL CL

VENICE CT

FLORENCE CT

VENICE CT

FLORENCE CT

Knights Enham Inf Sch

LAUNCELOT CL

AGRICOLA WY

CAERLEON

Finkley Down Farm Park

Shepherds Spring Jun & Inf Sch

KNOLL CT

CRICKETERS WY

THE OVAL

ANDOVER

47

CRICKETERS WY

BLACKBIRD CT 62
PLOVER GL 63
SWIFT CL 64

RIVER WAY

GREENWICH WAY

Wks

RIVER WAY

Works

QUEENSWAY

NORTH WY

KINGSWAY

Hennings Farm

SUTHERLAND CT

EDRICH SQ 13
FRY SQ 14
GRAVENEY SQ 15
HAMMOND SQ 16

WESTMARCH BSNS CTR

Icknield Special Sch

WALWORTH RD

WALWORTH IND EST

BEECHCROFT CL

Saw Mill

PILGRIMS WAY

Works

WALWORTH ENT CTR

CENTRAL WY

OX DRO

ARTISTS WAY

MOORE

A3093

CHURCHILL WAY

A3093

CROWN

WEST WY

DUKE CT

FOCUS

1 IMPERIAL CT
2 KNIGHTS CT

BERESFORD GATE

NORTHERN AVE

A3057

NEWBURY ST

Vigo Jun Sch

SEVILLE CRES

GRANADA PL

WALWORTH RD

FLINDERS CL

LIVINGSTONE

Cemy

SPRING MEWS 1
FORGE FIELD 2

MAJORCA MN

CORDOBA

VIGO RD

1 JELLICOE CT
2 RODNEY CT
3 MOUNTBATTEN CT
4 NAPIER WLK

5 NELSON CT
6 RODNEY CT
7 SOMERVILLE CT
8 TOVEY CT
9 DRAKE CT
10 HAWKE CT

B3400

Norman Gate Special Sch

Vigo Inf Sch

BLEAD CT

MAGELLAN

1 BEDSER SQ
2 BRADMAN SQ
3 COWDREY SQ
4 COMPTON SQ
5 DEXTER SQ
6 WORRELL SQ
7 WOOLLEY SQ
8 TATE SQ
9 VERITY SQ
10 SUTCLIFFE SQ
11 TRUEMAN SQ
12 STATHAM SQ

17 GODDARD SQ
18 HENDREN SQ
19 GRACE SQ
20 HUTTON SQ
21 HOBBS SQ
22 JARDINE SQ
23 SOBERS SQ
24 LAKER SQ
25 SHEPPARD SQ
26 LARWOOD SQ
27 SHACKLETON SQ
28 LOCK SQ
29 RHODES SQ
30 MARSHALL SQ

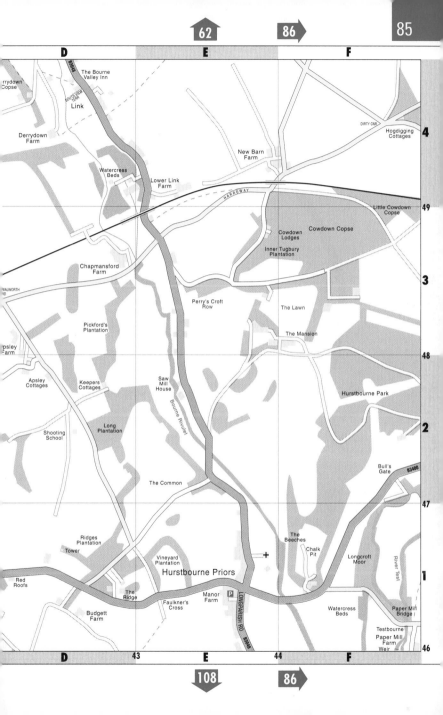

D   E   F

rrydown Copse

The Bourne Valley Inn

SOUTHVIEW TERR

Link

Derrydown Farm

Watercress Beds

Lower Link Farm

New Barn Farm

DIRTY CNR

Hogdigging Cottages

4

HARROWAY

Little Cowdown Copse

49

Cowdown Copse

Cowdown Lodges

Inner Tugbury Plantation

WALWORTH RD

Chapmansford Farm

3

Perry's Croft Row

The Lawn

Pickford's Plantation

The Mansion

psley Farm

48

Apsley Cottages

Keepers Cottages

Saw Mill House

Hurstbourne Park

Long Plantation

Bourne Rivulet

Shooting School

2

The Common

Bull's Gate

B3400

47

Ridges Plantation

Tower

Vineyard Plantation

The Beeches

Chalk Pit

Longcroft Moor

River Test

Red Roofs

Hurstbourne Priors

The Ridge

Faulkner's Cross

Manor Farm

P

LONGPARISH RD

B3048

Watercress Beds

Paper Mill Bridge

1

Budgett Farm

Testbourne Paper Mill Farm Weir

46

D   43   E   44   F

A **B** **C**

Court Farm

1 TOWN MILL
2 NORRIS HO
3 OVERTON HO
4 LAMPOOL HO
5 BUTLER LODGE
6 WALTHAM CT

The White Hart (PH)

Source of the River Test

Ashe House

Ashe

Hyde Hill Plantation

Ash Hill Row

LONDON RD

HIGH ST

Lib'y

B3051

B3400

Berrydown Court

Tidnock Farm

Water Tower

Berrydown Farm

BATTENS AVE

ELM PIECE RD

TWO GATE LA

THE GREEN

BORROW LA

PIDDEMAKERS LA

WINDMILL LA

WALTHAM RD

POUND RD

GREYHOUND LA

ALEXANDER

DELLANDS

CHARLE DOWN RD

POULTONS RD

POND LA

CHARLEDOWN

1 DALLENCE HO
2 MILLDOWN HO

Overton

Jackson's Copse

Sapley Farm House

Berrydown Copse

Burley Wood

Lampacre Plantation

Upper Ashe

BURLEY LA

WALTHAM LA

Woodside

White Hill

Bramdown Copse

Lower Whitehill Cottages

Northdown Plantation

Hazeldown Copse

Southley Farm

Bramdown

Quidhampton Southley Copse

Shelter Plantation

Craw Cop

Pilgrim's Copse

Upper Whitehill Farm

Southley Copse

Copse Farm

Litchfield Tunnel

Litchfield Copse

Keepers Cottage

Pilgrim's Farm

Golf Course

Cowage Copse

4 49 3 48 2 47 1 46

A   B   C

Breach
Farm

Breach
Cottages

Jeffery's
Copse

OSPREY
RD

LARK
PHEASANT CL
WOODPECKER CL
BLACKBIRD
JAY CL
SEAGULL CL
MAGPIE CL

SANDPIPER WAY
BITTERN
BRAMBL

4

Sewage
Works

Pardown

Small's
Copse

MALLARD
WOODMERE CROFT

49

Bull's Bushes
Copse

Pardown
Copse

Bull's Bushes
Farm

3

Little Stubbs
Copse

South
Wood

WINCHESTER RD

BEGGARWOOD

CH

Great Stubbs
Copse

48

Dean Heath
Copse

Waylarer's Walk

Golf
Course

Southwood
Farm

Kempshott Park

2

Ganderdown
Copse

The
Cedars

The Copse
(Caravan Site)

Peak Copse

Oakdown
Farm

47

7

Waylarer's Walk

CH

Golf Course

Rowle
Cops

1

The Sun Inn
(PH)

MAGENTHORN LA

Mast

Dummer

CH
F

Tel Ex

The Queen
(PH)

Dummer
Clump

Nutley

46

Cemy

57   A   58   B   59   C

A

B

C

Three Castles Path

Three Castles Path

UPTON GREY RD

Four Lanes End

Ford Farm

Bidden Water

Bidden Grange Farm

Lower Bidden Farm

BIDDEN RD

Dean Plantation

Bidden

4

49

Cleves Farm

CLIVES LA

Gaston Copse

BATH LA

Upton Grey House

Manor Farm

WOODMANFIELD

Little Dean Farm

LITTLE DEAN LA

3

Upton Grey

LITTLE HODDINGTON DR

Little Hoddington

The Hoddington Arms (PH)

PH

The Village Farm

MARSH LANE

Weston Mark

Hoddington Park

Tile Barn Farm

48

WESTON RD

HODDINGTON COTTS

Hoddington House

THE OLD ORCHARD 1
NASH MEADOWS 2

Hoddington Farm

Lee's Farm

2

Dean Farm House

Weston Patrick House

CHURCH VIEW

47

ALTON ROAD COTTS

B3349

Manor Farm

Dean Copse

Weston Patrick

Hoddington

Privett Copse

Wood Lane End

1

Little Park Copse

Westers Lane

Long La

B3349

A356 LA

46

69

A

70

B

71

C

95
73

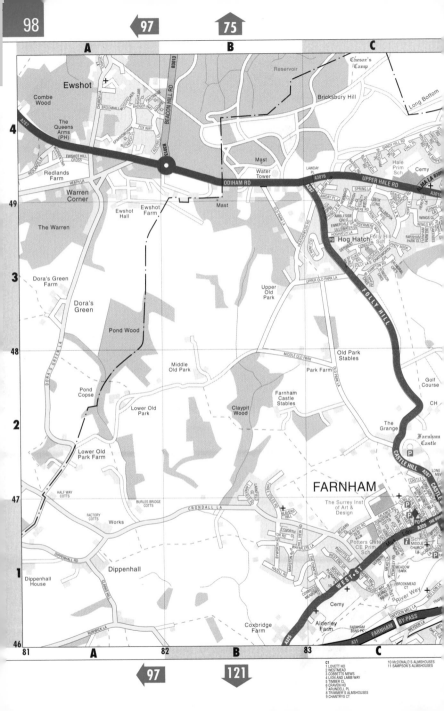

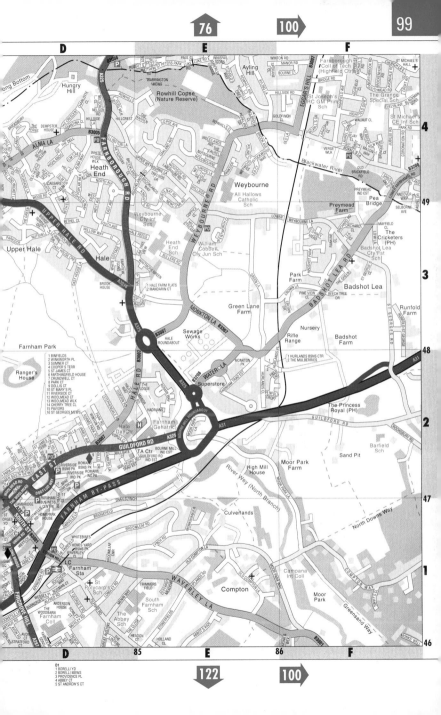

ASH RD A323 PO A323

A31

KING'S CT MANOR RD
KING'S AVE
ASH LODGE DR
RATEMAN GR

COMMERCIAL RD WOODCOTT TERR
ELSTON PL
ALLUMS
GILLIAN AVE

CARFAX EST
OXENDEN CT
ASH GREEN LA W

Bin Wood

Ash Manor Sch

St Michael's CE Jun Sch

PARK RD

CHARTERS CT
ORCHARD CL

LOWER FARNHAM RD

TONGHAM MEADOWS
ELM LA
THE ELMS
THE MOORS
FIELD WAY
THE GARDENS
POYLE LA

St Paul's CE Inf Sch

Poyle Farm

4

HAWTHORNE CL

Connaught Sec Sch

BLENHEIM CL

GRIEVE CL

THE CARDINALS
SOUTH SIDE

Poyle Farm

Park Prim Sch

PLACE CT
ASPEN RD
GLOUCESTER RD

Aldershot Park

B3208

RUSSELL CT

ORCHARD HO

POYLE RD

Tongham

49

GARBETTS WAY
MAITLAND

CRIPTON
MAITLAND

Crematorium

NEW RD

Blackwater Valley Footpath
Blackwater River

3

A331

GRANGE RD

Grange Farm

MANOR HOUSE FLATS

Manor Farm

MANOR FARM BSNS CTR

Poyle Park

Hog's Back Hotel

A3

Hog's Back

IPSLEY LODGE

48

A331

West Farm

Runfold Manor

Foxbury Farm

THORNBURY RD

SANDY CROSS

MANOR FIELDS

PUTTENHAM LA

FLOCK HILL

SEALE LA

Seale Lodge

Sand Pits

2

TONGHAM RD
THE WILLOWS

Runfold

WOODLANDS
WHITEWAYS END

GUILDFORD RD

Jolly Farmer (PH)

The Park

Sand Pits

Seale

North Downs Way

Payn First

47

N Downs Way

BINTON LA

Furze Hill

Binton Cottage

Binton Farm

Binton Wood

The Roughs

ESTON RD

SANDS RD

Club House

Golf Course

Owlshatch

1

Sandy Farm

The Sands

SANDS RD

Botany Hill

THE GREEN

PO

BOTANY HILL

Barley Mow (PH)

LITTLEWORTH RD

The Ridge

SALDIERS RING

Soldiers Ring

Crooksbury Hill

Coach Bottom

Shipton Bellinger
Cty Prim Sch

Shipton
Bellinger

BULFORD RD
KILSBY
FLATS

Manor
Farm

Old Coach Rd

HIGH ST

Parsonage
Farm

Gilbert's
Farm

Sewage
Works

SALISBURY RD

Snoddington
Manor

Pearl Wood

Lodge

Hills
Copse

Althorne
Cottage

Furze
Copse

Althorne
Farm

River Bourne

PARKHOUSE CROSS

A303

POTTER'S
CROSS

PARK HOUSE
MEWS

Winscott

B3084

PARKHOUSE
CNR

Down Barn

Park
Bridge

Spinney

Michael's
Wood

Yew
Grove

Cholderton
House

Home
Farm

The
Rectory

Cholderton
Park

Ann's
Wood

Cholderton

Anne's Farm
Cottages

Manor
Farm

Crown Inn
(PH)

Salisbury
Lodge

Cholderton
Lodge

AMESBURY RD

Yew Tree
Farm

Walnut
Cottage

GRATELEY RD

CHOLDERTON RD

A338

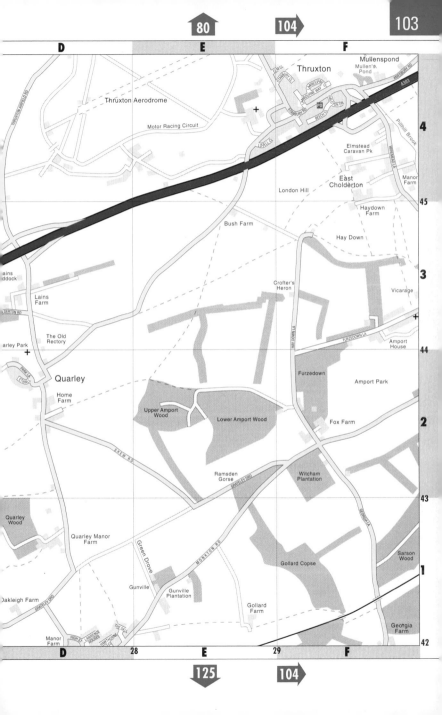

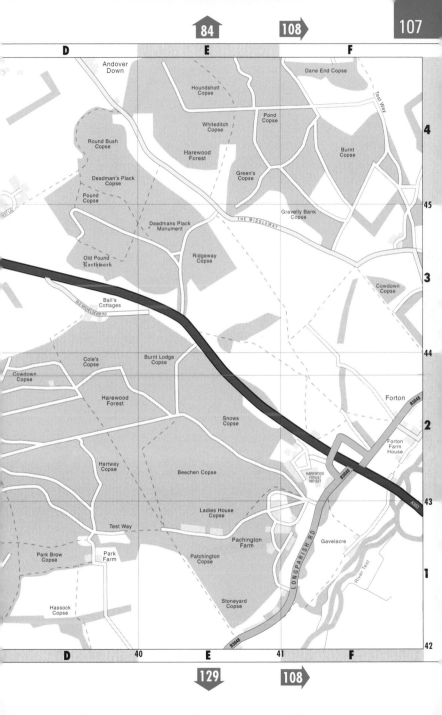

107
85

A   B   C

Three Halve Copse

Bourne Rivulet

LONGPARISH RD

DRURY LA

Tracy's Dell

Watercress Beds

Paul's Dell

Wood Walk Plantation

East Aston

Mill House

45

PORTWAY

Longparish House

Cricketers Inn

P Ø

River Test

Watercress Beds

Larkwhistle Farm

3

Longparish

Lower Mill

Vale Farm

Lower Farm

GLADSTONE TERR

THE MIDDLE WAY

Middleton Park

The Plough Inn

Middleton

THE WITHES

SOUTHBRIDGE RD

MILL LA

44

Middleton House

✛

Longparish Cty Prim Sch

Southside Farm

B3048

2

Drayton

TODDLE HILL LANE

THE AVENUE

Drayton Camp

Lodge Farm

43

A303

Drayton Down

Bransbury Manor Farm

1

Motel

Bransbury

River Dever

A3

Sewage Works

Playing Field

Weir

Bransbury Hill

42

42   A   43   B   44   C

107
130

D E F

4

45

3

44

2

43

1

42

Mile
Hurdle

Firgo Lane

Little
Firs

Big
Firs

Firgo
Farm

Firgo
Cottages

Tufton Warren
Cottages

Tufton Warren
Farm

Little
Wood

Tidbury
Rings

Upper Norton
Farm

Tidbury
Farm

Little
Bullington

TIDBURY
COTTS

Bullington
Cross
Inn
(PH)

A303

A303

A34

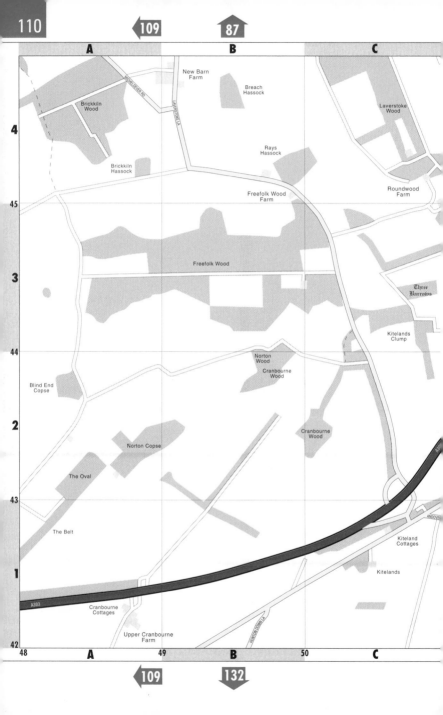

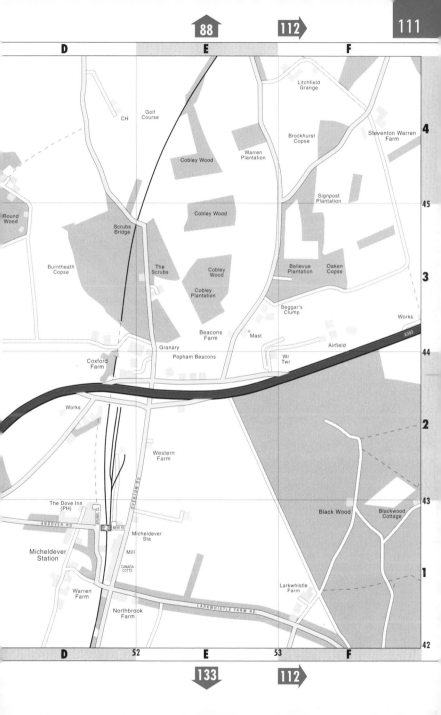

A **B** **C**

4

Ashen Grove
Copse

The Fox
(PH)

Wheatsh
Hotel

A303

45

Misholt
Copse

Waltham Trinleys

Hellier's
Copse

8

3

Cocksford Firs
East

Bramley
Wood

Cocksford
Down

A303

West Farm

44

Popham Court
Farm

Popham

2

Popham Court
Farm

Bittley
Copse

43

Black Wood

The Old
Vicarage

Vicarage
Farm

College Wood

BRADLEY
COTTS

Bradley
Farm

Manor Farm

1

Woodmancott

Rownest
Wood

THE CALVERT CTR

London
Lodge

A303

A303

Innersdown
Farm

42

54 **A** **55** **B** **56** **C**

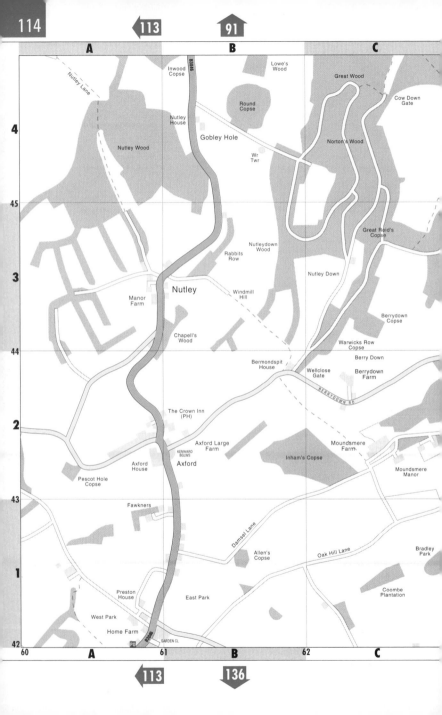

113
91

Nutley Lane

Inwood Copse

B3046

Lowe's Wood

Great Wood

Cow Down Gate

Round Copse

Nutley House

4

Gobley Hole

Nutley Wood

Norton's Wood

Wr Twr

45

Great Reid's Copse

Nutleydown Wood

Rabbits Row

Nutley Down

3

Nutley

Windmill Hill

Berrydown Copse

Manor Farm

Chapell's Wood

Warwicks Row Copse

44

Bermondspit House

Berry Down

Wellclose Gate

Berrydown Farm

BERRYDOWN RD

The Crown Inn (PH)

2

Axford Large Farm

Moundsmere Farm

KENWARD BGLWS

Inham's Copse

Moundsmere Manor

Axford House

Axford

Pescot Hole Copse

43

Fawkners

Damsel Lane

Allen's Copse

Oak Hill Lane

Bradley Park

1

Coombe Plantation

Preston House

East Park

West Park

Home Farm

PO

B3046

GARDEN CL

42

60 A 61 B 62 C

113
136

D   E   F

+ Hill Farm

Alley Lane

Ellisfield

Mast

Widmoor Farm

CHURCH LA

WINDSOR LA

Three Castles Path

FURZEN LA

Ellisfield Manor

Chatter's Row

GREEN LA

FARRIER'S FIELD

Park Field Copse

The Fox Inn (PH)

Upper Common

Smart's Copse

Merritt's Farm

Merritt's Copse

Oxlease Lane

Grange Farm

Herriard Grange

4

College Farm

BELL LA

45

CANNON CL

High Wood

Lower Common

COLLIER LA

Kit Lane

Cooper's Farm

Bushy Leane Copse

Scratchface Lane

Hurst Farm

Little Baldmore Lane

3

Ham Copse

BAGMORE LA

Beach Wood

AXFORD RD

Herriard Common

44

Preston Oak Hills

RED LA

Fir Plantation

2

Foster's Copse

Apple Croft Copse

Fliscombe's Copse

Brick Kiln Copse

Down Wood

Heathcraft's Copse

SPAIN LA

Spain Cottages

43

Lasham Hill

Southwood Farm

Bradley Hill

Down Wood

Home Farm

A339

Southwood Cottages

Three Castles Path

Burkham House

1

Burkham

Burkham Lodge

Wigdell Copse

42

D   64   E   65   F

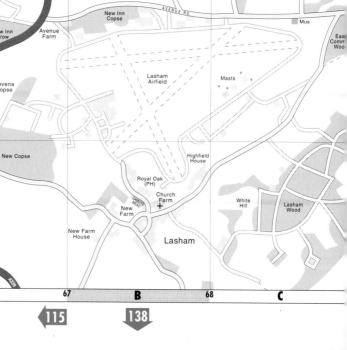

D
E
F

Long La

Webster La

B3349

Humbly Grove
Copse

Humbly Grove
House

Humbly Grove
Farm

Good
Hope
Farm

4

New Farm

Blounce

Bairns Fell
Farm

Elmtree
Farm

Holding
Corner

45

Closedown
House

3

Great Park

Swaineshill
Farm

PICKAXE LA

Bayman's
Barn

Weston Common

Powntley
Copse

Swaines
Hill
Manor
Farm

Closedown
Wood

44

Swaines
Hill
Manor

Lasham
Corner

Shrubs
Copse

Golden
Pot

Great
Hankins
Copse

2

Shalden Green

The
Golden Pot
(PH)

AYLESFIELD
FARM

Aylesfield
House

Ledgefield
Plantation

Withey
Copse

Shalden
Park
Farm

Ropers
Copse

Marlefield

43

Gason
Wood

NEW ODIHAM RD

Sunacres
Farm

Shalden Park
Wood

OLD ODIHAM RD

1

Little
Down
Copse

Lee Lands

CH

Manor
Farm

SOUTHWOOD RD

Stancombe La

B3349

Golf
Course

42

D
70
E
71
F

New Farm

Vinney
Copse

Sheephouse
Copse

Pickaxe
Copse

White House
Farm

Highnam
Copse

Sutton
Common

West
View

Great
Wood

Gaston
Copse

Little
Wood

Broadlane
Copse

Yarnhams
Farm

Hawkins
Wood

Beech Hangers Lane

Mast *

Liddenfield
Copse

Stowell
Copse

Dicket's
Plantation

Fielders
Copse

Yarnhams
Cottages

Stowell
Cottage

Ham Wood

Shrub Croft
Copse

* Masts

Spollycombe
Copse

Brockham Hill
Farm Cottages

Peakham
Copse

Holybourne
Down

Round
Wood

Brockham Hill
Barn

New Lane

Howard's
Lane

D
E
F

The Beeches

Sheephouse Copse

The Drove

Hangers Hyle Copse

High Wood

Stenes Copse

Isnage Farm

4

Crest Hill Farm

Silvester's Copse

45

Copse Hill Farm

Chalk Pit

astholes Copse

Rock House Farm

3

Hodges Farm

Lower Froyle

Shortlands Copse

The Prince of Wales (PH)

Blackacre Copse

Saintburyhill Farm

Saintbury Hill

Silvesters Farm

Husseys Farm

The Hanger

44

BARNFIELD

WESTBURN FIELDS

The White House

Brocas Farm

Crocks Farm

B.A.M.R.LA

The Anchor Inn (PH)

Coldrey Farm

HOLMWOOD COTTS

A31

Meml

COLDREY COTTS

Highway House

2

Rye Bridge

Blundens Farm

GID.LA

43

Cemy

Upper Froyle

River Wey

Isington Mill

THE SQUARE

Lord Mayor Treloar Sch

Froyle Mill

The Miller's House Farm

Isington

est End Farm

College Farm

Quarry Bottom

Isington Farm

1

Cotthouse Lane

Shrubbery House

Chestnut Copse

Gaston Copse

West End

Hen and Chicken (PH)

A31

Greatfield Cottages

D
76
E
77
F
42

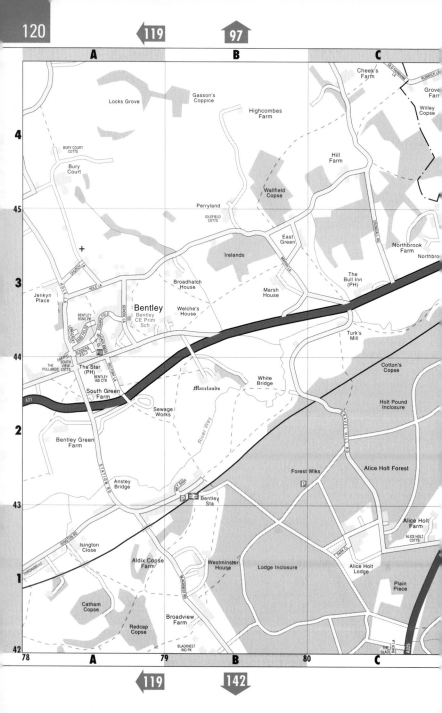

A   B   C

4

Locks Grove

Gasson's Coppice

Highcombes Farm

Cheek's Farm

Grove Farm

Willey Copse

Bury Court Cotts

Bury Court

Hill Farm

45

Perryland

IDLEFIELD COTTS

Wallfield Copse

East Green

Northbrook Farm

Northbro

3

Jenkyn Place

CHURCH LA

HOLE LA

Bentley

Broadhatch House

Welche's House

Irelands

Marsh House

MAIN LA

The Bull Inn (PH)

GRANGE RD

BENTLEY BSNS PK

Bentley CE Prim Sch

SCHOOL LA

Turk's Mill

44

THE POLLARDS COTTS

SOUTH VIEW COTTS

OAKWST

SANDERS FIELD

PO

The Star (PH)

BENTLEY IND CTR

BECKETTS LA

White Bridge

Cotton's Copse

South Green Farm

Marelands

Holt Pound Inclosure

A31

2

Bentley Green Farm

Sewage Works

River Wey

GRAVEL HILL RD

Forest Wlks

P

Alice Holt Forest

STATION RD

Anstey Bridge

MILL BANK

43

P

Bentley Sta

Alice Holt Farm

ALICE HOLT COTTS

THOROMBEAD

Isington Close

Aldix Copse Farm

BLACKNEST RD

Westminster House

Lodge Inclosure

PARK LA

Alice Holt Lodge

1

Catham Copse

Redcap Copse

Broadview Farm

Plain Piece

THE GLADE

PARK LA

A325

BLACKNEST IND PK

42

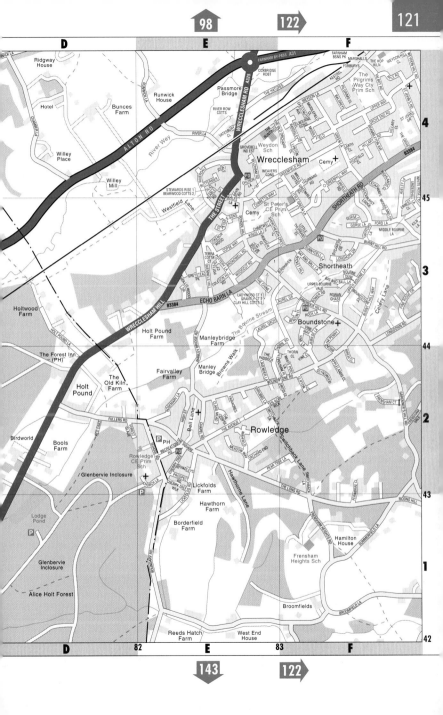

A
B
C

B3001

WAVERLEY LA

FRIGROVE HILL

RIDGWAY RD

A287

B3384

Priory Croft

Greenhills

Great Austins Ho

Abbey Rd

The Bourne Stream

Abbey Esks Pk

Ancora Farm House

Monk's Walk Farm

Priory Farm

Waverley Abbey House

Waverley Abb (remains of)

Bourne Heights

PO

Ridgeway Sch

Middle Bourne

Audley Ho

Vicara

Red Hill

Lodge Farm

Camp Site

4

45

Stream Farm Cl

The Bourne Cty Inf Sch

School La

Lodge Hill Rd

Lower Bourne

Black Lake

PO

The Bourne

Eldon Pl

Bournelands

Alice Holt Forest Bourne Wood

Nightingale Farm

River Wey (North Branch)

Tilfordmi Bridge

3

44

FRENSHAM RD

DENE LA

FRENSHAM RD

CLUMPS RD

GONG HILL

GONG HILL DR

Gong Hill

Tilford

Edgeborough

Edgeborough Sch

HEATH COTTS

Rural Life Ctr

Tilford Hou Farm

2

43

Kennel Farm

KENNEL LA

Keepers Field

THE REEDS RD

Tilford Reeds

Tankersford Common

More House Sch

MOORS HILL

HAMLASH COTTS

FIELD LA

Burtleys Copse

1

Shortfield Common

GORSE COTTS

SANDS LA

PO

Southview Cotts

Millbridge

Pierrepont Home Farm

River Wey (South Branch)

Meadow End Farm

Chuter's Firs

Tilford Commo

42

The Mariners (PH)

A287

Pierrepont Sch

84

A

85

B

86

C

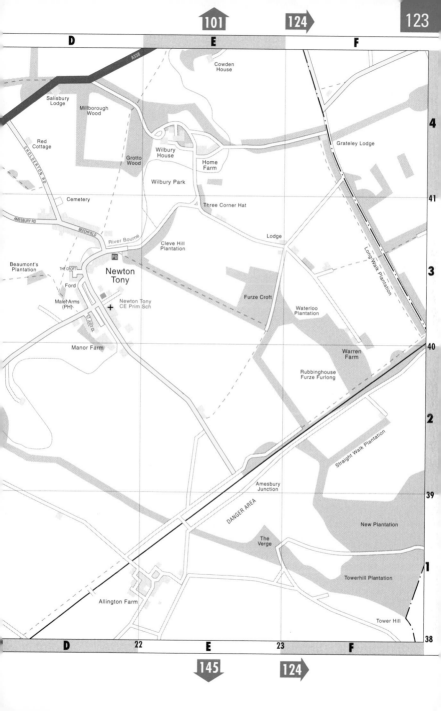

D

E

F

A338

Cowden
House

Salisbury
Lodge

Millborough
Wood

4

Red
Cottage

Grateley Lodge

Wilbury
House

Grotto
Wood

Home
Farm

Wilbury Park

Cemetery

41

Three Corner Hat

AMESBURY RD

BEECHFIELD

River Bourne

Cleve Hill
Plantation

Lodge

Long Walk Plantation

Beaumont's
Plantation

PO

THE CROFT

Newton
Tony

3

Ford

Furze Croft

Malet Arms
(PH)

Newton Tony
CE Prim Sch

Waterloo
Plantation

Manor Farm

40

Warren
Farm

Rubbinghouse
Furze Furlong

2

Straight Walk Plantation

Amesbury
Junction

39

DANGER AREA

New Plantation

The
Verge

1

Towerhill Plantation

Allington Farm

Tower Hill

38

D   E   F

Cemy
Grateley
Georgia Farm
Georgia LA.
Grateley Prim Sch
Grateley House Sch
STATION RD

4

Georgia Lane
Great Vinels Copse
Hurst Copse
Georgia Down

WALLOP RD

Lower Grateley Wood

Upper Grateley Wood

Georgia Lane

41

OLD STOCKBRIDGE RD

Red Lodge Farm
CARMEL RD
ckbarn arm

Oklahoma Farm

3

WALLOP RD

40

Sunnyside Farm
KING LA.
Poultry Farm

Park Farm

2

PARK DRO

The Sheiling

Craydown

DOWNS RD
Poultry Houses
CRAYDOWN LA
Works

39

ary Drove

Wallop Brook

KEYHAVEN COTTS
EVANS CL
POUND RD
APPLETON CL
KING LANE COTTS
HORSESHOE DRO

Tunlands Farm

Croft Farm

Townsend Farm

Pottery Farm
PH
STATION RD
Northern Farm
SALISBURY LA

CHIMES LA
Rosehill Farm
Middle Wallop Airfield

1

Over Wallop

A343
B3084

38

D   28   E   29   F

A   B   C

4

Old Prospect
Farm

Prospect
Farm

Eastover
Copse

Cossical
Copse

Stonehanger
Copse

41

Monxton
Oakcuts

Abbotts Ann Down

SALISBURY RD

Down Farm

Dunkirt
House

Chestnut
Cottage

3

Saxley Farm

OLD STOCKBRIDGE RD

Married
Quarters

Kentsboro

40

Towers
SYCAMORE
CRES

MAPLE
CL

Kentsboro
Farm

BEECH
CL

PINE CL

BIRCH
AVE

Married
Quarters

Upper Oakcuts
Copse

2

Mast

1 HAWTHORN HILL
2 POPLAR PATH
3 CHERRY WLK
4 ASH PATH
5 DANEBURY VIEW
6 LAUREL PL
7 HOLLY WLK

Mus of
Army Flying

39

Knock Wood

Down Farm

1

Middle Wallop
Airfield

Sewage
Works

38
30   A   31   B   32   C

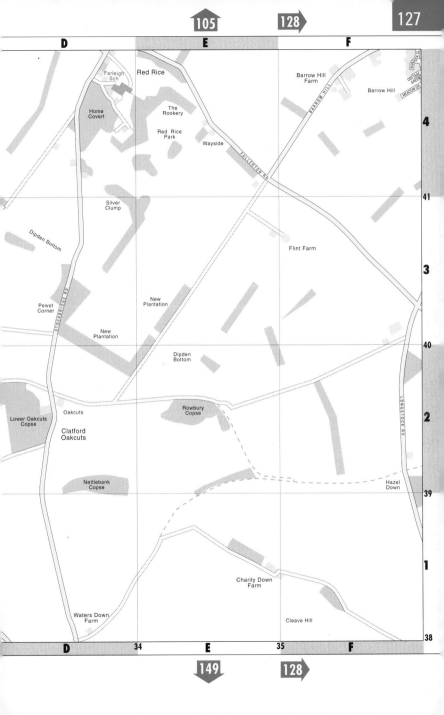

105
128

D E F

Farleigh Sch
Red Rice

Home Covert

The Rookery

Red Rice Park

Wayside

Barrow Hill Farm

Barrow Hill

BIRCH CL
COTTAGE GREEN
MEADOW DR

FULLERTON RD

BARROW HILL

4

41

Silver Clump

Dipden Bottom

Flint Farm

STOCKBRIDGE RD

3

Pewet Corner

New Plantation

New Plantation

Dipden Bottom

40

LONGSTOCK RD

Lower Oakcuts Copse

Oakcuts

Clatford Oakcuts

Rowbury Copse

2

Nettlebank Copse

Hazel Down

39

Charity Down Farm

1

Waters Down Farm

Cleave Hill

38

D 34 E 35 F

149
128

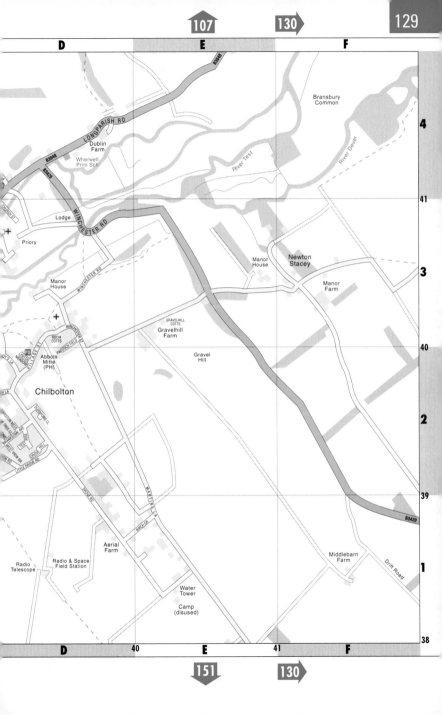

LONGPARISH RD
Dublin Farm
Wherwell Prim Sch
B3048
B3420
Lodge
WINCHESTER RD
Priory
Manor House
WINCHESTER RD
GRAVELHILL COTTS
Gravelhill Farm
Gravel Hill
Manor House
Newton Stacey
Manor Farm
River Test
River Dever
Bransbury Common

ROOM COTTS
PADDOCK FIELD
Abbots Mitre (PH)

Chilbolton

DUBLIN CL
LITTLE GROVE RD

BROOK RD

MARTINS LA

BIRCH GR

Aerial Farm

Radio Telescope
Radio & Space Field Station

Water Tower
Camp (disused)

Middlebarn Farm
Drift Road
B3420

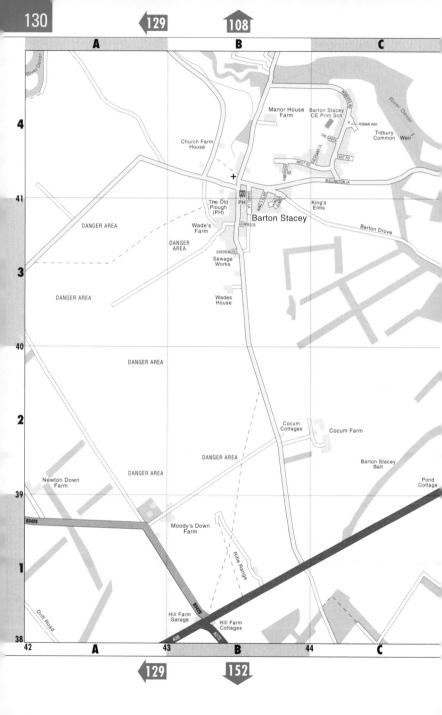

D   E   F

Black Wood

Works

Parkhill
Farm

4

41

Middle
Lodge

3

Shepherd's
Close

West
Stratton

Stratton
Park

The Bothy

West Stratton
Farm

Stratton
End

Winchester
Lodge

40

Northbrook House
Lodge

Northbrook
Dairy

Chapel Ave

Highways
Cottages

Cowdown
Wood

Northbrook

Micheldever

Highways

2

Cowdown
Farm

New
Farm

1 LANE END BUNGALOWS
2 MEADOW VIEW
3 SOUTHBROOK COTTS

South Down La

Micheldever
Prim Sch

P

DUKE ST
1 2 3

Highways
Nursery

39

Manor
Farm

South
Down

Half Moon and
Spread Eagle
(PH)

Dodsley
Wood

1

Cole's
Barn

WINCHESTER RD

Micheldever
Wood

Folly
Wood

38

Butcher's
Copse

A
B
C

Biddles
wood

Black
Wood

Embley
Wood

4

Lone Farm

Stratton
Park

41

Stratton
House

Whiteway
Farm

Norn's Copse

The Cowleys

Cross

3

Well House
Copse

Candover Copse

East Stratton
Farm

40

CHURCH BARN
RD

East Stratton

EAST
STRATTON

Hazely
Copse

Foxhill

The
Plough
Inn

NEW CHARE RD

STRATTON LA

BARING ST

2

Thorny
Down
Wood

Burnt
House
Copse

Black
Hut
Copse

COPSE LA

Duke's
Copse

NORTHINGTON
CORNER

39

South Down Lane

Totford Copse

South Down

STRATTON LA

Burcot Farm

1

Dodsley Wood

Wayfarer's Walk

38

54
A
55
B
56
C

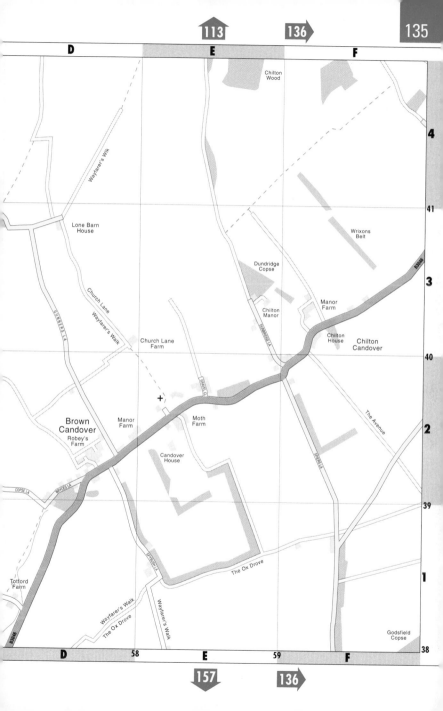

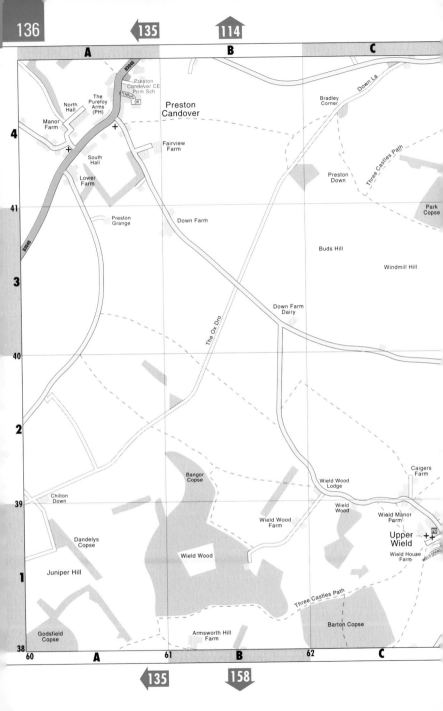

A B C

4

41

3

40

2

39

1

38

60 A 61 B 62 C

North Hall

Manor Farm

The Purefoy Arms (PH)

Preston Candover CE Prim Sch

STENBURY DR

B3046

Preston Candover

South Hall

Lower Farm

Fairview Farm

Preston Grange

B3046

Down Farm

Buds Hill

Bradley Corner

Down La

Preston Down

Three Castles Path

Park Copse

Windmill Hill

The Ox Dro

Down Farm Dairy

Chilton Down

Bangor Copse

Wield Wood Lodge

Wield Wood

Caigers Farm

Dandelys Copse

Wield Wood Farm

Wield Wood

Wield Manor Farm

Upper Wield

Wield House Farm

WIELD GRANGE

PO

Juniper Hill

Wield Wood

Three Castles Path

Godsfield Copse

Armsworth Hill Farm

Barton Copse

D **E** **F**

Wigdell
Copse

Tickley

Manor
Farm

Upper
Farm
Bradley

4

Bradley
Wood

South
Lease
Copse

Stubbins
Copse

41

Hunt's
Copse

Mayhew's
Wood

Powells Farm

BERRTWOOD LA

Rushmoor La

Bullfield La

Lower Wield
Farm

Lower Wield

3

Nicholas's
Farm

Laurel
Farm

Whites
Farm

Ashley Farm

Three Castles Path

40

Kings Farm

Mucklands La

The Yew
Tree
(PH)

Blue Ridge
Farm

WIELD
INDUSTRIES

Dirty La

2

Gastop Wood

Gaston
Grange

Holt End

HOLT END LA

Jennie Green La

39

Church
Farm

Lower College
Copse

1

Battle
Corner

WIELD RD

JENNIE GREEN LA

TRINITY RD

Deadhob
Copse

Medstead
Grange
Farm

Bannbridge
Farm

Red Barn
Farm

Trinity
House

Medstead
Grange

38

D 64 **E** 65 **F**

A   B   C

4

41

3

40

39

1

2

Bentworth

Nancole Copse

Haley Firs

Derby Dell Cottages

Station Cottages

Redens Copse

Rogussen's Row

Bylanders Copse

Crossing Cottage

Pumping Station

Shalden Lan Plantation

Haley La

Wadgett's Copse

Cockreads Copse

Binney Copse

BELLHANGER ENTERPRISES

Binsted Hill Wood

Drury Farm

Ham Farm

DRURY LA

GLEBE CL

GLEBE FIELDS

Summerley

Well Cottages

ASHLEY RD

Bentworth CE Prim Sch

The Sun Inn (PH)

Bentworth Lodge

PO

Well Copse

The Star Inn (PH)

CHURCH ST

East End Farm

Weller's Place Farm

VILLAGE ST

Childer Hill Farm

Heathcroft Farm

Mucklands La

Hall Farm

Childer Hill Copse

DENYERS COTTS

HOLT END

Tinker's La

Thedden Farm

Thedden Park

Holt End

Gadwick Dell Copse

Thedden Grange

Bentworth Hall

Gadwick Cottages

Collier's Wood

Wivelrod

Wivelrod Cottages

Hillside Piggeries

WELLHOUSE RD

Jennie Green La

WIVELROD RD

Wivelrod House

MEDSTEAD RD

Beec

The Homestead

Warem Farm House

A33'S HILL

66   A   67   B   68   C

38

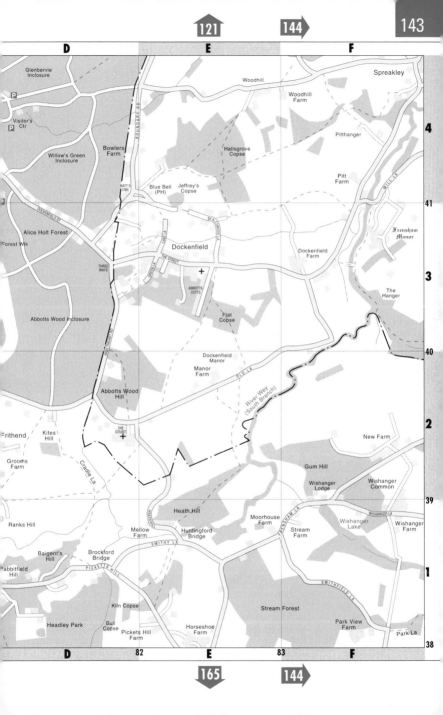

D
E
F

Glenbervie
Inclosure

Woodhill

Spreakley

Woodhill
Farm

P

Visitor's
Ctr

P

Pitthanger

4

Willow's Green
Inclosure

Bowlers
Farm

Halisgrove
Copse

Pitt
Farm

MILL LA

BATT'S
CNR

Blue Bell
(PH)

Jeffrey's
Copse

41

DOCKENFIELD RD

Alice Holt Forest

BEALES LA

Frensham
Manor

Forest Wlk

Dockenfield
Farm

THREE
WAYS

THE STREET

GREEN LA

Dockenfield

3

ABBOTTS
COTTS

The
Hanger

Abbotts Wood Inclosure

Flat
Copse

Dockenfield
Manor

40

Manor
Farm

OLD LA

HIGH ROAD

Abbotts Wood
Hill

River Wey
(South Branch)

Frithend

Kites
Hill

THE COURT

New Farm

2

Grooms
Farm

Gum Hill

Cradle La

Wishanger
Lodge

Wishanger
Common

WISHANGER LA

39

Ranks Hill

Heath Hill

Moorhouse
Farm

Wishanger
Lake

Wishanger
Farm

HEATH HILL

Mellow
Farm

Huntingford
Bridge

FRENSHAM LA

Stream
Farm

Baigent's
Hill

Brockford
Bridge

SMITHY LA

abbitfield
Hill

PICKETTS HILL

1

SMITHFIELD LA

Kiln Copse

Bull
Copse

Stream Forest

Park View
Farm

Headley Park

Pickets Hill
Farm

Horseshoe
Farm

Park La

38

D
82
E
83
F

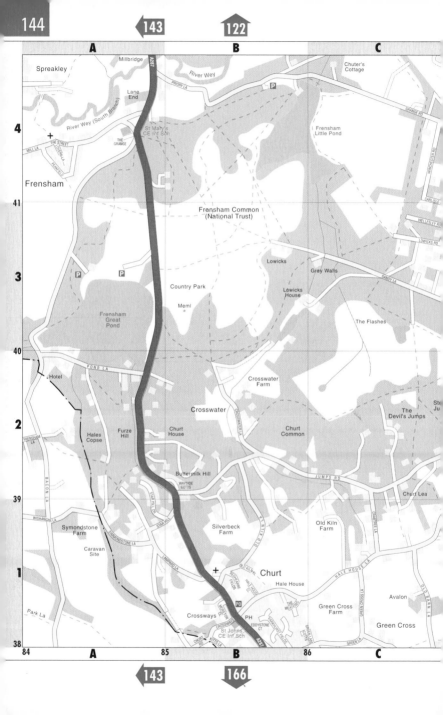

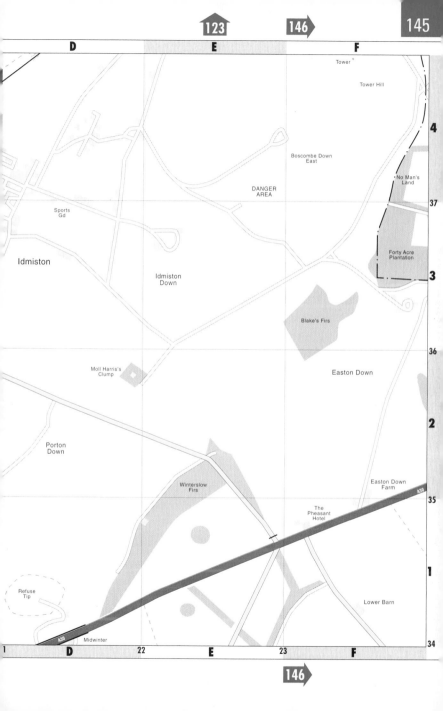

D **E** **F**

A343

PH
Kent's
Farm

Suddern
Farm

Middle Wallop
Airfield

SALISBURY LA
FRIARS
COTTS
CARUM CL
OBWE SQ
COTTAGE

Wallop
Prim Sch

SCHOOL LA

SCHOOL LANE
COTTS

4

Haydown
Farm

**Middle
Wallop**

KNOCKWOOD LA

Salisbury La

Farley
Farm

Goddard's
Farm

BENT CL

Hatchetts
Farm

37

Hill
Farm

FARLEY ST

Poultry
Houses

Wallop
House

Benham Dro

THE
CAUSEWAY

3

New Manor
Farm

HORLETTE LA

Boardgate
Farm

HIGH
ST

DUCKS LA

ROMSEY RD

Ashers
Farm

ALFRIDGE WALK

Bottom Rd

FIVE BELLS LA

Gastons
Farm

BUSTARDS
CNR

36

SPEED DRO

Wood Way

Testwood
Farm

WALLOP RD

2

Beech
Farm

A30

35

Kestrels
Farm

Newton

London
Cottage

1

SALISBURY RD

B3084

Kent's
Wood

34

D 28 **E** 29 **F**

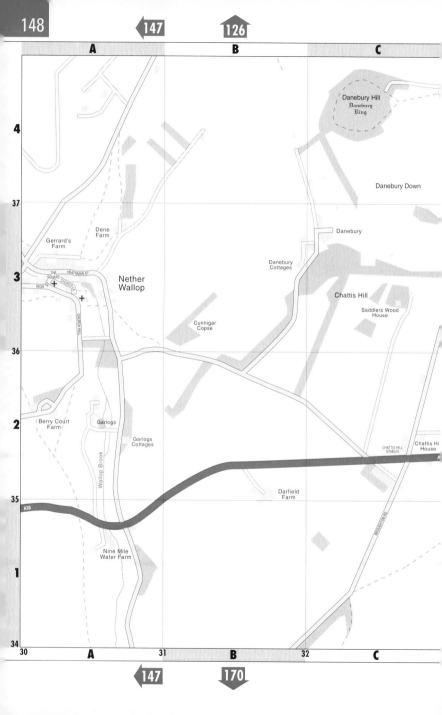

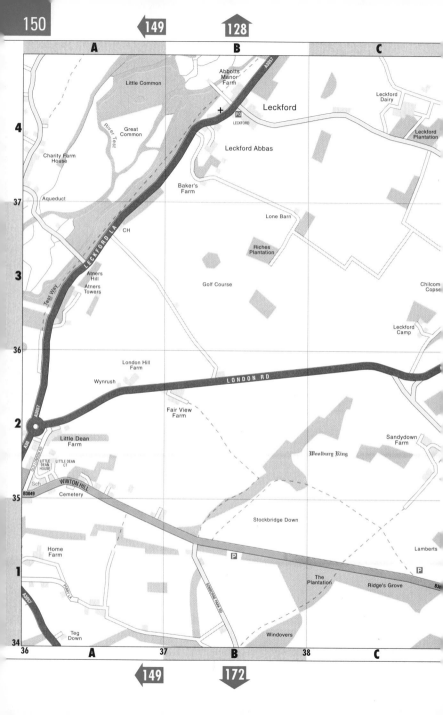

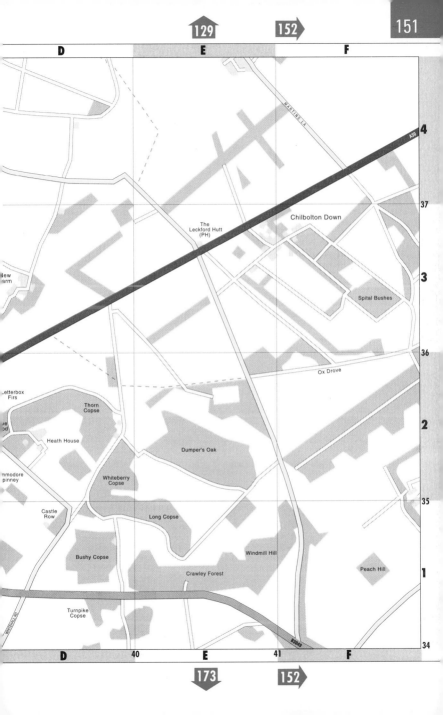

A30

A272

Dead Mans Belt

Brockley
Cottages

Hill Farm

4

A30

Barton Stacey Belt

Barton Stacey Belt

37

Barton
Ashes

Brockley Warren

3

Crawley Down

Ox Drove

Crawley
Clump

36

Warren
Wood

2

Warren
Cottages

35

New
Barn

NEW BARN
COTTS

HACKS LA

CRICKET CL

Crawley
Court

CRAWLEY
COTTS

Crawley

Cemy

Fox & Hounds
(PH)

1

Rack
Belt

Morns
Field

Beeches
Farm

34

42   A   43   B   44   C

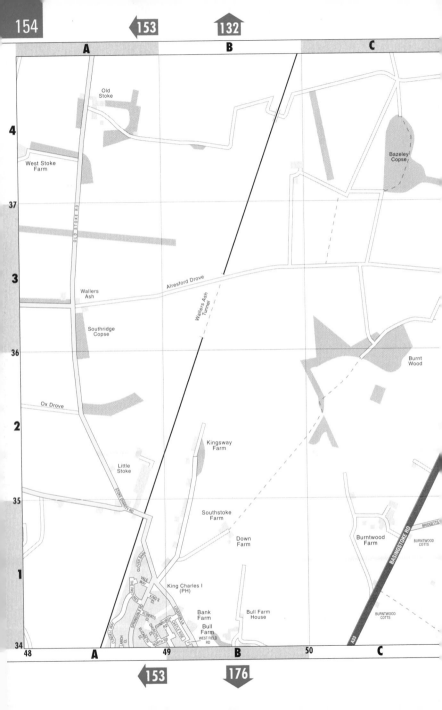

153 132

4

37

3

36

2

35

1

34

48 A 49 B 50 C

Old
Stoke

Bazeley
Copse

West Stoke
Farm

OLD STOKE RD

Alresford Drove

Wallers
Ash

Wallers Ash Tunnel

Southridge
Copse

Burnt
Wood

Ox Drove

Kingsway
Farm

Little
Stoke

STOKE CHARITY RD

Southstoke
Farm

BASINGSTOKE RD

BRIDGETS

Burntwood
Farm

BURNTWOOD
COTTS

Down
Farm

OLD LANE

VALE
WAY

KING'S
PL

THE PIGHTLE

EDINBURGH RD

ROBERTS
RD

CASTLE RISE

LARCH
CL

ROBERTS
RD

NORTH RD

CHAR EDINBURGH
RD

CASTLE RD

King Charles I
(PH)

Bank
Farm

Bull
Farm

WEST FIELD RD

Bull Farm
House

Bull Farm

A33

BURNTWOOD
COTTS

D E F

4

37

3

36

2

35

1

34

Winchester Rd
A33
M3

Micheldever
Wood

Long Wlk

Mill Lane
Copse

Newdown
Farm

Alresford Dro

Lunways Inn
(PH)

Hassock
Copse

BASINGSTOKE RD

Itchen
Wood

CHILLANDHAM LA

Shroner
Wood

Shroner Wood
House

Courtney's
Copse

Shroner Hill
Farm

The
Scrubbs

CHILLANDHAM LA

Rutherley
Copse

Chillandham
Farm

Bridget's
Farm

BRIDGETS LA

M3

Lone
Farm

D 52 E 53 F

A   B   C

4

Lawn
Copse

Northington
Down

Kites
Hill

Northington

Northington Down
Farm

Lawn
Cottage

+

Swarraton

37

Northfield
Plantation

Piggery

Newhouse
Farm

The Grange
Farm

3

Newhouse

New
Lodge

Swarraton
Lodge

The Grange
Park

East
Lodge

36

The Grange

The Grange
Lake

2

35

Lynch
Row

Abbotstone
Farm

Wayfarers Wlk

NORTHINGTON RD

Abbotstone

1

New
Cottages

Three Castles Path

Itchen Stoke
Down

Wayfarers Wlk

Watercress
Beds

Itchen Down
Farm

34

54   A   55   B   56   C

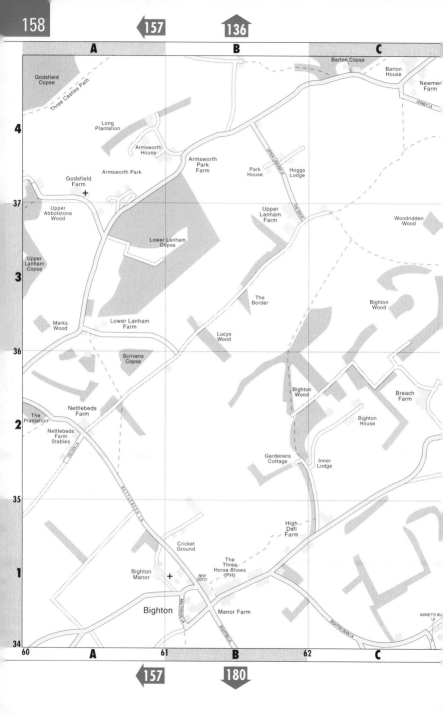

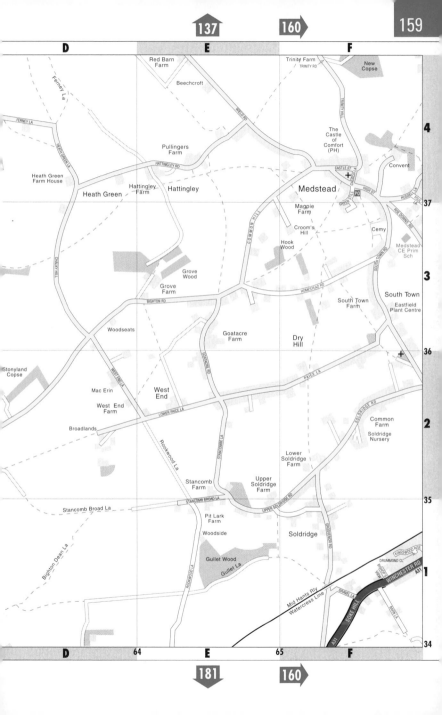

159
138

A   B   C

Bushy Leaze Wood

Meadow View Farm

Redwood Farm

Jennie Green La

The Abbey

Cemy

Old Park Farm

Mast

Redwood

Redwood Poultry Farm

RUSSELL LA

4

Spruce Copse

Foul La

The Hassock

Lodge Hill

37

Down Copse

Chawton Park Wood

Chawton Park Bungalow

Roe Downs Farm

BRICKILN LA

Brickiln Farm

Roedowns Cottage

High Wood

3

Redhill Copse

Gibbet Copse

Red Hill Farm

RED HILL

Mid Hants Rly
Watercress Line

Wr Twr   * Mast

36

Eighteen Acre Plantation

Firtree Copse

THE CRESCENT

BOYNESWOOD RD

Fourteen Acre Plantation

THE SHRAVE

BOYNESWOOD LA

Houghton's Piece

New Copse

Beverley Farm

Estevan Farm

2

Medstead & Four Marks Sta.

CHAWTON CL

WINCHESTER RD

Weathermore Copse

Weathermore La

Dell Piece

Woodlea Farm

STATION APP

PH

FAIRFIELD GREEN

MILLBRIDGE

Semaphore Farm

35

Four Marks

ALTON LA

BIGHTSTONE LA

Battles Copse

1

A31

ST FAITHS

Garden Ctr

Greenways Farm

Willis Farmhouse

WILLIS LA

Kitcombe La

Budgetts Farm

Crofters Farm

34

66   A   67   B   68   C

159
182

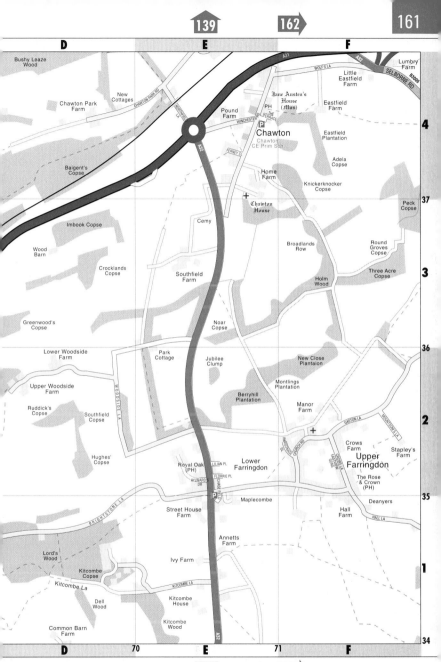

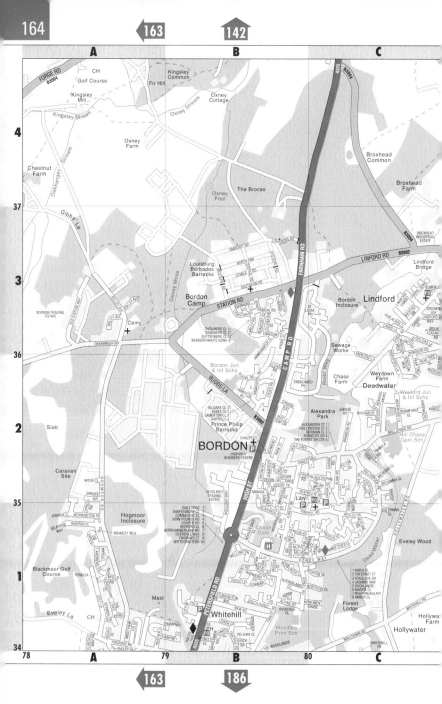

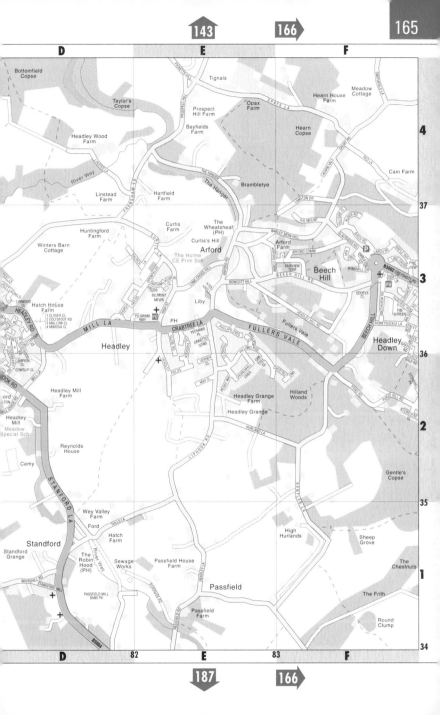

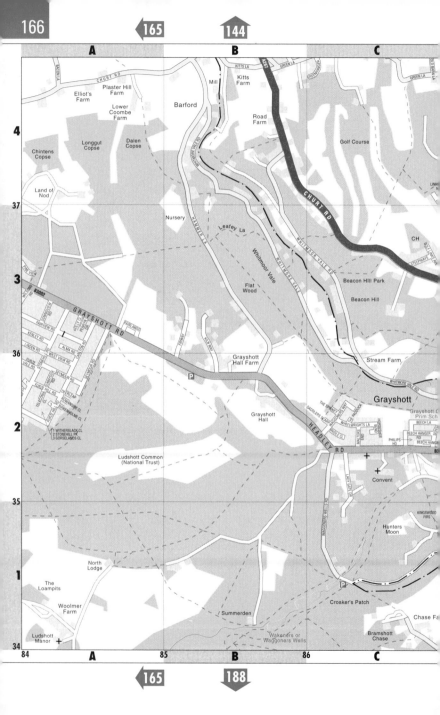

D   E   F

Green La
Valley Farm
Hyde Hill
Marchants Hill
Gravel Hanger
Beacon Hill
Marchants Hill Activity Ctr
4
Highcomb Copse
37
Highcomb Bottom
Meml
Highcombe Farm
Twizzletwig
3
Beacon Hill Cty First Sch
Hotel
TRIMMERS WOOD
The Beacon
Hindhead Common
Devil's Punch Bowl
PH
CHURT RD
Golden Valley
Hindhead
36
Meml
MEAD RD
Whitmore Vale Farm
1 THE KINGS PEACE
2 BEACON VIEW HO
3 THE SQUARE
4 OAKLEA HO
5 ROCKDALE HO
6 THE GABLES
7 SUMMERHOUSE CT
8 WOOLMER VIEW
HIGHFIELD CRES
ROYAL PAR
LONDON RD
Hind Head
2
VALE WOOD LA
CHURCH LA
GLEN RD
PH
HEADLEY RD
Libry
B3002
RUSSELL CT 1
HEATHER CT 2
BROOM SQUIRES 3
HINDHEAD HO 4
TYNDALLS EST
Tyndalls Wood
St Edmunds Sch
FORESTDALE
STONEY BOTTOM
Nutcombe Down
35
KINGSWOOD FIRS
MOWATT RD
Nutcombe Valley
PORTSMOUTH RD
KINGSWOOD FIRS
Kingswood Firs
KINGSWOOD LA
KINGSWOOD
HINDHEAD RD
Greensand Way
Royal Naval Sch
1
Mount Alvernia
Nutcombe
Chasemoor
Theo Grove Sch
Craig's Wood
Coombswell Copse
Amesbury Sch
STOATLEY HOLLOW
Haslemere
High Pitfold Farm
34
A3

D   88   E   89   F

189

East Winterslow

Howe Copse

Burretts Grove

Earthpits Wood

Ramshill Dro

Red La

Hill Farm

Ramshill House

Warren Farm

4

Cooper's Farm

Noad's Copse

Middle Winterslow

Birchen Copse

33

THE CAUSEWAY

STONE CL

THE FLASHETT

GUNVILLE HILL

EASTON COMMON HILL

The Monarch's Way

Little Buckholt Farm

PADDOCK

BROOK LOW END

PO

PH

THE COMMON

Robin Hill Farm

TYTHERLEY RD

Clarendon Way

Upper Noad's Copse

COMMON VALE

MEADFIELD RD

The Common

WITT RD

Lower Noad's Copse

3

Yarmley Farm

BENTLEY WAY

Witt's End

Elevage Breton

32

Richwellsted Copse

Hedgemoor Copse

Tanglewood

Picked Copse

2

Gravel Shoot Copse

Home Farm

Chickard Wood

Three Sisters Copse

Smokeway Copse

31

LIVERY RD

Northaw Sch

Hooping Oak Copse

Prior's Copse

1

Bentley Wood

PARK LA

Coalpits Copse

Beechways Copse

Redman's Gore

Park Copse

30

24   **A**   25   **B**   26   **C**

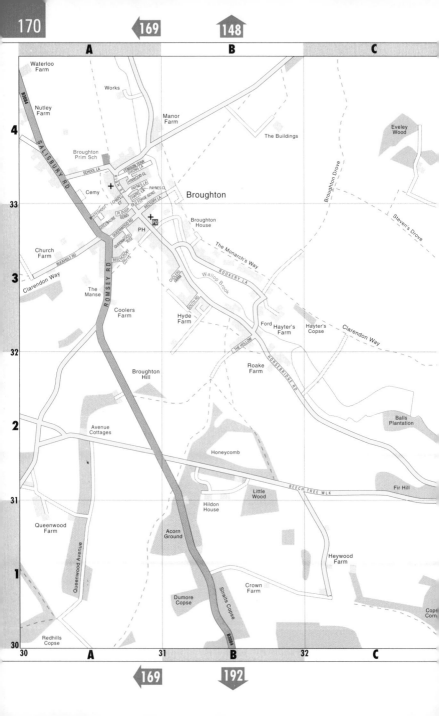

169
148

A   **B**   **C**

Waterloo Farm

Works

Nutley Farm

Manor Farm

The Buildings

Eveley Wood

4

Broughton Prim Sch

SCHOOL LA

Broughton Drive

SALISBURY RD

Cemy

VENDON TERR

HINWOOD CL

PAYNES LA

PAYNES CL

CHAPEL LA

OLD FORGE GDNS

Broughton

Steven's Drove

33

WHITECHURCH

CHAPEL CL

FLOUDS

RECTORY LA

Broughton House

QUEENWOOD RD

SHEEPMERE LA

PH

PO

GREENWOOD RISE

The Monarch's Way

Church Farm

BUCKHOLT RD

BEECHCROFT COTTS

ROOKERY LA

3

Clarendon Way

ROMSEY RD

The Manse

COOLERS GARTH

Wallop Brook

COOLERS

SOUTH RD

Coolers Farm

Hyde Farm

Ford

Hayter's Farm

Hayter's Copse

Clarendon Way

32

Broughton Hill

Roake Farm

THE HOLLOW

HORSEBRIDGE RD

Balls Plantation

2

Avenue Cottages

Honeycomb

BEECH TREE WLK

Fir Hill

31

Queenwood Farm

Little Wood

Queenwood Avenue

Hildon House

Acorn Ground

Heywood Farm

1

Crown Farm

Dumore Copse

Straits Copse

B3084

Cops Corn

30

Redhills Copse

30   **A**   **31**   **B**   **32**   **C**

169
192

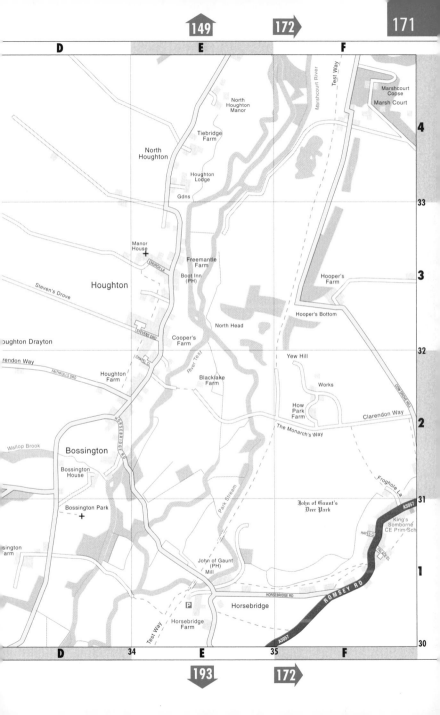

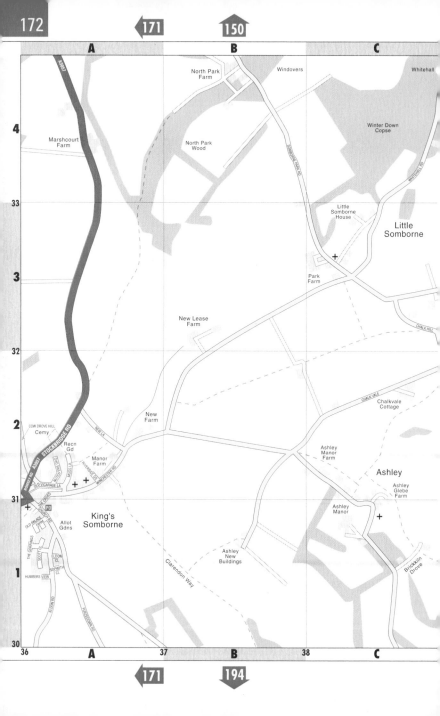

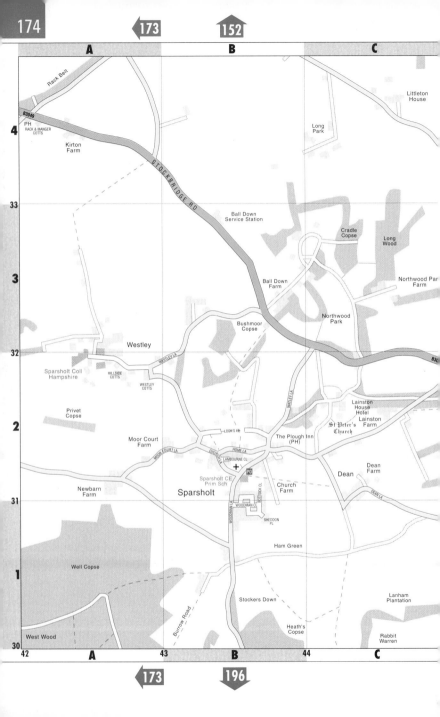

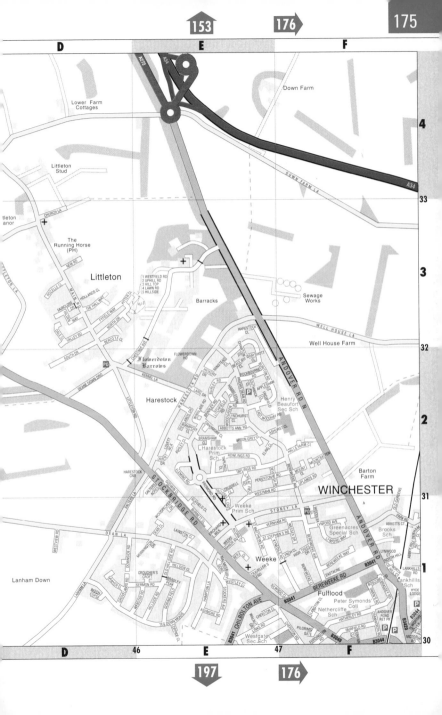

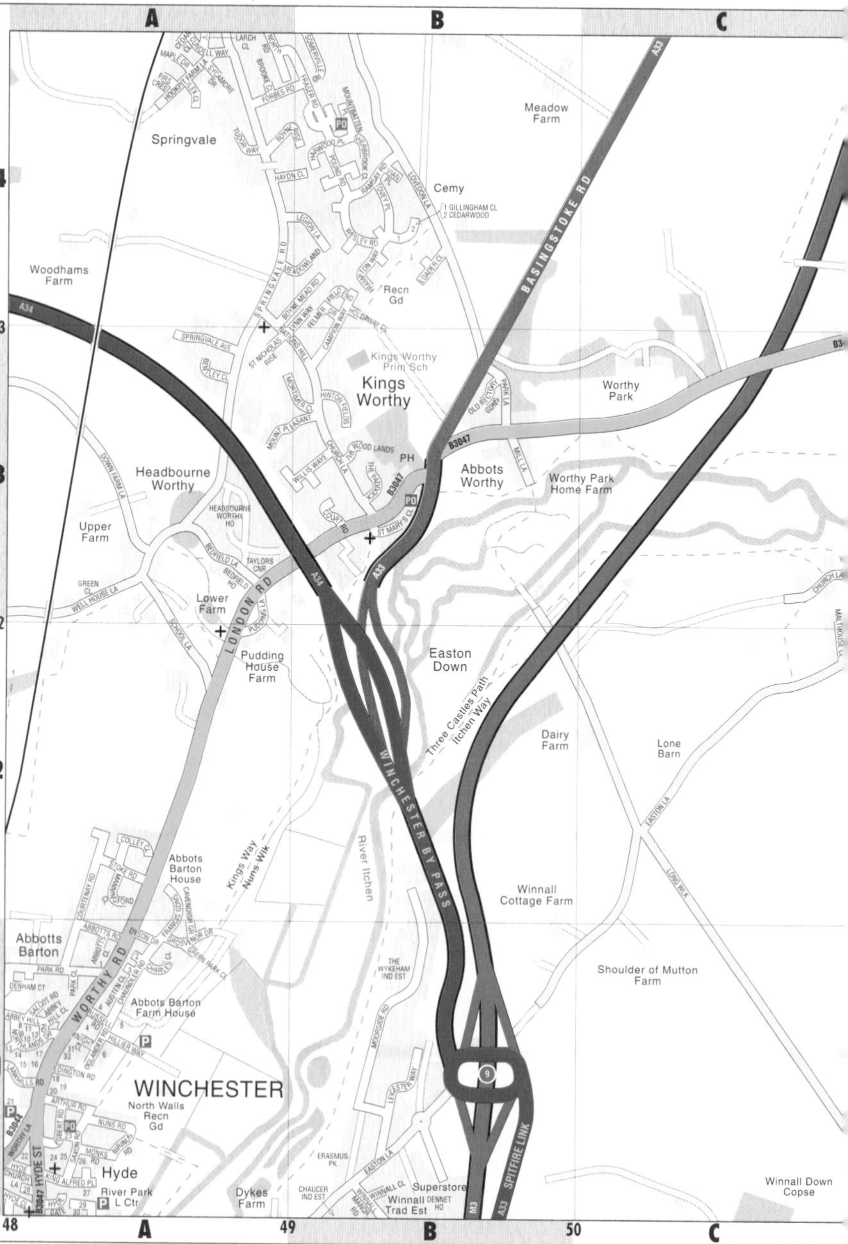

A1
1 PARK CT
2 HUSSEY CL
3 CORAM CL
4 CONEY GN
5 SIMONDS CT
6 COLBOURNE CT
7 COVENTRY CT
8 KENILWORTH CT
9 STRATFORD CT
10 MERIDEN CT
11 WARNER CT
12 ALTON CT
13 WARWICK CL
14 HYDE WICK CT
15 TWYFORD CT
16 FARINGDON CT
17 REGENT CT
18 WOODLANDS CT
19 DONNINGTON CT
20 THE TOLLGATE
21 HYDE LODGE
22 HYDE HOUSE GDNS
23 DANES RD
24 HYDE CHURCH PATH
25 BARTHOLOMEW CL
26 ST BEDE'S CT
27 ALSWITHA TERR
28 ROSEWARNE CT
29 KING ALFRED TERR

A1
30 ARLINGTON PL
31 DALZELL
32 YORK HO

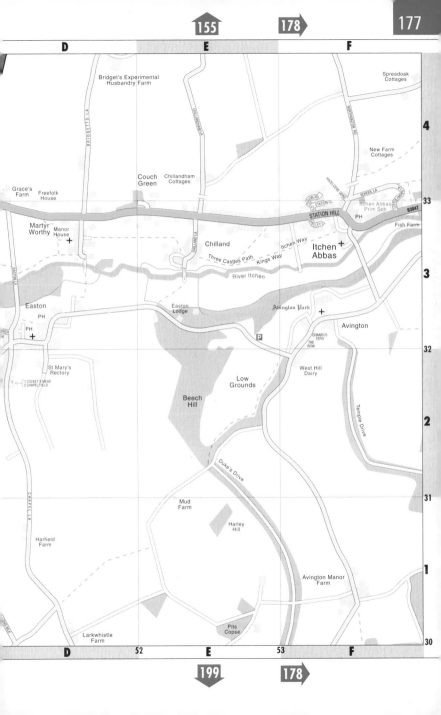

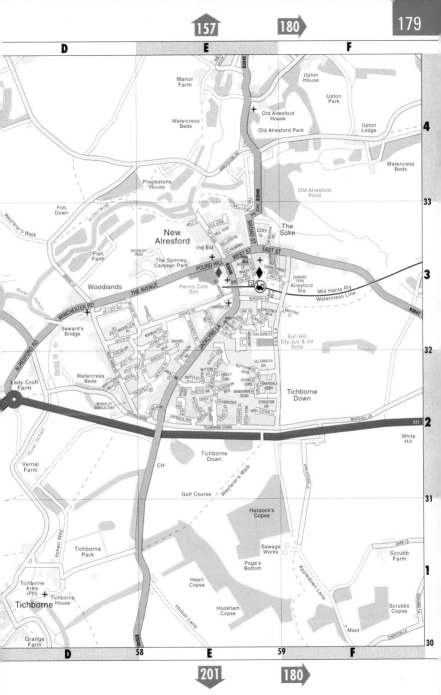

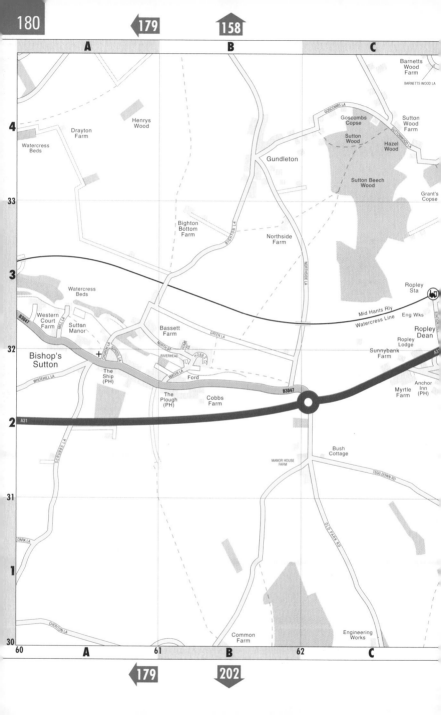

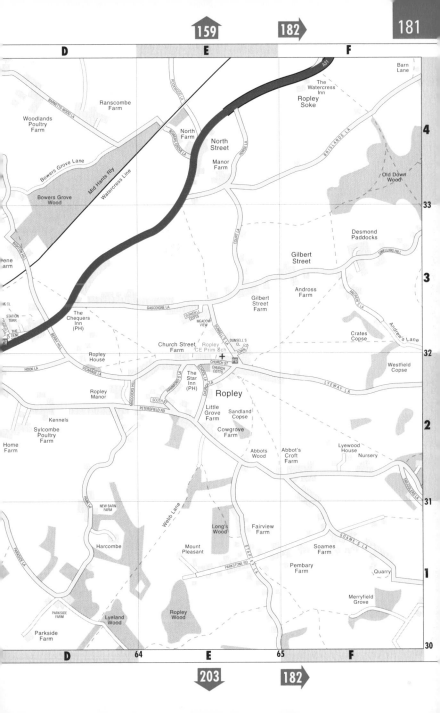

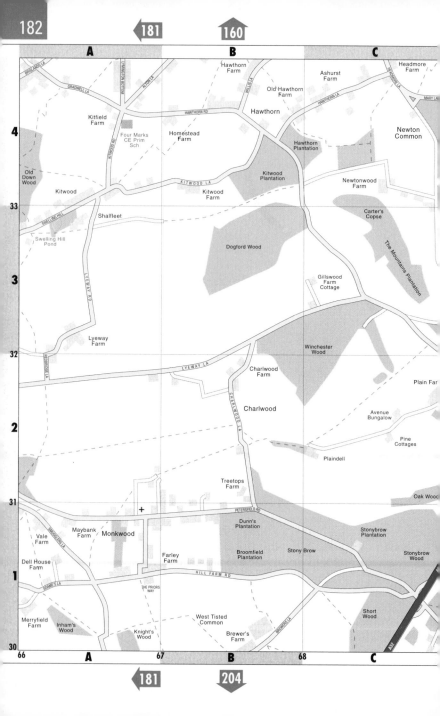

4

3

33

32

2

31

1

30

A

B

C

Brisland La

Gradwell La

Kitfield Farm

Four Marks CE Prim Sch

Homestead Farm

Hawthorn Rd

Hawthorn Farm

Old Hawthorn Farm

Ashurst Farm

Headmore Farm

Mary La

Hawthorn

Hawthorn La

Newton Common

Old Down Wood

Kitwood

Swelling Hill

Shalfleet

Kitwood La

Kitwood Farm

Kitwood Plantation

Hawthorn Plantation

Newtonwood Farm

Carter's Copse

Swelling Hill Pond

Dogford Wood

Gillswood Farm Cottage

The Mountains Plantation

Lyeway Rd

Lyeway Farm

Ridgefield La

Lyeway La

Charlwood Farm

Winchester Wood

Plain Far

Charlwood

Avenue Bungalow

Pine Cottages

Charlwood La

Plaindell

Treetops Farm

Oak Wood

Petersfield Rd

Maybank Farm

Monkwood

Dunn's Plantation

Stonybrow Plantation

Vale Farm

Dell House Farm

Farley Farm

Broomfield Plantation

Stony Brow

Stonybrow Wood

Hill Farm Rd

Smokey La

The Priors Way

Short Wood

Merryfield Farm

Inham's Wood

Knight's Wood

West Tisted Common

Brewer's Farm

Brislea La

A32

66

67

68

A

B

C

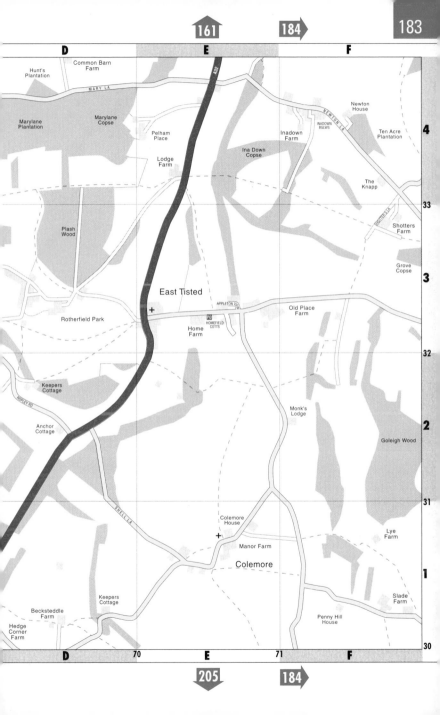

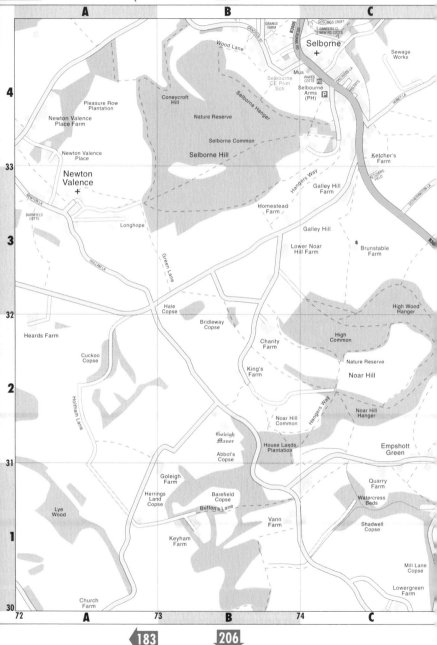

185
164

A   **B**   **C**

A325

MAYFLOWER RD

OAK TREE RD

THE

WALLDOWN RD

LIPHOOK RD

WHITEHILL PARK

PH

HOLLYWA
Green

St Matthew's
C E Prim
Sch

NETHERBY

FLETC

PLAYGROUND

WAY

CHASE RD

Round
Hill

Hollywater
Clump

Hollywater
Clump

4

DANGER AREA

The
Vicarage

Rifle Range

Fern Hill

Pa
H

33

DANGER AREA

Horsebush Hill

Linchboro
Park

BLACKMOOR RD

Cranmer
Bottom

PETERSFIELD RD

3

DANGER AREA

Woolmer
Cottages

Woolmer Forest

Queen's
Bank

Long Down

Brimstone Inclosure

Woolmer Pond
Cottage

Keepers
Cottage

32

Woolmer Pond

Woolmer
Down

Heife
Dow

BENHAM LA

WOOLMER
TERR

PO

Forest
Side Farm

WOOLMER RD

A325

Rifle Range

2

Inn

DANGER AREA

King's
Holt

LONGMOOR RD

PLUMER RD

KITCHENER RD

NETHERN RD

HOPESWOOD

HOLTMENT LA

31

Forest
Side

WHITE WAY

KIMBERLEY RD

ROBERTS RD

FRENCH RD

RAILWAY RD

HAM

OR HUNTERS RD

Broad
Hill

Longmoor
Camp

MOOR RD

1

Palmer's Ball

Longmoor
Inclosure

Weavers Down

A

Greatham
Moor

30

78   **A**   **79**   **B**   **80**   **C**

185
208

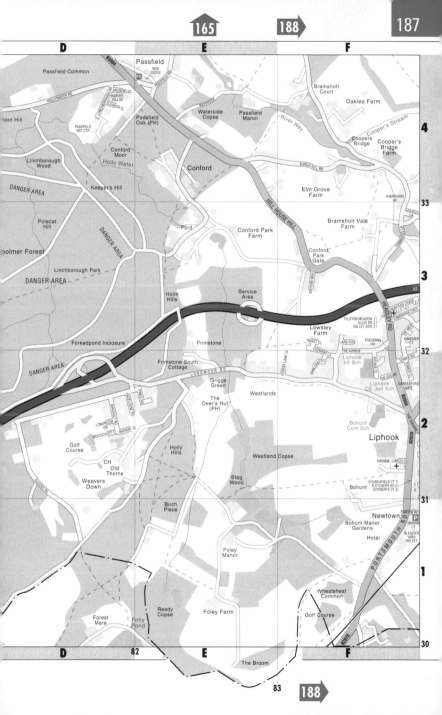

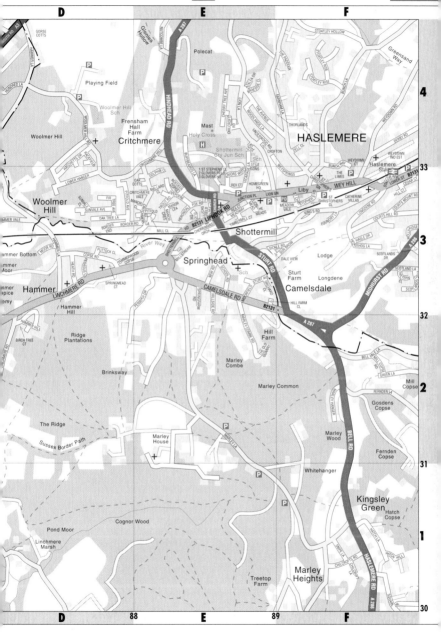

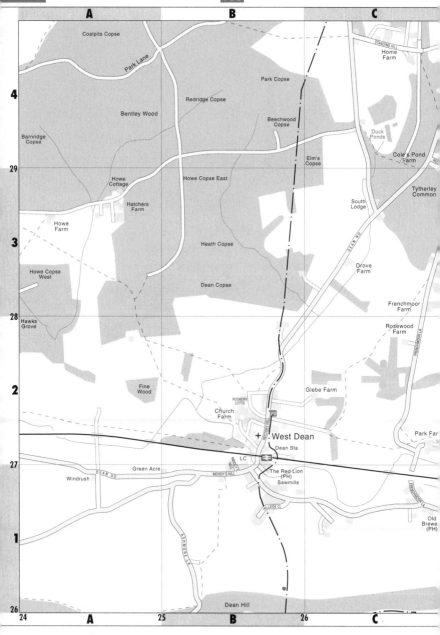

Coalpits Copse

Park Lane

Home Farm

STANDING HILL

Park Copse

4

Redridge Copse

Bentley Wood

Beechwood Copse

Duck Ponds

Cole's Pond Farm

Barnridge Copse

29

Howe Copse East

Howe Cottage

Elm's Copse

DEAN RD

South Lodge

Tytherley Common

Hatchers Farm

Howe Farm

3

Heath Copse

Drove Farm

Howe Copse West

Frenchmoor Farm

Dean Copse

28

Rosewood Farm

Hawks Grove

FRENCHMOOR LA

2

Fine Wood

Glebe Farm

ROOKERY COTTS

Church Farm

Park Far

PO

West Dean

Dean Sta

Green Acre

LC

Park Far

27

DEAN RD

MOODY'S HILL

The Red Lion (PH)

Windrush

Sawmills

FRENCHMOOR LA

HILLSIDE CL

Old Brewe (PH)

1

ASHWORTH LA

26

Dean Hill

24   A   25   B   26   C

A B C

4

29

3

28

2

27

1

26

30 A 31 B 32 C

Redhills Copse

Hackpits Copse

B3084

Deborah Copse

Pittleworth Manor

Pittleworth Farm

Little Bentley Farm

Great Bentley Farm

Holm Moor Copse

Bentley Firs

Blackpits Wood

The Bungalow

Lain Copse

Great Copse

Clapgate Copse

Spearywell Wood

Newlyns Farm

BACK LA

Snook's Copse

Blackmoor Firs

Bushy Copse

Culver Leaze

Woodland Walk

P

Cadbury Farm

Spearywell

Test Way

Dummer Copse

Mottisfont Abbey (National Trust)

Priory

Gardens

Abbey Farm

Keepers La

Benger's La

OLD BARN DRIVE

Mottisfont

PO

Drove Copse

Hatt La

Glebe Farm

River Dun

The Monarch's Way

River Test

CHURCH LA

Hatt Farm

Hatt Hill

Lockerley Endowed CE Prim Sch

Dunbridge

The School Farm

Butt's Green

Lockerley

LC

LC

Test Way

River Dun

Dunbridge Sta

PH

Mill Rise

LOCKERLEY RD

DUNBRIDGE RD

B3084

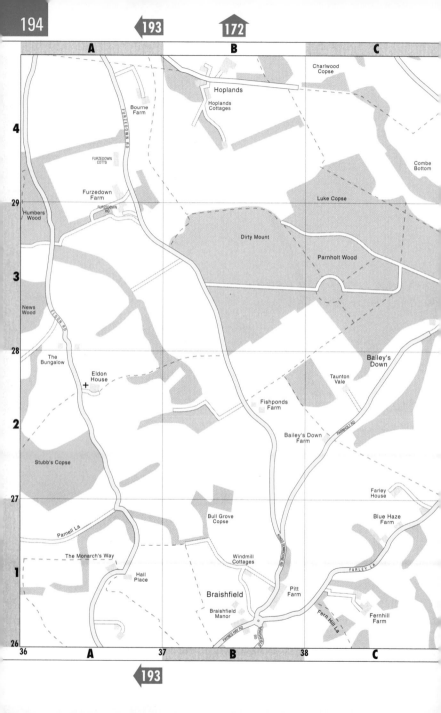

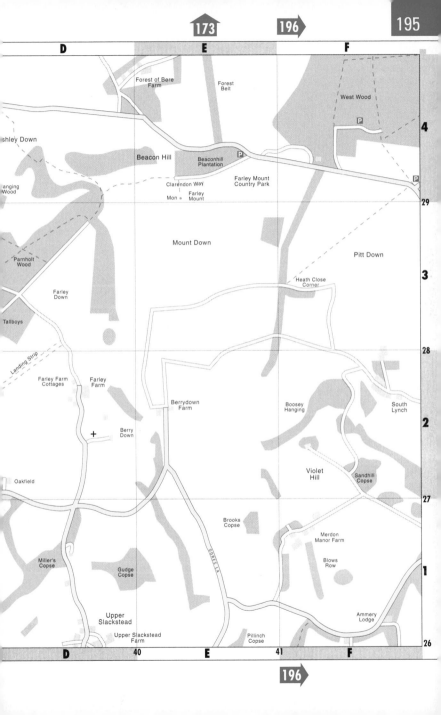

West Wood

Burrow
Copse

Crab Wood

Ashmore
Hill
Copse

Crabwood
Farm
House

Crabwood
House

Clarendon Way

SARUM RD

Pittdown
Plantation

Pitt Down

Little
Pittdown
Plantation

Enmill
House

Enmill
Barn

ENMILL LA

Vale Farm

Enmill
Farm

Pitt View

White House

Pages
Copse

Grovelands
Copse

Yew Tree

Pitt
Copse

MILLERS LA

Stopham's
Copse

MELKSHAM RD

SPARSHOLT RD

Larkfarm
Plantation

Southlynch
Plantation

Standon
Farm

Juniper
Bank

Nan Trodd's
Hill

Standon

Butcher's
Plantation

Down Farm

PORT LA

Merdon
Castle

A3090

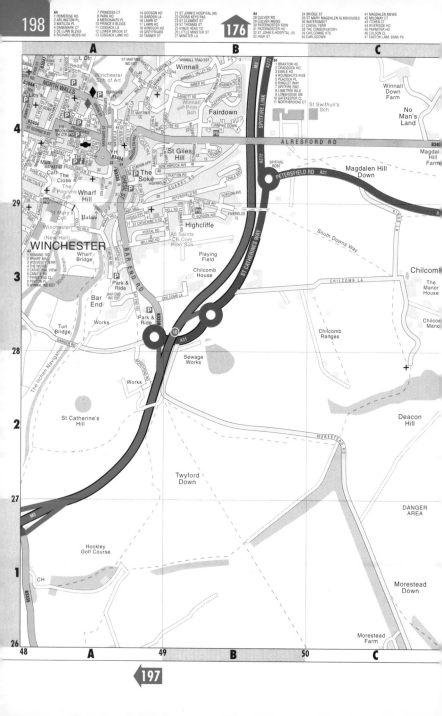

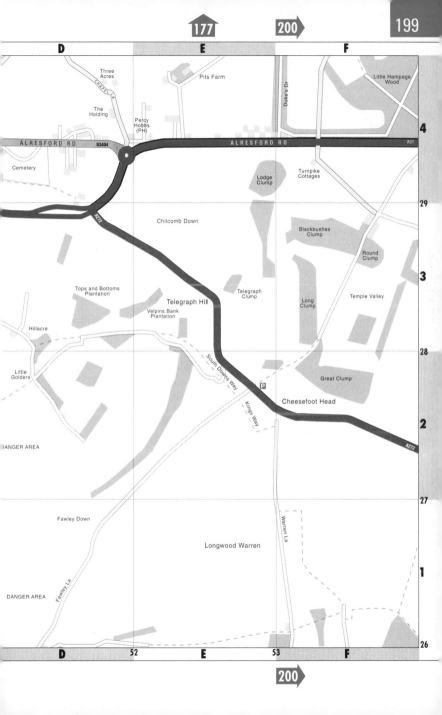

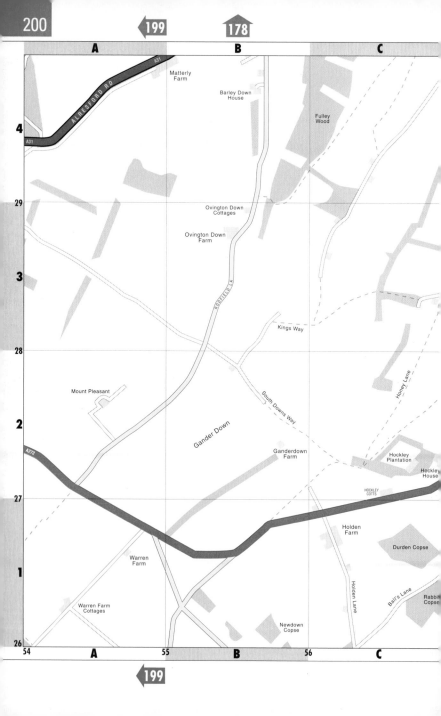

199
178

A **B** **C**

ALRESFORD RD

A31

Matterly
Farm

Barley Down
House

Fulley
Wood

4

A31

29

Ovington Down
Cottages

Ovington Down
Farm

Kings Way

3

28

Mount Pleasant

South Downs Way

Honey Lane

2

Gander Down

Ganderdown
Farm

Hockley
Plantation

Hockley
House

A272

HOCKLEY
COTTS

27

Holden
Farm

Durden Copse

Warren
Farm

Holden Lane

Ball's Lane

Rabbit
Copse

1

Warren Farm
Cottages

Newdown
Copse

26

54 **A** **55** **B** **56** **C**

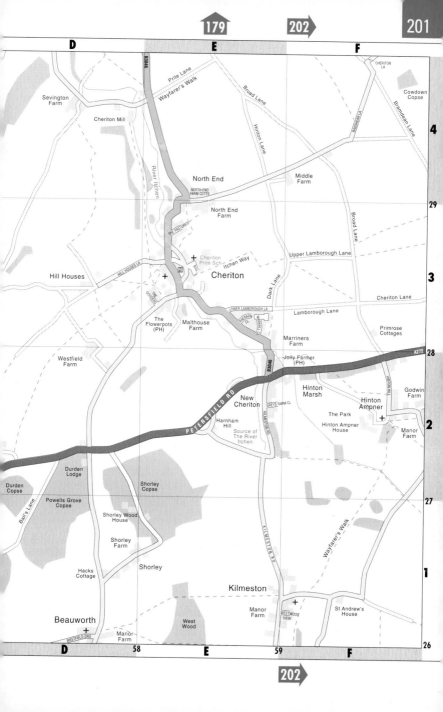

D E F

4

29

3

Cowdown
Copse

CHERITON
LA

Sevington
Farm

Cheriton Mill

Prite Lane

Wayfarer's Walk

Broad Lane

Hinton Lane

River Itchen

North End

Middle
Farm

NORTH END
FARM COTTS

North End
Farm

THE PASTURES

Hill Houses

MILL HOUSES LA

Cheriton
Prim Sch

Itchen Way

Cheriton

Upper Lamborough Lane

Dark Lane

Cheriton Lane

Broad Lane

28

The Flowerpots
(PH)

THE GODSELL

LOWER LAMBOROUGH LA

TICHBARN

Malthouse
Farm

Lamborough Lane

Primrose
Cottages

Westfield
Farm

Marriners
Farm

Jolly Farmer
(PH)

B3046

A272

Godwin
Farm

Hinton
Marsh

Hinton
Ampner

2

PETERSFIELD RD

New
Cheriton

GREYS FARM CL

KILMESTON RD

The Park

Hinton Ampner
House

Manor
Farm

Harnham
Hill

Source of
The River
Itchen

HINTON HILL

Durden
Lodge

Durden
Copse

Ball's Lane

Powells Grove
Copse

Shorley
Copse

Shorley Wood
House

27

Shorley
Farm

Shorley

KILMESTON RD

Wayfarer's Walk

1

Hacks
Cottage

Beauworth

WESTFIELD DRO

Manor
Farm

West
Wood

Kilmeston

Manor
Farm

WESTWOOD
VIEW

St Andrew's
House

26

D 58 E 59 F

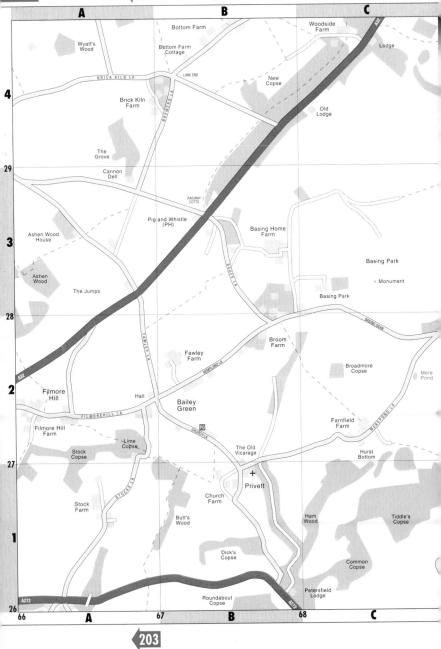

	A	B	C

4

Church Farm

Manor House

Five Ash Farm

Hawkley Hanger

Lowergreen Farm

Lower Green

Champlers Farm

Hawkley

PH

POCOCKS LA

29

Warren Farm

Tubb's Farm

Cheesecombe Farm

3

The Warren

Reston Hanger

Oakshott Farm

Oakshott Stream

Moore's Copse

Warren Corner

Windmill Cottage

Shaw Wood

Roundhills Hanger

WARREN LA

28

Parsons

Happersnapper Hanger

Oakshott

Lower Oakshott Farmhouse

GREEN LA

Hill Farm

Oakshott Hanger

Wheatham Hill

2

TROOPER BOTTOM

PH

WOODFIELD COTTS

Hangers Way

COTTAGE LA

Ringsgreen Copse

Rings Green

Ringsgreen Lane

Woodfield Copse

OLD LITTEN LA

Old Litten Lane

27

Ashford Hill

Shoulder of Mutton Hill

HIGH CROSS LA

COCKSHOTT LA

1

Wyke Green Farm

Week Green Farm

Lutcombe Bottom

Ashford Farm

ASHFORD CHACE

Bushy Hill

MILL LA

SGALWOOD LA

STONER HILL RD

Wyke Green Cottage

Little Langleys

26

Stoner Hill

72	A	73	B	74	C

D E F

Mabbotts
Adam's Wood
Uplands
Lowerbarn Copse
UPLAND LA
Scotland Farm
Farewells
Prouts Farm
Hurst Cottages
Oakshott Stream
Barefoots Farm
Wheatham Farm
Glascombe Hanger
Coldhayes Wood
Coldhayes
Steep Marsh Farm
Steep Marsh
The Moors
NINE ACRES

Hurst Farm
Park Lands Farm
SWAILING LA
Primmers
Lyss Place Farm
Lyss Place
Batt's Brook
Woolshers Cottage
Flexcombe
Gardner's Farm
Bowyer's Common
The Lodge

Ham Barn Farm
River Rother
Greatham Bridge
Berry Grove Farm
CHURCH ST
Burgates Farm
Burgates
ELM TERR
HOMEFIELD COTTS
HAWKLEY RD
Upper Green
The Blue Bell (PH)
THE GREEN
KILN
Brows Farm
CHILMARK CT
F2
1 MEADOW WLK
2 SPRINGFIELD
3 SCHOOL LA
4 COLLARD WAY
5 PORTLAND SQ
FARNHAM RD
Sewage Works
River Rother
Prince's Bridge
LC
Little Stodham House

Goleigh Farm House
A3
Moor Park Farm
Kippences
West Liss
THE ARCADE
STATION RD
Liss Sta
LC
BRIDGE MEADOWS
LONGMEAD
ROTHER HO
HILL BROW RD
B3006
MT WORTH
NURSERY FIELD
Andlers Ash Farm
Prince's Marsh
LC
STODHAM
Pruetts
Stodham Park
PAGE LEA

4
29
3
28
2
27
1
26

D 76 E 77 F

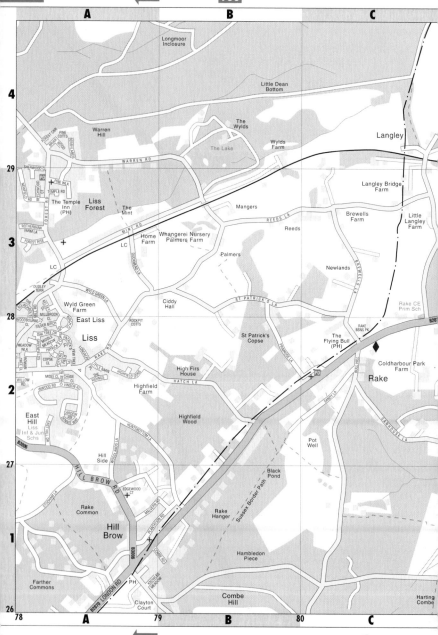

Longmoor
Inclosure

Little Dean
Bottom

The
Wylds

Warren
Hill

Langley

Wylds
Farm

The Lake

WARREN RD

SHERWOOD CL

Langley Bridge
Farm

The Temple
Inn
(PH)

Liss
Forest

The
Mint

Mangers

REEDS LA

Brewells
Farm

Little
Langley
Farm

ROTHERBANK
FARM LA

FOREST RISE

LC

Home
Farm

Whangerei Nursery
Palmers Farm

Reeds

LC

Palmers

Newlands

LC

DUDLEY
TERR

WYLD GREEN LA

Wyld Green
Farm

Ciddy
Hall

ST PATRICK S LA

Rake CE
Prim Sch

28

MILLBROOK
CL

SILVER BIRCH

East Liss

ROCKPIT
COTTS

RAKE
BSNS PK

B20

OAK TREE DR

Liss

St Patrick's
Copse

The Flying Bull
(PH)

MEADOW
WLK

COPSE
CL

Coldharbour Park
Farm

High Firs
House

Rake

WILLOW
RD

MOSS CL

VINSON RD

Highfield
Farm

HATCH LA

HIGHFIELD RD

East
Hill

Liss
Inf & Jun
Schs

Highfield
Wood

HUNTSBOTTOM LA

Pot
Well

B3006

27

Hill
Side

HILL BROW RD

EDGEWOOD
CT

Rake
Common

Black
Pond

Sussex Border Path

Hill
Brow

Rake
Hanger

1

B3006

B2070 LONDON RD

PH

Farther
Commons

Clayton
Court

Hambledon
Piece

Combe
Hill

Harting
Combe

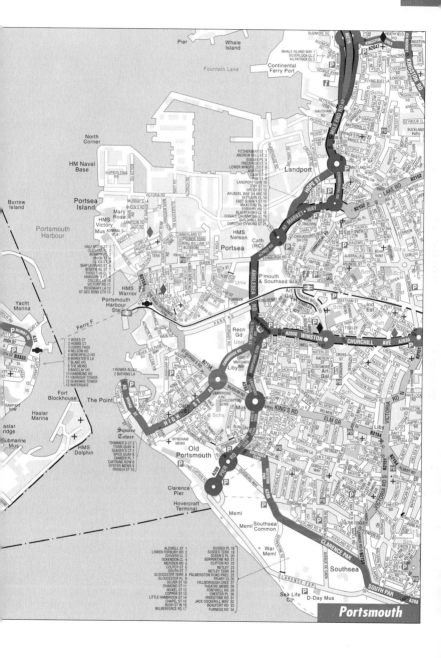

Portsmouth

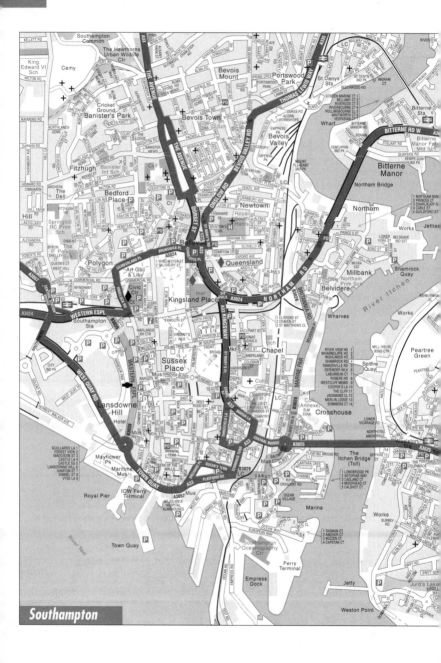

Southampton

Street names are listed alphabetically and show the locality, the Postcode District, the page number and a reference to the square in which the name falls on the map page

Victoria Gdns 9 Fleet GU13 .... 53 F1

Full street name
This may have been abbreviated on the map

Location Number
If present, this indicates the street's position on a congested area of the map instead of the name

Town, village or locality in which the street falls

Postcode District for the street name

Page number of the map on which the street name appears

Grid square in which the centre of the street falls

Schools, hospitals, sports centres, railway stations, shopping centres, industrial estates, public amenities and other places of interest are also listed.

Abbreviations used in the index

App	Approach	Cl	Close	Ent	Enterprise	La	Lane	Rdbt	Roundabout

App Approach
Arc Arcade
Ave Avenue
Bvd Boulevard
Bldgs Buildings
Bsns Pk Business Park
Bsns Ctr Business Centre
Bglws Bungalows
Ctr Centre
Cir Circus

Cl Close
Comm Common
Cnr Corner
Cotts Cottages
Cres Crescent
Ct Court
Ctyd Courtyard
Dr Drive
Dro Drove
E East
Emb Embankment

Ent Enterprise
Espl Esplanade
Est Estate
Gdns Gardens
Gn Green
Gr Grove
Hts Heights
Ho House
Ind Est Industrial Estate
Intc Interchange
Junc Junction

La Lane
N North
Orch Orchard
Par Parade
Pk Park
Pas Passage
Pl Place
Prec Precinct
Prom Promenade
Ret Pk Retail Park
Rd Road

Rdbt Roundabout
S South
Sq Square
Strs Stairs
Stps Steps
St Street, Saint
Terr Terrace
Trad Est Trading Estate
Wlk Walk
W West
Yd Yard

Town and village index

Abbotts Ann 105 D2
Aldermaston 9 F4
Aldershot 76 A1
Alton 139 F2
Amport 104 A3
Andover 106 B4
Appleshaw 81 D3
Arborfield 15 D4
Ash 77 F2
Ashford Hill 8 B1
Ashley 172 C2
Ashmansworth 40 C4
Axford 114 B2
Ball Hill 4 A2
Barton Stacey 130 B3
Basingstoke 68 C3
Baughurst 26 B4
Beacon Hill 167 D4
Beech Hill 13 D3
Bentley 120 A3
Bentworth 138 A3
Bighton 158 B1
Binsted 141 F3
Bishop's Green 6 C2
Bishop's Sutton 180 A2
Blackwater 35 D2
Bordon 164 B2
Bossington 171 D2
Bradley 137 D4
Braishfield 194 B1
Bramdean 202 B2
Bramley 28 C2
Bramshill 31 F4
Bramshott 188 A3
Brimpton 8 C3
Broughton 170 B4
Brown Candover 135 D2
Burghclere 22 B4
Buttermere 18 A4
Camberley 36 B4
Charlton 82 C2
Charter Alley 46 C4
Chawton 161 E4
Cheriton 201 E3
Chilbolton 129 D2
Chilcomb 198 C3
Chineham 48 C2
Cholderton 101 E1
Churt 144 B1
Chute Forest 58 B2

Cliddesden 91 F4
Cold Ash 2 C4
Colemore 183 E1
Combe 19 E4
Crawley 152 A1
Crondall 97 E4
Crookham Village 74 B3
Deane 66 A1
Dogmersfield 74 A3
Dummer 90 B1
East Dean 191 D1
East Stratton 134 A2
East Tisted 183 E3
East Tytherley 191 F4
East Woodhay 20 B4
East Worldham 162 C4
Ecchinswell 23 E2
Ellisfield 115 E4
Enborne 4 B4
Enham Alamein 83 E4
Eversley 15 F1
Ewshot 98 A4
Farleigh Wallop 91 F1
Farley Castle 15 D4
Farley Hill 15 D3
Farnborough 55 F1
Farnham 98 C2
Finchampstead 16 B1
Fleet 54 A1
Fosbury 17 F1
Four Marks 160 B1
Frensham 144 A4
Froxfield 205 F1
Fyfield 80 C1
Golden Pot 117 E2
Goodworth Clatford .. 105 F1
Grateley 125 D4
Grayshott 166 C2
Greatham 185 F1
Greenham 6 A4
Greywell 71 F2
Hamstead Marshall 3 F4
Hannington 44 C2
Hartley Wespall 30 A1
Hartley Wintney 52 C3
Haslemere 189 F4
Hatherden 59 E1
Hawkley 206 C4
Hawley 35 E2
Headley 165 D3

Headley, Nr Greenham . 7 E1
Heckfield 31 D3
Herriard 93 D1
High Cross 205 F1
Highclere 21 F3
Hill Brow 208 A1
Hindhead 167 E3
Hook 51 D1
Houghton 171 D3
Hurstbourne Priors ... 85 E1
Hurstbourne Tarrant .. 60 C4
Ibworth 45 F1
Idmiston 145 D3
Itchen Abbas 177 F3
Itchen Stoke 178 B3
Kilmeston 201 E1
Kimpton 80 A2
King's Somborne 172 A1
Kings Worthy 176 B3
Kingsclere 24 B1
Kingsley 142 A1
Kintbury 3 D4
Knights Enham 83 D3
Lasham 116 B1
Laverstoke 87 E3
Leckford 150 B4
Linchmere 188 C1
Lindford 165 C3
Liphook 188 A2
Liss 208 A2
Litchfield 63 E4
Little Somborne 172 C3
Littleton 175 D3
Lockerley 191 F1
Long Sutton 95 F2
Longmoor Camp 186 B1
Longparish 108 B3
Longstock 149 F3
Lower Froyle 119 E3
Ludgershall 57 D1
Mapledurwell 70 C2
Mattingley 51 E4
Medstead 159 F4
Micheldever 133 D2
Michelmersh 193 E1
Middle Wallop 147 F4
Middle Winterslow .. 168 A4
Monk Sherborne 47 D3
Monkwood 182 A1
Monxton 104 B3

Mortimer 11 F3
Mottisfont 192 C1
Mytchett 56 B2
Nether Wallop 148 A3
New Alresford 179 E3
Newbury 1 B2
Newnham 50 B1
Newton Tony 123 D3
Newton Valence 184 A3
Newtown 5 F2
North Tidworth 79 D4
North Waltham 89 F1
North Warnborough .. 72 B2
Northington 156 C4
Oakhanger 163 E3
Oakley 67 E1
Odiham 72 C1
Old Alresford 157 E1
Old Basing 70 B3
Old Burghclere 42 B4
Over Wallop 125 D1
Overton 88 A4
Ovington 178 C2
Oxenwood 17 D2
Padworth 10 C4
Pamber End 27 E1
Pamber Heath 10 B3
Penton Grafton 81 F2
Picket Piece 84 A1
Popham 112 C2
Preston Candover ... 136 B4
Privett 204 B1
Quarley 103 D2
Quidhampton 65 D1
Rake 208 C2
Ramsdell 46 B4
Riseley 14 A2
Ropley 181 E2
Rotherwick 50 C3
Sandhurst 35 D4
Seale 100 C2
Selborne 184 C4
Shalden 139 D4
Sherborne St John 47 F2
Sherfield on Loddon .. 29 F1
Shinfield 13 F4
Shipton Bellinger ... 101 E4
Silchester 10 C1
Smannell 83 F3
South Tidworth 78 C2

South Warnborough .. 95 D2
South Wonston 153 E3
Sparsholt 174 B2
St Mary Bourne 62 A1
Standon 196 A1
Steep Marsh 207 D1
Steventon 89 D2
Stockbridge 149 F2
Stoke 61 E2
Stratfield Mortimer ... 12 A3
Stratfield Saye 29 F4
Stratfield Turgis 30 A2
Sutton Scotney 131 E2
Swallowfield 14 A3
Sydmonton 43 D4
Tadley 27 D4
Tangley 58 C3
Thatcham 2 C1
Thruxton 103 F4
Tichborne 179 D1
Tilford 122 C2
Tongham 100 C3
Upper Bullington 131 E4
Upper Chute 57 F4
Upper Clatford 105 F2
Upper Farringdon ... 161 F2
Upper Froyle 119 D1
Upper Wield 136 C1
Upton Grey 94 A3
Vernham Dean 38 A3
West Dean 190 B2
West Tisted 203 E4
West Tytherley 169 D1
West Woodhay 3 D2
Weyhill 81 E1
Wherwell 128 C3
Whitchurch 86 B3
Wildhern 59 F1
Winchester 197 E3
Winchfield 52 B1
Winterbourne 1 B4
Wokingham 16 B4
Wonston 131 F2
Woodcott 41 E1
Woolton Hill 21 E4
Wootton St Lawrence .. 67 E4
Yateley 34 A3

Abbatt Cl SP11 .... 57 D1
Abberbury Cl (Almshouses)
  RG14 .... 1 B3
Abbetts La GU47 .... 35 F2
Abbey Bsns Pk GU9 ...... 122 B4
Abbey Cl RG14 .... 54 A1
Abbey Ctr Basingstoke RG24 . 48 A1
  Camberley GU15 .... 36 A3
  4 Farnham GU9 .... 99 D1
Abbey Hill Rd SO23 ...... 176 C1
Abbey Hill Rd SO23 ...... 175 F1
Abbey Pas SO23 .... 198 A4
Abbey Sch The GU9 .... 99 D1
Abbey St GU15 .... 99 D1
Abbey Way GU14 .... 56 A2
Abbot's Ride GU9 .... 99 E1
Abbots Cl Fleet GU13 ..... 54 A1
  North Tidworth SP9 .... 78 C4
Abbots Ct GU46 .... 34 B4
Abbots Rd Newbury RG14 .. 1 C1
  North Tidworth SP9 .... 78 C4
Abbotstone Rd SO24 ..... 179 E4
Abbotswood Cl RG26 ...... 26 C4
Abbott Cl RG23 .... 68 B1
Abbott's Ann Parochial
  Prim Sch SP11 .... 104 C2
Abbott's Ann Rd
  Abbotts Ann SP11 .... 104 B3
  Monxton SP11 .... 104 B3
  Abbotts Ann SP11 .... 104 B3
  Abbotts Ann Rd SO22 .. 175 E2
Abbotts Cl
  Abbotts Ann SP11 ...... 105 D2
  Winchester SO23 .... 176 A1
Abbotts Cotts GU34 ..... 143 E3
Abbotts Ct SO22 .... 175 F1
Abbotts Hill SP11 .... 105 D2
Abbotts Rd SO23 .... 176 A1
Abex Rd RG14 .... 2 A2
Abingdon Rd GU17 .... 35 D3
Above Town SP11 .... 105 F2
Academy Cl GU17, GU47 ... 36 B4
Accentors Cl GU34 ...... 139 F3
Acheulian Cl GU9 .... 122 A4
Achilles Cl RG24 .... 48 C2
Ackender Rd GU34 .... 139 F2
Acorn Cl RG23 .... 69 C3
Acorn Mews GU14 .... 55 F4
Acorn Rd RG27 .... 34 C3
Acre Almshouses **7** SP10 . 106 A4
Acre Ct SP10 .... 106 A4
Acre Path SP10 .... 106 A4
Acton Ho RG22 .... 68 C2
Adam Cl RG7 .... 9 E1
Adampur Rd SP9 .... 78 B2
Adams Cl RG29 .... 72 A2
Adams Dr GU13 .... 54 A1
Adams Ho GU34 .... 140 A2
Adams Park Rd GU9 .... 99 D2
Adams Way GU14 .... 140 A2
Addison Cl SO22 .... 197 E3
Addison Gdns RG29 .... 72 C2
Addison Rd GU14 .... 56 B4
Adelaide Cl SP9 .... 79 E4
Adelaide Rd SP10 .... 106 A4
Adlington Pl GU14 .... 56 B1
Admers Cres GU30 .... 188 A1
Admirals Way SP10 .... 83 E1
Admiralty Way GU47 ...... 35 E2
Adrian Cl RG27 .... 52 B3
Aerospace Byd GU11 ...... 76 C4
Aghemund Cl RG24 .... 48 C2
Agra Rd SP9 .... 78 B2
Agricola Wlk SP10 .... 83 D2
Ainger Cl GU12 .... 77 D2
Aintree Cl RG14 .... 2 A2
Airborne Forces Mus GU13 . 76 C3
Aircraft Espl GU14 .... 56 A1
Aird Cl RG20 .... 21 E4
Airlie Cnr SO22 .... 197 F3
Airlie Rd SO22 .... 197 F3
Ajax Cl RG24 .... 48 C2
Alamein Rd Aldershot GU11 . 76 C1
  Enham Alamein SP11 .... 83 D4
Alanbrooke Cl RG27 ...... 52 B3
Alanbrooke Rd GU11, GU12 . 77 D3
Albany Cl GU13 .... 75 F4
Albany Ct Camberley GU15 . 36 A1
  Fleet GU13 .... 54 A1
Albany Mews SP10 .... 105 F4
Albany Park Ind Est GU15 . 36 A1
Albany Pk GU15 .... 36 A1
Albany Pk Ind Est GU47 .. 35 F1
Albany Rd Andover SP11 . 105 F4
  Fleet GU13 .... 75 D4

Albert Rd Aldershot GU14 .. 76 C1
Alton GU34 .... 139 F1
Camberley GU13 .... 36 A3
Farnborough GU16 .... 56 A1
Newbury RG14 .... 1 C2
Albert St GU13 .... 54 A1
Albert Wlk **11** RG21 ...... 69 D2
Albion Pl RG27 .... 52 B3
Albion Rd GU46 .... 34 C4
Alder Cl Alton GU34 ..... 139 F3
  Ash GU12 .... 77 F4
Alder Gr GU46 .... 34 A2
Alder Rd GU35 .... 165 F3
Aldermaston Prim Sch RG26 . 9 E4
Aldermaston Rd
  Basingstoke RG23 .... 68 C4
  Pamber End RG26 .... 27 D2
  Sherborne St John RG26 .. 47 E3
Aldermaston Rd S RG22 .. 68 C4
Aldermany Ave RG22 ...... 91 D4
Alders Ct SO24 .... 179 E3
Aldershot Military Mus
  GU12 .... 77 D3
Aldershot Rd Ash GU12 .. 77 E1
  Fleet GU13 .... 75 F4
  Fleet, Church Crookham
  GU13 .... 75 E3
Aldershot Sta GU11 .... 76 C1
Alderwood RG24 .... 48 C2
Alderwood Dr RG27 ...... 51 D1
Aldrin Cl SP11 .... 82 C2
Aldrin Pl GU14 .... 55 F3
Aldwick Cl GU14 .... 55 F3
Aldworths Cres RG22 ..... 68 C2
Aldwych Cotts RG14 .... 1 B3
Alencon Link RG24 .... 69 D3
Alexander Ho **6** SP9 ..... 78 C4
Alexander Rd RG25 .... 88 A4
Alexander Terr RG29 ...... 72 B2
Alexandra Ave GU15 ...... 35 F3
Alexandra Ct Bordon GU35 .164 C2
  9 Farnborough GU14 ... 55 F4
Alexandra Rd
  Aldershot GU11 .... 76 B1
  Alton GU34 .... 139 F3
  Andover SP11 .... 105 F4
  Ash GU11 .... 77 F2
  Basingstoke RG21, RG24 . 68 C3
  Farnborough GU14 .... 56 A1
Alexandra Terr
  1 Winchester GU11 ...... 76 C1
  Winchester SO23 .... 197 F4
Alexandria Rd SO21 ..... 131 E3
Alfonso Cl GU9 .... 100 A4
Alfred Rd GU9 .... 100 C1
Alfred St GU11 .... 76 C1
Alice Holt Cotts GU10 .. 120 C1
Alice Rd GU11, GU12 ..... 76 C1
Alison Cl GU15 .... 55 E2
Alison Dr GU15 .... 36 B3
Alison Way GU11 .... 76 B1
Alison's Rd GU11 .... 76 C2
All Hallows Catholic Sch
  GU9 .... 99 E4
All Saints CE Com
  Prim Sch SO23 .... 198 A3
All Saints CE Jun Sch
  GU13 .... 54 B3
All Saints Cl GU15, GU16 . 35 E1
Allden Ave GU9 .... 100 A4
Allden Gdns GU12 .... 100 A4
Allee Dr GU30 .... 187 F3
Allen Cl Alton GU34 ..... 140 A3
  Basingstoke RG21 .... 68 C2
Allenby Rd GU17 .... 35 F3
Alliston Way
  Basingstoke RG22 .... 68 A2
  Whitchurch RG28 .... 86 B2
Allnutt Ave RG21 .... 69 E3
Alma Cl GU11 .... 77 D1
Alma La GU9 .... 99 D4
Alma Rd
  Bordon GU35 .... 164 C2
  Headley GU35 .... 166 A3
Alma Sq GU12 .... 77 D1
Alma Way GU9 .... 99 D4
Almond Ave RG14 .... 1 C3
Almond Cl
  2 Farnborough GU14 ... 55 F4
  Old Basing RG24 .... 70 A3
Almondale Ct GU13 .... 55 F3
Almshouses RG21 .... 69 D2
Almswood Rd RG26 .... 44 C4
Aloes The GU10 .... 122 A4
Alphington Ave
  GU15, GU16 .... 36 B1
Alphington Gn GU15 ...... 36 B1
Alpine Cl GU14 .... 55 D2
Alpine Ct RG21 .... 68 A2
Alresford Dro SO21 ...... 153 F3

Alresford Rd
  Chilcomb SO21, SO23 . 199 E4
  Ovington SO24 .... 178 C1
  Tichborne SO24 .... 178 C1
  Winchester SO21, SO23 . 198 B4
Alresford Sta SO21 ...... 179 E3
Alsace Wlk GU15 .... 35 F1
Alswitha Terr **17** SO23 ... 176 A1
Alton Bsns Ctr GU34 .... 140 A2
Alton Coll GU34 .... 139 F3
Alton Ct **12** SO23 .... 176 A1
Alton Inf Sch GU34 ...... 140 A2
Alton La GU34 .... 160 B1
Alton Rd Farnham GU10 . 121 D4
  Fleet GU13 .... 75 F4
  Odiham RG29 .... 95 D3
  South Warnborough RG25 . 95 D3
Alton Ride GU34 .... 140 A3
Alton Road Cotts RG25 .. 94 C2
Alton Sta GU34 .... 140 A2
Altona Gdns SP10 .... 82 C2
Alverstoke Gdns GU11 ... 76 B1
Amber Cl GU35 .... 164 C1
Amber Ct **2** GU12 .... 77 D1
Amber Gdns SP10 .... 105 E4
Amber Hill GU15 .... 36 C2
Amberley Cl RG14 .... 1 B2
Amberley Grange GU9 .... 99 E4
Amberwood Dr GU16 ..... 36 B4
Ambleside Cl
  Farnborough GU14 .... 55 E2
  Mytchett GU16 .... 36 B3
Ambleside Cres GU10 ... 98 C3
Ambrose Rd RG26 .... 26 C4
Amery Hill GU34 .... 139 F2
Amery Hill Sec Sch GU34 .139 F2
Amery St GU34 .... 139 F2
Amesbury Ho **3** SP9 ... 79 D3
Amesbury Rd
  Cholderton SP4 .... 101 D1
  Newton Tony SP4 .... 123 D3
  Penton Grafton SP11 .... 81 D1
Amesbury Sch GU26 ..... 167 F1
Amherst Rd GU35 .... 164 B3
Ampere Rd RG14 .... 1 C2
Amport CE Prim Sch SP11 .104 A3
Amport Cl Old Basing RG24 . 70 A4
  Winchester SO22 .... 175 E2
Amport Firs SP11 .... 104 A3
Ancells Ct GU13 .... 54 B3
Ancells Rd GU13 .... 54 B2
Anchor Meadow GU14 ... 55 E2
Anchor Rd RG20 .... 24 B1
Anchor Yd **16** RG21 ...... 69 D2
Anders Rd SO21 .... 153 F2
Anderson Ho GU9 .... 99 D1
Andlers Ash Rd GU33 ... 207 F2
Andover CE Prim Sch
  SP10 .... 106 A4
Andover District Hospl
  SP10 .... 82 C1
Andover Dr RG20 .... 4 A2
Andover Golf Club SP10 . 106 A3
Andover Ho **7** SP9 ...... 78 C3
Andover La SP11 .... 80 C3
Andover Rd
  Appleshaw SP11 .... 80 C3
  Blackwater GU17 .... 35 D3
  Deane RG25 .... 66 B1
  Fyfield SP11 .... 80 C3
  Kimpton SP11 .... 80 C3
  Ludgershall SP11 .... 80 C3
  Micheldever SO21 .... 111 D1
  Monxton SP11 .... 104 B3
  Newbury RG14, RG20 ... 5 D3
  Oakley RG25 .... 66 B1
  Penton Grafton SP11 .... 80 C3
  Winchester
  SO21, SO22, SO23 ...... 175 F1
  Wolverton RG N SO22 .. 175 F2
Andover Road Ret Pk
  SO23 .... 175 F1
Andover Sta SP10 .... 105 F4
Andover Way SP11 .... 80 C3
Andrew Cl RG29 .... 72 A2
Andrew Ct GU14 .... 55 E4
Andrew's La
  Long Sutton RG29 .... 95 F2
  Ropley SO24 .... 181 F3
Andrewartha Rd GU14 ... 56 B3
Andrews Cl GU33 .... 75 D3
Andrews Endowed CE
  Prim Sch GU34 .... 140 B3
Andrews Rd GU14 .... 55 E3
Andwell La
  Mapledurwell RG24 ...... 71 D3
  Newnham RG27 .... 71 D3
Angel Ct RG14 .... 1 C2
Angel Meadows RG29 .... 72 C2
Anglesey Bd GU12 .... 77 D1
Anglesey Ave GU14 .... 55 E4

Anglesey Cl Andover SP10 . 106 A3
Angora Way GU14 .... 55 E4
Annandale Dr GU10 ..... 122 A3
Anne Armstrong Cl GU14 . 77 D3
Annes Way GU13 .... 75 D3
Annettes Croft RG27 ..... 74 C2
Ansell Rd GU16 .... 36 B3
Anstey Cl RG21 .... 69 D1
Anstey Jun Sch GU34 ... 139 F2
Anstey La Alton GU34 ... 139 F4
  Shalden GU34 .... 139 F4
Anstey Mill Cl GU34 ..... 140 A3
Anstey Mill La GU34 ..... 140 A3
Anstey Rd GU34 .... 140 A3
Anton Cl RG23 .... 67 D1
Anton La SP10 .... 83 D3
Anton Mill Rd SP10 ...... 106 A4
Anton Rd SP10 .... 106 A3
Anton Schs SP10 .... 106 A3
Anton Trad Est SP10 .... 106 A4
Antonia Cl RG23 .... 68 A2
Antrim Cl RG21 .... 68 A2
Anzio Cl Aldershot GU11 . 76 C1
  North Tidworth SP9 .... 79 E3
Apex Dr GU15 .... 36 A1
Apollo Cl GU35 .... 164 C1
Apollo Ho **5** RG26 .... 9 E1
Apollo Rise GU14 .... 55 D2
Apple Tree Cl RG14 .... 1 C2
Apple Tree Gr SP10 .... 82 B1
Apple Way RG24 .... 70 A3
Appledore Mews GU14 ... 55 F4
Appledown Cl SO24 ..... 179 E2
Appledown La SO24 ..... 179 F2
Applegarth Cl RG21 .... 69 E2
Applelands Cl GU10 ..... 121 F2
Appleshaw CE Schs SP11 . 81 D4
Appleshaw Cl Tadley RG26 . 26 C4
  Winchester SO22 .... 175 E2
Appleshaw Dene SP11 ... 81 D3
Appleton Cl SO20 .... 125 E1
Appleton Mews SP10 ... 106 A3
Appleton View GU34 .... 183 E3
Appley Ct GU15 .... 35 F3
Appley Dr GU17 .... 35 F3
Approach Rd GU9 .... 99 D1
April Cl GU15 .... 36 A3
Apsley Cl SP10 .... 105 F3
Arbour Ct **15** SO22 ...... 197 F4
Arcade The
  11 Aldershot GU11 ...... 76 C1
  Liss GU33 .... 207 F3
  12 Newbury RG14 .... 1 C2
Archery Fields RG29 ...... 72 C2
Archery La SO22 .... 197 F4
Archery Rise GU14 .... 139 F1
Arcot Rd SP9 .... 78 C2
Ardglen Rd RG28 .... 86 B3
Ardrossan Ave GU16 ..... 36 A3
Arena L Ctr GU16 .... 36 A3
Arena La GU11 .... 76 B3
Arford Comm GU35 ..... 165 E3
Arford Rd GU35 .... 165 E3
Argent Terr GU17 .... 35 E4
Argente Cl GU13 .... 54 A2
Argyle Cl GU35 .... 164 B1
Argyle Rd RG14 .... 1 B1
Arkle Ave RG19 .... 2 B2
Arkwright Cl RG20 .... 21 E3
Arkwright Gate SP10 ..... 82 A1
Arle Cl SO24 .... 179 E3
Arle Gdns SO24 .... 179 E3
Arlebury Pk SO24 .... 179 E3
Arlington Pl **2** SO23 .... 198 A4
Arlington Terr GU11 .... 76 B1
Arlott Dr RG21 .... 69 D4
Armitage Dr GU15 .... 36 B1
Armstrong Cl SO21 ...... 153 F2
Armstrong Mall GU14 .... 55 D2
Armstrong Rd GU11 ...... 69 F4
Armstrong Rise SP10 .... 82 C2
Arne Cl RG22 .... 91 E4
Arnett Ave RG40 .... 16 B4
Arnewood Ave RG26 ..... 10 A1
Arnhem Cl GU11 .... 76 C2
Arnhem Rd RG14 .... 1 C2
Arran Cl RG23 .... 67 D1
Arrow Ind Est GU14 ...... 55 E1
Arrow La RG27 .... 52 A4
Arrow Rd GU14 .... 55 E1
Arthur Cl GU9 .... 98 C1
Arthur Rd
  Farnham GU11 .... 76 C1
  Newbury RG14 .... 1 B1
  Winchester SO23 .... 176 A1
Arthur St GU11 .... 76 C1
Artillery Rd
  Aldershot GU11 .... 76 C1
  Farnborough GU12 .... 77 D4
Artists Way SP10 .... 83 D1
Arun Ct **23** RG21 .... 69 E3

Arundel Cl Fleet GU13 .... 75 D4
  Liphook GU30 .... 187 D4
  New Alresford SO24 ..... 179 E2
Arundel Gdns RG22 .... 68 B4
Arundell Pl **7** GU9 .... 98 C3
Ascension Cl RG24 .... 48 B1
Ascot Cl Alton GU34 .... 140 A3
  Newbury RG14 .... 6 A4
Ash Church Rd GU12 ..... 77 F1
Ash Cl Ash GU12 .... 77 F2
  Blackwater GU17 .... 35 D3
  North Tidworth SP9 ...... 79 D4
Ash Ct **6** RG14 .... 1 A1
Ash Gr Kingsclere RG20 . 24 B1
  Liphook GU30 .... 188 A2
  Old Basing RG24 .... 70 B3
Ash Grange Cty Prim Sch
  GU11 .... 77 F1
Ash Green La W GU12 .. 100 B4
Ash Hill Rd GU12 .... 77 F2
Ash La Baughurst RG26 .. 26 C3
  Latchmere Green RG26 . 28 A3
Ash Lodge Cl GU12 .... 77 F1
Ash Lodge Dr GU12 .... 77 F1
Ash Manor Sch GU12 ... 100 B4
Ash Path SO20 .... 126 A2
Ash Rd Aldershot GU12 . 100 A4
  Bishop's Green RG14 ...... 6 C2
Ash St GU12 .... 77 F1
Ash Terr GU12 .... 77 F1
Ash Terr RG18 .... 2 A1
Ash Tree Cl GU14 .... 55 D2
Ash Tree Gr RG20 .... 3 F4
Ash Tree Rd SP10 .... 106 A4
Ash Vale Sta GU12 .... 77 F4
Ashbarn Cres SO22 ..... 197 E3
Ashbourne Way RG19 ..... 2 C2
Ashburton Cl SO24 ...... 179 E3
Ashburton Rd SO24 ..... 179 E3
Ashbury Dr GU15 .... 35 F1
Ashbury Rd GU35 .... 164 B1
Ashdell Rd GU34 .... 140 A2
Ashdene Cres GU12 .... 77 F2
Ashdene Rd GU12 .... 77 F1
Ashdown Ave GU14 .... 56 B3
Ashdown Terr SP9 .... 78 C2
Ashe Park Cotts RG25 ... 89 D4
Ashfield RG24 .... 48 C2
Ashfield Gn GU47 .... 34 B3
Ashfield Rd SP10 .... 105 E4
Ashfields SO20 .... 130 B3
Ashford Chace GU32 .... 206 C1
Ashford Hill Prim Sch RG19 . 8 B1
Ashford Hill Rd RG14 ...... 7 E1
Ashlawn Gdns SP10 ..... 106 A3
Ashlea RG27 .... 51 D1
Ashley Cl Camberley GU16 . 56 C3
  Crondall GU10 .... 97 E4
  Winchester SO22 .... 175 E2
Ashley Ct GU34 .... 140 A2
Ashley Dr GU47 .... 35 D2
Ashley Dro Burrstreet RG40 17 F3
  Owenwood RG40 .... 17 F3
Ashley Lodge RG21 .... 69 D2
Ashley Rd Bentworth GU34 .138 A3
  Farnborough GU14 .... 56 A2
Ashmead GU35 .... 164 B2
Ashmoor La RG24 .... 70 C3
Ashmore Green Rd RG18 . 2 C4
Ashmore La SP5 .... 190 B1
Ashmore Rd SO22 .... 175 E1
Ashridge GU14 .... 55 E4
Ashridge Ct **2** RG14 ...... 1 C1
Ashton Rd RG14 .... 1 C1
Ashurst Cl Tadley RG26 ... 26 C4
  Winchester SO22 .... 175 E2
Ashurst Rd GU12 .... 77 E2
Ashwell Ave GU15 .... 36 B3
Ashwood Dr RG14 .... 2 A2
Ashwood Way RG22 ...... 68 B4
Ashworth Ho Moat RG22 . 68 B4
Aspen Cl GU35 .... 164 B1
Aspen Gdns RG27 .... 51 D1
Aspen Ho GU12 .... 100 A4
Aspin Way GU47 .... 34 C3
Aster Cl SP10 .... 105 E3
Aster Rd RG22 .... 91 D4
Atbara Rd GU13 .... 75 D2
Atholl Ct SP10 .... 83 D2
Atholl Rd GU35 .... 164 B1
Attenborough Cl GU13 ... 54 A2
Attfield Cl GU12 .... 77 E1
Attlee Gdns RG27 .... 74 C2
Attwood Cl RG23 .... 68 C2
Attwoods Dro SO21 ...... 197 E1
Auchinleck Ho **3** SP9 .. 78 C4
Auchinleck Way GU11 .... 76 B1
Audley Cl RG14 .... 2 A3
Audley Ho GU12 .... 122 A4
Augustine Cl SP10 .... 82 B2

Augustus Dr RG23 .... 68 B4
Aukland Cl SP9 .... 79 D3
Auklet Cl RG25 .... 90 C4
Austen Ave SO22 .... 197 E2
Austen Cl SO23 .... 176 A1
Austen Gdns RG14 .... 5 F4
Austen Gr RG22 .... 68 C1
Austen Rd GU14 .... 55 F3
Austin's Cotts GU9 .... 98 C1
Avalan Ct SO22 .... 197 F3
Aveley La GU10 .... 122 A4
Avenue Cl Andover SP10 .... 105 F4
Liphook GU30 .... 187 F2
Avenue Rd
Farnborough GU14 .... 56 A2
Fleet GU13 .... 53 F1
Graysnott GU26 .... 167 D2
Lasham GU34 .... 116 B2
Avenue Sucy GU17 .... 35 F2
Avenue The
Aldershot GU12 .... 100 A4
Andover SP10 .... 105 F4
Barton Stacey SP11 .... 108 B2
Camberley GU17 .... 35 F3
Farleigh Wallop RG22 ...... 91 E1
Farnham GU10 .... 121 F2
Fleet GU13 .... 53 F1
Graysnott GU26 .... 167 D2
Haslemere GU27 .... 189 E4
Hatherden SP11 .... 59 F1
Liphook GU30 .... 187 F2
Mortimer RG7 .... 11 F3
New Alresford SO24 .... 179 E3
South Tidworth SP9 .... 78 C2
Avery Cl 1 GU11 .... 76 C1
Aviary Ct RG24 .... 69 F4
Aviemore Dr RG26 .... 67 D1
Avocet Cres GU17 .... 35 E4
Avon Cl Ash GU12 .... 77 E1
Farnborough GU14 .... 55 E4
Avon Ct 1 Andover SP11 ... 83 E1
Farnham GU9 .... 99 D1
Avon Rd Farnham GU9 ...... 99 D1
Oakley RG23 .... 67 D1
South Tidworth SP9 .... 78 C3
Avon Way RG14 .... 2 A2
Avon Wlk 7 RG21 .... 69 E3
Avondale GU12 .... 77 E4
Avondale Rd Aldershot GU9 .. 99 F4
Fleet GU13 .... 54 A1
Award Rd GU13 .... 74 C3
Axford La RG25 .... 115 D2
Ayjay Cl GU9 .... 99 F4
Aylesfield Farm GU34 ...... 117 F2
Aylesham Way GU46 .... 33 F3
Ayliffe Ho RG21 .... 68 B2
Ayling Cl GU11 .... 99 E4
Ayling Hill GU11 .... 76 B1
Ayling La GU11 .... 99 E4
Aylings Ct RG23 .... 68 A2
Aylward's Dr GU34 .... 161 E2
Aylwards Way SO20 .... 147 F3
Aylwin Cl RG21 .... 69 D1
Ayres La RG20 .... 22 C4
Ayrshire Gdns GU13 .... 54 A2
Azalea Ave GU35 .... 165 D3
Azalea Ct SP10 .... 105 E3
Azalea Dr GU27 .... 189 E4
Azalea Gdns GU13 .... 75 D3
Azalea Way GU35 .... 36 C3

Babbs Mead GU9 .... 98 C1
Babs Fields GU10 .... 120 A3
Bacchus Ho 10 RG26 .... 9 E1
Bach Cl RG22 .... 91 E4
Back La Appleshaw SP11 ... 81 E3
Binsted GU34 .... 142 C4
Brimpton RG26 .... 9 D3
Mottisfont SO51 .... 192 C3
Shinfield RG7 .... 13 F4
Silchester RG7 .... 11 D2
Southrope RG25 .... 116 B3
Vernham Dean SP11 .... 38 B3
Back St SO23 .... 197 F2
Bacon Cl GU15 .... 35 D3
Bacon La GU10 .... 144 A2
Badajos Rd GU11 .... 76 B2
Baden Powell Rd GU33 ..... 186 B1
Bader Cl GU34 .... 55 E4
Badger Farm Rd SO22 ..... 197 E2
Badger Way GU9 .... 98 A4
Badger's Bank RG24 .... 69 F4
Badgers Cl GU13 .... 74 C4
Badgers Copse GU16 .... 36 B2
Badgers Croft RG7 .... 11 F3
Badgers Holt GU46 .... 33 F3
Badgerwood Dr GU15 ...... 36 A1
Badshear La SO24 .... 201 F4
Badshot Lea City Fst Sch
GU9 .... 99 F3
Badshot Lea Rd GU11 .... 99 F3
Badshot Pk GU9 .... 99 F3
Bagmore La Bradley RG25 . 115 F3
Herriard RG25 .... 115 F3
Bagnols Way RG14 .... 1 B1
Bagwell La Odiham RG29 ... 73 E3
Winchfield RG29 .... 73 E3
Baigent Cl SO23 .... 198 B4
Bailey Cl Camberley GU16 .. 56 A4
Winchester SO22 .... 197 E3
Bailey Ho SO24 .... 179 E3
Baileys Ct GU15 .... 35 D2
Bailey Ave RG18 .... 2 C2
Bain Ave GU47 .... 35 F1
Baird Ave RG22 .... 68 C1
Baird Rd Arborfield RG2 .... 15 E4
Farnborough GU14 .... 56 A3
Bakehouse Mews 9 GU11 .. 76 C1
Charlton SP10 .... 82 B2
Bakers Field GU33 .... 185 F1
Baldreys GU10 .... 121 F4
Balfour Cres RG14 .... 5 D3
Balfour Dr GU33 .... 207 F2
Balintore Ct GU47 .... 35 D4
Balksbury Hill SP10 .... 105 E3
Balksbury Hill Ind Est
SP11 .... 105 F3
Balksbury Rd GU11 .... 105 F3
Balksbury Sch SP10 .... 105 E3
Ball and Wicket La GU9 .... 99 D4
Ballantyne Rd GU14 .... 55 F3
Ballard Cl RG22 .... 68 B2
Ballard Ct GU15 .... 36 C4
Ballard Rd GU15 .... 36 C4
Balmoral Cl Andover SP10 . 106 A4
Ash GU12 .... 77 F2
Balmoral Cres GU9 .... 98 C3
Balmoral Ct RG23 .... 68 B2
Balmoral Dr GU14 .... 56 B4
Balmoral Rd Andover SP10 . 106 A4

Badminal Way RG25 .... 91 D4
Bamber La GU34 .... 119 D2
Banbury Cl GU16 .... 56 C4
Band Hall Pl RG27 .... 51 D1
Bank Rd GU12 .... 77 D3
Bank Side RG40 .... 16 B3
Bankside GU9 .... 99 E4
Bannister Gdns
Eversley GU46 .... 33 E4
Yateley GU46 .... 34 B3
Bannister Pl RG19 .... 8 B3
Baptist Hill SP11 .... 61 F1
Bar End Ind Est SO23 ..... 198 A3
Bar End Rd SO23 .... 198 A3
Barbara Cl GU13 .... 75 D3
Barbel Ave RG21 .... 69 F3
Barberry Way GU17 .... 35 E1
Barbour Ct RG29 .... 95 E4
Barcelona Cl SP10 .... 83 D1
Bardsley Dr GU10 .... 121 F4
Bardwell Cl RG22 .... 68 B2
Baredown The RG27 .... 71 E4
Barfield Cl SO23 .... 198 A3
Barfield Rd RG18 .... 2 C2
Barfield Sch GU9 .... 99 F2
Barford Cl GU13 .... 75 E4
Barge Cl GU12 .... 77 E3
Barge La RG7 .... 13 E2
Baring Cl
East Stratton SO21 .... 134 A2
Itchen Abbas SO21 .... 178 A4
Baring Rd SO23 .... 198 A4
Barkham Ride RG40 .... 16 B4
Barley Down Dr SO22 ..... 197 E2
Barley Mow Cl RG27 .... 73 F4
Barley Mow Hill GU35 .... 165 E3
Barley Way GU33 .... 54 A3
Barlows La SP10 .... 105 F3
Barlows Rd RG26 .... 26 C4
Barn Cl GU16 .... 36 B3
Barn Close La RG20 .... 40 C4
Barn La Four Marks GU34 . 159 F1
Oakley RG22 .... 90 A4
Barn Meadow Cl GU13 ..... 74 C2
Barn The 16 GU34 .... 139 F2
Barnard Cl GU14 .... 56 B4
Barncroft Appleshaw SP11 . 81 D3
Farnham GU9 .... 99 D1
Barnes Cl Farnborough GU14 56 A2
Winchester SO23 .... 197 F3
Barnes Rd GU16 .... 56 B4
Barnet Side La GU34 ...... 205 E3
Barnetts Wood La SO24 .. 181 D4
Barnfield GU46 .... 34 A3
Barnfield Cl GU34 .... 119 D2
Barnfield Cotts GU34 ..... 184 A3
Barnfield Rise SP10 .... 105 F3
Barns The RG25 .... 113 E4
Barnside Way GU33 .... 207 F2
Barnsley Cl GU16 .... 56 C1

Baroda Rd SP9 .... 78 B2
Barossa Rd GU15 .... 36 A4
Barra Cl RG23 .... 67 D1
Barrack Rd GU11 .... 76 C1
Barracks Rd RG14 .... 6 B3
Barrett Ct RG21 .... 69 E1
Barrie Rd GU10 .... 98 C4
Barron Pl RG22 .... 68 B4
Barrow Hill SO20 .... 127 F4
Barry Way RG21 .... 91 E4
Bartholomew St RG14 .... 1 B1
Bartholomew Cl 2 SO23 . 176 A1
Bartlemy Cl RG14 .... 5 E4
Bartlemy Rd RG14 .... 5 E4
Bartlett Cl RG26 .... 29 D1
Bartley Way RG29 .... 72 B4
Bartok Cl RG22 .... 68 C1
Barton Cl Aldershot GU11 . 76 B1
Charlton SP10 .... 82 B2
Barton End 2 GU14 .... 139 F2
Barton Stacey CE
Prim Sch SO21 .... 130 C4
Barton's Ct RG29 .... 72 B4
Bartons La RG24 .... 70 A4
Bartons Way GU14 .... 55 D4
Basing Dean GU34 .... 204 C2
Basing Dr GU11 .... 99 F4
Basing Rd RG24 .... 70 A3
Basing Rd RG24 .... 69 F3
Basing View RG21 .... 69 E3
Basingbourne Cl GU13 ..... 75 D3
Basingbourne Rd GU13 .... 75 D3
Basingstoke Bsns Ctr RG22 . 68 C1
Basingstoke Canal Ctr GU16 56 C2
Basingstoke Coll Of Tech
Basingstoke RG24 .... 68 C3
Basingstoke RG24 .... 69 D2
Basingstoke Rd
Aldermaston RG26 .... 9 E4
Alton GU34 .... 139 E2
Kings Worthy SO23 .... 176 B4
Kingsclere RG20 .... 24 C1
Monk Sherborne RG26 ..... 46 C3
Ramsdell RG26 .... 46 A3
Swallowfield RG7 .... 14 A3
Basingstoke Sta RG24 ..... 69 D3
Bassenthwaite Gdns RG24 .. 83 E1
Bassett Cl GU12 .... 56 B4
Bat and Ball La GU9 .... 121 F3
Batchelor Dr RG24 .... 70 B3
Batchelors Barn Rd SP10 . 106 B4
Bateman Gr GU12 .... 100 B4
Bath Rd Camberley GU15 ... 36 A3
Newbury RG14 .... 1 A2
Thatcham RG18, RG19 ..... 2 C2
Batley Wood Bsns Pk W
RG29 .... 72 B4
Batsford SP11 .... 61 F1
Batt's Cnr GU35 .... 143 D4
Battens Ave RG25 .... 88 A4
Battend End RG14 .... 5 D3
Battery Hill SO22 .... 197 E3
Battle Cl RG14 .... 1 A2
Battle Rd RG14 .... 5 D3
Baughurst Rd
Baughurst RG26 .... 26 B3
Ramsdell RG26 .... 46 B4
Baverstocks GU34 .... 140 A3
Bawlings The GU15 .... 36 A3
Baxendales The RG14 .... 2 A1
Bayfield Ave GU15 .... 36 B1
Bayford Cl GU15 .... 35 F1
Baynard Cl RG21 .... 69 E4
Baywood Cl GU34 .... 55 D3
Bazaar Rd SP9 .... 78 B3
Beach Piece Way RG22 ..... 91 D4
Beach's Cres RG26 .... 27 F2
Beachdown Ho RG22 .... 68 B1
Beacon Cl GU9 .... 121 F3
Beacon Hill Ct GU26 ...... 167 D3
Beacon Hill Cty First Sch
GU26 .... 167 D3
Beacon Hill Rd
Beacon Hill GU26 .... 167 D3
Ewshot GU10 .... 75 E2
Fleet GU13 .... 75 E2
Beacon Pass Gdns GU34 ... 42 A4
Beacon View Ho GU26 .... 167 D2
Beaconsfield Rd RG21 ...... 69 D2
Beal's Pightle RG26 .... 46 C4
Beale's Cl SP10 .... 106 A4
Beale's Ct SP5 .... 169 D1
Beales La GU34 .... 121 E4
Bealeswood La GU35 ...... 143 E3
Beam Hollow GU9 .... 99 D4
Bear Ct RG24 .... 69 F4
Bear Hill RG20 .... 24 B1
Bear La Farnham GU11 ..... 99 D2
Newbury RG14 .... 1 C2
Bearwood Cotts GU10 .... 121 E4

Bearwood Gdns GU13 ...... 54 A1
Beatty Ct SP10 .... 106 B4
Beauclerk Gn RG27 .... 52 B1
Beaufort Rd Bordon GU35 . 164 B3
Farnham GU9 .... 99 D2
Fleet GU13 .... 75 D3
Winchester SO23 .... 197 F3
Beaulieu Cl GU15 .... 36 C4
Beaufront Rd GU15 .... 36 C4
Beaulieu Cl SO22 .... 175 E2
Beaulieu Ct
2 Andover SP10 .... 83 E1
22 Basingstoke RG21 ..... 69 E3
Blackwater GU17 .... 35 D1
Beaulieu Gdns GU47 .... 35 D3
Beaumaris Cl SP10 .... 105 F3
Beaumaris Par GU16 .... 56 B4
Beaumond Gn SO22 .... 197 F4
Beaumont Cl GU14 .... 76 B1
Beaumont Gr GU11 .... 76 B1
Beaumont Jun Sch GU11 .. 76 B1
Beaurepaire Cl RG26 .... 28 B2
Beaver End Est GU30 ...... 188 A2
Beaver La GU46 .... 34 B3
Beavers Cl Alton GU34 .... 139 F2
Farnham GU9 .... 98 C1
Bttadley RG26 .... 9 F1
Beavers Hill GU9 .... 98 B1
Beavers Mews GU35 ...... 164 C2
Beavers Rd GU9 .... 98 C1
Beck Gdns GU9 .... 98 C3
Beck Ind Est The GU12 ... 100 A4
Becket Ct RG22 .... 68 A2
Beckett Cl RG23 .... 68 A3
Beckett Rd GU10 .... 105 F4
Beddington Ct RG24 .... 70 A4
Bede Dr SP10 .... 82 B2
Bedfield La RG21 .... 69 D3
Bedford La SO23 .... 176 A3
Bedford Ave GU16 .... 56 B3
Bedford Cl Bordon GU35 .. 164 B1
Newbury RG14 .... 5 D3
Bedford Cres GU16 .... 56 B3
Bedford La GU16 .... 56 B3
Bedford Wlk 12 RG21 ...... 69 D3
Bedser Sq SP10 .... 83 D2
Beech Ave Camberley GU16 . 36 A2
Farnham GU10 .... 122 A3
Middle Wallop SO20 ...... 126 A2
Overton RG25 .... 65 D1
Penton Grafton SP11 ...... 82 A1
Thruxton SP11 .... 103 F4
Winchester SO22 .... 197 D2
Beech Copse SO22 .... 175 D1
Beech Ct Crondall GU10 ... 97 F1
5 Newbury RG14 .... 1 C2
Whitchurch RG28 .... 86 B3
Beech Down Prim Sch RG22 91 E4
Beech Dr GU17 .... 35 D2
Beech Gr SP11 .... 128 C4
Beech Hanger Ave RG27 .. 101 E1
Beech Hanger End GU26 .. 166 C2
Beech Hanger Rd GU26 ... 166 C2
Beech Hill GU35 .... 165 F3
Beech Hill Rd
Headley GU35 .... 165 E3
North Tidworth SP9 .... 79 D4
Shinfield RG7 .... 13 E4
Beech Ho RG24 .... 49 D2
Beech La GU26 .... 166 C2
Beech Ride Fleet GU13 .... 74 C4
Sandhurst GU47 .... 34 C4
Beech The GU17 .... 35 E4
Beech Tree Cl RG22 .... 90 A4
Beech Tree Dr GU9 .... 99 F3
Beech Tree Wlk
Broughton SO20 .... 170 B2
East Tytherley SO20 ..... 170 B2
Beech Way RG23 .... 68 B4
Beech Wlk SP10 .... 105 E4
Beechams Berry RG22 ..... 91 E4
Beechbrook Ave GU46 ..... 34 B3
Beechcrest View RG27 .... 51 D1
Beechcroft Cl Andover SP10 . 83 D1
Liphook GU30 .... 187 D2
Beechcroft Cotts SO20 .. 170 B2
Beeches The Andover SP10 105 F4
Ash GU16 .... 56 B1
Basingstoke RG24 .... 91 E3
Tadley RG26 .... 26 C4
Wonston SO21 .... 131 E2
Beechfield SP14 .... 123 D3
Beeching Cl GU12 .... 77 F2
Beechlands Rd GU34 ...... 160 A2
Beechnut Dr GU46 .... 34 C3
Beechnut Rd GU11 .... 76 C1

Beechwood RG24 .... 48 C2
Beechwood Cl
Basingstoke GU22 .... 91 E3
Fleet GU13 .... 74 C3
Beechwood Ct GU33 ...... 208 A3
Beechwood Dr GU34 ...... 139 E1
Beestons Cotts RG27 ...... 51 D1
Beethoven Rd RG22 .... 91 F4
Beeton's Ave GU11 .... 77 F2
Beggar's La SO23 .... 198 A4
Beggarwood La RG22 ...... 91 D3
Begonia Cl RG22 .... 91 D4
Belaga Cl SO20 .... 126 A3
Beldham Rd GU10 .... 121 E4
Belgrave Cl GU17 .... 35 D2
Belgrave Mews RG27 ...... 52 B3
Bell Cl GU16 .... 56 A3
Bell Hill Enborne RG20 ...... 4 C2
Newbury RG14 .... 4 C2
Bell Ho SO23 .... 179 E2
Bell Holt RG14 .... 5 D3
Bell La Blackwater GU17 ... 35 D3
Ellisfield RG25 .... 115 E4
Bell Meadow Rd RG27 ..... 51 D1
Bell Rd Andover SP10 ..... 106 B4
Basingstoke RG24 .... 69 F4
Linchmere GU27 .... 189 F2
Bell St Ludgershall SP11 ... 57 D1
Whitchurch RG28 .... 86 B3
Bell Vale La GU27 .... 189 F1
Belland Dr GU11 .... 76 B1
Belle Vue Cl GU12 .... 77 D1
Belle Vue Ent Ctr GU12 ... 77 E1
Belle Vue Inf Sch GU12 ... 77 D1
Belle Vue Rd
Aldershot GU12 .... 77 D1
Andover SP10 .... 106 A3
Old Basing RG24 .... 70 B3
Bellever Hill GU15 .... 36 B3
Bellevue RG28 .... 86 B3
Bellew Rd GU16 .... 56 C3
Bellhanger Ents GU34 .... 138 A3
Belmont Cl Andover SP10 . 106 A3
Farnborough GU14 .... 55 E4
Belmont Cotts RG14 .... 1 A3
Belmont Hts RG22 .... 91 E3
Belmont Mews
Camberley GU15 .... 36 A2
Headley GU35 .... 165 E3
Belmont Rd Andover SP10 . 106 A3
Camberley GU15 .... 36 A2
Belstone Mews GU14 ...... 55 F4
Belton Rd GU15 .... 36 B3
Belvedere Cl GU13 .... 53 E1
Belvedere Ct GU17 .... 35 D3
Belvedere Dr RG14 .... 5 F4
Belvedere Gdns RG24 ...... 49 D2
Belvedere Rd GU14 .... 56 A1
Belvoir Cl GU15 .... 36 B1
Bembridge Cl 3 GU12 ..... 77 D1
Benbow Ho SO24 .... 179 E2
Benen Gn SO24 .... 179 E2
Benett Gdns RG14 .... 1 B3
Benford Ct RG29 .... 72 C1
Benger's La SO51 .... 192 B1
Benham Newbury RG14 ..... 1 B3
Thatcham RG18 .... 14 A2
Benham La RG7 .... 14 A2
Benhams La GU33 .... 186 A2
Benin Rd SP9 .... 79 E3
Bennet Cl Alton GU34 ..... 139 F2
Basingstoke RG21 .... 69 E4
Bennett Ct GU15 .... 36 A3
Bensgreen La GU32 ...... 205 F2
Bent St SO20 .... 147 F4
Benta Cl SO20 .... 126 A3
Bentley Bsns Pk GU10 .... 120 A3
Bentley CE Prim Sch GU10 120 A3
Bentley Cl SO23 .... 176 A3
Bentley Copse GU15 .... 36 C2
Bentley Ind Ctr GU10 .... 120 A2
Bentley Ind Est GU10 .... 120 A2
Bentley Sta GU10 .... 120 B2
Bentley Way GU15 .... 168 A3
Bentworth CE Prim Sch
GU34 .... 138 A3
Benwell Cl RG29 .... 95 E4
Bercote Cl SO22 .... 175 D3
Bere Cl SO22 .... 175 E1
Bere Hill RG28 .... 86 B3
Bere Hill Cl RG28 .... 86 B3
Bere Hill Cres SP10 .... 106 B4
Beresford Cl Andover SP10 106 A3
Camberley GU14 .... 56 B3
Beresford Cres RG24 .... 69 F4
Beresford Gate SP10 .... 83 E1
Bereweeke Ave SO22 ..... 175 F1

Bereweeke Cl SO22 .... 175 F1
Bereweeke Rd SO22 .... 175 F1
Bereweeke Way SO22 ...... 175 F1
Berewyk Cl RG22 .... 91 D4
Berkeley Cl GU13 .... 54 A1
Berkeley Cres GU16 .... 56 C4
Berkeley Dr RG22 .... 91 F4
Berkeley Rd RG14 .... 1 B1
Berkshire Rd GU16 .... 36 B4
Bermuda Cl RG24 .... 48 B1
Bernard Ave GU34 .... 160 A1
Bernard Ct GU17 .... 35 F2
Bernstein Rd RG21 .... 91 E4
Berry Ct RG29 .... 72 A4
Berry Hill SO24 .... 181 D3
Berrybank GU17 .... 99 D3
Berrydown La Axford RG25 . 114 C2
  Overton RG25 .... 88 B4
Berrylands GU33 .... 208 A4
Berrywood La
  Bradley RG25 .... 137 D3
  Upper Wield RG25 .... 137 D3
Berwyn Cl RG23 .... 68 A2
Bessemer Rd RG23 .... 68 C1
Beta Rd GU14 .... 95 D3
Bethel Cl GU9 .... 99 D3
Bethel La GU9 .... 99 D3
Betjeman Wlk GU46 .... 33 F2
Beveren Cl GU33 .... 54 A2
Beverley Cl Ash GU12 .... 77 E1
  Basingstoke RG24 .... 69 D1
Beverley Cres GU14 .... 55 E1
Bevers The RG7 .... 11 F3
Bexmoor RG24 .... 70 A3
Bexmoor Way RG24 .... 70 A3
Beyne Rd SO22 .... 197 D2
Bible Fields RG25 .... 113 E4
Bicester Cl RG20 .... 86 B3
Bicknell Rd GU16 .... 36 B1
Bidden Rd Oldham RG29 .... 94 B4
  Upton Grey RG25 .... 94 B4
Biddesden La SP11 .... 57 D1
Bideford Cl GU14 .... 55 F4
Bietigheim Way GU15 .... 36 A3
Bigg's Hill Cotts RG20 .... 4 B2
Biggs La RG40 .... 15 F4
Bighton Dean La SO24 ...... 158 C1
Bighton Hill SO24 .... 144 C4
Bighton La Bighton SO24 .. 180 B4
  Bishop's Sutton SO24 ...... 180 B3
Bighton Rd GU34 .... 159 E3
Bilbao Ct SP10 .... 83 E1
Bilberry Ct **8** SO22 ...... 197 F4
Billing Ave RG40 .... 16 B3
Bilton Rd RG24 .... 48 C1
Binfields GU9 .... 99 D2
Binfields Ct RG24 .... 48 C1
Binfields Rdbt RG24 .... 48 C1
Bingley Ct GU34 .... 139 F2
Binley Bottom SP11 .... 61 F3
Binley Ct RG26 .... 27 D4
Binsted CE Prim Sch GU34 141 F4
Binsted Dr GU17 .... 35 D3
Binton La GU12 .... 100 B2
Birch Ave Fleet GU13 .... 53 F1
  Middle Wallop SO20 .... 126 A2
Birch Cl Bordon GU35 ...... 164 C1
  Camberley GU15 .... 36 B4
  Farnham GU10 .... 121 F2
  Liss GU33 .... 208 A2
Birch Ct **3** SO22 .... 197 E3
Birch Dr GU17 .... 35 D2
Birch Gr Bordon GU35 ...... 164 B1
  Chilbolton SO20 .... 129 C1
  Hook RG27 .... 51 D1
Birch Ho **4** GU14 .... 55 F4
Birch La RG7 .... 11 E3
Birch Rd Headley GU35 ... 165 F3
  Tadley RG26 .... 9 F2
  Wokingham RG40 .... 16 C4
Birch Tree Ct GU27 .... 189 D2
Birch Way GU12 .... 77 F4
Birches The
  Blackwater GU47 .... 34 C3
  Farnborough GU14 .... 55 D3
Birchett Rd Aldershot GU11 . 76 C1
  Farnborough GU14 .... 55 D4
Birchfields GU15 .... 36 A2
Birchland Cl RG7 .... 11 E3
Bircholt Rd GU30 .... 187 D2
Birchview Cl GU46 .... 34 A2
Birchwood RG24 .... 48 C2
Birchwood Rd RG14 .... 2 A2
Birdhaven GU9 .... 121 F3
Birdwood Rd GU47 .... 35 E4
Birdworld GU10 .... 121 D2
Birinus Rd SO23 .... 176 A1
Birkenholme Cl GU35 ...... 166 A2

Bisheare Gdns GU33 .... 207 F3
Bishop Challoner RC
  Sec Sch RG22 .... 68 B2
Bishop Ct SP10 .... 105 E4
Bishop Sumner Dr GU9 ..... 99 D3
Bishop's Mead GU9 .... 98 C1
Bishop's View GU34 .... 159 F1
Bishop's Way SP10 .... 105 F4
Bishops Cl Fleet GU13 .... 75 D3
  South Tidworth SP9 .... 78 C2
Bishops Rd GU9 .... 98 C3
Bishopswood Ct RG7 .... 9 E1
Bishopswood La RG26 .... 26 B4
Bishopswood Rd RG26 .... 9 E1
Bishopswood Schs RG26 ... 26 C4
Bittern Cl Basingstoke RG22 90 C4
  Sandhurst GU17 .... 35 D4
Black Dam Rdbt RG24 .... 69 F2
Black Dam Way RG24 .... 69 F2
Black Pond La GU9 .... 122 A3
Black Swan Bldgs **12** SO22 197 F4
Black Swan Yd **6** SP10 .. 106 A4
Blackberry Cl GU34 .... 160 B2
Blackberry La GU34 .... 160 B1
Blackberry Wlk RG22 .... 69 F4
Blackbird Cl
  Basingstoke RG22 .... 90 C4
  Sandhurst GU17 .... 35 D4
Blackbird Ct SP10 .... 83 D1
Blackbird La RG20 .... 6 C2
Blackbird Way GU34 .... 160 C1
Blackbushe Bsns Ctr GU17 34 A2
Blackbushes Rd RG27 .... 53 E4
Blackcap Pl GU15 .... 35 E4
Blackdown Ct RG22 .... 68 A2
Blackheath Rd GU9 .... 98 C4
Blackman Gdns GU11 .... 99 F4
Blackmoor Golf Course
  GU35 .... 164 A1
Blackmoor Ho GU33 .... 185 F3
Blackmoor Rd GU33 .... 186 A3
Blackmoor La GU32 .... 205 F2
Blacknest Golf Course
  GU34 .... 142 B3
Blanchard Ind Pk GU34 ... 142 B4
Blacknest Rd GU34 .... 120 B1
Blackstocks La
  Mapledurwell RG27 .... 71 D3
  Newnham RG27 .... 71 D3
Blackstone Cl GU14 .... 55 D3
Blackthorn Cl SO21 .... 153 E2
Blackthorn Cres GU14 .... 55 E4
Blackthorn Way RG21 .... 68 B3
Blackthorne Cl GU35 .... 164 C2
Blackwater Cl Ash GU12 .... 77 F1
  Basingstoke RG21 .... 69 E3
  Oakley RG23 .... 67 D1
Blackwater & Hawley Ltr Ctr
  GU47 .... 35 E2
Blackwater Sta GU47 .... 35 D2
Blackwater Way GU12 ..... 100 A4
Blackwater Way Ind Est
  GU10 .... 100 B4
Blackwell Rd SO21 .... 153 E2
Blair Rd **8** RG21 .... 69 D2
Blaire Pk GU46 .... 33 F4
Blaise Cl GU14 .... 56 A2
Blake Cl RG29 .... 95 E4
Blake's La RG7 .... 10 A1
Blake's Ride GU46 .... 33 F3
Blakes Cotts RG29 .... 72 C1
Blanket St GU34 .... 162 C4
Bleach's Yd Ind Est GU30 . 188 A1
Bledlow Cl RG14 .... 5 D3
Blendon Dr SP10 .... 82 B1
Blenheim Cl Alton GU34 ... 140 A2
  Four Marks GU34 .... 160 A2
  Tongham GU12 .... 100 B4
Blenheim Cres GU9 .... 98 C4
Blenheim Ct GU16 .... 56 A1
Blenheim Pk GU12 .... 77 D4
Blenheim Rd
  Farnborough GU12 .... 76 C4
  Newbury RG14 .... 1 B1
Blighton La GU10 .... 100 B2
Bliss Cl RG22 .... 68 C1
Block Cotts RG7 .... 10 C3
Bloomfieldhatch La RG7 ... 12 C4
Bloomsbury Way GU47 ...... 35 D2
Bloswod Dr RG28 .... 86 A3
Bloswood La RG28 .... 86 A3
Blue Ball Hill SO23 .... 198 A4
Blue Pryor Ct GU13 .... 74 C2
Blue Timbers Cl GU35 ..... 164 B1
Bluebell Rd GU35 .... 165 D3
Bluebell Wlk **1** GU13 ..... 53 F1
Bluehaven Wlk RG27 .... 50 C1
Blues Hayes Cl SP10 .... 106 A4
Bluethroat Cl GU15 .... 35 E4
Bluff Cove GU11 .... 77 D2
Blunden Cl RG24 .... 69 D1

Blunden Rd GU14 .... 55 E3
Blythwood Dr GU15 .... 36 A1
Boames La RG20 .... 4 B3
Boar's Bridge RG26 .... 27 F2
Bodmin Cl RG22 .... 68 A3
Bogmoor Cl GU34 .... 160 A1
Bohunt Com Sch GU30 .... 187 F2
Bohunt Manor Gdns GU30 187 F1
Bolle Rd GU34 .... 139 E1
Bolley Ave GU35 .... 164 A3
Bolton Cres RG23 .... 68 C2
Bond Cl RG21, RG23 .... 69 F4
Bone La RG14 .... 2 A2
Bonemill La RG14 .... 1 A1
Bonner Cotts SP5 .... 191 F4
Bonners Field GU10 .... 120 A3
Boon Way RG27 .... 67 D1
Borden Gates SP10 .... 106 A4
Border End GU27 .... 189 D3
Border Rd GU27 .... 189 D3
Borderside GU46 .... 33 F3
Bordon Cl RG26 .... 26 C4
Bordon Schs GU35 .... 164 B2
Bordon Trad Est GU35 ..... 164 A3
Boreen The GU35 .... 165 F3
Borelli Mews **2** GU34 ... 139 F1
Borelli Yd **1** GU11 .... 99 D1
Borkum Cl SP10 .... 82 C2
Borman Way SO21 .... 153 F2
Borodin Cl RG22 .... 91 F4
Borough The Crondall GU10 97 E3
  Farnham GU9 .... 98 C1
Borovere Cl GU34 .... 139 F1
Borovere Gdns GU34 .... 139 F1
Borovere La GU34 .... 139 F1
Boscobel Rd SO22 .... 175 F1
Boscowen Cl SP10 .... 106 B4
Bostock Cl SO21 .... 174 B2
Botany Hill Farnham GU10 100 A1
  Seale GU10 .... 100 A1
Botisdone Cl SP11 .... 38 B3
Bottle La RG27 .... 51 D4
Boulters Rd GU11 .... 76 C1
Boundary Rd Binsted GU10 121 E1
  Farnborough GU16 .... 56 A1
  Frensham GU10 .... 121 E1
  Grayshott GU26 .... 167 D2
  Newbury RG14 .... 1 C1
Boundstone Cl GU10 .... 121 F3
Boundstone Rd GU10 ...... 121 F2
Bounty Rd RG21 .... 69 D2
Bounty Rise RG21 .... 69 D2
Bourley Rd Aldershot GU13 . 75 F2
  Crondall GU13 .... 75 E2
  Fleet GU13 .... 75 E2
Bourne Arch RG18 .... 2 C2
Bourne Cl Aldershot GU9 ... 99 F4
  32 Andover SP10 .... 83 E1
  4 Basingstoke RG24 ..... 69 E3
Bourne Cty Inf Sch The
  GU10 .... 122 A3
Bourne Dene GU10 .... 121 F3
Bourne Field GU10 .... 47 F2
Bourne Firs GU10 .... 122 A3
Bourne Gr GU10 .... 122 B4
Bourne Grove Cl GU10 .... 122 B4
Bourne Grove Dr GU10 .... 122 B4
Bourne Hts GU10 .... 122 A4
Bourne La SP9 .... 101 F4
Bourne Meadow SP11 .... 62 A1
Bourne Mill Ind Est GU9 ... 99 F2
Bourne Pl GU34 .... 140 C4
Bourne Rd
  North Tidworth SP9 .... 78 C3
  Thatcham RG19 .... 2 C3
Bourne The GU13 .... 75 D3
Bourne View SP9 .... 78 B3
Bournemouth Rd SP11 .... 124 C3
Bow Dr RG26 .... 29 E1
Bow Field RG27 .... 51 E3
Bow Gdns RG24 .... 49 E4
Bow Gr RG26 .... 29 E1
Bowcott Hill GU35 .... 165 E3
Bowenhurst Gdns GU13 ... 75 D3
Bowenhurst La GU13 .... 74 B2
Bowenhurst Rd GU13 .... 75 D3
Bower Rd GU10 .... 121 F3
Bowers Grove La SO24 .... 181 E4
Bowers La SP11 .... 38 A4
Bowling Green Ct GU14 .... 56 B4
Bowling Green Dr RG24 .... 50 C1
Bowling Green Rd RG18 ...... 2 C3
Bowman Rd RG24 .... 49 D2
Bowmonts Rd RG26 .... 27 D4
Bowyer Cl **5** RG21 .... 69 D2
Boxall's Gr GU11 .... 99 F4
Boxall's La GU9 .... 99 F4
Boyce Cl RG22 .... 91 E4
Boyne Mead Rd SO23 ...... 176 B4

Boyne Rise SO23 .... 176 A4
Boyneswood Cl GU34 ...... 160 A2
Boyneswood La GU34 ...... 160 A2
Boyneswood Rd GU34 ...... 160 A2
Brabon Rd GU14 .... 55 E3
Bracebridge GU15 .... 35 E3
Bracher Cl SP10 .... 106 A4
Bracken Bank RG21 .... 69 F4
Bracken La Bordon GU46 .. 186 A4
  Yateley GU46 .... 33 F3
Brackenbury SP10 .... 82 B1
Brackendale Cl GU15 .... 36 B2
Brackendale Rd GU15 .... 36 A2
Brackens The RG22 .... 91 E3
Brackenwood Dr RG26 .... 9 F1
Bracklesham Cl GU14 .... 55 F3
Brackley Ave RG27 .... 52 B3
Brackley Way RG22 .... 68 B3
Bracknell La RG27 .... 52 B4
Bracraft La RG27 .... 52 B4
Bradley Cotts SO21 .... 112 A1
Bradley Peak SO22 .... 175 E1
Bradley Rd SO22 .... 175 E2
Bradman Sq SP10 .... 83 D2
Bradwell Cl SP10 .... 82 B2
Braemar Cl GU14 .... 56 A4
Braemar Dr RG23 .... 67 D1
Braeside Cl
  Haslemere GU27 .... 189 E4
  Winchester SO22 .... 197 D2
Braishfield Rd SO51 .... 194 B1
Bramble Bank GU14 .... 56 C3
Bramble Hill SO24 .... 179 E3
Bramble Way RG24 .... 70 B3
Brambles Cl Ash GU12 ...... 77 F1
  Four Marks GU34 .... 160 A1
Brambles The RG14 .... 5 E4
Brambleton Ave GU10 ..... 121 F4
Bramblewood Pl GU13 ...... 74 C3
Brambling Cl RG22 .... 91 E4
Bramblys Cl RG21 .... 69 D2
Bramblys Dr RG21 .... 69 D2
Bramdean Cl RG26 .... 26 C4
Bramdown Hts RG22 .... 91 D4
Bramley CE Prim Sch RG26 28 C2
Bramley Cl GU34 .... 140 A2
Bramley Green Rd RG26 .... 29 D1
Bramley La Blackwater GU17 34 C3
Bramley Rd GU34 .... 140 A2
Bramley Sta RG26 .... 28 C2
Bramley Wlk GU35 .... 164 A1
Bramling Ave GU46 .... 33 F3
Brampton Gdns RG22 .... 91 E3
Bramshaw Cl SO22 .... 175 E2
Bramshill Cl RG2 .... 15 E4
Bramshill Council Hos RG27 31 F4
Bramshill Ho (Police Coll)
  RG27 .... 32 A2
Bramshot Dr GU13 .... 54 A1
Bramshot La GU13 .... 54 C3
Bramshott Dr RG27 .... 51 D1
Brancaster Ave SP10 .... 82 B2
Brandon Cl GU34 .... 139 F2
Brandon Rd GU13 .... 74 C2
Brandy Bottom GU46 .... 34 A2
Brandy Mount SO24 .... 179 E3
Branksome Ave SO20 ...... 129 D2
Branksome Cl
  Camberley GU15 .... 36 B3
  Chilbolton SO20 .... 129 D2
  Winchester SO22 .... 197 D3
Branksome Hill Rd GU47 ... 35 E4
Branksome Park Rd GU15 .. 36 B3
Branksomewood Rd GU13 . 53 F1
Branson Rd GU35 .... 164 C2
Branton Cl RG22 .... 68 B2
Brassey Rd SO22 .... 175 F1
Braunfels Wlk RG14 .... 1 B1
Braxton Ho **1** SO23 ...... 198 B4
Breach Farm Cotts RG25 . 113 E2
Breach La
  Sherfield on Loddon RG24 . 49 F4
  Upper Chute SP11 .... 58 A4
Breachfield RG20 .... 22 B4
Brecon Rd GU14 .... 55 D4
Bremen Gdns SP10 .... 82 C2
Brendon Rd GU14 .... 55 D4
Bret Harte Rd GU15 .... 36 B1
Brew House La RG27 .... 52 B3
Brewells La GU33 .... 208 C2
Brewer Cl RG22 .... 68 B2
Brewers Cl GU14 .... 55 F3
Brewers La SO24 .... 204 B4
Brewery Comm RG7 .... 11 F4
Briar La GU34 .... 160 B2
Briar Way RG26 .... 27 D4
Briar Wood GU33 .... 208 A4

Briarlea Rd RG7 .... 11 E3
Briarleas Ct GU11 .... 77 D2
Briars Cl GU14 .... 55 D2
Briars The GU11 .... 77 F1
Briarwood RG40 .... 16 B3
Brick Kiln La Alton GU34 . 139 E2
  West Tisted SO24 .... 204 A4
Brickfields Cl RG24 .... 70 A4
Bricklin La GU34 .... 160 C3
Bricksbury Hill GU11 .... 99 F4
Bridge Cl RG29 .... 72 D4
Bridge Ct RG26 .... 27 D4
Bridge Meadows GU33 .... 207 F2
Bridge Rd Aldershot GU11 . 99 F4
  Camberley GU15 .... 35 F2
  Farnborough GU14 .... 55 E2
  New Alresford SO24 .... 179 D3
  North Warnborough RG29 . 72 B2
Bridge Sq GU9 .... 99 D1
Bridge St Andover SP10 ... 106 A4
  9 Newbury RG14 .... 1 C2
  Overton RG25 .... 88 A4
  34 Winchester SO23 .... 198 A4
Bridge Wlk GU46 .... 34 A4
Bridge Works GU15 .... 35 F2
Bridgefield GU11 .... 99 E4
Bridgemead GU16 .... 56 A4
Bridges The RG7 .... 11 D3
Bridgetts La SO21 .... 155 D1
Bridle Cl RG26 .... 166 C2
Bridle Ct **7** GU11 .... 76 B1
Brighton Hill Com Sch
  RG22 .... 68 B1
Brighton Hill Ctr RG22 ...... 91 E4
Brighton Hill Rdbt RG22 ... 68 B1
Brighton Rd GU10 .... 100 A4
Brighton Way RG22 .... 91 E4
Brightstone La GU34 .... 161 D1
Brightwells Rd GU9 .... 99 D1
Brimley Hill Ct RG20 .... 24 B1
Brimpton CE Prim Sch RG19 8 B3
Brimpton La RG19 .... 8 C2
Brimpton Rd Baughurst RG26 9 D1
  Brimpton RG7 .... 8 B4
Brindle Cl GU9 .... 99 F4
Brinksway GU13 .... 75 D4
Brinn's La GU47 .... 35 D3
Brinns Cotts GU15 .... 35 D3
Brisbane Cl SP9 .... 79 E4
Brislands La SO24 .... 181 F4
Bristow Cres GU15 .... 36 A2
Bristow Cty Fst Sch GU47 . 35 F1
  The Ashes RG26 .... 28 B2
Britannia Cl GU35 .... 164 C2
Brittain Ct GU17 .... 35 D4
Britten Cl GU12 .... 77 F1
Britten Rd RG22 .... 91 F4
Broad Chalke Down SO22 197 E2
Broad Ha'penny GU10 ..... 121 F3
Broad Leaze RG27 .... 51 D1
Broad Oak La RG29 .... 73 D2
Broad Rd SP11 .... 104 B2
Broad St SO24 .... 179 E3
Broad View La SO22 .... 197 D2
Broad Way RG7 .... 13 D2
Broad Wlk GU15 .... 36 B1
Broadacres GU13 .... 74 B4
Broadhalfpenny La RG7 ... 10 A1
Broadhurst Gr RG24 .... 69 F4
Broadlands Camberley GU16 56 B1
  Farnborough GU16 .... 56 B1
Broadlands Cl GU34 .... 120 A3
Broadmead GU14 .... 55 D2
Broadoak RG26 .... 27 D4
Broadview Cl GU34 .... 141 F4
Broadway RG28 .... 86 B2
Broadway The
  Andover SP10 .... 106 A4
  Newbury RG14 .... 1 C2
  Sandhurst GU17 .... 34 C4
  Winchester SO23 .... 198 A4
Broadwell Rd GU9 .... 121 E3
Brocas Dr RG21 .... 69 E4
Brockenhurst Dr GU46 .... 34 A3
Brockenhurst Rd GU9 .... 99 F4
Brockham Hill La GU34 ... 118 A1
Brockhurst Lodge GU10 .. 121 F4
Brocksby Cl GU46 .... 34 C3
Brockwood Bottom SO24 . 202 C1
Broken Way Burghclere RG14 6 A1
  Newtown RG14 .... 6 A1
Bromelia Cl RG26 .... 28 C2
Bronte Rise RG14 .... 5 F4
Brook Ave GU11 .... 99 F4
Brook Cl Ash GU12 .... 77 F2
  Fleet GU13 .... 75 D4
Brook Cotts
  King's Somborne SO51 .... 193 E3
  Yateley GU17, GU47 .... 34 A3
Brook Gdns GU14 .... 55 E1

Brook Gn RG26 .... 27 D4
Brook Ho Farnham GU11 ... 99 D3
  Newbury RG14 .... 1 C2
Brook Rd GU15 .... 35 F2
Brook The SO24 .... 179 E4
Brook Trad Est The GU12 ... 77 E1
Brooke Cl SO23 .... 176 A4
Brooke Ct GU16 .... 56 B3
Brookfield Rd GU12 .... 77 E2
Brookham Sch GU30 .... 188 B1
Brookhouse Rd GU14 ...... 55 E2
Brooklands GU11 .... 76 B1
Brooklands Cl GU9 .... 99 D4
Brooklands Rd GU9 .... 99 E4
Brooklands Way GU9 ...... 99 E4
Brookley Cl GU10 .... 100 A2
Brookly Gdns GU13 .... 54 A1
Brookmead Ct GU9 .... 98 C1
Brooks Cl RG28 .... 86 B2
Brooks Sch SO22 .... 175 F1
Brookside Farnham GU9 ... 99 D3
  Sandhurst GU15 .... 64 C3
Brookside Bsns Ctr RG7 ... 14 A3
Brookside Wlk RG26 .... 27 D4
Brookvale Cl RG21 .... 69 D3
Brookway Newbury RG14 .... 2 B1
  Upper Clatford SP10 ...... 105 E2
Brookwood Rd GU16 ...... 56 A2
Broom Acres Fleet GU13 ... 74 C3
  Sandhurst GU46 .... 34 C4
Broom Cl GU47 .... 35 E2
Broom Squires GU26 ...... 167 E2
Broome Cl GU46 .... 34 A4
Broomfield La GU10 ...... 121 F1
Broomfield Rd GU35 ...... 164 A1
Broomhill GU10, GU9 ...... 98 A4
Broomleaf Cnr GU9 .... 99 D1
Broomleaf Rd GU9 .... 99 D1
Broomrigg Rd GU13 .... 53 F1
Broomwood Way GU10 ... 122 A3
Brougham Pl GU9 .... 98 C4
Broughton Mews GU16 .... 36 B1
Broughton Rd SO20 .... 148 C1
Brown Croft RG24 .... 50 C1
Browning Cl RG24 .... 69 E4
Browning Dr SO22 .... 197 E4
Browning Rd GU13 .... 74 C2
Brownsover Rd GU14 ...... 55 D2
Broxhead Ind Est GU35 ... 164 C3
Bruan Rd GU14 .... 5 E4
Brummell Rd RG14 .... 1 B3
Brunel Cl SO21 .... 111 D1
Brunel Gate SP10 .... 82 A1
Brunel Rd RG22 .... 68 C3
Brunswick Rd RG22 .... 68 C1
Bruntile Cl GU14 .... 56 A1
Bryanstone Cl GU13 .... 75 D3
Bryce Gdns GU12 .... 100 A4
Bryces La SO21 .... 135 D2
Bryn Rd GU10 .... 121 E4
Buchan The GU15 .... 36 C4
Buchanan Dr RG40 .... 16 B4
Buckby La ■ RG21 .... 69 E3
Buckfast Cl RG24 .... 48 A1
Buckholt Rd SO20 .... 170 A3
Buckhurst Rd GU16 .... 56 B3
Buckingham Cl GU34 ..... 139 E2
Buckingham Ct RG22 ...... 91 D4
Buckingham Rd RG14 .... 1 B1
Buckland Ave RG22 .... 68 B1
Buckland Cl GU14 .... 56 A4
Buckland Par RG21 .... 68 B1
Buckskin La RG21 .... 68 A2
Budd's Cl RG21 .... 69 D2
Buddlesgate SO21 .... 131 E2
Budds La GU35 .... 164 B2
Buffbeards La GU27 .... 189 E4
Buffins Rd RG29 .... 72 B1
Bulbery SP11 .... 104 C2
Bulford Rd
  Shipton Bellinger SP9 .... 101 F4
  South Tidworth SP9 .... 78 B2
Bull Hill GU33 .... 208 C2
Bull La RG7 .... 13 F4
Buller Ct ■ GU14 .... 56 A1
Buller Rd GU11 .... 76 C2
Bullers Rd GU9 .... 99 E3
Bullfinch Cl GU15 .... 35 F4
Bullington La
  Barton Stacey SO21 ...... 130 C4
  Upper Bullington SO21 ... 131 E3
  Wonston SO21 .... 131 E3
Bulls Drove SP5 .... 191 D3
Bullsdown Cl RG27 .... 29 E1
Bullsdown Rd RG26 .... 29 D1
Bulpits Hill SP11 .... 38 B3
Bunch La GU27 .... 189 F4
Bungler's Hill RG7 .... 14 C3
Bunnian Pl RG24 .... 69 D3

Buntings GU34 .... 139 F3
Buntings The GU9 .... 121 E4
Burchell Rd RG14 .... 1 B3
Burchett Coppice RG40 .... 16 B4
Burdock Cl SO20 .... 127 F4
Burfield RG20 .... 21 E3
Burford Rd GU14 .... 35 F2
Burgess Cl RG29 .... 72 B1
Burgess La RG20 .... 3 D3
Burgess Rd RG21 .... 69 D3
Burgh Hill Rd GU34 .... 187 F4
Burghclere Prim Sch RG20 . 22 C3
Burghead Cl GU15 .... 35 D4
Burgoyne Rd GU16 .... 36 C3
Buriton Rd SO22 .... 175 E2
Burleigh Rd GU16 .... 56 A4
Burles Bridge Cotts GU9 .. 98 A1
Burley La RG25 .... 88 C3
Burley Rd SO22 .... 175 E2
Burley Way GU47 .... 35 D3
Burlington Ct
  ■ Aldershot GU11 .... 76 C1
  Blackwater GU15 .... 35 D2
Burnaby Cl RG22 .... 68 B2
Burne Cl SO21 .... 153 E1
Burnett Cl SO22 .... 175 E1
Burney Bit RG26 .... 27 E4
Burnham Copse Schs RG26 .. 9 F1
Burnham Manor GU10 ..... 36 C4
Burnham Rd RG26 .... 9 E1
Burnley Cl RG26 .... 26 C4
Burnmoor Meadow RG40 ... 16 B1
Burns Ave GU13 .... 75 D3
Burns Cl Basingstoke RG21 ... 69 E4
  Farnborough GU14 .... 55 E3
  South Wonston SO21 .... 153 F2
Burnsall Cl GU14 .... 55 D3
Burnside GU13 .... 54 A1
Burnt Hill Rd GU10 .... 121 F3
Burnt Hill Way GU9 ...... 121 F3
Burnt Oak RG40 .... 16 B4
Burntwood Cotts SO21 .. 154 C1
Burrell Rd GU14 .... 56 A4
Burrow Hill Sch GU15 ..... 36 B1
Burrowfields RG22 .... 91 D3
Burrowood Gdns GU12 .... 77 F2
Bursledon Cotts SP9 ..... 101 F4
Burton's Gdns RG24 .... 70 A4
Bury Court Cotts GU34 ... 120 A4
Bury Hill Cl SP10 .... 105 E2
Bury Rd RG22 .... 68 B3
Bury's Bank Rd
  Greenham RG19 .... 6 B4
  Thatcham RG19 .... 6 B4
Burydown Mead RG25 ..... 89 F1
Buryfields RG29 .... 72 C1
Buryfields Inf Sch RG29 ... 72 C1
Buryhill Flats SP10 .... 105 E2
Bushnells Dr RG20 .... 24 B2
Bushywarren La RG22 ...... 92 C1
Busk Cres GU14 .... 55 E2
Busket La SO23 .... 198 A4
Bustards Cnr SO20 .... 147 F3
Butler Cl RG22 .... 68 B2
Butler Lodge RG25 .... 88 A4
Butlers Cl SO51 .... 191 F1
Butson Cl RG14 .... 1 B2
Buttenshaw Ave RG7 .... 15 E4
Buttercup Cl GU35 .... 165 D3
Butterfield GU47 .... 35 F2
Butterfield Cl GU10 .... 121 E4
Buttermere Cl
  Bordon GU35 .... 164 B3
  Farnborough GU14 .... 55 E2
Buttermere Ct GU12 .... 77 E2
Buttermere Dr RG22 .... 68 A1
Buttermere Gdns SO24 .. 179 E2
Butterys Ct ■ SO24 ...... 139 F2
Butts Hill RG14 .... 57 F4
Butts Meadow RG27 .... 51 D1
Butts Prim Sch GU34 .... 139 F1
Butts Rd GU34 .... 139 F1
Butts The RG26 .... 27 D3
Butty The ■ RG21 .... 69 E3
By Pass Rd SO21 .... 131 D2
Byes La Silchester RG26 ... 27 F3
  Three Ashes RG26 .... 28 A4
Byfields Rd RG20 .... 24 B3
Byfleet Ave RG24 .... 70 A3
Byfrons The GU16 .... 56 C1
Byrd Gdns RG22 .... 91 E4
Byron Ave Camberley GU15 . 36 C2
  Winchester SO22 .... 197 E4
Byron Cl Basingstoke RG24 . 48 B1
  Fleet GU13 .... 75 D4
  Newbury RG14 .... 1 C4
  Yateley GU46 .... 33 F2
Byways GU46 .... 33 F3
Byworth Cl GU9 .... 98 B1
Byworth Rd GU9 .... 98 B1

Cabrol Rd GU14 .... 55 F3
Cabul Rd SP9 .... 78 B2
Cadet Way GU13 .... 75 D2
Cadnam Cl Aldershot GU10 100 A3
  Oakley RG23 .... 67 D1
Cadogan Rd GU12 .... 77 D4
Caerleon Cl GU26 .... 167 D3
Caerleon Dr SP10 .... 83 D2
Caernarvon Cl GU16 .... 56 B4
Caernarvon Cl RG23 .... 68 B3
Caesar Ct ■ GU11 .... 76 B1
Caesar Rd SP10 .... 83 D2
Caesar's Camp Rd GU15 ... 36 C4
Caesar's Cl GU15 .... 36 C4
Caesars Ct Camberley GU15 36 C4
  Farnham GU9 .... 99 D4
Cairn Cl GU15 .... 36 C2
Cairngorm Cl RG22 .... 68 A2
Cairngorm Pl GU14 .... 55 E4
Caithness Cl RG23 .... 67 D1
Caker Stream Rd GU34 .... 140 A2
Caker's La Alton GU34 .... 140 B1
  East Worldham GU34 .... 140 B1
Calard Dr RG18 .... 2 C2
Calard Rd RG18 .... 2 C3
Calcott Pk GU46 .... 34 A3
Calder Cl ■ SP10 .... 83 E1
Calender Cl GU34 .... 139 F1
California Ctry Pk RG40 ... 16 A4
Calleva Cl RG22 .... 91 D4
Calleva Pk RG26 .... 9 E1
Calne Ho ■ SP9 .... 78 C3
Calshot Way GU16 .... 56 C4
Calthorpe Hos RG27 .... 52 C4
Calthorpe Park Sec Sch
  GU13 .... 74 B4
Calthorpe Rd GU13 .... 53 F1
Calthorpe Sq ■ GU13 ..... 53 F1
Calton Gdns GU11 .... 100 A4
Calvecroft GU30 .... 188 A2
Calvert Cl GU12 .... 77 D1
Calvert Ctr The SO21 .... 112 B1
Calvin Cl GU15 .... 36 C2
Cam Wlk ■ RG21 .... 69 E3
Cambell Rd SP11 .... 108 B1
Camberley Cty Inf Sch GU9 36 A3
Camberley Heath
  Golf Course GU15 .... 36 C2
Camberley Sta GU15 .... 36 A3
Camberley Towers GU15 ... 36 A3
Camberry Cl RG21 .... 69 E2
Cambrian Cl GU17 .... 35 F3
Cambrian Rd GU14 .... 55 D4
Cambrian Way
  Basingstoke RG22 .... 68 A2
  Wokingham RG40 .... 16 C4
Cambridge Ct ■ GU14 .... 56 A1
Cambridge Military Hospl
  GU11 .... 76 C2
Cambridge Pl GU9 .... 99 D1
Cambridge Rd GU11 .... 76 B1
Cambridge Rd E GU16 ..... 56 A1
Cambridge Rd W GU16 .... 56 A1
Cambridge Sq GU15 .... 36 A3
Cambridge Wlk GU15 ...... 36 A3
Camden Wlk GU13 .... 54 B1
Camelot Cl SP10 .... 83 D1
Camelsdale Cty Prim Sch
  GU27 .... 189 E3
Camelsdale Rd GU27 .... 189 E3
Cameron Rd GU12 .... 77 D4
Camfield Cl RG21 .... 69 E1
Camlea Cl GU13 .... 69 E1
Camoys Mead GU34 ...... 116 B1
Camp Farm Rd GU11 .... 100 A3
Camp Hill GU11 .... 100 A3
Camp Rd Bordon GU35 ... 164 B2
  Farnborough GU17 .... 36 C4
  Padworth RG7 .... 11 D4
Campana Int Coll GU9 .... 99 F1
Campbell Cl
  Aldershot GU11 .... 100 A4
  Fleet GU13 .... 54 B1
  Yateley GU47 .... 34 B3
Campbell Pl GU16 .... 36 C2
Campbell Rd Aldershot GU11 76 C2
  Bramley RG27 .... 29 D1
  Camp St SP11 .... 124 C4
Campbell's Gn RG27 .... 11 F3
Campion Cl Hawley GU17 ... 35 F2
  Lindford GU35 .... 165 D2
Campion Way
  Hartley Wintney RG27 .... 52 B4
  Kings Worthy SO23 .... 176 B4
Campsie Cl RG23 .... 68 A2
Camrose Way RG21 .... 69 E2
Camus Cl GU13 .... 74 B3
Camwood Cl RG21 .... 69 E4
Canada Cotts SO21 .... 111 D1
Canada Way GU35 .... 164 B2

Canal Cl Farnborough GU11 . 77 D3
  North Warnborough RG29 .. 72 B2
Canal Cotts GU11 .... 77 F2
Canal View Rd RG14 .... 2 A2
Candleford Gate GU30 ... 188 F2
Candover Cl RG26 .... 26 C4
Canes La GU35 .... 164 C3
Canhouse La GU33 .... 208 C2
Canning Rd GU14 .... 77 D1
Cannon Cl Ellisfield RG25 ... 115 D3
  Sandhurst GU15 .... 35 E4
Canon S SO23 .... 197 F4
Canons Cl SP9 .... 78 C2
Canons Rd GU20 .... 24 B1
Cansfield End RG14 .... 1 B2
Canterbury Cl RG22 .... 91 D4
Canterbury Rd Ash GU12 ... 77 F2
  Farnborough GU14 .... 56 A1
Canute Rd ■ SO23 .... 198 A3
Capital Ho ■ SO22 .... 197 F4
Capper Rd GU15 .... 35 F4
Carbonel Cl RG22 .... 68 A3
Cardew Rd GU33 .... 208 A2
Cardinals The GU10 ...... 100 B4
Carfax Ave GU11 .... 100 B4
Carfax Est GU10 .... 100 B4
Cargate Ave GU11 .... 76 C1
Cargate Gr GU11 .... 76 C1
Cargate Hill GU11 .... 76 B1
Cargate Terr GU11 .... 76 B1
Carisbrooke Cl GU11 ...... 56 B4
Carisbrooke Ct
  Basingstoke RG22 .... 68 B3
  New Alresford SO24 .... 179 E2
Carleton Cl RG27 .... 50 C1
Carlinwark Dr GU15 .... 36 B4
Carlisle Cl GU15 .... 68 B3
Carlisle Rd GU10 .... 144 C4
Carlton Cl GU35 .... 36 C2
Carlton Cres GU13 .... 75 D3
Carlton Rd GU35 .... 166 A3
Carlyon Cl
  Farnborough GU14 .... 56 A2
  Mytchett GU14 .... 56 B2
Carmarthen Cl GU14 ...... 55 F4
Carmichael Way RG22 .... 91 E4
Carnegie Rd RG14 .... 1 C1
Carnival Sq ■ GU13 .... 53 F1
Carolina Pl RG40 .... 16 B4
Carpenter Rd SP11 .... 108 B1
Carter's Meadow SP10 ... 82 C1
Carters Wlk GU9 .... 99 D4
Carthagena SO21 .... 131 E2
Carthona Dr GU13 .... 74 C4
Carwarden House Sch GU15 36 C2
Cary Cl RG14 .... 1 C1
Cassino Cl GU11 .... 76 C1
Castle Ave SO23 .... 197 F4
Castle Bridge Cotts RG29 ... 72 B2
Castle Cl GU15 .... 36 B4
Castle Ct GU15 .... 98 C2
Castle Gr RG14 .... 1 A3
Castle Hill Farley Castle RG 15 D4
  Farnham GU9 .... 98 C3
  Winchester SO22 .... 197 F4
Castle Hill Schs RG23 ...... 68 B3
Castle Ind Pk RG22 .... 69 E4
Castle La RG14 .... 1 B3
Castle Rd Aldershot GU11 ... 76 B2
  Basingstoke RG21 .... 69 E4
  Camberley GU15 .... 36 B2
Castle Rise
  Kings Worthy SO23 ...... 154 B1
  North Warnborough RG29 .. 72 B2
Castle Sch The RG14 .... 1 B3
Castle Sq ■ RG21 .... 69 D3
Castle St Farnham GU9 .... 98 C2
  Fleet GU13 .... 74 C4
  Medstead GU34 .... 159 F4
Castlecraig Ct GU15 .... 35 D4
Caston's Yd ■ RG21 .... 69 D2
Castor Ct Fleet GU13 ...... 75 D3
  Yateley GU46 .... 33 F4
Caswall Ride GU46 .... 34 B4
Caswell Cl GU14 .... 55 D3
Catesby Gdns GU46 .... 33 F3
Cathedral View ■ SO23 . 198 A3
Catherine Ct ■ GU11 ...... 76 B1
Catherine Rd RG14 .... 1 C1
Catherine Villas GU27 .... 189 F3
Catkin Cl RG24 .... 48 C2

Cattle La SP11 .... 104 C3
Caunter Rd RG14 .... 1 A2
Causeway Gn RG27 .... 52 B3
Causeway The
  Heckfield RG27 .... 31 D4
  Middle Winterslow SP5 .. 168 A4
  Nether Wallop SO20 .... 147 F3
Cavalier Cl Newbury RG14 ... 2 A3
  Old Basing RG24 .... 70 B3
Cavalier Way GU34 .... 139 E1
Cavalry Ct ■ GU11 .... 76 B1
Cavan's Rd GU12 .... 77 D3
Cavell Ct RG24 .... 70 A4
Cavendish Ct
  Blackwater GU47 .... 35 D2
  Newbury RG14 .... 2 B3
Cavendish Gdns GU13 .... 74 C2
Cavendish Gr SO23 ...... 176 A2
Cavendish Mews GU11 .... 76 C1
Cavendish Rd GU15 .... 35 E3
Cavendish Rd
  Aldershot GU11 .... 76 C1
  Fleet GU13 .... 74 C2
Caves Farm Cl GU46 .... 34 C4
Caxton Cl SP10 .... 82 B1
Cayman Cl RG24 .... 48 B1
Cedar Ave GU47 .... 35 D3
Cedar Cl Aldershot GU10 . 100 B4
  Kings Worthy SO23 ...... 176 A4
  Tadley RG26 .... 27 D3
Cedar Ct GU27 .... 189 F3
Cedar Dr Fleet GU13 .... 54 B1
  Kingsclere RG20 .... 24 B1
Cedar La GU16 .... 56 A4
Cedar Rd GU14 .... 56 A2
Cedar Terr RG27 .... 52 A3
Cedar Tree Cl RG22 .... 90 A4
Cedar Way RG22 .... 68 B3
Cedar Wlk Andover SP10 . 105 E4
  ■ Winchester SO22 ...... 197 F4
Cedars Cl GU46 .... 34 B4
Cedars Sch The RG26 .... 9 F4
Cedars The GU13 .... 75 D4
Cedarways GU10 .... 121 F4
Cedarwood Chineham RG24 48 C2
  Kings Worthy SO23 ...... 176 B4
Celandine Ct GU46 .... 33 F4
Celandine Dr SP11 .... 105 F3
Cemetery Hill RG29 .... 72 C1
Cemetery Rd GU13 .... 74 C4
Central Rd GU35 .... 164 B3
Central Way SP10 .... 83 F1
Centre Dr RG24 .... 48 C1
Centurion Cl GU17 .... 35 D4
Centurion Way RG22 .... 91 D4
Chaffers Cl RG29 .... 95 E2
Chaffinch Cl
  Basingstoke RG22 .... 91 E4
  Sandhurst GU15 .... 35 D4
Chalcraft Cl GU30 .... 187 F2
Chalcrafts GU34 .... 140 A3
Chalet Cl GU35 .... 164 B2
Chalet Hill GU35 .... 164 B2
Chalfont Dr GU16 .... 56 A1
Chalford Rd RG14 .... 1 B1
Chalk Cl GU34 .... 160 A1
Chalk Hill SO20 .... 172 C3
Chalk Vale Ashley SO20 . 172 C2
  King's Somborne SO20 . 172 C2
  Old Basing RG24 .... 70 B3
Chalkcroft La SP11 .... 81 F2
Chalkpit La SP11 .... 104 B3
Chalkridge Prim Sch RG22 . 68 C1
Chalky Copse RG27 .... 51 D1
Chalky La RG27 .... 159 F3
Chalky La RG27 .... 73 F3
Challenor Cl RG40 .... 16 B4
Challis Cl RG22 .... 68 B1
Challis Cl SP11 .... 57 D1
Challoner Cl RG23 .... 68 B2
Chamber La GU10 .... 121 D4
Chamberlains Meadow
  RG27 .... 31 D3
Chambers Rd GU12 .... 77 E3
Chamomile Gdns GU14 .... 55 D3
Champion Way GU13 ...... 75 D3
Champney Cl GU35 .... 164 A1
Chandler Rd RG21 .... 69 D1
Chandlers La GU46 .... 34 A4
Chandlers Rd GU12 .... 77 F2
Chandos Rd RG14 .... 5 E4
Chandos Terr SO21 .... 177 F3
Chant Cl SP11 .... 128 C3
Chantreys GU13 .... 74 B4
Chantry Cl GU16 .... 36 A1
Chantry Ctr The SP10 .... 106 A4
Chantry Mews RG22 .... 91 D4
Chantry St SP10 .... 106 A4

Chantrys Ct 9 GU9 .... 98 C1
Chantrys The GU9 .... 98 C1
Chapel Cl Amport SP11 .... 104 A3
  Dummer RG22 .... 90 B1
  Old Basing RG24 .... 70 A4
Chapel Cotts SP11 .... 61 F1
Chapel Ct Broughton SO20 170 A4
  Wherwell SP11 .... 128 C3
Chapel Field SO21 .... 177 D2
Chapel Gdns GU35 .... 164 C3
Chapel Hill RG21 .... 69 D3
Chapel La Aldermaston RG26 10 B3
  Ashford RG7 .... 8 B1
  Baughurst RG26 .... 25 F2
  Broughton SO20 .... 170 A4
  Enham Alamein SP10 .... 83 D3
  Farnborough GU14 .... 55 E4
  Itchen Abbas SO21 .... 177 D2
  Riseley RG7 .... 14 A2
  Stoke SP11 .... 61 E2
Chapel Lodge RG40 .... 16 B3
Chapel Mead GU46 .... 33 E4
Chapel Pond Dr RG29 .... 72 B2
Chapel Rd Camberley GU17 . 35 F3
  Farnham GU9 .... 121 E2
  Silchester RG7 .... 11 D3
Chapel River Cl SP10 .... 105 F4
Chapel Row RG27 .... 52 B4
Chapel Sq GU47 .... 35 E3
Chapel St Farnborough GU16 56 A3
  North Waltham RG25 .... 89 F1
Chapman Wlk RG18 .... 2 C2
Chappell Cl GU30 .... 188 A2
Chapter Ho 14 GU34 .... 139 F2
Chapter Terr RG27 .... 52 B3
Charfield Cl SO22 .... 197 F3
Charlcot Cl RG28 .... 86 B2
Charldon Gn RG24 .... 70 A4
Charlecote Cl GU14 .... 56 A2
Charlecote Mews 10 SO22 197 F4
Charledown Cl RG25 .... 88 A4
Charledown Rd RG25 .... 88 A4
Charles Cl Hook RG27 .... 51 D1
  Winchester SO21 .... 176 A1
Charles Dalton Ct SP10 .... 106 A4
Charles St
  Basingstoke RG22 .... 68 C2
  Newbury RG14 .... 5 D3
Charlotte Cl Andover SP10 106 B4
  Farnham GU9 .... 99 D4
Charlton Down SP11 .... 59 F1
Charlton La RG7 .... 14 A3
Charlton Pl RG14 .... 1 C2
Charlton Rd SP10 .... 82 C1
Charlton Sports & L Ctr
  SP10 .... 82 B1
Charlwood La
  East Tisted SO24 .... 182 B2
  Ropley SO24 .... 182 B2
Charnwood Cl RG14 .... 1 B3
Charnwood Cl
  Andover SP10 .... 106 A3
  Basingstoke RG22 .... 68 A2
Chart House Rd GU11 .... 77 F4
Charter Rd RG14 .... 5 E4
Charters Ct GU12 .... 100 A4
Chartwell Camberley GU14 .. 56 B3
  Farnham GU10 .... 121 E3
Chartwell Gdns GU12 .... 77 D4
Chase Cl GU33 .... 208 A2
Chase Com Hospl GU35 .... 164 B1
Chase Ct GU35 .... 164 C3
Chase Field GU34 .... 161 E2
Chase Plain GU26 .... 167 D1
Chase Rd Lindford GU35 .... 164 C3
  Liss GU33 .... 208 A2
Chase The
  Farnborough GU14 .... 56 A3
  Newbury RG14 .... 1 B4
Chasewater Ct 7 GU11 ...... 76 C1
Chatfield Cl GU14 .... 56 A1
Chatham Rd SO22 .... 197 E3
Chatsworth Dr SP10 .... 105 F4
Chatsworth Gn RG22 .... 91 E3
Chatsworth Gr GU9 .... 98 C3
Chatsworth Hts GU35 .... 36 C4
Chatsworth Rd GU16 .... 56 B2
Chatter Alley GU13 .... 74 A4
Chatters The RG2 .... 15 D4
Chattis Hill Stables SO20 .. 148 C2
Chaucer Ave GU14 .... 82 B1
Chaucer Cl
  Basingstoke RG24 .... 48 B1
  South Wonston SO21 ...... 153 F3
Chaucer Cres RG14 .... 1 B3
Chaucer Gr GU15 .... 36 A3

Chaucer Ind Est SO23 ...... 176 B1
Chaucer Rd GU14 .... 55 E3
Chaundler Rd SO23 .... 176 A1
Chaundlers Croft GU10 ...... 97 E3
Chaundsingers Cotts 12
  GU34 .... 139 F2
Chaundsingers Rd GU34 ... 139 F2
Chawton CE Prim Sch
  GU34 .... 161 E4
Chawton Ct SO22 .... 175 E2
Chawton End Cl GU34 ...... 160 B2
Chawton Park Rd GU34 .... 139 E1
Cheam Hawtreys Sch RG26 24 A4
Cheap St RG14 .... 1 C1
Cheavley Cl SP10 .... 105 E4
Chelmer Ct 2 RG21 .... 69 E3
Chelsea Ho 6 RG21 .... 69 D3
Chequer La RG7 .... 13 E1
Chequers La GU46 .... 33 E4
Chequers Rd RG21 .... 69 E3
Cherberry Cl GU13 .... 54 A2
Cheriton Cl Tadley RG26 .... 26 C4
  Winchester SO22 .... 175 E1
Cheriton La SO24 .... 180 A1
Cheriton Prim Sch SO24 ... 201 E3
Cheriton Rd SO22 .... 197 F4
Cheriton Way GU47 .... 35 D3
Cherrimans Orch GU27 .... 189 E3
Cherry Cl Hook RG27 .... 51 D1
  Newbury RG14 .... 1 B2
Cherry Tree Ave
  Haslemere GU27 .... 189 E4
  North Tidworth SP9 .... 79 D4
Cherry Tree Cl
  Farnborough GU14 .... 55 D3
  Farnham GU9 .... 99 D2
Cherry Tree Rd
  Andover SP10 .... 82 C1
  Farnham GU10 .... 121 E2
Cherry Tree Wlk GU9 ...... 121 E2
Cherry Wlk SO20 .... 126 A2
Cherryhill Gr GU11 .... 76 B1
Cherryway GU34 .... 139 F3
Cherrywood RG24 .... 48 C2
Cherrywood Rd GU14 .... 55 F4
Chesil St SO23 .... 198 A4
Chesil Terr 37 SO23 .... 198 A4
Chesilton Cres GU13 .... 75 D3
Chester Cl Ash GU12 .... 77 F1
  Newbury RG14 .... 2 A1
Chester Pl RG21 .... 69 D2
Chester Rd Ash GU12 .... 77 F1
  Winchester SO23 .... 198 A4
Chester Way GU12 .... 100 B4
Chesterfield Rd RG21 .... 69 E2
Chesters Rd GU16 .... 36 C3
Chestnut Ave
  Aldershot GU12 .... 100 A4
  Andover SP10 .... 105 F3
  Camberley GU15 .... 36 C3
  Farnham GU10 .... 121 F4
  Littleton SO22 .... 175 D2
  North Tidworth SP9 .... 79 D4
Chestnut Bank RG24 .... 70 A4
Chestnut Cl Alton GU34 .... 139 F3
  Blackwater GU15 .... 35 E2
  Fleet GU13 .... 54 B2
  Grayshott GU26 .... 167 D2
  Liphook GU30 .... 188 A2
Chestnut Cres
  Middle Wallop SO20 .... 126 A2
  Newbury RG14 .... 1 C2
Chestnut Ct Aldershot GU11 77 D1
  Borden GU35 .... 164 C1
  7 Newbury RG14 .... 1 C2
Chestnut End GU35 .... 165 F2
Chestnut Gr GU13 .... 54 A1
Chestnut Rd GU13 .... 55 F3
Chestnut Wlk SO24 .... 179 E3
Cheswell Gdns GU13 .... 74 C3
Cheswycks Prep Sch GU14 . 56 C3
Chetwode Pl GU10 .... 100 A4
Chetwode Terr GU11 .... 76 B3
Cheviot Cl Basingstoke RG22 68 A2
  Farnborough GU14 .... 55 E4
  Fleet GU13 .... 54 A2
  Newbury RG14 .... 5 D3
Cheyne Way GU14 .... 55 E4
Chichester Cl SP10 .... 105 E4
Chichester Pl RG22 .... 68 C1
Chichester Rd GU12 .... 77 F2
Chilbolton Ave SO22 .... 197 E4
Chilcombe Hts 38 SO23 ... 198 A4
Chilcombe La
  Chilcomb SO23 .... 198 C3
  Winchester SO23 .... 198 B3
Chilcott La GU27 .... 189 F1
Chilcroft Rd GU27 .... 189 E4
Chilcrofts Rd GU27 .... 189 F1
Childerstone Cl GU30 ...... 188 A2

Chilham Cl GU14 .... 56 B4
Chilland La SO21 .... 177 E3
Chillandham La SO21 .... 155 E1
Chillingham Way GU15 ...... 36 A2
Chilmark Ct GU33 .... 207 F2
Chiltern Ave GU14 .... 55 D2
Chiltern Cl
  Farnborough GU14 .... 55 D2
  Haslemere GU27 .... 189 F3
  Newbury RG14 .... 5 D3
Chiltern Ct SO24 .... 179 E3
Chiltern Way RG22 .... 68 A2
Chiltlee Cl GU30 .... 188 A2
Chiltlee Manor GU30 .... 188 A2
Chiltley La GU30 .... 188 A1
Chiltley Way GU30 .... 188 A1
Chilton Farm Pk GU14 .... 55 D2
Chilton Ridge RG27 .... 91 D3
Chine The GU10 .... 121 E3
Chineham Bsns Pk RG24 ... 48 C2
Chineham District Ctr RG24 48 C1
Chineham La
  Basingstoke RG21 .... 69 E4
  Basingstoke, Popley RG24 . 48 A1
  Sherborne St John RG24 ... 48 A1
Chineham Park Cty Prim Sch
  RG24 .... 69 E4
Chingford Ave GU14 .... 56 A3
Chinnock Cl GU13 .... 74 C4
Chippendale Cl
  Baughurst RG26 .... 9 E1
  Blackwater GU17 .... 35 E2
Chipstead Cl
  Chine Cl GU13 .... 55 D2
Chivers Cl RG22 .... 68 B2
Chivers Dr RG40 .... 16 B4
Chobham Rd GU15 .... 36 B1
Cholderton Rd
  Cholderton SP4 .... 102 B2
  Grateley SP11 .... 124 C4
  Newton Tony SP4 .... 123 D4
  Quarley SP4 .... 102 B2
Chopin Rd RG22 .... 91 E4
Chrismas Ave GU12 .... 77 D1
Chrismas Pl GU12 .... 77 D1
Christchurch Cl RG27 .... 74 C2
Christchurch Dr GU17 .... 35 D3
Christchurch Gdns 1
  SO23 .... 197 F3
Christchurch Rd SO23 ...... 197 F3
Christie Hts RG14 .... 5 E4
Christie Wlk GU47 .... 34 A2
Christine Cl GU12 .... 77 E1
Christopher Ct RG14 .... 1 C1
Christy Ct RG26 .... 27 D4
Christy Est GU12 .... 77 E1
Chudleigh Ct 5 GU14 .... 55 F2
Church Ave GU14 .... 56 A2
Church Bank RG21 .... 133 F3
Church Brook RG26 .... 26 C3
Church Circ GU16 .... 56 A1
Church Cl Andover SP10 ... 106 A4
  Enborne RG20 .... 4 B3
Church Cotts Ropley SO24 181 E2
  Selborne GU35 .... 185 F4
Church Ct 7 GU13 .... 53 F1
Church Farm Barns RG7 .... 12 A3
Church Farm Cl RG25 .... 89 F1
Church Fields GU35 .... 165 D3
Church Gdns SP10 .... 101 F4
Church Gr GU13 .... 53 F1
Church Hill Aldershot GU12 100 A4
  Camberley GU15 .... 36 B3
  Nether Wallop SO20 .... 148 A3
Church Hill Terr GU10 .... 97 E3
Church La Alton GU34 ...... 140 B4
  Ash GU12 .... 77 F1
  4 Basingstoke RG21 .... 69 D3
  Basingstoke, Worting RG22 68 A2
  Baughurst RG26 .... 25 E1
  Bentley GU10 .... 120 A3
  Binsted GU9 .... 121 E2
  Bishop's Sutton SO24 ...... 180 A2
  Bramdean SO24 .... 202 B2
  Bramshott GU30 .... 188 A3
  Brimpton RG7 .... 8 B3
  Burghclere RG20 .... 22 C4
  Buttermere SN8 .... 18 B4
  Cliddesden RG22 .... 92 A4
  Combe RG17 .... 19 E3
  Dogmersfield GU13 .... 74 A3
  Ellisfield RG25 .... 115 E4
  Enborne RG20 .... 4 B4
  Ewshot GU9 .... 98 A4
  Farley Hill RG2 .... 15 D3
  Farnborough GU14 .... 55 E2
  Farnham GU10 .... 121 E4
  Finchampstead RG40 .... 16 B2
  Froxfield GU34 .... 204 B2
  Goodworth Clatford SP10 106 A1
  Grayshott GU26 .... 167 D2

Church La continued
  Greatham GU33 .... 185 F1
  Hartley Wintney RG27 .... 52 B3
  Headley GU35 .... 165 E3
  Heckfield RG27 .... 31 D3
  Houghton SO20 .... 171 E3
  Itchen Abbas SO21 .... 176 C3
  Kings Worthy SO23 .... 176 B3
  Littleton SO22 .... 175 D3
  Medstead GU34 .... 159 F4
  Mottisfont SO51 .... 192 C1
  Nether Wallop SO20 .... 148 A3
  Newbury RG14 .... 1 A2
  Old Basing RG24 .... 70 A3
  Ropley SO24 .... 181 E2
  Silchester RG7 .... 11 E1
  South Tidworth SP9 .... 78 C2
  Sparsholt SO21 .... 174 B2
  Upper Clatford SP10 .... 105 F2
  Vernham Dean SP11 .... 38 A4
  Woolton Hill RG20 .... 21 D4
Church La E GU9 .... 99 F4
Church La W GU11 .... 76 C1
Church Lands RG26 .... 28 B2
Church Pas GU9 .... 98 C1
Church Path GU12 .... 77 E1
Church Rd Aldermaston RG26 9 F4
  Aldershot GU12 .... 100 A4
  Bramshott GU30 .... 188 A3
  Camberley GU15 .... 36 A1
  Fleet GU13 .... 53 F1
  Haslemere GU27 .... 189 E3
  King's Somborne SO20 .... 172 A1
  Longstock SO20 .... 149 E4
  Michelmersh SO51 .... 193 E1
  Newbury RG14 .... 1 C3
  North Waltham RG25 .... 89 F1
  Overton RG25 .... 88 A4
  Pamber Heath RG26 .... 10 B1
  Sandhurst GU17 .... 35 E4
  Silchester RG7 .... 11 D2
  Tadley RG26 .... 26 C3
  Upper Farringdon GU34 ... 161 F2
Church Rd E GU14 .... 56 A1
Church Rd W GU14 .... 56 A1
Church Sq RG24 .... 69 D3
Church St Aldershot GU11 .. 76 B1
  Alton GU34 .... 139 F2
  Basingstoke RG21 .... 69 D2
  Basingstoke
  RG23, RG24, RG25 .... 69 D3
  Bentworth GU34 .... 138 A3
  Coombill GU10 .... 97 E3
  Hurstbourne Tarrant SP11 . 60 C4
  Liss GU33 .... 207 F3
  Micheldever SO21 .... 133 D2
  North Warnborough RG29 . 72 B2
  Ropley SO24 .... 181 E2
  Wherwell SP11 .... 129 D3
  Whitchurch RG28 .... 86 B2
Church View Ash GU10 .... 77 F1
  Hartley Wintney RG27 .... 52 B3
  Hook RG27 .... 51 D1
  South Warnborough RG25 . 94 C2
  Upper Clatford SP10 .... 105 F2
  Yateley GU47 .... 34 A4
Churchdale 23 GU11 .... 76 C1
Churchfield Ct GU30 .... 187 F2
Churchfields GU35 .... 142 A1
Churchill Ave
  Aldershot GU12 .... 100 A4
  Odiham RG29 .... 95 E4
Churchill Cl Alton GU34 .... 139 F1
  Farnborough GU14 .... 55 F4
  Four Marks GU34 .... 160 A1
  Hartley Wintney RG27 .... 52 A4
  North Tidworth SP9 .... 78 B4
  Odiham RG29 .... 95 E4
  Tadley RG26 .... 27 D4
Churchill Cres
  Farnborough GU14 .... 55 F4
  Headley GU35 .... 165 E2
Churchill Way Andover SP10 83 E1
  Basingstoke RG21 .... 69 D3
Churchill Way E RG21, RG25 69 E3
Churchill Way W
  Andover SP10 .... 82 C2
  Basingstoke RG22 .... 68 C3
Churchyard Cotts SO24 .... 179 E3
Churn Ct RG24 .... 70 A4
Churt Rd Beacon Hill GU26 166 C4
  Grayshott GU26 .... 166 C4
Churt Wynde GU26 .... 167 D4
Chute Cl RG26 .... 28 C2
City Bsns Ctr SO23 .... 198 A4
City Rd SO23 .... 197 F4
Claire Ct SP10 .... 105 F4
Clandon Ct GU14 .... 56 B2

Clanfield Ride GU17 .... 35 D3
Clappers Farm Rd RG27 ..... 11 F1
Clapps Gate Rd RG26 .... 10 B1
Clare Ct 11 GU13 .... 54 A1
Clare Mead GU14 .... 121 E2
Clare Wlk RG14 .... 5 D3
Claremont Ave GU16 .... 36 B3
Clarence Cl GU12 .... 77 D1
Clarence Ct 5 GU13 .... 54 A1
Clarence Dr GU15 .... 36 C4
Clarence Rd GU13 .... 54 A1
Clarendon Ave SP10 .... 105 E3
Clarendon Ct GU17 .... 35 D2
Clarendon Cty Schs SP9 ... 78 C3
Clarendon Gdns RG14 .... 1 C2
Clarendon Ho 6 GU13 .... 53 F1
Clarendon Terr SP9 .... 78 B2
Clarendon Rd GU16 .... 36 B3
Clarewood Dr GU16 .... 36 B3
Clarke Cres GU47 .... 35 E4
Clarke's La SP11 .... 58 C3
Clarks Hill GU9 .... 98 A1
Clatford CE Prim Sch SP11 106 A1
Clatford Manor SP10 .... 105 F2
Clatford Manor Ho SP10 .. 105 F2
Claudius Cl SP10 .... 83 D2
Claudius Dr RG22 .... 68 B4
Clausentum Rd SO23 .... 197 F3
Clay Hill Cotts GU10 .... 121 E3
Clay Hill Cres RG14 .... 2 A3
Clay's La Binsted GU34 ..... 141 D3
  East Worldham GU34 .... 140 C1
Claycart Rd Aldershot GU11 76 A2
  Aldershot GU11 .... 76 B2
Clayden Gdns GU17 .... 35 F3
Claypit La GU32 .... 205 E3
Claythorpe Rd
  RG23, RG24, RG25 .... 68 B2
Clayton Cl RG27 .... 52 B3
Clayton Rd GU17 .... 35 E3
Cleaver Rd RG21 .... 68 B2
Clem's Way SO51 .... 192 A3
Clemence Gdns RG28 .... 86 B3
Clements Cl GU34 .... 141 F4
Clere Ct RG20 .... 24 B3
Clere Gdns GU34 .... 48 C1
Clere Sch The RG20 .... 22 C4
Clerewater Pl RG19 .... 2 C2
Clevedge Way RG29 .... 72 B2
Clevedon Ct
  Camberley GU14 .... 56 C4
  Farnborough GU14 .... 56 A2
Cleveland Cl RG23 .... 68 A3
Cleveland Gr RG14 .... 1 B2
Cleves La RG25 .... 94 A3
Clewborough Dr GU15 .... 36 C3
Clewborough House
  Prep Sch GU15 .... 36 C3
Cliddesden Ct RG21, RG25 . 69 D3
Cliddesden La RG22 .... 91 E3
Cliddesden Prim Sch RG25 . 92 A3
Cliddesden Rd RG21 .... 69 D3
Clift House Ash GU10 .... 77 F1
Clifton Cl GU10 .... 121 F2
Clifton Gdns GU14 .... 56 B3
Clifton Hill SO22 .... 197 F4
Clifton Lodge No 1 13
  SO22 .... 197 F4
Clifton Lodge No 2 14
  SO22 .... 197 F4
Clifton Rd Newbury RG14 ..... 1 B3
  Winchester SO22 .... 197 F4
Clifton Terr SO22 .... 197 F4
Clifton Wlk 15 RG21 .... 69 D3
Clitherow Rd GU46 .... 34 B3
Clive Rd GU12 .... 77 D3
Clockhouse Rd GU14 .... 55 F2
Cloisters The
  18 Alton GU34 .... 139 F2
  Camberley GU16 .... 36 A1
Close The Camberley GU16 . 56 A4
  Farnham GU9 .... 99 D3
  Hatherden SP11 .... 59 E3
  Liphook GU30 .... 188 A3
  Monk Sherborne RG26 ...... 47 D1
  Sandhurst GU15 .... 35 E4
  Thatcham RG18 .... 2 C2
Closeworth Rd GU14 .... 77 E4
Clouston Rd GU14 .... 55 E3
Clovelly Dr GU26 .... 167 D4
Clovelly Pk GU26 .... 167 D4
Clovelly Rd GU26 .... 167 D4
Clover Bank SO23 .... 154 A3
Clover Cl GU35 .... 165 D1
Clover Field RG21 .... 69 F4
Clover La GU46 .... 33 F2
Clover Pk GU35 .... 165 D1
Club La SP9 .... 78 C2
Clubhouse Rd GU11 .... 76 A3
Clumps Rd GU10 .... 122 B2
Clyde Ct 33 SP11 .... 83 E1
Coach Hill SP11 .... 58 A2
Coach House Cl GU15 .... 36 B4
Coach House Gdns GU13 ... 54 A1

Coach Rd The
East Tytherley SP5 .... 191 F4
West Tytherley SP5 .... 191 F4
Coachman's Ct RG14 .... 1 C3
Coachways SP11 .... 106 A3
Coate Dr SO21 .... 153 E1
Coates Cl RG22 .... 68 C1
Cob Tree Cotts RG24 .... 70 C2
Cobbett Cl SO22 .... 197 E3
Cobbett Gn RG22 .... 68 C1
Cobbett's La GU46 .... 34 B3
Cobbetts Mews **3** GU9 .... 98 C1
Cobbetts Way GU11 .... 121 E3
Cock-a-Dobby GU46 .... 34 C4
Cocket's Mead SO21 .... 177 D2
Cockshott La GU32 .... 206 B1
Cody Rd GU14 .... 55 E2
Coe Cl GU11 .... 76 C1
Cokenor Wood GU10 .... 121 E3
Coker Cl SO22 .... 197 F4
Colbeck GU13 .... 75 D2
Colbourne Ct **6** SO23 ...... 176 A1
Colbred Cnr GU13 .... 54 B2
Cold Harbour Ct **12** SP10 .. 106 A4
Cold Harbour La GU14 .... 55 E4
Colden La SO24 .... 158 A2
Coldharbour RG25 .... 89 F1
Coldrey Cotts GU34 .... 119 E2
Colebrook Pl SO23 .... 198 A4
Colebrook St SO23 .... 198 A4
Colebrook Way GU10 .... 105 E4
Coleford Bridge Rd
Farnborough GU14 .... 56 B2
Mytchett GU16 .... 56 B2
Coleford Cl GU16 .... 56 B2
Coleford Paddocks GU14 .... 56 B2
Coleman Cl RG21 .... 69 E4
Coleman Rd GU12 .... 77 D1
Colenzo Dr SP10 .... 83 E1
Coleridge Ave GU46 .... 34 B3
Coleson Hill Rd GU9 .... 121 E3
Coleville Rd GU14 .... 55 E3
Coley La SP11 .... 128 C2
Coliseum Bsns Ctr GU17 ...... 35 F2
Collard Way **4** GU33 .... 207 F2
College Cl GU15 .... 36 A4
College Cres GU14 .... 55 D3
College Gdns GU9 .... 98 C1
College La RG25 .... 115 D3
College Piece RG7 .... 11 E3
College Rd Ash GU12 .... 77 F2
Basingstoke RG22 .... 68 C3
Sandhurst GU47 .... 35 E4
College Ride GU16 .... 36 B4
College St SO23 .... 198 A4
College Town Sch GU47 .... 35 E4
College Wlk SO23 .... 198 A3
Collegewater La GU34 .... 205 D2
Collier Cl GU14 .... 55 D3
Collingwood GU16 .... 56 B1
Collingwood Coll GU16 .... 36 C4
Collingwood Grange Cl
GU15 .... 36 C3
Collingwood Mount GU15 ... 36 C3
Collingwood Pl GU15 .... 36 C4
Collingwood Rise GU15 .... 36 C4
Collins Cl SP10 .... 82 C2
Collins Ct **1** SP9 .... 78 C4
Collyers Cres GU30 .... 188 B2
Colne Way
Ash GU14 .... 77 F1
22 Basingstoke RG21 .... 69 E3
Colson Cl **46** SO23 .... 198 A4
Colson Rd SO23 .... 198 A4
Coltsfoot Pl RG27 .... 51 E1
Coltsfoot Rd GU35 .... 165 D3
Columbia Ct RG40 .... 16 B4
Columbine Rd RG22 .... 91 F4
Columbus Dr GU14 .... 55 D2
Columbus Way SP10 .... 83 F1
Colwyn Cl GU46 .... 34 A3
Colyer Cl RG22 .... 68 B2
Combe La GU14 .... 55 E4
Combe La GU10 .... 208 A1
Combe Rise GU10 .... 122 A3
Comet Ho **11** RG26 .... 9 E1
Comfrey Cl GU14 .... 55 F4
Commercial Ctr The SP11 ..... 84 A2
Commercial Rd GU11 .... 100 A4
Commodore Ct GU11 .... 76 C4
Common Hill GU34 .... 159 E3
Common Rd RG19 .... 17 F3
Common The
Middle Wintershow SP5 ...... 168 A3
Ramsdell RG26 .... 26 C1
Common Vale SP5 .... 168 A3
Commonfield La RG40 .... 15 F4
Communications Rd RG14 .... 1 B3
Compass Field RG27 .... 51 D1
Complins GU34 .... 140 B3

Compton Cl Fleet GU13 ...... 75 D3
Hook RG27, RG29 .... 51 D1
Winchester SO22 .... 197 D2
Compton Place Bsns Ctr
GU47 .... 35 F2
Compton Rd Fleet GU13 ...... 75 D3
Winchester SO23 .... 197 F4
Compton Sq SP10 .... 83 E2
Compton Way
Farnham GU11 .... 99 F1
Winchester SO22 .... 197 D2
Conde Way GU35 .... 164 B1
Coney Gn **8** SO23 .... 176 A1
Congreve Cl RG7 .... 9 F4
Conholt Hill SP11 .... 37 F2
Conholt Rd SP10 .... 106 A3
Conifer Cl Baughurst RG26 .... 9 E1
Bordon GU35 .... 164 B1
Fleet GU13 .... 74 C3
Winchester SO22 .... 175 F1
Conifer Crest RG14 .... 5 D2
Conifer Dr GU15 .... 36 C3
Coniston Cl
Farnborough GU14 .... 55 E2
Thatcham RG19 .... 2 C2
Coniston Ct Ash GU12 .... 77 E2
6 Newbury RG14 .... 1 C2
Coniston Dr GU9 .... 98 C3
Coniston Gr SO24 .... 179 E2
Coniston Rd
Basingstoke RG22 .... 68 A1
Bordon GU35 .... 164 B3
Coniston Way GU13 .... 74 C3
Connaught Cl Bordon GU35 164 B1
Yateley GU46 .... 34 B3
Connaught Rd
Aldershot GU12 .... 77 D1
Camberley GU15 .... 36 B3
Fleet GU13 .... 54 A1
Kings Worthy SO21 .... 153 E1
Newbury RG14 .... 1 C2
Connaught Sec Sch GU12 .. 100 B4
Connop Way GU14 .... 36 B2
Conservatory The **38** SO23 198 A4
Constable Ct SP10 .... 83 D1
Constable Way RG22 .... 91 D3
Constables Gate SO22 ...... 197 F4
Constantine Way RG22 .... 91 D3
Constantius Ct RG27 .... 74 C2
Conway Cl GU15 .... 36 B1
Conway Dr
Farnborough GU14 .... 55 D2
Thatcham RG18 .... 2 C3
Cooks La SO51 .... 191 F1
Coolarne Rise GU15 .... 36 C3
Coolers Farm SP20 .... 170 B3
Coombe Cl GU16 .... 54 B1
Coombe Dr GU13 .... 54 B1
Coombe Rd GU46 .... 33 F4
Coombehurst Dr RG21 .... 69 D1
Cooper Ho GU16 .... 164 B1
Cooper's Hill GU46 .... 33 F2
Cooper's Terr GU9 .... 99 D2
Cooperage The **3** GU34 .. 139 F2
Coopers Cl SO51 .... 153 E1
Coopers La RG26 .... 28 C2
Cope Hall La RG14 .... 5 D4
Copes La RG27 .... 31 F4
Copland Cl RG22 .... 91 E4
Copnor RG20 .... 21 D4
Copnor Cl RG20 .... 21 D4
Coppice Cl Baughurst RG26 . 26 A4
Farnham GU10 .... 99 E3
Newbury RG14 .... 1 C2
Winchester SO22 .... 175 E1
Coppice Gdns GU46 .... 34 A3
Coppice Mews RG21 .... 68 C3
Coppice Rd RG20 .... 24 C1
Copse Ave GU9 .... 99 F3
Copse Cl Camberley GU16 .... 36 C3
Liss GU33 .... 208 A2
Copse End Camberley GU16 . 36 B3
Fleet GU13 .... 74 B4
Copse Field RG24 .... 70 A4
Copse La
Brown Candover SO21 .... 134 C2
Fleet GU13 .... 74 B4
Copse Rd Lichmere GU27 ... 189 D3
Overton RG25 .... 65 D1
Copse The
Farnborough GU14 .... 55 D2
Farnham GU10 .... 121 E2
Tadley RG26 .... 26 C4
Copse View Cl RG24 .... 49 E2
Copse Way Farnham GU10 . 121 E3
Wokingham RG40 .... 16 B4
Coram Cl **8** SO23 .... 176 A1
Cordale Rd RG21 .... 69 D2
Cordelia Gdns GU14 .... 56 B1

Cordwales Cty Mid Sch
GU15 .... 36 B4
Cordwalles Rd GU15 .... 36 B4
Corfe Cl SO24 .... 179 E2
Corfe Gdns GU15 .... 36 B1
Corfe Way GU16 .... 56 B1
Corfe Wlk RG21 .... 68 B3
Corfield Cl RG40 .... 16 B2
Coriander Cl GU14 .... 55 D2
Corinthian Cl
Basingstoke RG22 .... 91 D4
Knights Enham SP10 .... 83 D2
Cormorant Cl RG23 .... 90 C4
Cormorant Pl GU15 .... 35 E4
Cormunna Ct GU15 .... 35 D4
Cornelia Cl GU14 .... 55 D4
Cornfields Andover SP10 .... 106 B3
Yateley GU46 .... 33 F2
Cornfields The RG22 .... 91 E4
Cornish Cl RG22 .... 91 D4
Cornwall Cl RG22 .... 68 B2
Cornwall Gr GU15 .... 36 B4
Cornwall Rd GU35 .... 164 B1
Coronation Cl
Burghclere RG20 .... 22 B4
Odiham RG29 .... 72 C2
Coronation Rd
Aldershot GU12 .... 99 F4
Basingstoke RG23 .... 69 E3
Ludgershall SP11 .... 57 D1
North Tidworth SP9 .... 78 C4
Yateley GU46 .... 34 B4
Corporation Cotts **1** RG14 .. 1 C2
Correlli Rd RG22 .... 91 F4
Corringway GU13 .... 75 D3
Corry Rd GU26 .... 167 D3
Coruna Main SP10 .... 83 D1
Cossack La **11** SO23 ...... 198 A4
Cossack Lane Ho **19** SO23 198 A4
Coster Cl RG14 .... 1 A3
Cotswold Cl
Basingstoke RG23 .... 68 A2
Farnborough GU14 .... 55 E4
Cotswold Ct **19** GU13 ...... 53 F1
Cottage Gdns GU14 .... 55 E2
Cottage Gn
Goodworth Clatford SP11 .. 128 A4
Hartley Wintney RG27 .... 52 B3
Cottage La GU12 .... 206 C2
Cottage Rd SO20 .... 147 E4
Cottington Cl RG20 .... 24 B1
Cottle Cl RG21 .... 69 D1
Cottonworth Cotts SP11 .... 126 C2
Cottrell Cl GU12 .... 77 E4
Cottrell Flats GU12 .... 77 D4
Coulsdon Cotts SO24 .... 157 E3
Council Hos Baughurst RG26 25 F1
Little Somborne SO24 .... 173 D3
Council Hos The
Baughurst RG26 .... 25 F2
Highclere RG20 .... 21 F4
Council Rd RG21 .... 69 D2
Court Cl GU30 .... 188 A2
Court Dro RG25 .... 64 C1
Court Gdns GU15 .... 36 A3
Court La
Little Somborne SO24 .... 173 D3
Ropley SO24 .... 181 E3
Court Moor Sch GU13 .... 74 C4
Court Rd Aldershot GU11 ..... 76 C1
Kings Worthy SO23 .... 176 B3
Court The GU35 .... 143 D2
Courtenay Rd Farnham GU9 99 E4
Winchester SO23 .... 176 A2
Courtlands Rd RG14 .... 1 C1
Courtmoor Ave GU13 .... 75 D4
Courts Hill Rd GU27 .... 189 E4
Courts Mount Rd GU27 ...... 189 F3
Courtyard The GU30 .... 188 C1
Cove Inf Sch GU14 .... 55 E3
Cove Jun Sch GU14 .... 55 E3
Cove Rd Farnborough GU14 . 55 E2
Fleet GU13 .... 54 B2
Cove Sch GU14 .... 55 E3
Coventry Cl RG22 .... 91 D4
Coventry **7** SO23 .... 176 A1
Covert The GU14 .... 55 C4
Coverts The RG26 .... 26 C1
Coverts The GU15 .... 55 F4
Covey Way SO24 .... 179 D2
Cow Drove Hill SO20 .... 172 A2
Cow La SP11 .... 80 B4
Cowdown Farm Cotts
SP10 .... 106 C3
Cowdown La SP10 .... 106 B2
Cowdray Pk GU34 .... 139 F1
Cowdrey Cl RG21 .... 69 D1
Cowdrey Sq SP10 .... 83 D2
Cowfold La RG27 .... 72 A3
Cowley Dr SO21 .... 153 E1
Cowslade RG14 .... 1 A3
Cowslip Bank RG21 .... 69 F4

Cowslip Cl GU35 .... 165 D2
Coxbridge Meadows GU9 ..... 98 C1
Coxbridge Rdbt GU10 .... 121 E4
Coxeter Rd RG14 .... 1 B2
Coxheath Rd GU13 .... 74 C3
Coxmoor Cl GU13 .... 75 E3
Crabb Hill RG26 .... 25 E1
Crabtree Gdns GU35 .... 165 E3
Crabtree La Churt GU10 ..... 144 C1
Headley GU35 .... 165 E3
Crabtree Rd GU47 .... 35 F1
Craddock Ho **2** SO23 ..... 198 B4
Crake Pl GU47 .... 35 D4
Cramptons GU34 .... 139 D1
Cranberry Wlk GU47 .... 35 E2
Cranbourne Ct RG21 .... 69 D1
Cranbourne La RG23 .... 68 C1
Cranbourne Sec Sch RG21 . 68 C2
Cranbrook Ct GU13 .... 54 A2
Crane Ct GU15 .... 35 D4
Cranes Rd RG26 .... 47 F2
Cranesfield RG26 .... 47 F2
Cranford Ave GU13 .... 74 C3
Cranford Dr GU34 .... 140 B3
Cranford Park Dr GU46 .... 34 A3
Cranleigh Ct GU14 .... 55 E2
Cranmere Ct GU14 .... 76 B1
Cranmore Cl GU16 .... 56 B2
Cranmore Gdns GU16 .... 56 B1
Cranmore La GU11 .... 76 B1
Cranmore Rd GU16 .... 56 C2
Cranworth Rd SO22 .... 175 F1
Craven Cl GU14 .... 122 A3
Craven Ct GU47 .... 35 E2
Craven Dene RG14 .... 1 C2
Craven Ho **6** GU9 .... 98 C1
Craven Rd RG14 .... 1 B1
Crawford Gdns GU17 .... 35 F3
Crawford Pl RG14 .... 1 B2
Crawleys La SP11 .... 57 D2
Crawleys Rd SP11 .... 57 D2
Crawley Cotts SO22 .... 152 A1
Crawley Dr GU16 .... 36 B3
Crawley Hill GU15 .... 36 B3
Crawley Ridge GU15 .... 36 B3
Crawley Ridge Cty Mid Sch
GU15 .... 36 B4
Crawley Wood Cl GU15 .... 36 B3
Crawts Rd RG25 .... 88 A4
Craydown La SO20 .... 125 F1
Credon Cl GU14 .... 55 D2
Crerar Cl GU14 .... 55 D2
Crescent Cl SO22 .... 197 D2
Crescent La GU12 .... 77 F3
Crescent The
Andover SP10 .... 105 E4
Crookham Village GU13 ...... 74 B3
Farnborough GU14 .... 56 A2
Farnham GU11 .... 99 F1
Four Marks GU34 .... 160 A2
Goodworth Clatford SP11 .. 105 F1
Hurstbourne Tarrant SP11 .. 60 C4
Mortimer RG7 .... 11 E3
Cress Gdns SP10, SP11 .... 105 F3
Cresswell Rd RG14 .... 2 A2
Cricket Cl SO21 .... 152 A1
Cricket Hill RG40 .... 16 B1
Cricket Hill La GU17, GU46 . 34 B2
Cricket La GU10 .... 122 A3
Cricket Lea GU35 .... 164 C3
Cricketers Way SP10 .... 83 E1
Cricklade Coll SP10 .... 106 A4
Crimea Rd GU11 .... 76 C1
Cripley Rd GU14 .... 55 D3
Cripstead La SO23 .... 197 F3
Critchmere Hill GU27 .... 189 E4
Critchmere La GU27 .... 189 E3
Critchmere Vale GU27 .... 189 E3
Crockford La RG24 .... 48 B1
Croft Ave SP11 .... 106 A3
Croft Gdns
Alton GU34 .... 139 F2
Andover SP10 .... 106 A3
Croft La
Crondall GU10 .... 97 E3
Newbury RG14 .... 1 B2
Yateley GU46 .... 34 A4
Croft Rd
Aldershot GU9 .... 99 F4
Mortimer RG7 .... 11 E3
Newbury RG14 .... 1 A1
Oakley RG23 .... 67 D1
Croft The
Fleet GU13 .... 74 B4
Newton Tony SP4 .... 123 D3
Crofter's Cl GU46 .... 34 C4
Crofters Meadow RG21 .... 69 F4
Crofton GU27 .... 189 E4
Crofts The RG22 .... 91 E3
Cromwell Cl RG24 .... 70 A3
Cromwell Pl RG14 .... 1 C2

Cromwell Rd
Basingstoke RG24 .... 69 D3
Camberley GU15 .... 36 A4
Newbury RG14 .... 2 A3
Winchester SO22 .... 197 F3
Cromwell Terr RG14 .... 1 A3
Cromwell Way GU14 .... 56 A4
Crondall Cl GU47 .... 35 F2
Crondall Rd GU46 .... 34 A4
Crondall La GU9 .... 98 B1
Crondall Prim Sch GU10 ...... 97 E3
Crondall Rd Bentley GU10 . 120 C3
Crondall GU13 .... 74 B2
Crookham Village GU13 .... 74 B2
Crookham CE Inf Sch GU13 74 C2
Crookham Ct RG26 .... 26 C3
Crookham Jun Sch GU13 ..... 75 D2
Crookham Rd GU13 .... 74 C4
Crookham Reach GU10 .... 74 C3
Crooksbury Rd GU12 .... 100 A2
Cropmark Way RG22 .... 91 E4
Crosby Gdns GU46 .... 33 F4
Crosby Hill Dr GU15 .... 36 B4
Crosby Way GU9 .... 98 C1
Cross Farm Cty Fst Sch
GU16 .... 56 B3
Cross Gdns GU16 .... 56 B3
Cross Keys Pas **22** SO23 . 198 A4
Cross La Andover SP11 ...... 105 F4
Ashmansworth RG20 .... 41 D4
Beech Hill RG7 .... 13 D4
Camberley GU15 .... 56 B3
Cross & Pillory La **6** GU34 139 F2
Cross Rd GU12 .... 77 F2
Cross St Aldershot GU11 ...... 76 C1
Basingstoke RG21 .... 69 D3
Farnborough GU14 .... 77 D4
Winchester SO23 .... 197 F4
Cross The SO20 .... 172 A2
Crossborough Gdns RG24 .... 69 E2
Crossborough Hill RG21 .... 69 E2
Crosswater La GU10 .... 144 B2
Crossways Aldershot GU12 .. 77 D1
Churt GU10 .... 144 B1
Crookham Village GU13 ...... 74 B3
Whitchurch RG28 .... 86 B3
Crossways The SP10 .... 105 F4
Croucher's Croft SO22 ...... 175 E1
Crowder Terr SO22 .... 197 F4
Crowfield Dr RG19 .... 2 C2
Crowley Dr GU34 .... 140 A2
Crown Cres RG24 .... 70 A3
Crown Dr GU9 .... 99 F3
Crown Gdns GU13 .... 75 D4
Crown La Farnham GU11 ...... 99 F3
Medstead RG27 .... 71 E4
Old Basing RG24 .... 70 A3
Crown Way SP10 .... 83 E1
Crows La GU34 .... 161 F2
Crowthorne Rd GU47 .... 35 E4
Croyde Cl GU14 .... 55 E3
Croye Cl SP10 .... 105 F4
Cruikshank Lea GU15 .... 35 E2
Crundwell Cl GU13 .... 99 D2
Cuckoo Cl RG25 .... 89 F1
Cufaude La RG24 .... 48 C4
Cuffelle Cl RG24 .... 49 D2
Cufoude La RG24 .... 48 C2
Cullen Cl GU47 .... 34 A3
Cullens Mews **4** GU11 ...... 76 C1
Culley View SO24 .... 179 E2
Culver Mews **29** SO23 .... 198 A4
Culver Rd Basingstoke RG21 69 D2
Newbury RG14 .... 5 E4
28 Winchester SO23 .... 198 A4
Culverlands Cres GU12 .... 77 F2
Culverwell Gdns **21** SO23 . 197 F4
Cumberland Ave RG22 .... 68 C1
Cundell Way SO23 .... 154 A1
Cundellway SO23 .... 176 A4
Cunningham Ho **4** SP9 ... 78 C4
Cunnington Rd GU14 .... 56 B1
Curlew Cl RG21 .... 68 C4
Curlews GU34 .... 139 F2
Curleys Way RG7 .... 14 A3
Curling Way RG14 .... 2 A2
Curly Bridge Cl GU14 .... 55 E4
Curnock Ct RG14 .... 1 B1
Curtis Cl GU35 .... 165 E3
Curtis Ct GU13 .... 75 D3
Curtis La GU35 .... 165 E3
Curtis Rd GU34 .... 140 A2
Curzon Dr GU13 .... 75 D3
Cusden Dr SP10 .... 83 D1
Cuthbert Rd GU14 .... 77 F3
Cutts Rd GU12 .... 77 D4
Cuxhaven Way SP10 .... 82 C2
Cygnet Cl RG19 .... 2 C2

Cygnet Ct Fleet GU13 .... 54 A2
Newbury RG14 .... 1 B2
Cygnets GU13 .... 54 A2
Cypress CI RG40 .... 16 C4
Cypress Dr GU13 .... 54 B1
Cypress Gr Andover SP10 .... 105 E4
Ash GU12 .... 77 E4
Cypress Rd GU35 .... 164 A1
Cypress Way
Blackwater GU17 .... 34 C3
Grayshott GU26 .... 167 D1
Cyprus Rd RG22 .... 91 E3
Cyril Vokins Rd RG14 .... 2 B1

Dacre CI SP10 .... 82 B2
Daffodil CI RG22 .... 91 D4
Dahlia CI RG22 .... 91 D4
Dahlia Ct SP10 .... 105 E3
Dairy Wlk RG27 .... 52 B3
Dalby Cres RG14 .... 6 A4
Dale CI Farnham GU10 .... 121 E4
Littleton SO22 .... 175 D3
Dale Gdns GU17, GU47 ...... 34 C4
Dale View GU27 .... 189 F3
Dalewood RG22 .... 68 A2
Dallence Ho RG25 .... 88 A4
Dalley Ct GU15 .... 35 D4
Dalzell **31** SO23 .... 176 A1
Damsel Path **12** RG21 ...... 69 E3
Dance's La RG28 .... 86 B3
Dancers Meadow RG26 ...... 47 F2
Dances CI SP10 .... 83 D1
Danebury Rd RG22 .... 91 E3
Danebury Ring SO20 .... 148 C4
Danebury View SO20 .... 126 A2
Danebury Wlk GU16 .... 56 B4
Danegeld CI SP10 .... 83 D2
Danehurst PI SP10 .... 105 E4
Danemark Ct **4** SO23 ...... 198 A4
Danes Rd **22** SO23 .... 176 A1
Danes The RG21 .... 69 E3
Daneshill Dr RG24 .... 70 A4
Daneshill East Ind Est RG21 69 F4
Daneshill Rdbt RG21 .... 69 F4
Daneshill Sch RG27 .... 30 B2
Daneshill West Ind Est
RG21 .... 69 E4
Daniel Rd RG28 .... 86 B2
Dankworth Rd RG22 .... 91 E4
Danley La GU27 .... 188 C2
Danvers Dr GU13 .... 74 C2
Daphne Dr GU13 .... 74 C2
Darby Green La GU46 .... 34 C3
Darby Green Rd GU17 .... 34 C3
Darcy Ho RG22 .... 68 B1
Dare's Cnr GU13 .... 74 C1
Dare's La GU13 .... 74 C1
Darent Ct **28** RG21 .... 69 E3
Dark La
Bishop's Sutton SO24 ...... 179 F1
Sherborne St John RG26 .... 47 F2
Darlington Rd RG21 .... 69 D4
Darracott CI GU15 .... 36 C4
Darset Ave GU13 .... 54 A1
Dart CI Thatcham RG18 .... 2 C3
Wokingham RG40 .... 16 B3
Dart Ct **30** SP10 .... 83 E1
Dart Rd GU14 .... 55 D3
Dartmoor Wlk RG22 .... 68 B2
Dartmouth Way RG22 .... 68 B2
Dartmouth Wlk RG22 .... 68 B2
Darvill Rd SO24 .... 181 D3
Darvills La GU9 .... 99 D1
Darwin Gr GU12 .... 77 D2
Dashwood CI GU34 .... 139 E1
Dasna Rd SP9 .... 78 B3
Daunch CI SP9 .... 78 B4
Dauntsey Dro SP11 .... 81 D2
Dauntsey La SP11 .... 81 D1
Davis Gdns GU15 .... 35 E4
Davy CI RG22 .... 91 D3
Dawn Gdns SO22 .... 197 E3
Dawnay Rd Camberley GU47 35 F4
Sandhurst GU15 .... 35 F4
Days Meadow RG20 .... 21 D4
De Lunn Bldgs **5** SO23 .. 198 A4
De Montfort Rd RG14 .... 1 B3
De-lucy Ave SO24 .... 179 D3
Deadbrook La GU11 .... 77 E2
Deadmans La RG19 .... 5 F3
Deadmoor La RG14 .... 5 E1
Dean CI SO22 .... 175 E1
Dean La Sparsholt SO22 .... 175 D1
Winchester SO22 .... 175 D1
Dean Par GU15 .... 36 B4
Dean Rd West Dean SP5 .... 190 A1
West Tytherley SP5 .... 190 C3
Dean Rise SP11 .... 60 C4
Dean Sta SP5 .... 190 B2
Dean Terr SP11 .... 38 B3
Dean The SO24 .... 179 E3
Deane Down Dro SO22 ...... 175 D2
Deane's Ct RG21 .... 69 E3
Deanes Cotts RG25 .... 66 A1
Deans CI SP9 .... 78 C2
Deanswood Rd RG26 .... 26 C4
Decouttere CI GU13 .... 74 C2
Deedman CI GU12 .... 77 F1
Deep La RG22 .... 68 C3
Deep Well Dr GU15 .... 36 B3
Deepdene Farnham GU10 .. 122 A4
Haslemere GU27 .... 189 E3
Deer Rock Rd GU15 .... 36 B4
Deerfield Ct RG26 .... 29 D1
Deerleap GU35 .... 166 A2
Delibes Rd RG22 .... 91 F4
Dell CI RG22 .... 68 C1
Dell CI GU27 .... 189 F4
Dell Cotts SO24 .... 202 C1
Dell Gr GU15 .... 36 B1
Dell Rd Andover SP10 .... 82 C1
Finchampstead RG40 .... 16 C2
Winchester SO23 .... 198 B3
Dell The Farnham GU9 .... 99 D4
Grateley SP11 .... 103 E1
Kingsclere RG20 .... 24 B1
Old Basing RG24 .... 70 B3
Vernham Dean SP11 .... 38 A3
Yateley GU47 .... 34 A3
Dellands RG25 .... 88 A4
Dellands La RG25 .... 88 A4
Dellfield Froxfield GU32 .... 205 F1
Oakley RG23 .... 67 E2
Delville CI GU14 .... 55 D2
Dempster Ho GU9 .... 99 D4
Denby Ct **3** GU46 .... 56 A1
Dene CI Bordon GU35 .... 164 B1
Farnham GU10 .... 122 B3
Ropley SO24 .... 181 D3
Dene Ct SP10 .... 106 A4
Dene La GU10 .... 122 B3
Dene La W GU10 .... 122 B3
Dene Path SP10 .... 106 A4
Dene Rd Andover SP10 ...... 106 A4
Farnborough GU14 .... 55 E2
Dene The SO24 .... 181 D3
Dene Way RG14 .... 1 C3
Denham Ct SO23 .... 175 F1
Denham Ct SO23 .... 176 A1
Denham Dr
Basingstoke RG22 .... 68 B1
Yateley GU17 .... 34 A3
Denham Terr SP11 .... 61 F1
Denman CI GU13 .... 54 B1
Denmark Rd RG14 .... 1 C2
Denmark Sq GU11 .... 77 E1
Denmark St GU12 .... 77 D1
Denmead RG26 .... 26 C4
Dennet Ho RG23 .... 176 B1
Denning CI GU10 .... 74 C4
Dennis Way GU33 .... 208 A2
Dennistoun CI GU15 .... 36 A3
Denton Way GU15 .... 36 A1
Denyers Cotts GU34 .... 138 A2
Deptford La Greywell RG29 .. 72 A2
Odiham RG29 .... 72 A2
Derby Rd Haslemere GU27 189 F4
Newbury RG14 .... 1 B1
Derbyfields RG29 .... 72 B3
Derek Horn Ct GU47 .... 35 F3
Derry Rd GU14 .... 55 E4
Derwent Ave GU12 .... 77 E2
Derwent CI Bordon GU35 .. 164 B3
Farnborough GU14 .... 55 E2
Farnham GU10, GU9 .... 98 C3
Derwent Ct **37** SP10 .... 83 E1
Derwent Gdns SO24 .... 179 E2
Derwent Rd
Basingstoke RG21 .... 68 A1
Thatcham RG19 .... 2 C2
Devenish Rd SO22 .... 175 E2
Dever CI SO21 .... 133 D2
Dever Way RG22 .... 67 E2
Devils La GU30 .... 188 B2
Devizes Ho **10** SP9 .... 78 C4
Devon CI Fleet GU13 .... 54 A2
Sandhurst GU15 .... 35 D4
Devon Rd GU35 .... 164 B2
Devonshire Dr GU16 .... 36 B4
Devonshire PI
Aldershot GU11 .... 76 B1
7 Basingstoke RG21 ...... 69 D2
Dewpond Wlk RG21 .... 69 F4
Dexter Sq SP10 .... 83 E2
Dexter Way GU13 .... 54 A2
Diamond Hill GU15 .... 36 B4
Diamond Ridge GU16 .... 36 A4
Diana CI RG22 .... 68 C2
Dibley CI RG22 .... 68 B2
Dickens La RG24 .... 70 A2
Dickens Way GU17 .... 34 A3
Dickens Wlk RG14 .... 5 F4
Dickenson Wlk SO24 .... 179 E2
Dicker's La GU34 .... 140 A2
Digby Rd RG14 .... 1 B2
Dilly La RG27 .... 52 B2
Dine CI SP11 .... 60 C4
Dingley Way GU11 .... 76 C4
Dinorben Ave GU13 .... 74 C4
Dinorben Beeches GU13 .... 74 C4
Dinorben CI GU13 .... 74 C4
Dippenhall Rd GU10 .... 98 A1
Dippenhall St GU10 .... 97 E3
Dirty Cnr SP11 .... 85 F4
Ditchfield La RG40 .... 16 B4
Divers CI GU34 .... 139 F3
Dixons La SO20 .... 170 A4
Dockenfield St GU35 .... 143 D3
Doctors Dro SP11 .... 60 B4
Dodsells Well RG40 .... 16 B4
Dogflud Way GU9 .... 99 D2
Dogmersfield CE Prim Sch
RG27 .... 74 A4
Doiley Bottom SP11 .... 40 B1
Doiley Hill SP11 .... 40 B2
Dollis CI GU9 .... 99 D2
Dollis Dr GU9 .... 99 D2
Dollis Gn RG26 .... 28 C2
Dolman Rd RG14 .... 1 C2
Dolomans La SP11 .... 60 C4
Dolphin CI GU27 .... 189 E3
Dolton Mews RG14 .... 1 B2
Doman Rd GU15 .... 35 F2
Dome AI SO23 .... 198 A4
Dominica CI RG24 .... 48 B1
Domum Rd SO23 .... 198 A3
Donnington Castle RG14 .... 1 B4
Donnington CI GU15 .... 35 F2
Donnington Ct **19** SO23 .. 176 A1
Donnington Hospital RG14 .. 1 B3
Donnington Lodge RG14 .... 1 B3
Donnington Pk RG14 .... 1 B3
Donnington Sq RG14 .... 1 B3
Dora's Green La GU9 .... 98 A2
Dorcas CI GU47 .... 35 F2
Dorchester CI RG22 .... 68 A3
Dorchester Rd RG27 .... 51 D1
Dorchester Way RG29 .... 72 A2
Doreen CI GU14 .... 55 E4
Dorian Gr SO24 .... 179 D2
Dormer CI RG14 .... 5 D3
Dorothy Ct RG14 .... 2 A2
Dorrel CI RG22 .... 91 D3
Dorset CI GU15 .... 36 B4
Dorset Rd GU12 .... 77 F3
Doswell Way RG21 .... 69 E3
Douai CI GU14 .... 56 A2
Doublet CI RG19 .... 2 C2
Doughty Way SP10 .... 83 F1
Douglas Gr GU10 .... 122 A3
Douglas PI GU14 .... 55 F3
Douglas Ride RG20 .... 21 E4
Douro CI RG7 .... 10 A3
Dove CI Andover SP10 .... 83 D1
Basingstoke RG22 .... 67 F1
Dove Ct GU34 .... 140 A3
Dove House Special Sch
RG21 .... 69 E4
Dover CI
Basingstoke RG22 .... 68 B3
New Alresford SO24 .... 179 E2
Doveton Way RG14 .... 1 C2
Dowden Gr GU34 .... 140 A3
Down Farm La SO23 .... 175 F4
Down Gate SO24 .... 179 E2
Down La RG25 .... 71 E1
Down Rd SP11 .... 80 A2
Down St RG25 .... 90 B1
Downing St GU9 .... 98 C1
Downlands Rd SO22 .... 197 D2
Downlands Way SO21 .... 153 E2
Downs La SN8 .... 18 A4
Downs Way GU34 .... 139 E1
Downside CI RG26 .... 167 D4
Downside Cotts SP11 .... 124 C4
Downside Rd SO22 .... 175 D1
Downsland Par RG22 .... 68 C2
Downsland Rd RG24 .... 69 D2
Downsview Rd GU35 .... 166 A3
Downsview La GU26 .... 167 D3
Downview Rd SP11 .... 52 A4
Doyle Gdns GU46 .... 34 A2
Dragonfly Dr RG21 .... 69 F4
Dragoon Ct **12** RG21 ...... 76 B1
Drake Ave GU16 .... 56 C1
Drake CI RG40 .... 16 B4
Drake Ct SP10 .... 83 E1
Drayman's Way GU34 .... 139 F2
Drayton St SO22 .... 197 E3
Drift Rd Bordon GU35 .... 186 A4
Selborne GU35 .... 186 A4
Driftway Rd RG27 .... 51 E1
Drive The Farnham GU10 .. 121 F4
Newbury RG14 .... 5 E4
Oakley RG23 .... 67 D1
Old Alresford SO24 .... 158 B3
Drove Hill SO20 .... 129 D2
Drove La SO24 .... 179 D3
Drove Rd SP11 .... 129 D2
Drovers Way SP10 .... 106 A4
Drovers Way GU10 .... 98 C3
Droxford Cres RG26 .... 26 C4
Drummond CI
Four Marks GU34 .... 159 F1
Winchester SO22 .... 197 F3
Drury CI SP11 .... 108 B4
Drury La Bentworth GU34 . 138 A3
Mortimer RG7 .... 11 F3
Dryden CI RG24 .... 48 B1
Dryden Rd GU14 .... 55 D3
Dryden Way GU30 .... 187 F3
Du Maurier CI GU13 .... 74 C2
Duchess CI GU34 .... 139 F2
Duck St SP11 .... 104 C2
Ducklands GU35 .... 164 C1
Duckmead La GU33 .... 208 A3
Ducks La SO20 .... 147 F3
Duddon Way **18** RG21 ... 69 E3
Dudley CI Basingstoke RG23 68 A3
Bordon GU35 .... 164 B1
Dudley Ct GU13 .... 75 D3
Dudley Terr GU33 .... 208 A3
Duke CI SP10 .... 83 E1
Duke St SO21 .... 133 D2
Duke Terr GU11 .... 76 C2
Dukes CI Alton GU34 .... 139 E1
Farnham GU9 .... 98 C3
Dukes Mead GU13 .... 53 E1
Dukes Ride RG26 .... 27 F4
Dukes Wlk GU12 .... 98 C3
Dumas CI GU46 .... 34 A3
Dummer Down La RG25 .... 113 E4
Dummer La SP11 .... 104 C2
Dunbar Rd GU16 .... 56 B4
Dunbridge La
Brown Candover SO24 .... 135 E3
Mottisfont SO51 .... 192 B1
Dunbridge Sta SO51 .... 192 B1
Duncan CI SP10 .... 106 B4
Duncan's CI SP11 .... 80 C1
Dundaff CI GU15 .... 36 C3
Dunedin CI SP9 .... 79 D3
Dungells Farm CI GU46 .... 34 A2
Dungells La GU46 .... 34 A2
Dunhills La
Enham Alamein SP10 .... 83 E4
Smannell SP10 .... 83 E4
Dunkirt La SP11 .... 104 C2
Dunley's Hill RG29 .... 72 B2
Dunmow Hill GU13 .... 54 A1
Dunmow Rd SP10 .... 106 A3
Dunnell's La SO24 .... 181 E3
Dunnsford Cres RG23 .... 68 B4
Dunsmore Gdns GU46 .... 33 F3
Dunstall Pk GU14 .... 55 F4
Dunstan's Dro SP11 .... 39 E1
Durbidges RG19 .... 24 B4
Durham Way RG22 .... 91 D4
Durnford CI SO20 .... 129 D2
Durngate PI SO23 .... 198 A4
Durngate Terr SO23 .... 198 A4
Durnsford Ave GU13 .... 75 D4
Dyson Dr SO23 .... 176 A1
Dysons CI RG14 .... 1 B2

Eagle CI Alton GU34 .... 139 F3
Basingstoke RG22 .... 90 C4
Eagle Ct RG21 .... 69 F3
Eagle Rd RG19 .... 6 C1
Eames La GU33 .... 206 C4
Eardley Ave SP10 .... 82 B1
Earle Ho **8** SO23 .... 198 B4
Earls Gr GU15 .... 36 B3
Earlsbourne GU13 .... 75 D2
Earlsdown **40** SO23 ...... 198 A4
East Ave GU9 .... 99 D3
East Dean Rd SO51 .... 191 F1
East Gn GU15 .... 35 D2
East Hill Dr GU33 .... 208 A2
East La SO24 .... 178 C2
East Portway SP10 .... 82 B1
East Rd SO21 .... 130 C4
East Ring GU10 .... 100 C4
East St Andover SP10 .... 106 A4
Farnham GU9 .... 99 D2
New Alresford SO24 .... 179 E3
East Station Rd GU12 .... 76 C1
East Stratton SO21 .... 134 A2
East Tree CI RG25 .... 90 A4
East View RG27 .... 52 A2
East Woodhay Rd SO22 .... 175 E2
Eastacre SO22 .... 175 F1
Eastbrooke Rd GU14 .... 140 A2
Eastern Ave SO21 .... 106 A4
Eastern Rd Aldershot GU12 .. 77 E3
Bordon GU35 .... 164 B3
Eastfield Ave RG24 .... 69 E3
Eastfield CI **9** SP10 .... 106 A4
Eastfield Ho SP10 .... 106 A4
Eastfield Lodge SP10 .... 106 A4
Eastfield Rd SP10 .... 106 A4
Eastgate St SO23 .... 198 A4
Eastlyn Rd RG26 .... 10 B3
Eastmead GU14 .... 55 F2
Easton Common Hill SP5 . 168 B3
Easton La SO21 .... 177 D3
Easton Lane Bsns Pk **17**
SO23 .... 198 A4
Eastrop La RG21 .... 69 E3
Eastrop Rdbt RG24 .... 69 E3
Eastrop Way RG21 .... 69 E3
Eastview Gdns GU34 .... 161 F2
Eastville SP11 .... 81 E4
Ebble Ct SP9 .... 35 F2
Ebble CI SP9 .... 78 C4
Ebden Rd SO23 .... 198 A4
Ecchinswell Rd
Ecchinswell RG20 .... 24 A3
Kingsclere RG20 .... 24 A4
Ecchinswell & Sydmonton
CE Prim Sch RG20 .... 23 F2
Echo Barn La GU10 .... 121 E3
Eddeys CI GU35 .... 165 F3
Eddeys La GU35 .... 165 F3
Eddy Rd GU12 .... 77 D3
Eddystone Ct GU10 .... 144 B3
Edgar Rd SO23 .... 198 A3
Edgar Villas SO23 .... 197 F3
Edgeborough Sch GU10 .... 122 A2
Edgecombe La RG14 .... 2 A1
Edgehill CI RG21 .... 68 B2
Edgewood CI GU33 .... 208 A1
Edinburgh CI Bath GU12 .... 77 F2
Kings Worthy SO23 .... 154 A1
Edington Rd SO23 .... 176 A1
Edison Rd RG23 .... 68 C4
Edney CI GU33 .... 208 A3
Edric's Gn SP4 .... 101 E1
Edrich Sq SP11 .... 83 D2
Egbert Rd SO23 .... 197 F4
Egerton Rd GU13 .... 54 B1
Eggars CI **21** GU11 .... 76 C1
Eggar's Hill GU9 .... 99 F4
Eggars's Sec Sch GU34 .... 140 A1
Eggars CI GU34 .... 140 A1
Eggars Field GU10 .... 120 A4
Eggleton CI GU13 .... 74 C1
Eglinton Rd GU10 .... 144 C1
Eight Bells RG14 .... 1 B1
Eights The SP11 .... 104 A4
Eland Rd GU12 .... 77 D3
Elane Ho SP11 .... 57 D1
Elbe Way SP10 .... 83 E1
Elbow Cnr RG21 .... 69 D2
Elder CI SO22 .... 197 E2
Elderberry Bank RG24 .... 69 F3
Elderberry Rd GU35 .... 165 D4
Eldergrove GU14 .... 56 B1
Eldon CI SO20 .... 172 A1
Eldon Dr GU10 .... 122 A4
Eldon PI GU9 .... 122 A4
Eldon Rd Braishfield SO20 194 A1
King's Somborne SO20 .... 194 A3
Eleanor CI GU30 .... 187 D3
Elgar CI RG22 .... 91 F1
Elgin Rd GU46 .... 34 B2
Elgin Way GU16 .... 56 B4
Elgrath Dr RG40 .... 16 B3
Eling CI SO22 .... 175 E1
Eliot CI GU15 .... 36 C1
Eliot Dr RG27 .... 189 E2
Elizabeth Ave RG14 .... 1 C1
Elizabeth CI SO23 .... 154 A1
Elizabeth Dr GU13 .... 75 D1
Elizabeth Par GU46 .... 34 A2

Elizabeth Rd RG23 .... 68 C2
Elizabethan Rise RG25 .... 89 F1
Elkington Cl RG20 .... 22 C4
Ellen Gdns RG26 .... 28 C2
Elleray Ct GU12 .... 77 F3
Elles Cl GU14 .... 55 F2
Elles Rd GU14 .... 55 F1
Ellingham Cl SO24 .... 179 E3
Ellington Cl GU10 .... 105 D4
Ellington Dr RG22 .... 91 E4
Elliot Park Ind Est GU12 .... 77 E1
Ellison Way GU11 .... 100 B4
Elm Bank GU46 .... 34 A4
Elm Bank Rd SP10 .... 106 A3
Elm Bottom Cross RG26 .... 47 E1
Elm Cl Bordon GU35 .... 164 C2
Middle Wallop SO20 ...... 126 A2
Thruxton SP11 .... 103 E4
Elm Cotts RG14 .... 4 B1
Elm Cres GU9 .... 99 D4
Elm Ct Andover SP10 .... 106 A4
Ludgershall SP11 .... 57 D1
Winchester SO22 .... 197 F4
Elm Gr Farnham GU11 ...... 99 D4
Kingsclere RG20 .... 24 B1
Elm Grove Flats RG20 .... 24 B1
Elm Gr Pk RG20 .... 24 B1
Elm Grove Rd GU14 .... 55 F2
Elm La GU10 .... 100 B4
Elm Piece Ho RG25 .... 88 A4
Elm Pl GU10 .... 100 A4
Elm Rd Farnham GU9 .... 99 D4
New Alresford SO24 ..... 179 E3
Overton RG25 .... 65 D1
Sherborne St John RG26 .. 47 F1
Winchester SO22 .... 197 F4
Elm Terr GU33 .... 207 F3
Elm View GU12 .... 77 F2
Elmay Ho SP11 .... 57 D1
Elmcroft Cl GU16 .... 56 B4
Elmfield Ct GU35 .... 164 C3
Elmhurst RG26 .... 27 D4
Elmhurst Ballet Sch GU15 .. 36 A3
Elmhurst Rd RG18 .... 2 C3
Elms Rd Aldershot GU11 .... 76 C1
Fleet GU13 .... 75 E4
Hook RG27 .... 51 D1
Elms The Andover SP11 .... 105 F4
Ash GU10 .... 100 B4
Blackwater GU15 .... 35 D2
Elmsleigh Rd GU14 .... 55 E2
Elmsley Ct GU14 .... 55 E2
Elmstead Caravan Pk SP11 103 F4
Elmwood RG24 .... 48 C2
Elmwood Cl GU14 .... 139 E1
Elmwood Par RG22 .... 64 B4
Elmwood Way RG21 .... 68 B4
Elsenwood Cres GU15 .... 36 C3
Elsenwood Dr GU15 .... 36 C4
Elsley Cl GU14 .... 56 B3
Elstead Rd GU11 .... 100 C2
Elston Pl GU12 .... 100 A4
Elston Rd GU10 .... 100 A4
Elvetham Cl GU13 .... 54 A2
Elvetham La RG27 .... 53 D4
Elvetham Pl GU13 .... 53 F2
Elvetham Rd GU13 .... 53 F2
Ely Cl GU14 .... 56 C4
Embleton Rd GU35 .... 165 F3
Emden Rd SP10 .... 82 C2
Empress Ave GU14 .... 55 F3
Enborne CE Prim Sch RG20 .. 4 B3
Enborne Gr RG14 .... 1 B1
Enborne Lodge Sch RG14 .... 4 C3
Enborne Pl RG14 .... 1 B1
Enborne Rd RG14 .... 1 A1
Enborne St Enborne RG14 .. 4 C2
Newbury RG14 .... 4 C2
Enborne Way RG7 .... 8 B3
Enbourne Gate RG14 .... 1 A1
Enfield Rd GU12 .... 77 F3
Engineers Rd RG19 .... 6 C3
Enham La SP11 .... 83 D2
Enmill La SO22 .... 196 C3
Ennerdale Cl RG22 .... 68 A1
Ennerdale Gdns SO24 .... 179 E2
Ennerdale Gr GU9 .... 98 C3
Ennerdale Rd GU35 .... 164 B3
Ennerdale Way RG19 .... 2 C2
Enterprise Ct RG21 .... 69 E4
Enterprise Ho RG23 .... 68 A2
Epsom Cl GU14 .... 36 A4
Epsom Cres RG14 .... 1 C1
Epsom Down GU34 .... 139 F1
Erasmus Pk SO23 .... 176 B1
Erica Cotts GU26 .... 167 D3
Erleigh Dene RG14 .... 1 A1
Erles Rd GU30 .... 188 A2
Ermine Wlk RG19 .... 2 C2
Ernest Cl GU10 .... 121 F3
Erskine Cl RG26 .... 10 B1

Erskine Rd SO22 .... 197 F4
Esher Cl RG23 .... 68 B1
Eskdale Ct GU12 .... 77 E2
Essex Cl Bordon GU35 ...... 164 B2
Camberley GU16 .... 56 C4
Essex Rd Basingstoke RG21 .. 69 D3
Bordon GU35 .... 164 B2
Essex St RG14 .... 5 D4
Ethelbert Ave SP10 .... 82 B2
Eton Cl RG22 .... 91 D3
Eton Pl GU9 .... 98 C4
Ettrick Ct GU14 .... 76 C4
Etwall SP11 .... 103 D2
Europa Cl RG26 .... 28 C2
Euskirchen Way RG22 .... 68 B3
Evans Cl SO20 .... 125 D1
Eveley Cl GU35 .... 164 A1
Evelyn Ave GU9 .... 99 F4
Evelyn Mews SO24 .... 179 E3
Evelyn Wood's Rd GU12 ..... 77 D3
Evenlode Way GU15 .... 35 D4
Everest Rd GU15 .... 36 A4
Evergreen Rd GU15 .... 36 B1
Eversfield Cl SP11 .... 105 F4
Eversley Pl SO22 .... 197 E3
Eversley Rd Arborfield RG40 15 F3
Eversley GU46 .... 33 D4
Eversley St RG7 .... 15 F1
Evesham Wlk RG24 .... 48 A1
Evingar Gdns RG28 .... 86 B3
Evingar Rd RG28 .... 86 B3
Ewhurst Rd RG26 .... 46 A3
Ewins Cl GU12 .... 77 F1
Ewshot Hill La GU13 .... 75 D1
Ewshot Hill Cross GU9 .... 98 A4
Ewshot La GU10 .... 74 B1
Exbury Way SP10 .... 105 F4
Exeter Ct RG22 .... 91 D4
Exeter Gdns GU14 .... 33 F4
Exeter Rd GU12 .... 77 F2
Exmoor Ct RG22 .... 68 A2
Express Way RG14 .... 2 B1

Fabers Yd SO22 .... 197 F4
Fabian Cl RG24 .... 69 D2
Factory Cotts GU9 .... 98 A1
Fair Cl RG28 .... 86 B2
Fair Close Ho RG14 .... 1 C1
Fair Oak La RG26 .... 29 E4
Fair Piece SP11 .... 128 C3
Fair View SO24 .... 179 E2
Fairacre RG20 .... 21 E4
Fairacres GU11 .... 121 E2
Fairclose Dr SO22 .... 175 D3
Faircrosse Cl GU17 .... 35 D4
Fairdown Cl SO23 .... 198 B4
Fairfax Ind Est GU11 .... 77 E1
Fairfax Mews GU16 .... 56 A1
Fairfax Pl RG14 .... 2 B3
Fairfax Rd GU14 .... 56 A4
Fairfield RG28 .... 86 B3
Fairfield Dr GU13 .... 36 B2
Fairfield Gn GU34 .... 160 B2
Fairfield Rd SO21, SO22 ... 175 F1
Fairfield The GU9 .... 99 D1
Fairfields Ct RG28 .... 69 D2
Fairfields Prim Sch RG21 ... 69 D2
Fairfields Rd RG21 .... 69 D2
Fairholm Gdns GU11 .... 99 D1
Fairholme Par RG27 .... 51 D1
Fairland Cl GU13 .... 75 D4
Fairlands GU35 .... 166 A3
Fairlawn Ho RG14 .... 1 B1
Fairlawn Rd RG26 .... 27 D4
Fairlight Gdns GU34 .... 160 B2
Fairmead Cl GU17 .... 35 E4
Fairmead Ct GU15 .... 36 A2
Fairmile GU13 .... 74 C3
Fairoak Way RG26 .... 9 D1
Fairthorne Ho RG22 .... 68 C2
Fairthorne Rise RG24 .... 70 B3
Fairview RG14 .... 5 E4
Fairview Gdns GU14 .... 99 D3
Fairview Meadow RG22 ...... 90 A4
Fairview Rd Ash GU12 .... 77 F2
Headley GU35 .... 166 A3
Fairview Terr GU35 .... 166 A3
Fairway Cl GU30 .... 187 D2
Fairway The Bordon GU35 . 164 A1
Camberley GU16 .... 36 C2
Farnham GU9 .... 99 D4
Hawley GU13 .... 75 F4
Fairways Beacon Hill GU26 166 C3
Thruxton SP11 .... 81 D1
Faithfulls Dro SO20 .... 171 D2
Falaise Cl Aldershot GU12 .. 76 C1
North Tidworth SP9 .... 78 A3
Falaise Rd
Middle Wallop SO20 ...... 126 A2
North Tidworth SP9 .... 79 E3
Falcon Bsns Pk RG40 .... 15 F3

Falcon Cl Basingstoke RG23 . 67 F1
North Tidworth SP9 .... 78 C4
Falcon Coppice RG20 .... 21 E4
Falcon Ct Alton GU34 .... 139 F3
Camberley GU16 .... 36 A1
Falcon Fields RG7 .... 9 F1
Falcon House Gdns RG20 ... 4 A1
Falcon Rd SP9 .... 78 C4
Falcon View SO22 .... 197 E2
Falcon Way GU46 .... 33 F3
Falkland Ct GU12 .... 77 E1
Falkland Cty Prim Sch RG14 . 5 E3
Falkland Dr RG14 .... 5 E4
Falkland Garth RG14 .... 5 D4
Falkland Rd
Basingstoke RG24 .... 48 B1
Newbury RG14 .... 5 D3
Falkner Ho GU13 .... 54 B2
Falkner Rd GU9 .... 98 C1
Falkners Cl GU13 .... 54 B2
Fallow Field SO22 .... 197 E2
Fallowfield GU13 .... 54 B2
Falmouth Cl GU15 .... 36 C2
Fantails GU34 .... 139 F3
Faraday Cl RG40 .... 15 E4
Faraday Ct RG24 .... 69 E4
Faraday Pk SP10 .... 82 A1
Faraday Rd
Farnborough GU16 .... 56 A3
Newbury RG14 .... 1 C2
Farcrosse Cl GU47 .... 35 D4
Fareham Dr GU46 .... 33 F4
Faringdon Cl [16] SO23 ...... 176 A1
Farleigh House Sch RG22 ... 91 F1
Farleigh La Dummer RG25 .. 91 D1
Farleigh Wallop RG22 ...... 91 D1
Farleigh Rd GU9 .... 92 A4
Farleigh Rise RG21 .... 69 E1
Farleigh Sch SP11 .... 127 D4
Farley Cl SO22 .... 197 D2
Farley Ct GU14 .... 56 A1
Farley Hill Prim Sch RG2 ... 15 D3
Farley La SO51 .... 194 C1
Farley Mount Ctry Pk SO21 195 E4
Farley Mount Rd SO21 ...... 196 A2
Farley St SO20 .... 147 F3
Farm Cl GU46 .... 34 A3
Farm Cotts RG22 .... 68 B4
Farm Ct GU15 .... 36 B1
Farm Dr GU13 .... 54 A2
Farm Ground Cl RG27 .... 51 E1
Farm La GU10 .... 97 E3
Farm Rd Abbotts Ann SP11 105 D3
Aldershot GU12 .... 77 E2
Camberley GU46 .... 36 B1
Farm View GU46 .... 34 A3
Farm View Dr RG24 .... 49 D2
Farmhouse Way GU13 .... 74 C3
Farnborough Bsns Ctr GU14 55 E3
Farnborough Coll of Tech
GU14 .... 56 A1
Farnborough Coll of Tech
(Highfield Ctr) GU14 .... 55 F3
Farnborough Gate Ret Pk
GU14 .... 56 A4
Farnborough Grange Inf Sch
GU14 .... 55 F4
Farnborough Hill
(Girls Public Sch) GU14 .. 56 A3
Farnborough Ind Est GU14 . 55 F2
Farnborough North Sta
GU14 .... 56 A3
Farnborough Rd
Aldershot GU11 .... 76 B2
Farnborough GU14 .... 76 B2
Farnborough (Sixth Form)
Coll GU14 .... 55 F3
Farnborough St GU14 .... 56 A3
Farnborough Sta GU14 ...... 55 F3
Farnham Bsns Ctr GU9 ...... 99 D2
Farnham Bsns Pk GU9 .... 98 C1
Farnham By-Pass GU9 .... 99 D1
Farnham Coll GU9 .... 99 D1
Farnham Hospl (Geriatric)
GU9 .... 99 E2
Farnham La GU27 .... 189 F4
Farnham Park Cl GU9 .... 98 C3
Farnham Park Dr GU9 .... 98 C3
Farnham Rd Bordon GU35 164 B3
Dogmersfield RG27 .... 73 E1
Fleet GU13 .... 73 E1
Liss GU33 .... 207 F2
Odiham RG29 .... 73 E1
Farnham Sta GU9 .... 99 D1
Farnham Trad Est GU9 .... 99 E2
Faroe Cl RG24 .... 48 B1
Farrell Cl GU15 .... 35 F4
Farrier's Field RG25 .... 115 D4
Farringdon Way RG26 .... 26 C4
Farrs Ave SP10 .... 106 A4
Farthing Fields GU33 .... 165 E3

Farthinghold Ho GU9 .... 99 D2
Fawconer Rd RG20 .... 24 B1
Fawley La GU34 .... 204 A2
Fayrewood Chase RG22 ..... 91 D4
Feathers La [4] RG21 .... 69 D2
Feilden Ct RG20 .... 24 B1
Felbridge Cl GU16 .... 56 A1
Feld Way RG24 .... 70 A4
Fellows Rd GU14 .... 56 A1
Felmer Dr SO23 .... 176 B4
Fencott Pl RG24 .... 69 D3
Fennel Cl Chineham RG24 .. 49 D2
Farnborough GU13 .... 54 C2
Newbury RG14 .... 2 A3
Ferbies GU13 .... 75 D3
Ferguson Cl RG21 .... 69 D1
Fern Cl GU16 .... 36 C2
Fern Ct GU12 .... 77 E1
Fern Dr GU13 .... 74 C3
Fernbank RG40 .... 16 A3
Fernbrae Cl GU10 .... 121 F2
Ferncote Rd GU35 .... 164 C2
Ferndale Gdns RG27 .... 51 D1
Ferndale Rd Andover SP10 . 82 C1
Farnborough GU14 .... 54 C3
Ferndown Cl GU34 .... 140 A2
Ferndown Gdns GU14 .... 55 E2
Ferney Cl GU34 .... 161 E4
Ferney La SO24 .... 159 D4
Fernhill Cl
Farnborough GU14 .... 35 E1
Farnham GU9 .... 98 C3
Fernhill Dr GU9 .... 98 C3
Fernhill Ho GU14 .... 56 A1
Fernhill La
Farnborough GU47 .... 35 E1
Farnham GU9 .... 98 C3
Fernhill Prim Sch GU47 ..... 35 E1
Fernhill Rd GU14 .... 55 E3
Fernhill Sch GU14 .... 35 E1
Fernhill Wlk GU14 .... 35 E1
Ferniehurst GU15 .... 36 B2
Fernlea GU35 .... 164 A1
Ferns Mead GU9 .... 98 C1
Ferns The GU9 .... 99 D4
Ferrell Field RG27 .... 50 C1
Ferrier Gr RG14 .... 1 A1
Fiddlers Field GU34 .... 139 D4
Field End Farnham GU9 ...... 99 E2
Kings Worthy SO23 .... 176 B4
Field Gate Dr RG20 .... 24 B1
Field Gn GU34 .... 160 B1
Field Path GU14 .... 35 E1
Field Pl GU30 .... 188 A2
Field Rd GU14 .... 35 E1
Field Stores App GU11 .... 77 D2
Field Way Aldershot GU12 .. 77 E2
Tongham GU12 .... 100 B4
Fielders The GU46 .... 33 E4
Fielding Ave [2] GU46 .... 33 F3
Fieldgate Ctr RG20 .... 24 B1
Fielding Rd GU17 .... 35 E3
Fieldridge RG14 .... 2 A3
Fieldway GU13 .... 74 A4
Fifehead Gotts SO20 .... 147 E4
Fifield La GU10 .... 122 A1
Fifth Ave GU14 .... 56 B4
Fifth Rd RG14 .... 1 B1
Fifth St RG14 .... 6 B3
Filmorehill La GU34 .... 204 A2
Finch Cl RG26 .... 27 D4
Finchampstead CE Prim Sch
RG40 .... 16 B2
Finchampstead Rd
Wokingham RG40, RG41 ... 16 B3
Wokingham RG40 .... 16 B4
Finches Gn GU34 .... 139 F3
Findhorn Cl GU17 .... 35 D4
Findings The GU14 .... 55 E4
Fingle Dr SP10 .... 105 F4
Finkley Down Farm Pk SP10 83 F2
Finkley Rd Smannell SP10 .. 84 B4
St Mary Bourne SP10 .... 84 B4
Finnart Cl GU15 .... 55 E4
Fintry Pl GU14 .... 55 E4
Fintry Wlk GU14 .... 55 E4
Fircon Cl SO23 .... 198 B4
Fir Acre Rd GU12 .... 77 F3
Fir Cottage Rd RG40 .... 16 B4
Fir Dr GU14 .... 35 D2
Fir Gr GU35 .... 164 A1
Fir Tree Alley [6] GU11 .... 76 C1
Fir Tree Cnr RG26 .... 9 E1
Fir Tree La RG14 .... 2 B2
Fir Tree Piece RG26 .... 45 D2
Fir Tree Prim Sch RG14 .... 2 B2
Fir Tree Rd GU9 .... 99 D1
Fircrofts [3] GU13 .... 54 A1
Fire Station Rd GU11 .... 76 C2
Fire Thorn Cl GU13 .... 74 B4
Firfield Rd GU10 .... 121 F4

Firglen Dr GU46 .... 34 A4
Firgrove Ct
[6] Farnborough GU14 .... 55 F2
Farnham GU9 .... 99 D1
Firgrove Hill GU9 .... 99 D1
Firgrove Par [7] GU14 .... 55 F2
Firgrove Rd Bordon GU35 . 164 A1
Eversley GU46 .... 33 F3
Firlands Ave GU16 .... 36 A3
Firs Cl Farnborough GU14 .. 56 A1
Wokingham RG40 .... 16 B4
Firs Cres SO23 .... 176 A4
Firs End RG7 .... 11 E3
Firs La RG29 .... 72 B1
Firs The Andover SP10 ...... 105 F4
Thatcham RG18 .... 2 C2
Firs Way
Basingstoke RG22 .... 68 A4
Whitchurch RG28 .... 86 B3
First St RG14 .... 6 C3
First Cl RG26 .... 27 F4
Firtree Cl GU46 .... 34 B4
Firview GU30 .... 187 F2
Firway GU26 .... 166 B3
Firwood Ct GU15 .... 36 A3
Firwood Dr GU15 .... 36 A3
Fisher Cl SP10 .... 106 B4
Fisherman's La RG26 .... 9 F4
Fishermen's Cl GU11 .... 77 E3
Fiske Cl RG22 .... 68 B2
Fiske Ct GU46 .... 34 B3
Fitzroy Rd GU13 .... 53 E1
Five Acres Cl GU35 .... 164 C3
Five Ash Rd GU34 .... 160 A2
Five Bells La SO20 .... 147 F3
Five Bridges Rd SO22 .... 197 F2
Five Lanes SP11 .... 61 F1
Five Lanes End RG27 .... 71 D1
Fivefields Cl SO23 .... 198 B4
Fivefields Rd SO23 .... 198 B4
Fiveways
Basingstoke RG22 .... 68 A1
Camberley GU15 .... 36 B3
Flashett The SP5 .... 168 A3
Flats The GU47 .... 35 D2
Flaxfield Ct RG21 .... 69 D3
Flaxfield Rd RG21 .... 69 D3
Fleet Bsns Pk GU13 .... 75 D2
Fleet Hill RG40 .... 16 A1
Fleet Hospl GU13 .... 53 F1
Fleet Inf Sch GU13 .... 75 E4
Fleet Pond (Nature Reserve)
GU13 .... 54 B2
Fleet Rd Aldershot GU14 .... 76 B3
Farnborough GU14 .... 54 C2
Fleet GU13 .... 54 A1
Hartley Wintney RG27 ...... 53 D2
Fleet Sta GU13 .... 54 A1
Fleming Cl Arborfield RG2 .. 15 E4
Farnborough GU14 .... 56 A3
Fleming Rd RG14 .... 1 C2
Flensburg Ct SP10 .... 82 C2
Fletcher Cl RG23 .... 68 B1
Fletchers Field GU30 .... 188 A2
Fletchers Ho GU30 .... 187 F2
Flexford Cl RG20 .... 21 E3
Flinders Cl SP10 .... 83 F1
Flint Cl SP10 .... 105 F3
Flint La Chute Forest SP11 .. 81 F4
Penton Grafton SP11 .... 81 F4
Floral Way SP10 .... 105 E4
Floreat Gdns RG14 .... 1 B1
Florence Cl GU46 .... 34 A3
Florence Ct SP10 .... 83 D2
Florence Portal Cl RG28 .... 87 D3
Florence Rd Fleet GU13 ..... 75 D4
Sandhurst GU47 .... 35 E4
Florence Way RG22 .... 68 B4
Florrie Pl GU34 .... 161 E2
Flowerdew Ct SP10 .... 106 A3
Flowerdown Ho SO22 .... 175 E2
Focus 303 SP10 .... 83 E1
Folly Cotts RG20 .... 22 C4
Folly Gr GU35 .... 98 C3
Folly Hill Cty Inf Sch GU9 .. 98 C3
Folly La GU9 .... 98 C3
Folly La N GU9 .... 98 C3
Folly La S GU9 .... 98 C3
Folly The RG14 .... 1 C1
Fontwell Dr GU34 .... 139 F1
Fontwell Rd RG14 .... 1 C1
Forbes Chase GU17 .... 35 D4
Forbes Rd SO23 .... 176 A4
Forbury La RG20 .... 3 D4
Forbury GU10 .... 121 F4

Ford La Farnham GU9 .... 121 F3
Odiham RG29 .... 95 D3
South Warnborough RG29 .. 94 C4
Swallowfield RG7 .... 14 C1
Fordington Ave SO22 .... 197 F4
Fordington Rd SO22 .... 175 F1
Forehead The RG7 .... 12 B2
Foreman Pk GU12 .... 77 F1
Foreman Rd GU12 .... 77 F1
Forest CI RG26 .... 9 E1
Forest Cnr GU33 .... 208 A4
Forest **2** SP9 .... 79 D4
Forest Dean GU13 .... 54 B2
Forest Dr Chineham RG24 ... 48 C2
  Farnham GU9 .... 122 A2
  North Tidworth SP9 .... 79 D4
Forest End GU13 .... 74 C3
Forest End Rd GU47 .... 34 C4
Forest Glade GU10 .... 121 D2
Forest Hills GU17 .... 35 F2
Forest La Andover SP10 ... 106 C3
  Lindford GU35 .... 165 D3
  Tadley RG26 .... 27 D3
  Upper Chute SP11 .... 57 F4
Forest Lane CI GU30 .... 187 F2
Forest Rd Bordon GU35 ... 164 B1
  Greatham GU33 .... 207 F4
  Liss GU33 .... 208 A3
Forest Rise GU33 .... 208 A3
Forest Sh Ctr The GU35 ... 164 C2
Forestdale GU26 .... 167 E2
Forge CI Bramley RG26 ...... 29 D1
  Farnham GU9 .... 99 D2
Forge Ct GU46 .... 34 A4
Forge Field SP10 .... 83 D1
Forge La GU11 .... 76 C3
Forge Rd Kingsley GU35 ... 142 C1
  Kingsley GU35 .... 164 A4
Forsters RG26 .... 9 E4
Fort Hill Com Sch RG23 .... 68 B3
Fort Narrien GU47 .... 35 E4
Forth CI GU14 .... 55 D3
Forth CI **38** SP10 .... 83 E1
Fortrose CI GU47 .... 35 D4
Fossewood Dr GU15 .... 36 A4
Fosters Bsns Pk RG27 .... 71 F4
Foul La GU34 .... 159 F4
Foundry La GU27 .... 189 F3
Foundry Rd SP10 .... 105 E2
Fountains CI RG24 .... 48 A1
Four Acre Coppice RG27 .... 51 E1
Four Houses Cnr RG7 .... 11 E4
Four Lanes CI RG24 .... 49 D2
Four Lanes Cty Schs RG24 .. 48 C2
Four Lanes End RG24 .... 49 D1
Four Marks CE Prim Sch
  GU34 .... 182 A4
Four Oaks RG20 .... 21 E3
Four Ways GU35 .... 142 C4
Fourth St RG14 .... 6 B3
Fowler Rd GU14 .... 55 E2
Fowler's Rd GU11 .... 77 D3
Fox Dr GU46 .... 34 A4
Fox Heath GU14 .... 55 D2
Fox La Eversley GU46 .... 33 E4
  Oakley RG22 .... 67 E2
  Winchester SO22 .... 197 E3
Fox Rd Farnham GU10 ...... 122 A4
  Haslemere GU27 .... 189 E3
Fox Way GU9 .... 98 A4
Fox Yd GU9 .... 98 C1
Fox's La RG20 .... 24 B1
Foxborough RG7 .... 14 A3
Foxcote RG40 .... 16 C4
Foxcote CI SP10 .... 82 B1
Foxcote La SP10 .... 82 B2
Foxcote Rd SP10 .... 82 B2
Foxcroft GU13 .... 75 D3
Foxdown RG25 .... 65 D1
Foxdown CI GU15 .... 36 A3
Foxglove CI RG22 .... 91 D4
Foxglove Dr GU35 .... 164 C1
Foxhill Cres GU15 .... 36 C4
Foxhunter Way RG19 .... 2 B2
Foxhurst Rd GU12 .... 77 F2
Foxley CI GU15 .... 35 D3
Foxmoor CI RG23 .... 67 E2
Foxwood GU13 .... 54 B2
Foye La GU13 .... 75 D3
Foyle Pk RG21 .... 69 D1
Foyle Rd SP11 .... 80 B2
Frampton Way GU34 .... 176 B4
France Hill Cty Sec Sch
  GU15 .... 36 A1
France Hill Dr GU15 .... 36 A3
Frances Rd RG21 .... 69 D2
Francis Ct GU14 .... 55 E2
Francis Gdns SO23 .... 176 A2

Francis Way GU15 .... 36 C2
Franklin Ave
  Hartley Wintney RG27 ...... 52 B4
  Tadley RG26 .... 9 F1
Fraser CI RG24 .... 70 A3
Fraser Mead GU15 .... 35 E3
Fraser Rd SO23 .... 176 B4
Fraynes Croft GU13 .... 74 C4
Frederick St GU11 .... 76 C3
Freelands Dr GU13 .... 74 C3
Freemantle CI RG21 .... 69 E4
French Gdns GU47 .... 35 D2
French Rd GU33 .... 186 B2
Frenchmans Creek GU13 ... 74 C2
Frenchmoor La
  East Dean SP5 .... 190 C1
  West Tytherley SP5 .... 190 C2
Frensham Ave GU13 .... 54 B1
Frensham CI GU46 .... 33 F3
Frensham Ct GU10 .... 121 F2
Frensham Heights Rd
  GU10 .... 121 F1
Frensham Heights Sch
  GU10 .... 121 F1
Frensham La Headley GU35 165 D3
  Lindford GU35 .... 165 D3
Frensham Rd GU10 .... 122 A3
Frensham Vale GU10 .... 122 A3
Frescade Cres RG21 .... 69 D2
Freshwood Dr GU47 .... 34 A2
Friars Ct GU46 .... 34 B4
Friars Rd RG14 .... 5 F3
Friarsgate SO23 .... 198 A4
Friend Ave GU12 .... 77 D1
Friesian CI GU13 .... 54 B1
Frimley Bsns Pk
  Camberley GU14 .... 56 A4
  Farnborough GU14 .... 55 F4
Frimley CE Fst & Mid Sch
  GU14 .... 56 B4
Frimley Green Rd GU14 ...... 56 B4
Frimley Grove Gdns GU16 .. 36 B1
Frimley High St GU16 .... 56 A4
Frimley Park Hospl GU15 ... 36 A1
Frimley Rd Ash GU12 .... 77 E3
  Camberley GU15 .... 35 F2
Frimley Sta GU16 .... 56 B4
Frinton End Rd GU35 .... 142 C3
Frith Hill Rd GU15 .... 36 C1
Frithmead CI RG21 .... 69 D1
Frog La
  Latchmere Green RG26 ..... 27 F3
  Mapledurwell RG24 .... 70 C2
  Rotherwick RG27 .... 50 B3
Frogmore Com Sch GU46 ... 34 B3
Frogmore Ct GU47 .... 35 D2
Frogmore Gr GU17 .... 35 D2
Frogmore Park Dr
  GU15, GU16 .... 35 D2
Frogmore Rd GU17 .... 35 D2
Frogmore Schs GU17 .... 34 C3
Frogs Hole RG20 .... 24 B1
Frome CI Basingstoke RG21 . 69 E3
  Oakley RG22 .... 67 E1
Fromond Rd SO22 .... 175 E2
Froud CI RG27 .... 71 F4
Fruchold CE Inf Sch GU22 205 F1
Froxfield CI SO22 .... 175 E2
Froyle La RG29 .... 95 D2
Fry Sq SP10 .... 83 D1
Fry's Acre GU12 .... 77 F2
Fry's La GU46 .... 34 B4
Fugelmere Rd GU13 .... 54 B1
Fugelmere Wlk GU13 .... 54 B1
Fulbrook Way RG29 .... 95 E4
Fullfood Ct **2** SO22 .... 197 F4
Fulham Ho **19** RG20 .... 69 D3
Fullers La RG20 .... 21 D4
Fullers Rd Binsted GU10 ... 121 D2
  Farnham GU10 .... 121 D2
Fullers Vale GU35 .... 165 E3
Fullerton Rd
  Goodworth Clatford SP11 . 127 E4
  Upper Clatford SP11 .... 127 E4
  Wherwell SP11 .... 127 E4
Fullerton Way RG26 .... 27 D4
Fulmar CI RG22 .... 90 C4
Furley CI SO23 .... 198 A4
Further Vell-Mead GU13 .... 74 C2
Furze CI GU12 .... 77 F4
Furze Hill Rd
  Headley GU35 .... 166 A2
  South Tidworth SP9 .... 78 C3
Furze Rd RG7 .... 9 E1
Furze Vale Rd GU35 .... 166 A2
Furzedown Cotts SO20 ... 194 A4
Furzedown Ho SO20 .... 194 A3
Furzedown La SP11 .... 103 F3
Furzedown Rd SO20 .... 194 A4
Furzen La RG25 .... 115 D4
Fuzzy Dro RG22 .... 90 C4

Fyfield CI GU17 .... 35 D3
Fyfield La Appleshaw SP11 . 81 D2
Fyfield SP11 .... 81 D2
Fyfield Rd Fyfield SP11 ...... 81 D1
  Thruxton SP11 .... 81 D1
Fylingdales CI RG21 .... 68 A2

Gable End **3** GU14 .... 55 F2
Gables CI GU14 .... 55 F2
Gables Rd GU13 .... 74 C2
Gables The Grayshott GU26 167 D2
  Whitchurch RG28 .... 86 C3
Gabriel Dr GU16 .... 36 C2
Gabriels The RG14 .... 5 D3
Gaffney CI GU11 .... 77 D4
Gage CI RG21 .... 69 F4
Gainsborough CI
  Camberley GU15 .... 36 B4
  Farnborough GU14 .... 56 A1
Gainsborough Ct
  Andover SP10 .... 82 C1
  3 Fleet GU51 .... 54 A1
Gainsborough Rd
  RG21, RG23 .... 69 E1
Galahad CI SP10 .... 106 A4
Gales Ct SP10 .... 82 B1
Galileo Pk SP10 .... 82 B3
Gallaghers Mead SP10 .... 105 E4
Galley La RG19 .... 24 B4
Gallop The GU46 .... 34 A4
Galloway CI
  Basingstoke RG24 .... 68 A2
  Fleet GU13 .... 54 B2
Galloway Ctr The RG14 ...... 2 B1
Gallwey Rd GU11 .... 77 D2
Gally Hill Rd GU13 .... 74 C2
Galway Rd GU46 .... 34 A2
Gander Dr RG22 .... 68 B4
Ganders CI GU34 .... 184 C4
Gangbridge La SP11 .... 61 F2
Gannet CI RG23 .... 90 C4
Gar St SO22 .... 197 F4
Garbett Rd SO23 .... 198 B4
Garbetts Way GU12 .... 100 B3
Garden CI
  10 Andover SP11 .... 106 A4
  Ellisfield RG25 .... 114 A1
  Farnborough GU14 .... 55 E2
  Hook RG27 .... 50 C1
  Kingsclere RG20 .... 24 B1
Garden Close La RG14 .... 5 D2
Garden La **18** SO23 .... 198 A4
Gardener's Hill Rd GU10 .. 121 F2
Gardeners Gn SP9 .... 101 E4
Gardens The GU10 .... 100 B4
Garfield Rd GU15 .... 36 A3
Garford Cres RG14 .... 5 D4
Garnet Field GU17, GU46 ... 33 F3
Garnet Rd GU35 .... 164 C1
Garnier Rd SO23 .... 198 A3
Garrett CI RG20 .... 24 B1
Garrett Rd RG40 .... 16 B4
Garrick Way GU16 .... 56 B4
Garson Mede SO20 .... 129 D2
Garth CI Bordon GU35 ...... 164 B2
  Farnham GU10 .... 121 F4
Garth Rd RG7 .... 11 F3
Garth The Alton GU34 ...... 140 A2
  Ash GU12 .... 77 E1
  Farnborough GU14 .... 55 D2
Gascoigne La SO24 .... 181 E3
Gaskell CI GU34 .... 140 B3
Gason Hill Rd SP9 .... 78 C4
Gaston La
  South Warnborough RG29 . 95 D3
  Upper Farringdon GU34 .. 161 F2
Gaston's Wood Ind Est
  RG21 .... 69 E4
Gatekeeper CI **10** SO23 .. 198 B4
Gates The GU13 .... 54 B2
Gauvain CI GU34 .... 140 A1
Gawaine CI SP10 .... 83 D2
Gaywood Dr RG14 .... 2 A2
Geale's Almshouses **11**
  GU34 .... 139 F2
Geale's Cres GU34 .... 140 A3
Geale's Ct GU34 .... 140 A3
Geffery's Fields RG24 .... 69 E3
General Johnson Ct **6**
  SO22 .... 197 E3
Genoa Ct SP10 .... 83 D2
Gentles La
  Bramshott GU30 .... 165 F2
  Headley GU35 .... 165 F2
George Eyston Dr SO22 ... 197 E3
George Gdns GU11 .... 100 A4
George Rd Fleet GU13 .... 54 A1
  North Tidworth SP9 .... 78 C4
George St Basingstoke RG22 68 C3
  Kingsclere RG20 .... 24 B1
George Yd SP10 .... 106 A4

George Yd The SO24 .... 179 E3
Georgia CI SP10 .... 105 F3
Georgia La Amport SP11 ... 103 F1
  Grateley SO20 .... 125 D4
Georgian CI GU15 .... 36 B4
Georgina **6** GU13 .... 54 A1
Georgina Gdns RG26 .... 27 D4
Gerald Sq GU34 .... 140 A3
Gershwin Ct RG22 .... 91 E4
Gershwin Rd RG22 .... 91 E4
Gibbet La GU15 .... 36 C4
Gibbons CI GU17 .... 35 D4
Gibbs CI RG40 .... 16 B3
Gibbs Way GU46 .... 33 F2
Gid La GU34 .... 119 D2
Giffard Dr GU14 .... 55 E3
Giffards Meadow GU9 .... 99 E1
Gilbard Ct RG24 .... 49 D2
Gilbert CI RG24 .... 48 B1
Gilbert Rd GU15 .... 36 A1
Gilbert White Way GU34 .. 139 F3
Gilbert's Gn SP4 .... 101 F4
Gilberts Mead CI SP10 .... 105 E2
Giles CI RG14 .... 5 B1
Giles CI RG26 .... 27 D4
Giles Hill SO23 .... 198 A4
Giles Rd RG26 .... 27 D4
Gillham's La GU27 .... 188 C3
Gillian Ave GU12 .... 100 A4
Gillian CI GU11 .... 100 A4
Gillies Dr RG22 .... 68 B4
Gillingham CI SO23 .... 176 B4
Gilmour Gdns GU34 .... 140 A3
Gilroy CI RG14 .... 5 D2
Gisborne CI SP9 .... 79 D3
Glade CI RG24 .... 48 C1
Glade The Binsted GU10 ... 120 C1
  Farnham GU9 .... 99 D4
  Newbury RG14 .... 5 E4
Gladiator Way GU11 .... 76 C4
Gladstone Terr SP11 .... 108 A3
Glamis CI Camberley GU14 . 56 B4
  Oakley RG23 .... 67 D1
Glaston Hill Rd GU46 .... 33 D4
Glastonbury CI RG21 .... 69 D4
Glayshers Hill GU35 .... 165 F3
Glebe CI Bentworth GU34 . 138 A3
  Dummer RG22 .... 90 B1
  Tadley RG26 .... 27 D4
Glebe Ct GU13 .... 53 F1
Glebe Fields GU34 .... 138 A3
Glebe La Basingstoke RG24 . 68 A2
  Hartley Wintney RG27 ...... 52 B3
Glebe Meadow
  East Dean SP5 .... 191 D1
  Overton RG25 .... 88 A4
Glebe Rd Crondall GU10 .... 97 E3
  Farnborough GU14 .... 55 E3
  Headley GU35 .... 165 E3
Glebe The GU17 .... 35 D3
Glebefields RG14 .... 1 C3
Glebeland Rd GU17 .... 35 D4
Glebelands SP10 .... 106 A1
Glen CI Andover SP10 ...... 105 F4
  Beacon Hill GU26 .... 167 D3
Glen Court Flats GU26 .... 167 D3
Glen Rd Beacon Hill GU26 167 D3
  Fleet GU13 .... 167 D2
  Grayshott GU26 .... 167 D2
Glen The RG26 .... 10 B1
Glena Ave GU46 .... 33 F2
Glenapp Grange RG7 .... 11 E3
Glenavon Gdns GU46 .... 34 A2
Glencoe CI GU16 .... 56 C4
Glendale Ave RG14 .... 5 D3
Glendale Pk GU13 .... 53 E1
Glendale Rd RG26 .... 9 F1
Gleneagles Dr GU14 .... 55 D2
Glenhurst CI GU47 .... 35 D2
Glenlea GU20 .... 167 E1
Glenlea Hollow GU27 ...... 189 E4
Glenmount Rd GU16 .... 56 C1
Glenville Gdns GU26 .... 167 E2
Globe Farm La GU46 .... 34 C3
Glorney Mead GU9 .... 99 F3
Gloucester CI
  Camberley GU16 .... 56 B3
  Four Marks GU34 .... 160 A1
Gloucester Dr RG22 .... 91 D4
Gloucester Rd
  Aldershot GU12 .... 100 A4
  Newbury RG14 .... 1 B1
Glovers Field GU27 .... 189 E3
Glovers Rd GU27 .... 189 E3
Glynswood Camberley GU15 36 B2
  Farnham GU10 .... 121 F2
Goat La RG21 .... 69 E3
Goatacre Rd GU34 .... 159 E2
Goch Way SP10 .... 82 C1
Godalming Rd GU8 .... 189 D4
Goddard Sq SP10 .... 83 E1
Goddards CI RG24 .... 49 E4
Goddards Firs RG22 .... 90 B4

Goddards La
  Camberley GU17 .... 35 F2
  Sherfield on Loddon RG24 . 49 E4
Goddards Mead SP11 ...... 105 F4
Godden Cres GU14 .... 55 E2
Godson Ho **14** SO23 ...... 198 A4
Godwin CI SO22 .... 175 E1
Gold La GU11 .... 77 E2
Goldcrest CI **1** GU46 .... 33 F3
Golden Fields GU30 .... 188 A2
Golden Lion Rdbt RG21 .... 69 D1
Goldenfields CI GU30 ...... 188 A2
Goldfinch CI GU10, GU9 ... 99 F4
Goldfinch La RG20 .... 6 B2
Goldfinch Way SO21 .... 153 F3
Goldhill GU10, GU9 .... 122 A3
Goldney Rd GU15 .... 36 C2
Goldwell Dr RG14 .... 1 B2
Golf Dr GU15 .... 36 B2
Golf La GU35 .... 164 A1
Golf Links Ave GU26 .... 166 C3
Gondreville Gdns GU13 ..... 74 C2
Gong Hill Dr GU10 .... 122 A2
Goodboy's La RG7 .... 12 C4
Goodens The SO24 .... 201 E3
Goodman CI RG21 .... 68 C2
Goodwin Wlk RG14 .... 5 D3
Goodwood CI Alton GU34 .139 F1
  Camberley GU15 .... 36 A4
Goodwood PI GU10 .... 56 B2
Goodwood Way RG14 .... 2 A1
Goodwyns CI SP9 .... 101 E4
Goodwyns Gn GU34 .... 140 A3
Goodyers GU34 .... 140 A2
Goose Gn RG27 .... 50 C1
Goose La RG27 .... 51 D1
Gooserye Ct GU30 .... 187 F2
Gordon Ave
  Camberley GU15 .... 36 A2
  Fleet GU13 .... 75 D3
  Winchester SO23 .... 198 B3
Gordon CI RG24 .... 69 E4
Gordon Cres GU15 .... 36 A2
Gordon Ct RG14 .... 5 C3
Gordon Rd Aldershot GU11 . 76 C1
  Camberley GU15 .... 36 A2
  Farnborough GU11 .... 77 D4
  Newbury RG14 .... 5 B4
  Thatcham RG18 .... 2 C3
  Winchester SO23 .... 198 A4
Gordon Wlk GU17, GU46 ... 34 B3
Gore End Rd RG20 .... 3 F2
Goring Field SO22 .... 175 E1
Gorrings The SO20 .... 172 A1
Gorse CI GU9 .... 121 F3
Gorse Cotts
  Frensham GU10 .... 122 A1
  Haslemere GU27 .... 189 D4
Gorse La GU10 .... 121 F3
Gorse Rd GU15 .... 36 B1
Gorse Ride N RG40 .... 16 B4
Gorse Ride S RG40 .... 16 B3
Gorse Ride Schs RG40 ...... 16 B4
Gorsedown CI GU35 .... 164 A1
Gorselands Farnham GU9 ... 99 F4
  Newbury RG14 .... 5 D2
  Tadley RG26 .... 26 C4
  Yateley GU46 .... 34 A2
Gorselands CI Ash GU12 .... 77 F3
  Headley GU35 .... 166 A2
Gorseway GU13 .... 75 D2
Gort CI GU12 .... 77 E4
Goscombs La SO24 .... 180 C4
Goslings Croft GU34 .... 184 C4
Gothic Ct GU17 .... 35 D4
Gough Rd GU13 .... 53 F1
Gough's Meadow GU47 ..... 34 C4
Govenor's Rd GU15 .... 35 E3
Government House Rd
  GU11 .... 77 D4
Government Rd
  Aldershot GU11 .... 77 E2
  Farnborough GU11 .... 77 E2
Gower CI RG21 .... 69 D4
Gower Cres RG27 .... 51 D1
Gower Pk GU47 .... 34 C4
Grace Bennett CI GU14 ..... 55 F4
Grace Reynolds Wlk GU15 . 36 A2
Grace Sq SP10 .... 83 E1
Gracemere Cres RG25 .... 90 C4
Gracious Rd GU34 .... 184 B4
Gradwell La SO24 .... 182 A4
Grafton CI GU35 .... 164 C3
Grafton PI SP11 .... 81 F2
Grafton Rd SO23 .... 197 F3
Grafton Way RG24 .... 68 B2
Grainger CI RG23 .... 190 C4
Grammarsham La RG25 ..... 92 A1
Grampian Way RG21 .... 90 C4

Granada Pl SP10 .... 83 E1
Granary The RG14 .... 1 B2
Grand Ave GU15 .... 36 A3
Grand Par RG27 .... 51 D1
Grand Trunk Rd SP9 .... 78 B2
Grange Cl Fyfield SP11 .... 80 C1
 New Alresford SO24 .... 179 E3
 Winchester SO23 .... 197 F2
Grange Ct RG14 .... 1 C1
Grange Farm GU34 .... 184 B4
Grange Farm Rd GU11 .... 77 F2
Grange Jun Sch GU14 .... 55 F4
Grange La RG27 .... 52 A3
Grange Rd Ash GU11 .... 77 F1
 Camberley GU16 .... 36 B3
 Farnborough GU14 .... 55 F4
 Fleet GU13 .... 74 C3
 New Alresford SO24 .... 179 E3
 Tilford GU10 .... 144 C4
 Tongham GU12 .... 100 B3
 Winchester SO23 .... 197 F2
Grange Special Sch The
 GU11 .... 99 F4
Grange The
 Frensham GU10 .... 144 A4
 Newbury RG14 .... 5 D3
 Northington SO21 .... 156 C3
Grantley Dr GU13 .... 74 C4
Grantly Cl GU11 .... 121 E3
Granville Pl SO23 .... 198 A3
Grasmere Cl GU35 .... 164 B3
Grasmere Rd
 Farnborough GU14 .... 55 E2
 Farnham GU10 .... 98 C3
Graspan Rd SP11 .... 57 D1
Grateley Dro Amport SP11 . 103 E2
 Grateley SP11 .... 103 D1
Grateley House Sch SO20 . 125 D4
Grateley Prim Sch SP11 ... 125 D4
Grateley Rd SP4 .... 101 E1
Grateley Sta SP11 .... 124 C4
Grattons Cl SO21 .... 131 E3
Gravel Cl SO24 .... 135 E2
Gravel Hill Rd GU10 .... 120 C2
Gravel La
 Barton Stacey SO21 .... 130 B4
 Ropley SO24 .... 159 F1
Gravel Rd
 Farnborough GU11 .... 77 D4
 Farnham GU9 .... 98 C4
 Fleet GU13 .... 75 D3
Gravellhill Cotts SO20 ...... 129 E3
Gravelly Cl Ball Hill RG26 ... 3 F2
 Tadley RG26 .... 27 D3
Graveney Sq SP10 .... 83 D1
Grayshot Dr GU15 .... 35 D3
Grayshott CE Prim Sch
 GU26 .... 166 C2
Grayshott Cl SO22 .... 175 E2
Grayshott Laurels GU35 .... 165 D3
Grayshott Rd GU35 .... 166 A3
Grayswood Dr GU16 .... 56 C1
Great Austins Ho GU9 ...... 122 A4
Great Austins Rd GU9 ...... 122 B4
Great Binfields Rd
 Chineham RG24 .... 49 D1
 Old Basing RG24 .... 70 A4
Great Field Rd SO22 .... 175 E2
Great La RG28 .... 86 B2
Great Minster St SO23 ...... 198 A4
Great Oaks Chase RG24 ... 48 C1
Great Sheldons Coppice
 RG27 .... 51 D1
Greatfield Cl GU14 .... 55 F4
Greatfield Rd GU14 .... 55 F4
Greatham Prim Sch GU33 . 185 F1
Grebe Cl Alton GU34 .... 139 F3
 Basingstoke RG22 .... 90 C4
Green Acre GU11 .... 76 B1
Green Acres
 Barton Stacey SO21 .... 130 B3
 Farnham GU11 .... 100 A1
Green Cl
 Kings Worthy SO23 .... 176 A3
 Old Alresford SO24 .... 157 E1
 South Wonston SO21 ...... 153 F2
Green Croft Special Sch
 GU16 .... 56 A3
Green Cross La GU10 ...... 144 B1
Green Dro SP11 .... 60 A1
Green End GU46 .... 34 A4
Green Glades GU13 .... 74 C3
Green Jacket Cl SO22 ...... 197 F3
Green La
 Bishop's Sutton SO24 ...... 180 B3
 Blackwater GU17 .... 34 C2
 Blackwater GU47 .... 35 E2
 Churt GU10 .... 144 B2
 Ellisfield RG25 .... 115 D4
 Farnham GU9 .... 99 E3

Green La continued
 Farnham, Wrecclesham
 GU10 .... 121 F4
 Frensham GU35 .... 143 E3
 Froxfield GU32 .... 205 F3
 Hartley Wintney RG27 ...... 52 B3
 Monxton SP11 .... 104 B3
 Newbury RG14 .... 1 B1
 Pamber End RG26 .... 27 E2
 Rotherwick RG27 .... 50 C3
 Sandhurst GU17 .... 35 D4
 Stoke SP11 .... 61 D3
 West End Green RG26 ...... 29 E4
Green Lane Cl GU15 .... 36 A4
Green Lane Cotts GU10 .... 144 C1
Green Leys GU33 .... 74 C2
Green Meadows La SP10 . 106 A1
Green Park Cl SO23 .... 176 A1
Green Springs GU10 .... 97 E4
Green St GU34 .... 163 F4
Green Stile GU34 .... 159 F4
Green The
 Barton Stacey SO21 .... 130 C4
 Camberley GU14 .... 56 B3
 Charlton SP10 .... 82 C1
 Farnham GU10, GU9 .... 99 F3
 Farnham, Upper Hale GU9 .. 99 D3
 Kimpton SP11 .... 80 B1
 Liss GU33 .... 207 F3
 Overton RG25 .... 88 A4
 Seale GU10 .... 100 B1
 Tadley RG26 .... 27 D3
 Whitchurch RG28 .... 86 B3
Green Way GU12 .... 77 E2
Green's School La GU14 ... 55 F2
Greenacre Broughton SO20 170 A3
 Kingsclere RG20 .... 24 B1
Greenacres Bordon GU33 ... 164 C2
 Woolton Hill RG20 .... 21 E4
Greenacres Special Sch
 SO22 .... 175 F1
Greenways Ho RG14 .... 1 B1
Greenways The RG23 ...... 67 E1
Greenbank Way GU15 ...... 36 A1
Greenbirch Cl RG22 .... 90 C4
Greencroft 2 GU14 .... 55 F2
Greenfield Cl GU30 .... 188 A3
Greenfield Rd GU9 .... 121 F4
Greenfields GU33 .... 208 A2
Greenfields Ave GU34 ...... 139 F2
Greenfields Jun Sch RG27 .. 52 B3
Greenham Ct RG19 .... 6 A4
Greenham Court Prim Sch
 RG14 .... 5 F4
Greenham Mill RG14 .... 1 C2
Greenham Rd RG14 .... 5 F4
Greenhanger GU46 .... 166 C4
Greenham GU46 .... 33 F3
Greenhill Cl
 Farnham GU10, GU9 .... 121 F4
 Winchester SO22 .... 197 F4
Greenhill Rd Farnham GU9 122 A4
 Winchester SO22 .... 197 F4
Greenhill Terr SO22 .... 197 F4
Greenhill Way GU9 .... 121 F4
Greenhills GU9 .... 122 B4
Greenlands Rd
 Camberley GU15 .... 35 F1
 Kingsclere RG20 .... 24 B1
 Newbury RG14 .... 5 F4
Greenleas GU15 .... 36 B1
Greenleas Cl GU47 .... 34 A4
Greensey SP11 .... 81 D3
Greenway Basingstoke RG22 68 B2
 Sherfield on Loddon RG2 e .. 49 E4
Greenways Fleet GU13 ...... 74 C3
 Woolton Hill RG14 .... 4 B1
Greenwich Way SP10 .... 83 D1
Greenwood Dr RG24 .... 48 C2
Greenwoods RG28 .... 86 B3
Gregan Ct 16 GU11 .... 77 D4
Gregory Cl RG21 .... 69 E4
Gregory Ho RG27 .... 51 D1
Greig Cl RG22 .... 68 C1
Grenadier Rd GU12 .... 77 F2
Grenadiers Way GU14 ...... 55 D2
Grensell Cl GU46 .... 33 E4
Grenville Cl GU30 .... 188 A2
Grenville Dr GU13 .... 74 C4
Grenville Gdns GU16 .... 56 B3
Gresham Ct GU14 .... 77 D4
Gresham Ind Est GU12 ...... 77 E1
Gresham Way GU16 .... 56 B3
Gresley Rd RG21 .... 69 E3
Grey House Sch The RG27 .. 52 B3
Greyberry Copse Rd RG19 .. 6 A4
Greyfriars 18 SO23 .... 198 A4
Greyhound Cl GU12 .... 77 E1
Greyhound La RG25 .... 88 A4
Greys Ct 6 GU11 .... 76 B1

Greys Farm Cl SO24 .... 201 E2
Greystead Pk GU9 .... 121 E3
Greywell Cl RG26 .... 26 C4
Greywell St RG29 .... 71 F2
Grieve Cl GU10 .... 100 B4
Griffin Way N RG27 .... 51 D1
Griffin Way S RG27 .... 51 E1
Griffon Cl GU14 .... 55 D2
Groombridge Pl RG14 .... 1 B3
Grosvenor Cl RG22 .... 91 D3
Grosvenor Ct GU47 .... 35 D2
Grosvenor Dr SO23 .... 176 A1
Grosvenor Lawn RG14 .... 1 B1
Grosvenor Rd
 Aldershot GU11 .... 76 C1
 Medstead GU34 .... 159 F1
Grove Cl RG21 .... 69 E2
Grove Cross Rd GU15 .... 36 A1
Grove Cty Prim Sch The
 GU15 .... 36 B1
Grove End Way RG14 .... 121 F4
Grove Park Ind Est GU34 . 140 A2
Grove Pk GU34 .... 140 A2
Grove Rd Alton GU34 .... 139 F1
 Ash GU12 .... 77 F2
 Basingstoke RG21 .... 69 E1
 Beacon Hill GU26 .... 167 D3
 Camberley GU16 .... 36 B3
 Fleet GU13 .... 75 D3
 Newbury RG14 .... 1 B3
Grove Sch The GU26 .... 167 D1
Grove The Aldershot GU11 ... 76 C1
 Camberley GU16 .... 36 A1
 Farnborough GU16, GU17 ... 56 A1
 Hartley Wintney RG27 ...... 52 B3
 Liphook GU30 .... 187 F2
 Penton Grafton SP11 .... 81 F2
Grovebell Ind Est GU10 ... 121 E4
Grovefields Ave GU16 .... 36 A1
Groveland Rd RG14 .... 1 B3
Grovelands GU9 .... 122 B4
Grovelands Rd SO22 .... 175 D1
Groves Cl SO21 .... 153 E2
Guernsey Cl RG24 .... 48 B1
Guernsey Dr GU14 .... 54 A2
Guildford Rd
 Aldershot GU10 .... 100 A4
 Camberley GU16 .... 56 C3
 Farnham GU10, GU9 .... 99 F2
 Fleet GU13 .... 54 B1
 Mytchett GU16 .... 56 C3
Guildford Rd E GU14 .... 56 A1
Guildford Rd Ind Est
 GU10, GU9 .... 99 E2
Guildford Rd Trad Est
 GU10, GU9 .... 99 D2
Guildford Rd W GU16 .... 56 A1
Guillemont Fields GU14 ... 55 D3
Guillemont Jun Sch GU14 ... 55 D4
Guinea Ct RG24 .... 49 D2
Gun Hill GU11 .... 76 C2
Gunners La SO51 .... 135 D3
Gunns Farm GU30 .... 188 A1
Gunville Hill SP5 .... 168 A3
Gunville Rd SP5 .... 168 A3
Gurdons GU34 .... 139 E1
Gurkha Mus The SO22 ...... 197 F4
Gurkha Sq GU13 .... 74 C4
Gurney Cl RG21 .... 69 E4
Gurney Ct RG29 .... 72 C1
Guttridge La RG26 .... 26 C4
Gwyn Cl RG14 .... 5 E4

H J Cones Cres GU12 .... 77 D2
Hacks La SO21 .... 152 A2
Hackups La SO51 .... 193 E1
Hackwood Cl SP10 .... 105 E4
Hackwood Cotts RG21 ...... 69 E1
Hackwood La RG25 .... 92 B3
Hackwood Rd RG21 .... 69 E1
Hackwood Road Rdbt RG21 69 D2
Hadleigh Gdns GU16 .... 56 B3
Hadleigh Pl 3 RG21 .... 69 D3
Hadleys GU9 .... 121 E2
Hadrian Rd SP10 .... 83 D2
Hadrians Ct RG24 .... 99 E2
Hadrians Way RG23 .... 68 B4
Hagley Rd GU13 .... 53 F1
Haig La GU13 .... 75 D3
Haig Rd Aldershot GU12 ...... 77 D1
 Andover SP10 .... 105 F4
 New Alresford SO24 .... 179 E3
 Sandhurst GU17 .... 35 E3
Hailstone Rd RG21 .... 69 D4
Haining Gdns GU16 .... 56 C2
Halcyon Dr SP11 .... 82 B4
Hale Day Ctr GU9 .... 99 D2
Hale Farm Flats GU9 .... 99 D3
Hale House Cl GU10 .... 144 B1
Hale House La GU10 .... 144 C1
Hale Pl GU9 .... 99 E3
Hale Prim Sch GU9 .... 98 C4

Hale Rd GU9 .... 99 E2
Hale Reeds GU9 .... 99 E3
Hale Way GU14 .... 56 A4
Half Way Cotts GU9 .... 98 A2
Halifax Cl Andover SP10 ... 82 C1
 Farnborough GU14 .... 55 E2
Halimote Rd GU11 .... 76 C1
Halimote Rd GU11 .... 76 C1
Hall Cl GU15 .... 36 B3
Hall Farm Cres GU46 .... 34 A3
Hall La Selborne GU34 ...... 162 A1
 Upper Farringdon GU34 .. 162 A1
 Yateley GU17 .... 34 A3
Hall Rd GU34 .... 140 A3
Hall Way The SO22 .... 175 D3
Halliday Cl RG21 .... 69 D1
Hallmark Cl GU15 .... 35 E4
Halpin Ho RG7 .... 14 A2
Halstead Ho RG26 .... 9 E1
Halton Rd SP9 .... 79 E4
Ham La RG26 .... 25 F3
Hamble Ave GU17 .... 35 D3
Hamble Cl RG23 .... 67 D1
Hamble Ct
40 Andover SP10 .... 83 E1
17 Basingstoke RG21 .... 69 E3
Hamble Dr RG26 .... 27 D4
Hambledon Cl SO22 .... 175 E2
Hambleton Cl RG16 .... 36 C2
Hambridge La RG14 .... 2 B1
Hambridge Rd RG14 .... 2 A1
Hamburg Cl SP10 .... 82 C2
Hamelyn Cl 6 RG21 .... 69 D2
Hamelyn Rd RG21 .... 69 D2
Hamesmoor Rd GU16 .... 56 B2
Hamesmoor Way GU16 ...... 56 B2
Hamilton Cl
 Basingstoke RG22 .... 68 C4
 Bordon GU35 .... 164 C2
Hamilton Ct
 Farnborough GU47 .... 35 E1
 Newbury RG14 .... 5 F4
Hamilton Rd Bordon GU13 186 B1
 Fleet GU13 .... 75 D3
Hamlash Cotts GU10 .... 122 A1
Hamlash La GU10 .... 122 A1
Hammer Hill GU27 .... 189 D2
Hammer La
 Bramshott GU27 .... 188 C3
 Grayshott GU26 .... 166 B3
 Headley GU26 .... 166 B3
 Linchmere GU27 .... 189 D3
Hammer Vale GU27 .... 189 D4
Hammersly Rd GU11 .... 76 C4
Hammerwood Copse GU27 189 D3
Hammett Heath RG7 .... 11 F3
Hammond Rd 10 RG21 ...... 69 D2
Hammond Sq SP10 .... 83 D1
Hampdens The RG14 .... 5 D3
Hampshire Cl RG22 .... 68 A2
Hampshire Cross SP9 .... 78 C3
Hampshire Golf Club The
 SP10 .... 106 B1
Hampshire Ho GU30 .... 187 F4
Hampshire Int Bsns Pk
 RG24 .... 48 C2
Hampshire Rd
 Bordon GU35 .... 164 B2
 Camberley GU16 .... 36 B4
Hampstead Ho 20 RG21 ...... 69 D3
Hampton Cl RG13 .... 75 D2
Hampton Ct RG22 .... 68 B3
Hampton La SO22 .... 175 E1
Hampton Rd Farnham GU9 .. 98 C3
 Newbury RG14 .... 1 B1
Hanbury Way GU15 .... 36 A2
Handcroft Cl GU10 .... 97 E4
Handel Cl RG21 .... 68 C1
Handford La GU46 .... 34 A3
Hanger Rd RG26 .... 9 E1
Hanger The GU35 .... 165 E4
Hangerfield Cl GU46 .... 34 A1
Hanmore Rd RG24 .... 48 C2
Hannam's Farm GU11 .... 77 E3
Hanover Cl Andover SP10 ... 105 E3
 Camberley GU16 .... 36 B4
 Yateley GU17, GU46 .... 34 A4
Hanover Gdns
 Basingstoke RG21 .... 69 D1
 Farnborough GU14 .... 55 E2
Hanover Ho 14 SP10 .... 106 A4
Hanover Mead RG14 .... 5 D3
Hanson Cl GU15 .... 36 C4
Hanson Rd SP10 .... 82 C1
Harbour Rd GU14 .... 55 F4
Harcourt Rd GU47 .... 35 F3
Harding's La RG22 .... 54 A4
Hardy Ave GU46 .... 34 A2
Hardy La RG21 .... 69 D2

Hardyfair Cl SP11 .... 81 E1
Hardys Field RG20 .... 24 B2
Hare's La RG27 .... 52 C4
Harebell Cl RG27 .... 52 B4
Harebell Gdns RG27 .... 52 B4
Harestock Cl SO22 .... 175 E3
Harestock Cnr SO22 .... 175 E2
Harestock Prim Sch SO22 . 175 E2
Harestock Rd SO22 .... 175 E3
Harewood Forest Ind Est
 SP10 .... 107 F2
Harfield Cl RG27 .... 51 D1
Harlech Cl RG22 .... 68 B3
Harlech Rd GU11 .... 35 D2
Harlington Way GU11 .... 53 F1
Harmsworth Rd RG26 .... 26 C4
Harold Gdns GU34 .... 140 A3
Harold Jackson Terr RG21 .. 69 E2
Harpdon Par GU46 .... 34 A4
Harpton Cl GU46 .... 34 A4
Harriet Costello Sec Sch
 RG21 .... 69 E2
Harrington Cl RG14 .... 2 B3
Harris Cl GU30 .... 187 F1
Harris Hill RG22 .... 91 D4
Harrow Down SO22 .... 197 E2
Harrow La SP10 .... 82 A1
Harrow Way Andover SP10 .. 82 B1
 Oakley RG23 .... 66 C2
Penton Grafton SP11 .... 82 A1
Harrow Way Com Sch SP10 82 B1
Harrow Way The RG22 .... 68 C1
Harroway RG28 .... 85 E4
Hart Cl GU14 .... 55 E4
Hart Ctr 12 GU13 .... 53 F1
Hart L Ctr GU13 .... 74 B4
Hart The GU9 .... 98 C1
Hartfield Ho 6 GU13 .... 53 F1
Hartford Bridge Flats GU46 33 E1
Hartford Ct RG27 .... 52 B3
Hartford Rd RG27 .... 52 B4
Hartford Rise GU15 .... 36 A3
Hartford Terr RG27 .... 52 B3
Hartland Pl GU14 .... 55 F3
Hartley Cl GU35 .... 34 C3
Hartley Gdns RG26 .... 26 C4
Hartley La RG26 .... 30 A1
Hartley Meadow RG28 .... 86 A3
Hartley Mews RG27 .... 52 B4
Hartley Rd GU46 .... 33 F3
Harts Cotts RG20 .... 22 B3
Harts La RG20 .... 22 B3
Harts Leap Cl GU47 .... 34 C4
Harts Leap Rd GU46 .... 34 C4
Harts Yd GU9 .... 98 C1
Hartshill Rd RG26 .... 9 E1
Hartsleaf Cl GU13 .... 74 C4
Hartswood RG24 .... 48 C1
Harvest Cl
 Winchester SO22 .... 197 E2
 Yateley GU46 .... 33 F2
Harvest Cres GU13 .... 54 A3
Harvest Gn RG14 .... 1 B1
Harvest Way RG21 .... 69 F4
Harvey Rd GU14 .... 55 D3
Harvey Villas GU30 .... 187 D4
Harveys Field RG25 .... 88 A4
Harwood Pl SO23 .... 176 B4
Harwood Rise RG14 .... 4 B1
Hasle Dr GU27 .... 189 F3
Haslemere Rd
 Linchmere GU27 .... 189 F1
 Liphook GU30 .... 188 A2
Haslemere Sta GU27 .... 189 F3
Hassocks Workshops The
 RG21 .... 69 F4
Hastards La GU34 .... 184 C4
Hasted Dr SO24 .... 179 E2
Hastings Cl
 Basingstoke RG22 .... 68 A3
 Camberley GU15 .... 56 C4
Hatch Hill GU27 .... 189 F1
Hatch La Linchmere GU27 .. 189 F1
 Liss GU33 .... 208 B2
 Old Basing RG24 .... 70 B3
Hatchbury La SP11 .... 38 B3
Hatches The
 Camberley GU16 .... 56 B3
 Farnham GU10 .... 121 E4
Hatchet La GU11 .... 59 D1
Hatchetts Dr GU27 .... 189 D4
Hatchwarren Gdns RG22 .... 91 E4
Hatchwarren Gdns RG22 .... 91 F4
Hatchwarren La RG22 .... 91 E3
Hatchwarren Ret Pk RG22 .. 91 D3
Hatchwarren Schs RG22 ..... 91 F4
Hatfield Ct GU17 .... 35 F3
Hatfield Gdns GU16 .... 56 B2

Hatherden SP11 .... 59 E1
Hatherden CE Prim Sch
  SP11 .... 59 E1
Hatherden Cl [8] SP10 .... 106 A4
Hatherley Rd SO22 .... 175 F1
Hatherwood GU7 .... 34 B3
Hatt La SO51 .... 192 C1
Hattingley Rd GU34 .... 159 E4
Haughurst Hill RG26 .... 9 D1
Havelock Ho GU12 .... 77 D4
Haven Way GU9 .... 99 D2
Haweswater Cl GU35 ...... 164 B3
Haweswater Ct GU11 ...... 77 E3
Hawk Cl RG22 .... 90 C4
Hawk Conservancy The
  SP11 .... 104 A4
Hawke Cl SP10 .... 83 E1
Hawkes Cl RG27 .... 52 B4
Hawkfield La RG21 .... 69 D2
Hawkins Gr GU13 .... 74 B3
Hawkins Way GU13 .... 75 E4
Hawkley Dr RG26 .... 27 D4
Hawkley Rd Hawkley GU33 .. 207 E3
  Liss GU33 .... 207 E3
Hawks Mead GU33 .... 207 F3
Hawkshaw Cl GU30 .... 188 A2
Hawkswood Ave GU16 ..... 36 B1
Hawkwell GU13 .... 75 D2
Hawley Cl GU14 .... 55 E4
Hawley Garden Cotts GU15 ... 35 D3
Hawley Gn GU17 .... 35 E2
Hawley Green Farm GU17 ... 35 E2
Hawley La GU14 .... 55 F4
Hawley Lodge GU17 .... 35 E1
Hawley Place Sch GU17 ... 35 E1
Hawley Prim Sch GU17 .... 35 E1
Hawley Rd Blackwater GU17 ... 35 E2
  Farnborough GU17 ..... 35 E2
  Hawley GU17 .... 35 E2
Hawthorn Cl
  Micheldever SO21 ...... 133 D1
  New Alresford SO24 .... 179 E3
Hawthorn Cres GU17 ...... 35 E2
Hawthorn Hill SO20 .... 126 A2
Hawthorn La SO24 .... 182 C4
Hawthorn Rd
  Camberley GU15 .... 36 B1
  Four Marks SO24 .... 182 B4
  Newbury RG14 .... 1 C2
  North Tidworth SP9 .... 79 D4
Hawthorn Way RG23 ...... 68 B4
Hawthorne Cl
  Aldershot GU10 .... 100 B4
  Grateley SP11 .... 103 E1
Hawthorns GU34 .... 139 F3
Hawthorns Sch RG22 ...... 68 B1
Hawthorns The RG26 ...... 26 B4
Hay Down La SP11 .... 103 F3
Haydn Cl SO23 .... 176 A4
Haydn Rd RG22 .... 91 E4
Haydock Cl GU34 .... 139 F1
Haydown Leas SP11 ...... 38 B3
Hayes Cl SO20 .... 171 F1
Hayley La RG29 .... 95 E2
Haywarden Pl RG27 ...... 52 B4
Haywood Dr GU13 .... 75 D4
Hazel Ave GU14 .... 55 E2
Hazel Cl Andover SP10 ... 105 E3
  Oakley RG23 .... 67 D1
Hazel Coppice RG27 ..... 51 D1
Hazel Gn RG26 .... 9 D1
Hazel Gr Haslemere GU26 ... 167 E1
  Winchester SO22 ...... 197 E3
Hazel Rd Four Marks GU34 ... 160 B2
  Mytchett GU16 .... 56 C1
Hazelbank RG40 .... 16 B3
Hazeldene RG24 .... 48 C1
Hazeldene Gdns SO21 ... 177 F4
Hazeldene Rd GU30 ..... 187 D2
Hazeley Cl RG27 .... 52 B4
Hazeley Lea RG27 .... 31 F2
Hazell Rd GU9 .... 98 B1
Hazelwood Cl RG23 ..... 68 B4
Hazelwood Dr RG23 ..... 68 B4
Hazlebank Cl GU30 ..... 188 A2
Hazlebank Mews GU30 ... 188 A2
Headbourne Worthy Ho
  SO23 .... 176 A3
Headington Ct RG22 .... 91 E4
Headley Fields GU35 .... 165 E2
Headley Hill Rd GU35 ... 165 F3
Headley La GU30 .... 166 E1
Headley Rd Grayshott GU26 166 C2
  Lindford GU35 .... 165 D3
  Liphook GU30 .... 187 D4
Headmore La GU34 ..... 160 C1
Headon Ct GU9 .... 99 D1
Hearmon Cl GU47 .... 34 B3

Hearn Vale GU35 .... 165 F4
Hearsey Gdns GU47 ...... 34 C3
Heath Cl Beacon Hill GU35 167 D4
  Farnham GU9 .... 99 D4
Heath Cnr GU15 .... 36 C2
Heath Cotts
  Beacon Hill GU26 ...... 167 D3
  Frensham GU10 .... 122 A2
Heath Ct RG26 .... 9 E1
Heath End Rd
  Baughurst RG26 .... 9 E1
  Tadley RG26 .... 9 E1
Heath End Sch GU9 ..... 99 E3
Heath Green La GU34 ... 159 D4
Heath Hill GU35 .... 164 A1
Heath La Buttermere SN8 ... 18 B3
  Crondall GU10 .... 97 F3
  Farnham GU9 .... 99 D4
Heath Rd Linchmere GU27 189 D3
  Pamber Heath RG26 .... 10 B1
Heath Ride RG40 .... 16 C3
Heath Rise RG41 .... 36 A3
Heath Vale SP10 .... 106 A4
Heathcote Cl GU12 ..... 77 F2
Heathcote Rd Ash GU12 77 F2
  Bordon GU35 .... 164 C2
  Camberley GU15 ...... 36 A3
Heather Cl Aldershot GU11 ... 76 B1
  Ash GU12 .... 77 F3
  Bordon GU35 .... 164 A1
  Farnham GU9 .... 121 D3
  Wokingham RG40 ..... 16 B4
Heather Cotts GU12 .... 77 F4
Heather Ct
  [22] Aldershot GU11 .... 76 C1
  Hindhead GU26 .... 167 E2
Heather Dr Andover SP10 ... 105 F4
  Fleet GU13 .... 74 C3
  Lindford GU35 .... 164 C3
  Tadley RG26 .... 9 E1
Heather Gdns GU14 .... 55 E2
Heather Gr RG27 .... 52 B4
Heather La RG27 .... 71 E3
Heather Mead GU14 ... 36 B1
Heather Mead Ct GU15 36 B1
Heather Row La
  Mapledurwell RG27 ... 71 F3
  Newnham RG27 .... 71 F3
Heather Way
  Basingstoke RG22 ..... 91 D4
  Hindhead GU26 .... 167 E2
Heatherdale Rd GU15 .. 36 A3
Heatherley Cl GU17 .... 35 F3
Heatherley Rd GU17 ... 35 F3
Heatherly Cl GU15 ..... 35 E3
Heatherside Schs GU13 75 D4
Heathfield RG7 .... 11 F3
Heathfield Cl GU13 .... 74 C4
Heathfield Rd RG22 .... 91 E4
Heathland St GU13 .... 76 C1
Heathlands Baughurst RG26 ... 9 E1
  Highclere RG20 .... 21 F4
Heathlands Ct GU46 ... 34 B2
Heathman St SO20 .... 148 A3
Heathrow Copse RG26 ... 26 A4
Heathside La GU26 .... 167 D3
Heathside Way RG27 ... 52 B4
Heathvale Bridge Rd GU12 .. 77 F3
Heathview RG27 .... 51 E1
Heathway GU16 .... 36 A3
Heathway Cl GU16 .... 36 A3
Heathwood Cl GU46 ... 34 A4
Heathyfields Rd GU9 .. 98 C3
Heddon Wlk GU14 ..... 55 F4
Hedge Croft GU46 .... 33 F3
Hedge End Rd SP10 ... 106 A3
Hedge Way RG14 ...... 2 A2
Hedgehog La GU27 ... 189 F3
Hedgerows The RG24 ... 70 A4
Hedges Cl SP9 .... 101 E4
Heenan Cl GU16 ...... 56 B4
Heights The GU15 .... 36 B3
Hele Cl RG24 .... 69 D1
Helen Ct GU14 .... 55 F4
Helford Ct [30] SP10 ... 83 E1
Helston Cl GU14 ..... 56 C4
Hendon Rd GU35 .... 164 B1
Hendren Sq SP10 ..... 83 E1
Hengest Cl SP10 ..... 82 B2
Henley Cl GU14 ...... 55 E4
Henley Dr GU16 ...... 56 B4
Henley Gdns GU17 ... 34 A3
Henry Beaufort Sec Sch
  SO22 .... 175 F2
Henry Randell's Almshouses
  GU15 .... 35 E2
Henshaw Cres RG14 ... 5 D4
Henwick Cl RG18 ..... 2 C3
Henwick La RG18 ..... 2 C2
Hepplewhite Cl RG26 .. 9 E1
Hepplewhite Dr RG22 .. 91 D4

Hepworth Cl SP10 ...... 83 D1
Hepworth Croft GU15 ... 35 E3
Herald Ct [26] GU11, GU12 ... 76 C1
Herbert Rd GU13 ...... 53 F1
Herbs End GU14 .... 55 D3
Hereford Cl RG29 ...... 72 B1
Hereford La GU9 ...... 98 C4
Hereford Mead GU34 ... 54 A2
Hereford Rd RG23 ..... 68 B3
Herewood Cl RG14 .... 1 B2
Heritage Pk RG22 .... 91 D3
Hermes Cl GU13 ...... 54 B1
Hermitage Cl
  Camberley GU15 ...... 36 B1
  Farnborough GU16 ... 56 A1
Heron Cl Alton GU34 .. 139 F3
  Fleet GU13 .... 75 E3
  Mytchett GU16 .... 56 B2
Heron Park RG24 ..... 48 C1
Heron Rise SP10 ..... 106 A3
Heron Way
  Basingstoke RG22 .... 90 C4
  Thatcham RG19 ...... 2 C2
Heron Wood Rd GU12 . 100 A4
Herondale GU27 ..... 189 E3
Herrett St GU12 ..... 100 A4
Herretts Gdns GU12 .. 77 D1
Herriard Way RG26 ... 27 D4
Herridge Cl RG26 .... 29 D1
Herriot Cl GU46 ..... 34 A2
Hewshott Gr GU30 ... 188 B3
Hewshott La GU30 ... 188 B3
Hexagon The SP10 ... 105 E3
Hibiscus Gr GU35 .... 164 C1
Hickory Dr SO22 .... 175 E2
Hicks La GU46 ...... 34 C3
Hides Cl RG28 ...... 86 B2
High Beeches GU15 .. 36 A1
High Copse GU9 ..... 98 C4
High Crissels GU17 .. 35 D4
High Cross GU32 ... 205 F1
High Cross La GU32 . 205 E1
High Dr RG23 ...... 68 B1
High Park Rd GU9 ... 99 D2
High Pitfold GU26 ... 167 D1
High St
  Aldershot GU11, GU12 ... 76 C1
  Alton GU34 .... 139 F2
  Andover SP10 .... 106 A4
  Bordon GU35 .... 164 B2
  Broughton SO20 ..... 170 A4
  Camberley GU15 ..... 36 A3
  Farnborough GU12 ... 77 D4
  Farnham GU9 .... 121 E2
  Grateley SO20 ...... 125 E3
  Hartley Wintney RG27 52 B3
  Headley GU35 .... 165 E3
  Medstead GU34 ..... 159 F4
  Nether Wallop SO20 . 148 A3
  Odiham RG29 .... 72 C2
  Overton RG25 ...... 88 A4
  Sandhurst GU46 .... 34 B4
  Shipton Bellinger SP9 101 F4
  Stockbridge SO20 ... 149 F2
  Upton Grey SO24, SO23 197 F4
  [33] Winchester
    SO21, SO23 ...... 198 A4
  Winchester SO23 ... 175 F1
High Thicket Rd GU35 143 D3
High Trees Dr SO22 .. 175 F1
High View Cl GU14 ... 55 F1
High View Lodge [2] GU11 ... 76 C1
High View Rd GU14 .. 55 F1
Highams Cl RG20 ... 24 B1
Highbury Cres GU16 . 36 C4
Highbury Rd SP10 ... 105 E2
Highclere Castle RG20 21 F1
Highclere Park Gdns RG20 21 F1
Highclere Rd GU12 ... 100 A4
Highclere St RG20 ... 21 F1
Highcliffe Rd SO23 .. 198 B3
Highdown SO21 ..... 154 A1
Highdowns RG22 ... 91 D3
Higher Mead RG24 .. 69 F4
Highfield Ave
  Aldershot GU10, GU9 99 F4
  Newbury RG14 ...... 1 C1
Highfield Chase RG21 68 C3
Highfield Cl Aldershot GU9 ... 99 F4
  Farnborough GU14 ... 55 E2
  Farnham GU9 .... 121 D3
Highfield Cres GU26 . 167 E2
Highfield Gdns GU33 . 208 A2
Highfield La GU30 ... 188 B2
Highfield Path GU14 . 55 E2
Highfield Rd
  Farnborough GU14 .. 55 E2
  Newbury RG14 ...... 1 B1
Highfield Sch GU30 . 188 B1
Highfield Terr [17] SO22 197 F4
Highgate GU16 ...... 56 A3

Highgate La GU14 ..... 56 A3
Highland Dr Fleet GU13 .. 54 A2
  Oakley RG23 .... 67 D1
Highland Rd Aldershot GU12 77 D1
  Camberley GU16 ..... 36 B4
Highlands Cl GU10 ... 121 F4
Highlands Rd
  Andover SP10 .... 106 B4
  Basingstoke RG23 ... 68 A2
  Farnham GU11 ...... 99 D4
Highmoors RG24 .... 48 C2
Highmount Cl SO23 . 198 B4
Highridge GU34 .... 139 E2
Highrove GU14 ..... 55 F4
Highview Bsns Ctr GU35 . 164 B2
Highwood Cl Newbury RG14 . 1 C3
  Yateley GU46 .... 34 A2
Highwood Ridge RG22 91 D3
Highworth Cotts RG26 9 D1
Hilary Ho [9] RG14 .. 1 C1
Hilden Way SO22 ... 175 D3
Hilder Gdns GU16 ... 56 A2
Hill Brow Rd
  Hill Brow GU33 ..... 208 A1
  Liss GU33 .... 208 A1
Hill Cl RG14 .... 1 A1
Hill Corner Farm Est GU14 . 55 D4
Hill Crest Dr GU9 ... 121 E3
Hill Croft GU27 .... 189 F3
Hill Farm Cl GU27 .. 189 E3
Hill Farm Rd SO24 .. 182 B1
Hill House Hill GU30 187 F3
Hill Houses La SO24 . 201 D3
Hill Meadow RG25 ... 65 D1
Hill Rd Barton Stacey SP11 108 A1
  Beacon Hill GU26 ... 167 D3
  Farnham GU11 ...... 99 D4
  Grayshott GU26 ..... 167 D2
  Newbury RG14 ...... 1 B2
  Oakley RG22 .... 90 A4
Hill Sq RG24 ...... 49 D1
Hill Terr SO24 ..... 179 E3
Hill Top SO22 ..... 175 E3
Hill Top Ave SP9 .. 78 C4
Hill View Rd
  Basingstoke RG22 .. 68 C2
  Farnham GU9 ...... 98 B1
Hilland Rise GU35 .. 165 E3
Hillary Cl GU9 .... 121 F4
Hillary Rd Basingstoke RG21 69 D4
  Farnham GU9 ...... 121 F4
Hillbrook Rise GU9 . 98 C3
Hillbury Ave SP10 .. 105 F3
Hillcrest Farnham GU9 99 D4
  Fleet GU13 .... 54 A2
  Tadley RG26 .... 9 F1
Hillcrest Cotts RG14 . 1 B4
Hillcrest Cl RG21 ... 68 A3
Hillcrest Rd GU15 ... 36 C4
Hillcrest Wlk GU43 . 68 A3
Hillfield GU17 ..... 34 B3
Hillgarth GU20 .... 167 D3
Hillhouse La RG19, RG20 7 F1
Hillier Way SO23 ... 176 A1
Hillsborough Ct GU14 . 55 E4
Hillside Abbotts Ann SP11 . 104 C2
  Baughurst RG26 .... 26 A2
  Littleton SO22 ..... 175 E4
  Sandhurst GU46 .... 35 E4
  Upton SP11 .... 38 C1
Hillside Cl Alton GU34 .. 139 F3
  Headley GU35 ..... 165 F3
  West Dean SP5 .... 190 B1
  Winchester SO22 .. 175 E1
Hillside Cotts
  Farnborough GU47 .. 35 E1
  Sparsholt SO21 .... 174 A2
Hillside Cres GU16 .. 56 B4
Hillside Ct SP11 .... 105 D4
Hillside La GU9 .... 99 D4
Hillside Rd
  Aldershot GU9 ..... 99 F4
  Ash GU12 .... 77 F2
  Farnham GU10 ..... 122 A2
  Farnham, Weybourne GU9 99 F4
  Linchmere GU27 ... 189 E3
  Odiham RG29 ...... 72 D2
  Winchester SO22 .. 175 E1
Hillside Villas SP10 . 82 C1
Hillstead Ct RG21 ... 69 D2
Hilltop Rd RG25 ... 65 D1
Hilltop View GU46 .. 33 F3
Hindell Cl GU14 ... 55 E2
Hindhead Ho GU26 . 167 E2
Hindhead Rd GU27 . 167 E1
Hinstock Cl GU14 .. 55 E3
Hinton Ampner Ho SO24 . 201 F2
Hinton Cl RG26 .... 26 C4
Hinton Hill SO24 .. 201 F2
Hinwood Cl SO20 .. 170 A4

Hitches La
  Crookham Village GU13 ... 74 B4
  Fleet GU13 .... 74 B4
Hobbs Cl SO24 ...... 180 A2
Hobbs Sq SP10 ..... 83 E1
Hockford La RG7 .... 8 C2
Hockley Cotts SO24 ... 200 C2
Hockley Golf Course SO23 198 A1
Hoddington Cotts RG25 ... 94 B2
Hogarth Cl
  Basingstoke RG24 ... 69 F2
  Sandhurst GU15 .... 35 E3
Hogarth Ct SP10 .... 82 C1
Hoghatch La GU9 ... 98 C3
Hogmoor Rd GU35 . 164 A2
Hogwood Ind Est RG2 15 F3
Hogwood La RG40 .. 15 F3
Holbeche Cl RG46 .. 33 F3
Holbein Cl RG21 ... 69 E2
Holborne Rd RG14 .. 5 D3
Holbrook Cl GU11, GU12 ... 99 E4
Holbrook Way GU10, GU9 ... 99 F4
Holbury La
  East Tytherley SO51 . 191 E2
  Lockerley SO51 .... 191 E2
Holdaway Cl SO23 . 176 B4
Holder Rd GU14 ... 77 E1
Hole La GU10 ..... 120 A3
Holland Cl GU9 ... 99 E1
Holland Dr SP10 .. 82 C2
Holland Gdns GU13 75 D4
Hollands Cl SO22 . 175 D3
Hollies The RG14 .. 5 D3
Hollin's Wlk [14] RG21 69 D3
Hollington La RG20 . 21 D2
Hollis Wood Dr GU9 121 E3
Hollow The SO20 .. 170 B3
Holly Acre GU47 .. 34 A3
Holly Ave GU15 ... 36 C2
Holly Bush La GU12 77 E3
Holly Cl Aldershot GU12 77 D1
  Bramley RG26 ..... 29 D1
  Eversley GU46 .... 33 D4
  Farnborough GU14 . 55 F2
  Headley GU35 ..... 166 A3
Holly Cross RG26 .. 28 C2
Holly Dr RG24 ..... 70 B3
Holly Gr RG26 .... 10 B1
Holly Hedge Cl GU15 36 B1
Holly Hedge Rd GU15 36 B1
Holly La RG26 .... 27 F4
Holly Lodge Mid Sch GU12 . 77 E4
Holly Rd Aldershot GU12 77 D1
  Farnborough GU14 . 55 F2
Holly Way GU17 .. 35 D2
Holly Wlk Andover SP10 ... 105 E3
  Middle Wallop SO20 126 A2
Hollybrook Ct GU35 164 C2
Hollybrook Pk GU35 164 C2
Hollybush Ind Pk GU12 77 E3
Hollybush La Eversley GU46 33 E4
  Ramsdell RG26 .... 26 B1
Hollycombe Cl GU30 188 A1
Hollyfields Cl GU15 . 35 F3
Hollyhock Cl RG22 . 91 D4
Hollyridge GU27 ... 189 F3
Hollytree Gdns GU14 56 A4
Hollytrees GU13 ... 74 C3
Hollywater Rd
  Bordon GU35 ..... 164 C1
  Liphook GU30 .... 187 D4
Holmbrook Cl GU14 55 D2
Holmbrook Gdns GU14 55 D2
Holme CE Prim Sch The
  GU35 .... 165 E3
Holmes Cl RG22 ... 91 E3
Holmes Ct SP10 ... 105 F4
Holmwood Cotts GU34 119 F2
Holmwood Terr RG27 52 B3
Holst Cl RG22 .... 91 F4
Holt Cl GU14 .... 56 A4
Holt Cotts RG26 .. 25 E4
Holt End La GU34 . 138 A2
Holt La Baughurst RG26 25 E2
  Hook RG27 ...... 51 E1
  Tangley SP11 .... 59 E1
Holt Pound La GU10 121 D3
Holt Way RG27 ... 51 E1
Holtwood Rd RG20 . 3 F2
Holy Barn Cl RG22 68 A1
Holy Cross Hospl GU27 189 F4
Holyrood Ct RG23 . 68 A2
Holywell Cl GU14 . 55 D2
Home Cl SO24 .... 180 B3
Home Farm Bsns Ctr SP5 ... 191 F3
Home Farm Cl GU16 56 C1
Home Farm Gdns SP10 82 B2
Home Farm La RG26 26 C2
Home Farm Rd RG27 52 B3
Home La SO21 ... 174 B2
Home Mead RG25 . 89 F3

Home Mead Cl RG14 ...... 5 E4
Home Park Rd GU46 ...... 34 A3
Homefield Cotts
  East Tisted GU34 ...... 183 E5
  Liss GU33 ...... 207 F3
Homegreen Ho GU27 ...... 189 F3
Homelea Cl GU14 ...... 55 F4
Homeleigh Cres GU12 ...... 77 F4
Homepark Ho GU11 ...... 99 D1
Homerise Ho **1** SO23 ...... 198 A4
Homestead Rd GU34 ...... 159 F3
Homesteads Rd RG22 ...... 91 D4
Hone Hill GU17 ...... 34 C4
Hones Yard Bsns Pk GU9 ...... 99 D1
Honey La GU34 ...... 185 D4
Honeybottom Rd RG26 ...... 9 F1
Honeycritch La GU32 ...... 206 B2
Honeysuckle Cl
  Winchester SO22 ...... 197 F2
  Yateley GU46 ...... 33 F3
Honeysuckle La GU35 ...... 165 F3
Honister Gdns GU13 ...... 54 B1
Honysuckle Cl RG22 ...... 91 D4
Hood Cl SP10, SP11 ...... 106 B4
Hook La Baughurst RG26 ...... 25 F4
  Oakley RG23 ...... 67 D4
  Ropley SO24 ...... 181 D2
  Wooton St Lawrence RG23 ...... 67 D4
Hook Rd Greywell RG29 ...... 72 A3
  Hook RG29 ...... 72 A4
  Kingsclere RG20 ...... 24 C1
  North Warnborough RG29 ...... 72 A3
  Rotherwick RG27 ...... 51 D3
Hook Sta RG29 ...... 72 A4
Hookpit Farm La SO23 ...... 176 A4
Hookstile La GU9 ...... 99 D1
Hookwood La GU11 ...... 58 A4
Hoopers Way RG23 ...... 67 D1
Hoopersmead RG25 ...... 92 A4
Hop Garden Rd RG27 ...... 50 C1
Hop Gdn GU13 ...... 74 C2
Hop Kiln The GU10 ...... 121 F4
Hope Fountain GU16 ...... 36 C2
Hope Grant's Rd GU12 ...... 76 C2
Hope La GU9 ...... 98 C3
Hopeman Cl GU47 ...... 35 D4
Hopeswood GU33 ...... 186 A1
Hopfield Rd RG27 ...... 52 B3
Hopkinson Way SP10 ...... 82 A1
Hopton Garth RG24 ...... 49 D1
Hopwood Cl RG14 ...... 2 A2
Horizon West Ind Est RG14 ...... 2 A2
Horn Rd GU14 ...... 55 E3
Hornbeam Cl
  Farnborough GU14 ...... 55 D3
  South Moreton SO21 ...... 153 F2
Hornbeam Pl RG27 ...... 51 D1
Hornbeams RG7 ...... 14 A3
Hornes Field Ct GU13 ...... 74 C2
Horris Hill RG14 ...... 5 E2
Horse La SO24 ...... 181 E4
Horsebridge Rd
  Broughton SO20 ...... 170 B2
  Houghton SO20 ...... 171 D2
  King's Somborne SO20 ...... 171 E1
Horseshoe Bend GU26 ...... 166 C2
Horseshoe Cl GU16 ...... 36 B4
Horseshoe Cres
  Bordon GU35 ...... 164 C2
  Camberley GU16 ...... 36 B4
Horseshoe La Ash GU12 ...... 77 F4
  Hurstbourne Tarrant SP11 ...... 60 B4
Horshells Dro SO20 ...... 125 E1
Horwood Gdns RG23 ...... 68 C1
Hosketts La SO20 ...... 147 F3
Hospital Hill GU11, GU12 ...... 76 C2
Hospital Rd GU11 ...... 76 C2
Houghton Lodge Gdns
  SO20 ...... 171 E4
Hound Green Ho RG27 ...... 31 D2
Houndmills Rd RG22 ...... 68 C3
Houndmills Rdbt RG22 ...... 68 C4
House Plat Ct GU13 ...... 74 C2
Houseman Rd GU14 ...... 55 E3
Howard Cl GU13 ...... 54 B1
Howard Cole Way GU11 ...... 76 B1
Howard Dr GU13 ...... 54 C2
Howard Rd
  Basingstoke RG22 ...... 69 E2
  Newbury RG14 ...... 1 C1
Howard View RG21 ...... 68 B2
Howard's La GU34 ...... 140 B4
Howes Gdns GU13 ...... 74 C3
Hubbard Rd RG21 ...... 68 C4
Hubert Rd SO23 ...... 197 F2
Huddington Glade GU46 ...... 33 F3
Hudsons Meadow RG27 ...... 31 D1
Huish La RG24 ...... 70 A2
Hulbert Way RG22 ...... 68 B1
Hullam La GU34 ...... 184 A3

Humber Cl RG18 ...... 2 C3
Humber Cl **11** SP10 ...... 83 E1
Humber La SP9 ...... 78 B2
Humber Way GU17 ...... 35 D4
Humbers View SO20 ...... 172 A1
Humberstone Rd SP10 ...... 106 A3
Humphrey Pk GU13 ...... 74 C2
Hundred Acre Cnr SP10 ...... 105 D4
Hungerford Cl GU15 ...... 35 D4
Hungerford La
  Hatherden SP10 ...... 82 C4
  Knights Enham SP10 ...... 82 C4
  Tangley SP11 ...... 37 F1
  Upper Chute SP11 ...... 37 F1
Hungerford Rd SN8 ...... 18 A3
Hunnels Cl GU13 ...... 74 C2
Hunt Cl SO21 ...... 153 F2
Hunt's Cotts RG14 ...... 1 B3
Hunter Rd GU14 ...... 55 E2
Hunters Cl RG23 ...... 67 E2
Hunters Rd GU33 ...... 186 B1
Hunting Gate SP10 ...... 105 E4
Huntingdon House Dr
  GU26 ...... 167 E2
Huntingford Cl GU26 ...... 167 D4
Hunton Down La
  Upper Bullington SO21 ...... 132 B3
  Wonston SO21 ...... 132 B3
Hunton La SO21 ...... 132 A2
Hunts Cl RG27 ...... 51 E1
Hunts Cotts RG27 ...... 52 B4
Huntsbottom La
  Hill Brow GU33 ...... 208 A2
  Liss GU33 ...... 208 A2
Huntsman's Mews GU16 ...... 56 B2
Huntsmead GU34 ...... 140 A2
Huntsmoor Rd RG26 ...... 26 B4
Hurland La GU35 ...... 165 E2
Hurlands Bsns Ctr GU9 ...... 99 E2
Hurlands Cl GU9 ...... 99 E2
Hurlands Pl GU9 ...... 99 E2
Hurne Cl **28** RG21 ...... 69 E3
Hurst Cl GU30 ...... 187 F3
Hurst Com Sch The RG26 ...... 9 D1
Hurst La GU34 ...... 205 D2
Hurst Rd Aldershot GU12 ...... 77 D2
  Farnborough GU14 ...... 55 F4
Hurst The RG27 ...... 73 F4
Hurstbourne Tarrant
  CE Prim Sch SP11 ...... 60 C3
Hurstmere Cl GU26 ...... 167 D2
Hussar Cl **1** GU11 ...... 76 B1
Hussell La GU34 ...... 160 A4
Hussey Cl **2** SO23 ...... 176 A1
Husseys La GU34 ...... 119 E3
Hutton Cl RG14 ...... 1 C1
Hutton Rd GU13 ...... 77 F3
Hutton Sq SP10 ...... 83 E1
Hyacinth Cl RG22 ...... 91 D4
Hyde Abbey Rd SO23 ...... 198 A4
Hyde Church La SO23 ...... 176 A1
Hyde Church Path **24** SO23 ...... 176 A1
Hyde Cl SO23 ...... 175 F1
Hyde End La RG7 ...... 8 A3
Hyde Gate SO23 ...... 176 A1
Hyde House Gdns **22** SO23 ...... 176 A1
Hyde La Crondall GU10 ...... 97 E4
  Ecchinswell RG20 ...... 23 F4
Hyde Lodge SO22 ...... 175 F1
Hyde St SO23 ...... 176 A1
Hydes Platt RG26 ...... 27 F4
Hyson Cres SP11 ...... 57 D1
Hythe Cl RG26 ...... 26 C4

Iberian Way GU15 ...... 36 C3
Ibworth La RG26 ...... 45 E2
Icknield Ho **60** SP10 ...... 83 E1
Icknield Special Sch SP10 ...... 83 E1
Icknield Way SP10 ...... 83 D2
Iden Ct RG14 ...... 1 C2
Idlefield Cotts GU10 ...... 120 B3
Ilchester Cl **8** RG14 ...... 1 C1
Ilex Cl Pamber Heath RG26 ...... 10 B1
  Yateley GU46 ...... 33 F3
Illingworth Cl RG26 ...... 29 D1
Imadene Cl GU35 ...... 164 C2
Imadene Cres GU35 ...... 164 C2
Imber Rd SO23 ...... 198 B4
Imjin Cl GU11 ...... 76 C2
Imperial Ct SP10 ...... 83 F1
Impstone Rd RG26 ...... 10 B1
Imran Ct GU12 ...... 100 A4
Inadown Bglws GU34 ...... 183 F4
Ingle Dell GU15 ...... 36 A2
Ingle Glen RG40 ...... 14 C4
Inglewood Dr RG22 ...... 91 D3
Inhams Rd GU34 ...... 140 B3
Inhams Row SO24 ...... 157 E1
Inhams Way RG7 ...... 8 B1
Inhurst House Sch RG26 ...... 9 F1
Inhurst La RG26 ...... 26 A4

Inhurst Way RG26 ...... 9 E1
Inkpen Gdns RG24 ...... 70 A4
Innisfail Gdns GU9 ...... 99 E4
Institute Rd GU12 ...... 77 D1
Instow Gdns GU14 ...... 55 F4
Intec Bsns Ctr RG24 ...... 69 F4
Inverness Way GU47 ...... 35 D4
Invincible Rd GU14 ...... 55 F2
Inwood Rd GU33 ...... 208 A2
Ipoh Cl SO20 ...... 126 A3
Ipsley Lodge GU12 ...... 100 B3
Iris Cl RG22 ...... 91 D4
Irvine Dr GU14 ...... 55 E4
Irwell Cl **24** RG21 ...... 69 E3
Isaac Newton Rd RG40 ...... 15 F4
Isington La GU34 ...... 119 F1
Isington Rd GU34 ...... 119 F1
Isis Way GU47 ...... 35 D4
Island Farm Rd RG7 ...... 11 E4
Itchel La GU10 ...... 97 E4
Itchen Abbas Prim Sch
  SO21 ...... 177 F3
Itchen Cl RG23 ...... 67 D1
Itchen Ct
  45 Andover SP10 ...... 83 E1
  45 Winchester SO23 ...... 198 A4
Itchen View SO24 ...... 178 B3
Ivanhoe Rd RG40 ...... 15 F3
Ivar Gdns RG24 ...... 49 D1
Ively Rd GU14 ...... 55 D1
Ives Cl GU46 ...... 33 F4
Ivy Cl SO22 ...... 197 F3
Ivy Down La RG23 ...... 66 C2
Ivy La GU9 ...... 98 C1
Ivy Rd GU14 ...... 77 E1
Ivyhole Hill RG27 ...... 53 D4
Ivyhouse La GU27 ...... 205 F2

Jacaranda Rd GU35 ...... 164 B1
Jack St RG14 ...... 1 C2
Jackdaw Cl RG22 ...... 90 C4
Jacklyns Cl SO24 ...... 179 E2
Jacklyns La SO24 ...... 179 E3
Jacob's Yd **18** RG21 ...... 69 D2
Jagdalik Rd SP9 ...... 78 C2
James Cl RG21 ...... 69 E4
James Rd Camberley GU47 ...... 35 F1
  Farnborough GU14 ...... 77 D4
James Way GU47 ...... 35 F1
Jamrud Rd SP9 ...... 78 B3
Jan Smuts Cl GU33 ...... 186 B1
Jane Austen's Ho (Mus)
  GU34 ...... 161 E4
Japonica Cl GU12 ...... 77 E1
Jardine Sq SP10 ...... 83 E1
Jarvis Cl GU34 ...... 33 D4
Jasmine Cl SP10 ...... 105 F3
Jasmine Rd RG22 ...... 91 D4
Jasmine Way GU35 ...... 164 C1
Jays Cl RG21 ...... 69 D1
Jays Nest Cl GU17 ...... 35 D2
Jean Orr Ct GU13 ...... 75 D3
Jefferson Rd RG21 ...... 69 E4
Jellicoe Ct SP10 ...... 83 E1
Jenkins Pl GU12 ...... 77 D4
Jenkyn Pl GU10 ...... 120 A3
Jennet Way GU34 ...... 140 A3
Jenine Green La SO24 ...... 137 F1
Jenny's Wlk GU46 ...... 34 B3
Jenson Gdns SP10 ...... 105 F4
Jerrymoor Hill RG40 ...... 16 B4
Jersey Cl
  Basingstoke RG24 ...... 48 B1
  Fleet GU13 ...... 54 A2
Jervis Ct SP10 ...... 83 E1
Jesmond Dene RG14 ...... 1 B2
Jesse Cl GU46 ...... 34 B3
Jessett Dr GU13 ...... 74 C2
Jesty Rd SO24 ...... 179 D2
Jewry St SO23 ...... 198 A4
Jibbs Meadow RG26 ...... 28 C2
Jobson Cl RG28 ...... 86 B3
John Boys Ho RG14 ...... 5 D3
John Childs Cl RG14 ...... 1 C1
John Cl GU9 ...... 99 D4
John Eddie Ct RG22 ...... 68 B2
John Hanson Com Sch
  SP10 ...... 105 F4
John Hunt of Everest
  Com Sch RG22 ...... 48 B1
John Kimber's Almshouses
  RG14 ...... 1 B2
John Morgan Cl RG27 ...... 51 D1
John Pounds Ho GU35 ...... 164 B1
John Rankin Schs RG14 ...... 5 D4
Johnson Way GU13 ...... 75 D3
Joices Yd **13** RG21 ...... 69 D2
Jollies The GU10 ...... 97 E3
Jonathan Hill RG14 ...... 1 A1
Jouldings La RG2 ...... 15 D2

Joule Rd Andover SP10 ...... 82 A1
  Basingstoke RG21 ...... 68 C4
Joy's La SO20 ...... 129 D2
Jubilee Cl
  Farnborough GU14 ...... 55 D2
  Litchfield RG28 ...... 42 B1
  Pamber Heath RG26 ...... 10 B1
Jubilee Cotts RG7 ...... 14 A2
Jubilee Dr GU12 ...... 77 F3
Jubilee Hall Rd GU14 ...... 56 A2
Jubilee Ho GU35 ...... 164 C2
Jubilee La Farnham GU10 ...... 121 F3
  Grayshott GU26 ...... 167 D2
Jubilee Rd Aldershot GU11 ...... 99 F4
  Basingstoke RG22 ...... 69 D2
  Finchampstead RG40 ...... 16 B2
  Mytchett GU14 ...... 56 C1
  Newbury RG14 ...... 1 C1
Jumps Rd GU10 ...... 144 C2
Junction Pl GU27 ...... 189 E3
Junction Rd GU10 ...... 106 A4
Junction Terr RG14 ...... 2 A1
June Dr RG22 ...... 68 A3
Juniper Cl Bordon GU35 ...... 164 A1
  Chineham RG24 ...... 49 D2
  Winchester SO22 ...... 197 E3
Juniper Cl **1** SP9 ...... 79 C4
Juniper Rd GU14 ...... 55 D3
Jupiter Ho **8** RG26 ...... 9 E1

Karachi Rd GU13 ...... 78 C4
Kashmir Ct **6** GU16 ...... 56 A1
Kathleen Cl RG21 ...... 69 D1
Kay Cres GU35 ...... 165 F3
Keable Rd GU9 ...... 121 E4
Keats Cl Basingstoke RG24 ...... 69 E4
  South Wonston SO21 ...... 153 E2
  Winchester SO21, SO22 ...... 197 E2
Keats Gdns GU13 ...... 54 A1
Keats Way GU46 ...... 33 F2
Keble St SO22 ...... 197 E3
Keeper's Hill SP11 ...... 104 A3
Keepers La SO51 ...... 192 B1
Keeps Mead RG20 ...... 24 B2
Keith Lucas Rd GU14 ...... 55 E1
Kellynch Cl GU34 ...... 139 F2
Kellys Wlk SP10 ...... 105 F4
Kelsey Ave RG40 ...... 16 B3
Kelsey Cl GU33 ...... 208 A3
Kelsey Gr GU47 ...... 34 B3
Kelvin Cl RG40 ...... 15 E4
Kelvin Hill GU22 ...... 68 C1
Kelvin Rd RG14 ...... 1 C2
Kemmitt Way SP10 ...... 105 F3
Kempland La GU34 ...... 204 B2
Kempshott Gdns RG22 ...... 91 D4
Kempshott Gr RG21 ...... 68 A2
Kempshott La RG22 ...... 91 D4
Kempshott Schs RG22 ...... 91 D4
Kempton Cl Alton GU34 ...... 139 F1
  Newbury RG14 ...... 1 B2
Kendal Cl GU14 ...... 55 E2
Kendal Gdns RG23 ...... 68 A1
Kendrick Rd RG14 ...... 5 D3
Kenilworth Cres GU11 ...... 54 B1
Kenilworth Ct **8** SO23 ...... 176 A1
Kenilworth Rd
  Basingstoke RG22 ...... 68 B3
  Farnborough GU14 ...... 55 D3
Kenley Rd GU35 ...... 164 A3
Kenmore Cl Camberley GU16 ...... 56 A4
  Fleet GU13 ...... 75 D3
Kennedy Cl RG14 ...... 5 D3
Kennel La Frensham GU10 ...... 122 A1
  Littleton SO22 ...... 175 E2
Kennels La GU14 ...... 55 D1
Kennet Cl Ash GU12 ...... 77 F2
  21 Basingstoke RG21 ...... 69 E3
  6 Newbury RG14 ...... 1 C1
Kennet Ctr The RG14 ...... 1 C1
Kennet Pl **15** RG21 ...... 69 D2
Kennet Rd Newbury RG14 ...... 1 B1
  North Tidworth SP9 ...... 79 D4
Kennet Side RG14 ...... 1 C1
Kennet Way RG23 ...... 164 A3
Kensington Ho **10** RG21 ...... 69 D3
Kent Rd Bordon GU35 ...... 164 A3
  Fleet GU13 ...... 75 D3
Kenton Cl GU15 ...... 36 B1
Kenward Bglws RG25 ...... 114 B2
Kenwith Ave GU13 ...... 54 B1
Kenyons Yd SP11 ...... 105 F4
Keogh Cl GU35 ...... 164 B1
Kerchers Field RG25 ...... 88 A4
Kerfield Way RG27 ...... 51 D1
Kerfield SO22 ...... 197 E4
Kerfield Mews SO22 ...... 197 E4
Kerridge Ind Est GU35 ...... 140 A2

Kerry Cl RG13 ...... 54 A3
Kersey Cres RG14 ...... 1 B3
Kestrel Cres RG29 ...... 95 E4
Kestrel Cl Ewshot GU9 ...... 98 A4
  North Tidworth SP9 ...... 79 D4
  Thatcham RG19 ...... 2 C2
  Winchester SO22 ...... 197 E2
Kestrel Ct GU34 ...... 139 F3
Kestrel Ho GU10 ...... 121 F4
Kestrel Rd RG23 ...... 67 F1
Ketchers Field GU34 ...... 184 C3
Ketelbey Rise RG22 ...... 91 F4
Kevin Cl RG20 ...... 24 C1
Kevins Dr GU13 ...... 34 B4
Kevins Gr GU13 ...... 54 A1
Kew Wlk SP10 ...... 105 F4
Keyhaven Cotts SO20 ...... 125 E1
Keynes Cl GU13 ...... 75 D2
Kildare Cl GU35 ...... 164 B2
Kildare Rd GU35 ...... 164 B2
Kilham La SO22 ...... 197 D3
Kilmarnock Gdns GU15 ...... 36 B1
Kilmeston Rd
  Cheriton SO24 ...... 201 E2
  Kilmeston SO24 ...... 201 E1
Kilmore Dr GU15 ...... 36 C2
Kilmuir Cl GU15 ...... 35 D4
Kiln Cl GU35 ...... 207 F3
Kiln Gdns RG27 ...... 52 B3
Kiln Hill RG7 ...... 14 C4
Kiln La Farnham GU10, GU9 ...... 122 A3
  Monk Sherborne RG26 ...... 47 D3
  Old Alresford SO24 ...... 157 E1
  Stratfield Mortimer RG7 ...... 12 A3
Kiln Rd Newbury RG14 ...... 2 A3
  Sherborne St John RG26 ...... 47 F2
Kiln Ride RG40 ...... 16 C4
Kiln Ride Extension RG40 ...... 16 C3
Kiln Way Aldershot GU11 ...... 99 F4
  Grayshott GU26 ...... 166 B3
Kilns The GU34 ...... 140 A2
Kilsby Flats SP9 ...... 101 F4
Kimball Rd RG22 ...... 68 C1
Kimber Cl RG24 ...... 48 C1
Kimber's Cl RG14 ...... 1 B2
Kimberley SO23 ...... 75 D2
Kimberley Cl SP10 ...... 82 B1
Kimberley Rd GU33 ...... 186 B1
Kimberly Rd RG22 ...... 68 C2
Kimbers Dr RG14 ...... 1 A3
Kimbers La Farnham GU11 ...... 99 D2
  Pamber End RG26 ...... 27 D3
Kimpton CE Prim Sch SP11 ...... 80 B1
King Alfred Pl SO23 ...... 176 A1
King Alfred Terr **23** SO23 ...... 176 A1
King Alfred's Coll SO22 ...... 197 F4
King Arthur's Way SP10 ...... 83 D2
King George Rd SP10 ...... 105 F4
King Harold Ct SO23 ...... 197 F3
King John Cl RG20 ...... 24 B1
King John Rd RG20 ...... 24 B1
King Johns Rd RG29 ...... 72 B2
King La SO20 ...... 125 E2
King Lane Cotts SO20 ...... 125 E1
King's Somborne
  CE Prim Sch SO20 ...... 171 F1
King St Mortimer RG7 ...... 11 F3
  Odiham RG29 ...... 72 C1
King's Cl SO23 ...... 154 A1
King's Cres GU16 ...... 36 A4
King's Ct GU12 ...... 100 B4
King's Elms SO21 ...... 130 B4
King's Hill GU34 ...... 138 B1
King's La GU32 ...... 205 E2
King's Meadow RG25 ...... 88 A4
King's Rd Aldershot GU11 ...... 76 B1
  Basingstoke RG23 ...... 68 C2
  Haslemere GU27 ...... 189 F3
  R. GU16 ...... 36 A4
King's Wlk GU15 ...... 35 E3
Kingfisher Cl
  Bordon GU35 ...... 164 C1
  Farnborough GU14 ...... 55 D3
  Fleet GU13 ...... 75 D3
  Whitchurch RG28 ...... 86 B3
Kingfisher Court Ind Est
  RG14 ...... 2 A2
Kingfisher Ct GU34 ...... 139 F3
Kingfisher Dr GU46 ...... 33 F3
Kingfisher Wlk GU12 ...... 77 E1
Kingfishers SP9 ...... 101 F4
Kings Ave Ash GU10 ...... 100 B4
  Winchester SO22 ...... 197 F3
Kings Furlong Ctr RG24 ...... 69 D2
Kings Furlong Dr RG22 ...... 68 C2
Kings Furlong Schs RG22 ...... 68 C2
Kings Head **25** SO23 ...... 198 A4

Kings Keep GU13 .... 75 D3
Kings La Chilcomb SO23 .... 198 C3
Farnham GU10 .... 121 E3
Kings Mead RG14 .... 5 D3
Kings Meadow SP10 .... 106 A4
Kings Orch RG22 .... 90 A4
Kings Par 2 GU13 .... 54 A1
Kings Peace The GU26 .. 167 D2
Kings Pightle RG24 .... 48 C2
Kings Rd Alton GU34 .... 139 E2
Enham Alamein SP10 ...... 83 D4
Fleet GU13 .... 54 A1
Newbury RG14 .... 1 C1
Silchester RG7 .... 10 C1
Kings Road W RG14 .... 1 C1
Kings Sch SO22 .... 197 D4
Kings Sch The RG21 .... 69 D2
Kings Somborne Rd SO51 194 B1
Kings Wlk RG28 .... 86 B3
Kings Worthy Prim Sch
SO23 .... 176 B3
Kings Yd SP10 .... 106 A4
Kingsbridge Copse RG27 .... 71 F4
Kingsbridge Rd
Shinfield RG7 .... 13 F3
Swallowfield RG7 .... 13 F3
Kingsbridge Rd RG14 .... 1 B1
Kingsclear Pk GU15 .... 36 A2
Kingsclere CE Prim Sch
RG20 .... 24 B2
Kingsclere Pk RG20 .... 24 B2
Kingsclere Rd
Basingstoke RG21, RG23 ... 69 D3
Monk Sherborne RG26 .... 47 F1
Overton RG25 .... 65 D1
Upper Wootton RG26 .... 46 C1
Kingscroft GU13 .... 75 D4
Kingsdale CE 7 SO22 .... 197 F4
Kingsgate Rd SO23 .... 197 F3
Kingsgate St SO23 .... 198 A3
Kingsholt Cotts GU33 .... 185 F2
Kingsland Grange RG14 .... 5 E4
Kingsland Ind Pk
RG21, RG24 .... 48 C1
Kingsland Rd GU34 .... 139 F2
Kingsley Ave GU15 .... 36 A2
Kingsley Bglws GU24 .... 179 D2
Kingsley Bsns Pk GU35 ..... 142 B1
Kingsley Cl RG14 .... 1 C3
Kingsley Pk RG28 .... 86 B3
Kingsley Pl SO22 .... 197 F3
Kingsley Rd Eversley GU46 .. 33 D4
Farnborough GU14 .... 55 E3
Kingsmead Camberley GU14 56 B4
Farnborough GU14 .... 55 F2
Upper Clatford SP10 .... 105 E2
Kingsmead Cotts GU34 ...... 140 A2
Kingsmead Sh Ctr 9 GU14 56 B4
Kingsmill Rd RG21 .... 69 D1
Kingston Rd GU15 .... 36 B4
Kingstons Ind Est GU12 ...... 77 E1
Kingsvale Ct RG21 .... 68 C2
Kingsway Aldershot GU11 ... 76 B1
Andover SP10 .... 83 F1
Blackwater GU17 .... 35 E3
Kingsway Gdns SP10 .... 83 D2
Kingswood 8 GU13 .... 54 A1
Kingswood Firs GU26 .... 167 D1
Kingswood La GU26 .... 167 D1
Kingswood Rise GU34 .... 159 F1
Kintyre Cl RG23 .... 67 D1
Kipling Cl GU46 .... 34 A2
Kipling Wlk RG22 .... 68 C2
Kirk Knoll GU35 .... 165 E3
Kirkby Ct GU15 .... 36 B1
Kirkee Rd SP9 .... 78 C3
Kitchener Rd GU33 .... 186 B1
Kitchener's Rd GU12 .... 77 D3
Kitcombe La GU34 .... 161 E1
Kitt's La GU10 .... 203 E1
Kitts La GU10 .... 166 B4
Kitwood La SO24 .... 182 B4
Kitwood Rd SO24 .... 182 A4
Knapp La RG26 .... 27 D3
Knight Cl SO23 .... 176 A1
Knight St RG21 .... 68 C2
Knights Cl SP10 .... 83 F1
Knights Enham Schs SP11 .. 83 D2
Knights La RG20 .... 4 A2
Knights Rd GU11 .... 99 E4
Knights Way GU14 .... 139 E2
Knights Yd SP11 .... 60 C4
Knightsbridge Dr RG19 .... 6 C2
Knightsbridge Rd
Camberley GU15 .... 36 B4
Enham Alamein SP10 .... 83 E4
Knock Hundred La GU27 .. 189 D4

Knockwood La SO20 .... 147 F4
Knoll Cl GU13 .... 54 A1
Knoll Ct GU13 .... 54 A2
Knoll Rd Camberley GU15 .... 36 A3
Fleet GU13 .... 54 A1
Knoll Wlk GU15 .... 36 A3
Knollys Rd Aldershot GU11 .. 76 B2
Pamber Heath RG26 .... 10 B1
Knowle Cres RG20 .... 24 B1
Knowles Meadow GU33 .... 208 A1
Knowlings The RG28 .... 86 B2
Kohat Cl SP9 .... 78 B1
Kohat Ct 10 GU11 .... 76 B1
Kohat Rd SP9 .... 78 C3
Kohima Cl GU11 .... 76 C1
Krooner Rd GU47 .... 35 F2
Kurnool Mortar Cross Roads
GU15 .... 35 F3
Kyftle Court Flat RG14 .... 1 B1
Kynegils Rd SO22 .... 175 F1

Laburnam Gdns GU13 .... 75 D3
Laburnum Cl GU11 .... 76 C1
Laburnum Gr RG14 .... 1 C2
Laburnum Pas 3 GU11 ...... 76 C1
Laburnum Rd
Aldershot GU11 .... 76 C1
Farnham GU9 .... 99 E4
Laburnum Way RG21 .... 105 E4
Laburnums The GU46 .... 34 C3
Ladwell Cl RG14 .... 5 D3
Lady Godley Cl SP9 .... 78 C3
Ladyplace Ct 4 GU34 .... 139 F2
Ladywell La GU34 .... 179 E3
Ladywood Ave GU14 .... 55 D2
Ladywood Ct GU10 .... 121 E3
Laffan's Rd GU11 .... 76 B3
Laffans Rd RG29 .... 95 F4
Lahore Cl SP9 .... 78 C4
Lahore Rd SP9 .... 78 C4
Lake Ct RG26 .... 27 D4
Lake Dr GU35 .... 164 C2
Lake La GU10 .... 143 E3
Lake Rd GU16 .... 56 C3
Lake Side The GU17 .... 35 D2
Lakeland Dr GU15 .... 36 A4
Lakelands RG26 .... 26 A4
Laker Sq SP10 .... 83 E1
Lakeside Cl Ash GU12 .... 77 E2
Charlton SP10 .... 82 B2
Lakeside Cl GU13 .... 54 A2
Lakeside Cty Prim Sch
GU15 .... 36 B1
Lakeside Gdns GU14 .... 55 D4
Lakeside Rd Ash GU12 .... 77 E2
Farnborough GU11 .... 76 C4
Lama Ho GU12 .... 77 D1
Lamb Cl SP10 .... 106 B4
Lamb's Lane Prim Sch RG7 13 F4
Lambdens Wlk RG26 .... 26 C4
Lambdown App SP9 .... 79 E3
Lambdown Terr SP9 .... 79 E4
Lambert Cres GU15 .... 35 D2
Lambert Ct RG14 .... 1 C3
Lambourn Rd RG14 .... 1 A3
Lambourne Cl
Sparsholt SO21 .... 174 B2
Thruxton SP11 .... 103 F4
Lambourne Way
Thruxton SP11 .... 103 F4
Tongham GU10 .... 100 B4
Lambs Cl RG25 .... 88 A4
Lambs La RG7 .... 13 F4
Lambs Row GU21, RG23 .... 69 F4
Lamerton Cl GU35 .... 164 B2
Lamerton Rd GU35 .... 164 B2
Lamp Acres RG14 .... 1 C3
Lampard Cl RG27 .... 50 C3
Lampard Ho RG25 .... 88 A4
Lanark Cl GU16 .... 36 B1
Lancashire Cotts SP11 .... 59 E1
Lancaster Ave GU10 .... 122 A4
Lancaster Cl SP10 .... 82 C1
Lancaster Dr GU10 .... 36 A3
Lancaster Pl GU14 .... 69 D3
Lancaster Way GU12 .... 56 A4
Lancer Ct 5 GU11 .... 76 B1
Landale Cl SP11 .... 83 D4
Lands End La GU35 .... 164 C3
Landseer Cl
Basingstoke RG21 .... 69 E2
Sandhurst GU15 .... 35 E3
Landseer Ct SP10 .... 82 C1
Lane End Bramley RG26 .... 29 D1
West Tisted RG26 .... 204 B4
Lane End Bglws SO21 .... 133 D2
Lane The RG26 .... 27 D4
Langdale Cl GU14 .... 55 E2
Langdale Dr GU12 .... 77 E3

Langham Ct GU10 .... 122 A4
Langham Rd GU34 .... 139 F2
Langley Cl GU13 .... 74 C2
Langley Dr GU15 .... 36 A3
Langton Ct SO22 .... 175 F1
Langton Dr GU35 .... 165 F4
Langtons Ct SO24 .... 179 F3
Lanham La Sparsholt SO22 196 C4
Winchester SO22 .... 196 C4
Lankhills Sch SO22 .... 175 F1
Lankhills Rd SO22 .... 176 A1
Lansdowne Ave
Andover SP10 .... 105 F3
Winchester SO23 .... 197 F3
Lansdowne Ct 3 SO22 .... 197 F3
Lansdowne Rd
Aldershot GU11 .... 76 C1
Alton GU34 .... 140 A3
Camberley GU6 .... 56 C4
Lansley Rd RG24 .... 69 D4
Lantern Ct SO22 .... 197 F3
Lapin La RG22 .... 91 D3
Larch Cl Camberley GU16 .... 36 B4
Kings Worthy SO23 .... 154 A1
Liphook SO20 .... 187 F2
Middle Wallop SO20 .... 126 A2
Newbury RG14 .... 1 A3
Larch Dr Andover SP10 ..... 105 E4
Kingsclere RG20 .... 24 B1
Larch Way GU14 .... 55 D2
Larches Way GU46 .... 33 F4
Larchfield Rd GU33 .... 75 D3
Larchwood RG24 .... 48 C2
Larchwood Glade GU15 .... 36 C4
Larg Dr SO22 .... 175 E2
Lark Cl Andover SP11 .... 83 D1
Basingstoke RG22 .... 90 C2
North Tidworth SP9 .... 79 F3
Lark Hill Rise SO22 .... 197 E2
Lark Rise GU34 .... 187 F3
Larkfield RG24 .... 48 C1
Larkfield Cl GU9 .... 98 B1
Larkfield Rd GU9 .... 98 B1
Larks Barrow Hill RG28 ...... 63 E1
Larkspur Cl GU9 .... 99 F4
Larkwhistle Farm Rd
SO21 .... 111 E1
Larmer Cl GU13 .... 74 B4
Larwood Sq SP10 .... 83 E1
Lasham Airfield GU34 .... 116 B2
Latchwood La GU9 .... 122 A3
Latham Ave GU15 .... 36 A1
Lauder Cl GU15 .... 35 F1
Launcelot Cl SP11 .... 83 D2
Laundry La Camberley GU17 35 E3
Heckfield RG27 .... 31 D3
Sandhurst GU17 .... 35 E3
Laurel Cl Camberley GU15 .. 36 A2
Farnborough GU14 .... 55 D2
North Warnborough RG29 .. 72 B2
Laurel Gdns GU9 .... 99 F4
Laurel Grove GU10 .... 121 E3
Laurel Pl SO20 .... 126 A2
Laurels The Andover SP10 .. 82 C1
Basingstoke RG21 .... 69 E2
Farnham GU11 .... 99 E4
Fleet GU33 .... 54 A1
Lavell's La RG26 .... 29 D4
Lavender Cl SP10 .... 105 F3
Lavender Gdns GU35 .... 164 B2
Lavender La GU10 .... 121 E2
Lavender Rd RG22 .... 91 D4
Laverdale GU14 .... 55 D2
Laverstoke La RG28 .... 87 D2
Laverstoke Prim Sch RG28 . 87 D3
Lawday Link GU9 .... 98 C4
Lawday Pl GU9 .... 98 C4
Lawday Pl La GU9 .... 98 C4
Lawford Cres GU46 .... 34 A3
Lawn Ho 17 SO23 .... 198 A4
Lawn Rd SO22 .... 175 E2
Lawn St 16 SO23 .... 198 A4
Lawns The GU14 .... 55 E2
Lawrence Cl Andover SP10 .. 82 C1
Basingstoke RG24 .... 48 B1
Lawrence Hos SP11 .... 103 D1
Lawrence Lodge GU15 .... 36 A4
Lawrence Rd GU13 .... 74 C4
Lawrence Way GU47 .... 35 F2
Lawrenncedale Ct RG22 .... 68 C2
Laws Terr GU11 .... 77 D2
Lay Field RG27 .... 50 C1
Le Borowe GU13 .... 74 C2
Le Marchant Rd RG16 .... 36 B2
Lea Cl
Ash GU11 .... 77 F1
Basingstoke RG21 .... 69 E3
Farnham GU11 .... 99 F3
Lea Ct GU9 .... 99 E4
Lea Rd GU15 .... 35 F1
Lea Springs GU13 .... 74 B4

Lea The Fleet GU13 .... 74 C4
Wokingham RG40 .... 16 B4
Lea Way GU12 .... 77 E2
Lea Wood Rd GU13 .... 74 C4
Leaden Vere RG29 .... 95 E2
Leckford SO20 .... 150 B4
Leckford La Leckford SO20 150 A3
Stockbridge SO20 .... 150 A3
Ledger Cl GU13 .... 74 B4
Lee Ct GU11 .... 100 A4
Lefroy Ave RG21 .... 69 E4
Lefroy's Field GU10 .... 97 E4
Legge Cres GU14 .... 55 D1
Legion La SO23 .... 176 B4
Lehar Cl RG22 .... 91 E4
Leicester Pl SP10 .... 106 A4
Leicester Way SO23 .... 176 B1
Leigh Cl SP10 .... 106 B4
Leigh Field RG7 .... 11 E4
Leigh Gdns SP10 .... 106 B4
Leigh La GU9 .... 122 B4
Leigh Rd SP10 .... 106 B4
Leipzig Rd GU13 .... 75 D2
Lemon Gr GU35 .... 164 B1
Len Smart Ct RG21 .... 69 E4
Lendore Rd GU16 .... 56 A4
Lennel Gdns GU13 .... 75 D3
Lennon Way RG22 .... 91 D4
Lennox Rd RG21 .... 69 E4
Lennox Rd GU11 .... 68 C1
Lent Hill Cl 6 SO20 .... 197 E3
Lenten St GU34 .... 139 F2
Leonard Cl GU14 .... 56 A4
Leopold Ave GU14 .... 55 F3
Leslie Southern Ct 18 RG14 .. 1 C2
Lestock Way GU13 .... 54 B1
Levern Dr GU9 .... 99 D3
Levignen Cl GU13 .... 74 B3
Lewendon Rd RG14 .... 1 B3
Lewis Cl RG21 .... 69 E4
Lewis Wlk RG14 .... 5 D3
Ley Rd GU14 .... 55 F4
Leys Gdns RG14 .... 1 B2
Leyton Way SP10 .... 105 F3
Lickfolds Rd GU10 .... 121 E2
Liddell Cl RG40 .... 16 B2
Lightfoot Gr RG21 .... 69 D1
Lightsfield RG22 .... 91 D3
Lilac Cl GU35 .... 164 B1
Lilac Way RG23 .... 68 B3
Lilian Pl GU34 .... 161 E2
Lillywhite Cres SP10 .... 83 D2
Lily Cl RG22 .... 91 D4
Limbrey Hill RG29 .... 94 B4
Lime Ave GU34 .... 139 F3
Camberley GU15 .... 36 C3
Lime Cl RG14 .... 2 A2
Lime Cres GU11 .... 100 A4
Lime Gdns RG21 .... 69 E3
Lime Gr GU34 .... 139 F3
Lime Kiln Cotts The GU34 .. 42 B4
Lime Rd SO24 .... 179 E3
Lime St GU11 .... 76 B2
Lime Tree Way RG24 .... 48 C2
Lime Wlk SP10 .... 105 E3
Limecroft GU17 .... 34 A3
Limekiln Rd SP11 .... 58 A2
Limes Cl Bramshott GU30 . 188 A4
Liss GU33 .... 208 A2
Limes Rd GU14 .... 55 D3
Limes The
Basingstoke RG22 .... 91 D4
Bramley RG26 .... 26 C4
Haslemere GU27 .... 189 F3
Limetree Ave RG20 .... 21 F1
Limetree Wlk 3 SO23 ..... 198 B4
Limington House Sch RG22 68 B2
Linchmere Rd GU27 .... 189 D3
Lincoln Cl Basingstoke RG22 91 D4
Camberley GU15 .... 36 C2
Lincoln Ct Liphook GU30 .. 188 A2
Newbury RG14 .... 1 B1
Lincoln Gn GU34 .... 139 F1
Linden Ave Odiham RG29 ... 72 C2
Old Basing RG24 .... 70 A3
Linden Cl Ludgershall SP11 .. 57 D1
Newbury RG14 .... 1 B2
Linden Ct
Camberley GU15, GU16 .... 36 B4
Old Basing RG24 .... 70 A3
Linden Dr GU33 .... 207 F2
Linden Rd
Bishop's Green RG20 .... 6 B2
Headley GU35 .... 166 A3
Lindens The GU9 .... 99 D1
Lindford Chase GU35 .... 164 C3
Lindford Rd GU35 .... 164 C3
Lindford Wey GU35 .... 164 C3
Lindum Cl GU11 .... 76 C1
Lindum Dene GU11 .... 76 C1

Linford Rd GU35 .... 164 C3
Ling Cres GU35 .... 165 F3
Lingfield Cl Alton GU34 .... 139 F1
Old Basing RG24 .... 70 B3
Lingfield Rd RG14 .... 6 A4
Lingman Gro GU13 .... 75 D3
Link Ho 4 RG14 .... 1 C1
Link Rd Alton GU34 .... 140 A3
Kingsclere RG20 .... 24 C1
Newbury RG14 .... 1 C1
Link The Andover SP10 ..... 105 E4
Yateley GU17 .... 34 A4
Link View RG14 .... 1 B4
Link Way Oakley RG22 .... 67 D1
Thatcham RG18 .... 2 C2
Linklater's Cotts GU13 .... 54 C4
Links Rd SO22 .... 175 E1
Links The GU33 .... 164 A1
Links Way GU14 .... 55 D2
Linkside E GU26 .... 167 D4
Linkside N GU26 .... 166 C4
Linkside S GU26 .... 167 D3
Linkway Camberley GU15 .... 36 A2
Fleet GU13 .... 74 C3
Linkway Par GU13 .... 74 C3
Linnel La RG22 .... 68 A1
Linnet Cl RG22 .... 91 C3
Linnet La RG19 .... 6 B2
Linnets Rd SO24 .... 179 E2
Linnets Way GU34 .... 139 F3
Linsford Bsns Pk GU16 .... 56 B2
Linsford La GU16 .... 56 B2
Linsley Gdns SO24 .... 179 E2
Linstead Rd GU14 .... 55 E4
Linsted La GU35 .... 165 D4
Linton Cl RG26 .... 27 D4
Linton Dr SP10 .... 83 D1
Lion and Lamb Way 4 GU9 98 C1
Lion and Lamb Yd GU9 .... 98 C1
Lion Cl Haslemere GU27 ... 189 E4
Overton RG25 .... 88 A4
Lion Ct RG21 .... 69 F3
Lion Gn GU27 .... 189 E3
Lion La GU27 .... 189 E4
Lion Mead GU27 .... 189 E3
Lion Way GU13 .... 75 D3
Lions Field GU35 .... 163 E2
Lions Hall 25 SO22 .... 197 F4
Liphook CE Jun Sch GU30 187 F2
Liphook Inf Sch GU30 .... 187 F2
Liphook Rd Bordon GU35 .. 186 B4
Bramshott GU30 .... 165 E2
Haslemere GU27 .... 189 E3
Headley GU35 .... 166 B2
Linchmere GU27 .... 188 C2
Lindford GU35 .... 164 C3
Liphook Sta GU30 .... 188 A1
Lipscombe Cl RG14 .... 1 B1
Lipscombe Rise GU34 .... 139 F3
Lisa Ct 1 RG21 .... 69 F2
Liskeard Dr GU14 .... 55 E3
Lisle Cl Newbury RG14 .... 1 B3
Winchester SO22 .... 197 D2
Lismoyne Cl GU13 .... 53 F1
Liss Schs GU33 .... 208 A2
Liss Sta GU33 .... 207 F2
Lister Rd RG23 .... 68 C1
Litchfield Cl SP10 .... 82 B2
Litchfield Ho RG26 .... 26 C4
Litchfield Rd SO22 .... 175 E2
Litten The RG20 .... 24 B1
Little Aldershot La RG7 .... 8 C1
Little Austins Rd GU10 ..... 122 A4
Little Barn Pl GU33 .... 208 A2
Little Copse Andover SP10 . 105 F3
Fleet GU13 .... 74 C4
Little Copse Chase RG24 .... 48 C1
Little Croft GU34 .... 34 A3
Little Dean Ct SO20 .... 150 A2
Little Dean Ho SO20 .... 150 A2
Little Dean La
South Warnborough RG25 .. 94 C3
Upton Grey RG25 .... 94 C3
Little Drove Rd SO20 .... 129 D2
Little Fallow RG24 .... 70 A4
Little Green La GU10 .... 121 F3
Little Hatherden SP11 .... 59 F1
Little Hayes La SO21 .... 177 F4
Little Hoddington RG25 ...... 94 B3
Little Hoddington Cl RG25 . 94 B3
Little Knowl Hill RG20 .... 24 C2
Little London Rd RG26 .... 27 F4
Little Minster St 28 SO23 . 198 A4
Little Paddock GU35 .... 36 C4
Little Thurbans Cl GU10 ... 121 E3
Little Vigo GU46 .... 33 F2
Little Wellington St GU11 ... 76 B2
Little-Ann Bridge Farm
SP11 .... 105 E3
Littlefield Cl GU12 .... 77 F3

Littlefield Gdns GU12 .... 77 F1
Littlefield Rd GU34 .... 140 A2
Littlefield Sch GU30 .... 188 A1
Littleton Cotts SP11 .... 80 B2
Littleton La SO21 .... 175 D3
Littleton Rd SO22 .... 175 D2
Littleworth Rd GU10 .... 100 B1
Litton Gdns RG23 .... 67 D1
Livery Rd SP5 .... 168 A1
Livingstone Rd
  Andover SP10 .... 83 F1
  Newbury RG14 .... 1 C1
Lock Rd GU12 .... 77 D3
Lock Sq SP10 .... 83 E1
Lock's La SO21 .... 174 B2
Locke Cl SP11 .... 124 C4
Locke Rd GU30 .... 188 A2
Locke's Dro SP11 .... 60 A4
Lockerley Endowed
  CE Prim Sch SO51 .... 192 A1
Lockerley Rd SO51 .... 192 A1
Lockram La RG7 .... 12 A4
Lockwood Cl GU14 .... 55 E4
Loddon Bsns Ctr The RG24 .. 69 F4
Loddon Cl SO25 .... 36 C3
Loddon Ct RG21 .... 69 E1
Loddon Ctr RG24 .... 69 F4
Loddon Dr RG21 .... 69 E3
Loddon Mall 24 RG21 .... 69 D3
Loddon Rd GU14 .... 55 D3
Loddon Sch The RG24 .... 49 E3
Loddon Way GU12 .... 77 F1
Lodge Cl SP10 .... 105 F4
Lodge Dr SP11 .... 81 E1
Lodge Gr GU46 .... 34 B3
Lodge Hill Cl GU9 .... 122 A3
Lodge Hill Rd GU9 .... 122 B3
Lodge La SP11 .... 58 A2
Lodge The Farnham GU9 .... 99 E2
  Newbury RG14 .... 1 C2
Lodsworth GU14 .... 55 D2
Loggon Rd RG21 .... 69 D1
Loman Rd GU16 .... 56 C2
Lomond Cl RG23 .... 67 D1
Londlandes GU13 .... 74 C2
London Rd Alton GU34 .... 140 B3
  Andover SP10 .... 106 B4
  Andover SP10 .... 106 C4
  Basingstoke RG21 .... 69 E2
  Blackwater GU15 .... 35 E3
  Camberley GU15 .... 36 A3
  Camberley GU15 .... 36 B4
  Hartley Wintney RG27 .... 52 B3
  Hill Brow GU33 .... 208 A1
  Hook RG27 .... 51 E1
  Kings Worthy SO23 ...... 176 A3
  Laverstoke RG28 .... 87 D3
  Liphook GU30 .... 188 A3
  Newbury RG14 .... 2 A2
  Odiham RG29 .... 72 C2
  Odiham RG29 .... 72 C3
  Old Basing RG24 .... 70 B3
  Overton RG25 .... 88 A4
  Stockbridge SO20 ...... 150 B2
  Whitchurch RG28 .... 86 C3
London St Andover SP10 .. 106 A4
  Basingstoke RG21 .... 69 D2
  Whitchurch RG28 .... 86 B3
Long Beech Dr GU14 .... 55 D2
Long Bridge GU9 .... 99 D1
Long Cl SO22 .... 197 F3
Long Copse Chase RG24 .... 48 C2
Long Cross Hill GU35 ...... 165 E3
Long Cross La RG22 .... 91 D3
Long Gdn Mews GU9 .... 98 C1
Long Gdn Way GU9 .... 98 C1
Long Gdn Wlk GU9 .... 98 C1
Long Gdn Wlk E GU9 .... 98 C1
Long Gdn Wlk W GU9 .... 98 C1
Long Gr RG26 .... 9 D1
Long Hill GU11 .... 100 B1
Long La Chineham RG24 .... 49 D1
  Long Sutton RG29 ...... 96 A3
  Newbury RG14 .... 2 A4
  Odiham RG29 .... 96 A3
Long Leaze SP11 .... 61 E2
Long Rd The GU9 .... 121 F2
Long Sutton CE Prim Sch
  RG29 .... 95 F2
Long Wlk SO21 .... 176 C2
Longacre Ash GU12 .... 77 F1
  Liss GU33 .... 208 A2
  Newbury RG14 .... 5 D4
Longacre Rise RG24 .... 48 C1
Longbarrow Cl SO21 ...... 153 F2
Longbridge Cl RG26 .... 29 F1
Longbridge Rd RG26 .... 28 C2
Longcroft GU10 .... 120 A3
Longcroft Cl 4
  RG21, RG24, RG25 .... 69 D2
Longcroft Rd RG20 .... 24 B2

Longdene Rd GU27 .... 189 F3
Longdown GU13 .... 74 C3
Longdown Cl GU10 ...... 122 A3
Longdown Lodge GU46 .. 34 C4
Longdown Rd GU10 ...... 122 A3
Longfellow Par
  RG21, RG24, RG25 ...... 69 E4
Longfield Cl
  Farnborough GU14 .... 55 F4
  North Waltham RG25 ...... 89 F1
Longfield Rd Ash GU11 .... 77 F1
  Winchester SO23 .... 198 B4
Longford Cl GU15 .... 36 A2
Longhope Dr GU9 .... 121 F3
Longhouse Gn 9 SO23 .... 198 B4
Longleat Sq GU16 .... 56 A2
Longley Rd GU9 .... 99 D1
Longmead Fleet GU13 .... 75 D3
  Liss GU33 .... 207 F2
  Woolton Hill RG20 .... 4 B1
Longmeadow GU17 .... 36 B2
Longmoor Dr GU30 ...... 187 D2
Longmoor La RG7 .... 11 F4
Longmoor Rd
  Basingstoke RG21 .... 69 D2
  Bordon GU33 .... 186 A2
  Greatham GU33 .... 186 A2
  Liphook GU30 .... 187 E2
Longparish CE Prim Sch
  SP11 .... 108 A2
Longparish Cl 11 SP10 .. 106 A4
Longparish Rd
  Hurstbourne Priors SP10 .. 85 E1
  Longparish SP11 .... 107 F1
  Wherwell SP11 .... 107 F1
Longs Cl RG28 .... 86 B3
Longstock Cl Andover SP10 105 F4
  Chineham RG24 .... 49 D2
Longstock Ct 15 SP10 .. 106 A4
Longstock Rd
  Goodworth Clatford SP11 128 A4
  Wherwell SP11 .... 128 A4
Longwater La Eversley GU46 33 E4
  Finchampstead RG40 ...... 16 B2
Longwater Rd
  Eversley RG40 .... 16 B1
  Finchampstead RG40 ...... 16 B1
Lopcombe Corner SP4 .... 146 A2
Lord Mayor Treloar
  Coll of F Ed GU34 ...... 140 A3
Lord Mayor Treloar Coll
  GU34 .... 119 D1
Lord Wandsworth Coll
  RG29 .... 95 F1
Lordsfield Rd RG25 .... 88 A4
Lordswood RG26 .... 27 F4
Lorraine Cty Fst Sch
  GU15, GU17 .... 36 B4
Lorraine Rd GU15 .... 36 B4
Louisburg Rd GU35 ...... 164 B3
Louise Margaret Rd GU11 .. 76 C2
Loundyes Cl RG18 .... 2 C2
Love La
  Andover SP10 .... 106 A4
  Kingsclere RG20 .... 24 B1
  Newbury RG14 .... 1 C3
  Odiham RG29 .... 72 B1
Lovedon La SO23 .... 176 B4
Lovegroves RG40 .... 49 D2
Lovell Cl
  South Wonston SO21 .. 153 F2
  Thruxton SP11 .... 103 E4
Lovells Wlk SO24 ...... 179 E3
Loveridge Cl
  Basingstoke RG21 .... 69 D1
  Knights Enham SP10 ...... 83 D2
Lovers La GU10 .... 144 A4
Lovett Wood RG7 .... 11 E3
Lovett No 1 GU9 .... 98 C1
Lovett Wlk SO22 .... 175 E2
Lovington La SO24 .... 178 B2
Low La GU9 .... 99 F3
Lowa Cl SP9 .... 78 C3
Lowa Rd SP9 .... 78 C3
Lowden Cl SO22 .... 197 E2
Lower Brook St
  Basingstoke RG21 .... 68 C3
  12 Winchester SO23 ...... 198 A4
Lower Canes GU46 .... 33 F3
Lower Charles St GU16 .... 36 A3
Lower Chestnut Dr RG22 .. 68 C2
Lower Church La GU9 ...... 98 C1
Lower Church Rd GU46 .. 34 B4
Lower Comm RG27 .... 15 E1
Lower Evingar Rd RG28 .. 86 B3
Lower Farm Ct RG19 ...... 2 B1
Lower Farnham Rd GU10 .. 100 A4
Lower Hanger GU27 ...... 189 D3
Lower Lamborough La
  SO24 .... 201 A3
Lower Moor GU46 .... 34 A3

Lower Neatham Mill La
  Alton GU34 .... 140 B3
  Alton, Neatham GU34 .. 140 C3
Lower Nelson St GU11 .... 76 C1
Lower Newport Rd GU12 .. 77 D1
Lower Paice La GU34 .... 159 E2
Lower Raymond Almshouses
  RG14 .... 1 B1
Lower Sandhurst Rd RG40 .. 16 C1
Lower South View GU9 .... 99 D2
Lower St GU27 .... 189 F3
Lower Stanmore La SO23 . 197 F3
Lower Turk St GU34 ...... 139 F2
Lower Way RG19 .... 2 C2
Lower Weybourne La GU9 .. 99 F3
Lower Wote St RG24 ...... 69 D3
Lowicks Rd GU10 .... 144 C3
Lowlands Rd
  Basingstoke RG22 .... 68 A2
  Blackwater GU15 .... 35 D2
Lowry Cl GU15 .... 35 D3
Lowry Ct SP10 .... 82 C1
Loxwood Ave GU13 ...... 74 C4
Loyalty La RG24 .... 70 A3
Lubeck Dr SP10 .... 82 C2
Lucas Cl GU46 .... 34 A3
Lucas Field GU27 ...... 189 E3
Ludgershall Castle Prim Sch
  SP11 .... 57 D1
Ludgershall Rd SP9 ...... 78 C4
Ludlow Cl Basingstoke RG22 68 B3
  Camberley GU16 .... 56 C4
  Newbury RG14 .... 2 B2
Ludlow Gdns RG22 .... 91 D3
Ludshott Gr GU35 ...... 165 F3
Luke Rd GU9 .... 99 E4
Luke Rd E GU9 .... 99 E4
Lulworth Cl GU14 .... 55 F4
Lundy Cl RG24 .... 44 C3
Lune Cl 8 RG21 .... 69 E3
Lune Ct 48 SP10 .... 83 E1
Lupin Cl RG22 .... 91 D4
Lutyens Cl Basingstoke RG21 69 F4
  Chineham RG24 .... 48 C1
Lyall Pl GU9 .... 98 C4
Lych Gate Cl GU47 ...... 34 B4
Lydc Cl RG23 .... 67 D1
Lydford Cl Camberley GU16 . 56 C4
  Farnborough GU14 ...... 55 F4
Lye Copse Ave GU14 ...... 55 F4
Lyeway Cl
  East Tisted SO24 ...... 182 B2
  Ropley SO24 .... 182 B2
Lyeway Rd
  Four Marks SO24 ...... 182 A3
  Ropley SO24 .... 182 A3
Lyford Rd RG21 .... 69 D3
Lymington Ave GU46 ...... 34 A3
Lymington Bottom GU34 .. 160 A1
Lymington Bottom Rd
  Four Marks GU34 ...... 160 A2
  Medstead GU34 .... 160 A2
Lymington Cl
  Basingstoke RG22 .... 91 D4
  Four Marks GU34 ...... 160 A1
Lymington Rise GU34 .... 160 A1
Lyn Cl 6 RG22 .... 69 E3
Lynch Cl SO22 .... 175 F1
Lynch Hill RG28 .... 86 B3
Lynch Hill Pk RG28 ...... 86 B3
Lynchford La GU11 ...... 99 E1
Lynch The Overton RG25 .. 87 F4
  Whitchurch RG28 .... 86 B3
Lynchborough Rd GU30 .. 187 D4
Lynchford Rd
  Farnborough GU12 ...... 77 D4
  Farnborough GU12 ...... 77 F4
Lyndale Dr GU13 .... 54 B1
Lyndford Terr GU13 ...... 74 C4
Lyndhurst Ave
  Aldershot GU10 .... 100 A3
  Blackwater GU17 .... 35 D3
Lyndhurst Cl SO22 ...... 175 E2
Lyndhurst Dr RG22 ...... 91 E3
Lyndhurst Sch GU17 .... 35 F3
Lyndsey Cl GU13 .... 54 C2
Lynford Ave SO22 ...... 175 F1
Lynford Way SO22 ...... 175 F1
Lynn Way GU14 .... 55 E4
Lynton Cl GU10 .... 121 F4
Lynton Ct RG14 .... 1 C2
Lynton Meadow SO20 .... 129 D2
Lynton Rd GU35 .... 164 B2
Lynwood Cl GU35 ...... 165 D3
Lynwood Ct SO22 ...... 175 F1
Lynwood Dr Andover SP10 105 F4
  Mytchett GU16 .... 56 C2
Lynwood Gdns RG27 ...... 51 D1
Lyon Way GU16 .... 36 A1
Lyon Way Ind Est GU16 .. 36 A1
Lyse Ct GU33 .... 207 F2

Lysons Ave GU12 .... 77 E4
Lysons Rd GU11 .... 76 C1
Lytham Cl GU35 .... 164 A1
Lytton Rd RG24 .... 69 E3

Mabbs La RG27 .... 52 B2
Mac Callum Rd
  Enham Alamein SP10 ...... 83 D4
  Smannell SP10 .... 83 D4
Macadam Way SP10 ...... 82 A1
Macdonald Rd GU9 ...... 98 C4
MacDonald's Almshouses 10
  GU9 .... 98 C1
Macklin Rd 16 SO22 .... 197 F4
Macrae Rd GU46 .... 34 A3
Maddocks Hill SO24 .... 181 D2
Madeira Ct RG24 .... 48 B1
Madeira Pl 8 RG14 ...... 1 C1
Madeley Rd GU13 .... 75 D3
Madox Brown End GU47 .. 35 E3
Madrid Rd SP10 .... 83 E1
Magdalen Hill SO23 ...... 198 A4
Magdalen Mews 41 SO23 . 198 A4
Magellan Cl SP10 .... 83 F1
Magnolia Cl SP10 ...... 105 F4
Magnolia Ho RG24 ...... 48 A1
Magnolia Way GU13 ...... 75 D4
Magnus Dr RG22 .... 91 D4
Magpie Cl Basingstoke RG22 90 C4
  Bordon GU35 .... 164 C1
  Ewshot GU9 .... 98 A4
  Thatcham RG19 .... 2 C2
Mahler Cl RG22 .... 91 F4
Maida Rd GU11 .... 76 C2
Maidenthorn La RG22 .... 90 A1
Main Rd Littleton SO22 .. 175 D3
  Tadley RG26 .... 27 D3
Main St RG19 .... 6 C3
Maitland Rd GU14 ...... 76 C4
Maitlands Cl GU11, GU12 .. 100 B3
Majendie Cl RG14 .... 1 A3
Majestic Rd RG22 .... 91 D4
Majorca Ave SP10 .... 83 E1
Makins Ct SO24 .... 179 E3
Maldive Rd RG24 .... 48 B1
Malham Gdns RG22 ...... 91 D3
Mall The Andover SP10 .. 106 A4
  South Tidworth SP9 ...... 78 B2
Mallard Cl Andover SP10 .. 83 D1
  Ash GU11 .... 77 D1
  Basingstoke RG22 .... 90 C4
  Haslemere GU27 .... 189 E3
  New Alresford SO24 ...... 179 E3
Mallard Way 4 GU46 ...... 33 F3
Mallards GU34 .... 139 F3
Mallow Cl GU35 .... 165 D3
Malmesbury Gdns SO22 .. 175 E1
Malmesbury Ho 2 SP9 .... 79 D3
Malpass Rd SO21 ...... 153 C1
Malshanger La RG23 ...... 67 D2
Malt Ho RG24 .... 48 B1
Malt Ho 22 SO22 ...... 197 F4
Malta Cl RG24 .... 48 A1
Maltbys GU34 .... 184 C4
Malters End GU26 .... 166 C2
Malthouse Bridge Cotts
  GU13 .... 74 B3
Malthouse Cl Fleet GU13 .. 74 C3
  Itchen Abbas SO21 ...... 176 C2
Malthouse Cotts RG29 .... 72 B2
Malthouse Ct GU30 ...... 188 A2
Malthouse La
  Bighton SO24 .... 158 B1
  Smannell SP10 .... 83 E4
  Tadley RG26 .... 27 D3
  Upper Chute SP11 ...... 58 A4
Malthouse Meadows GU30 188 A2
Malthouse Mews GU34 .... 140 B3
Maltings Cl GU34 ...... 139 F2
Maltings The GU30 ...... 188 A2
Malvern Cl RG22 .... 68 A2
Malvern Ct RG14 .... 1 B1
Malvern Rd
  Farnborough GU14 ...... 55 D4
  Hawley GU47 .... 34 B1
  Hill Brow GU33 .... 208 A1
Mandarin Ct Farnham GU11 99 D3
  Newbury RG14 .... 2 A1
Mandora Rd GU11 ...... 76 C2
Manfield Rd GU14 .... 77 F1
Manica Cl GU35 .... 164 B2
Manley Bridge Rd GU10 .. 121 E3
Manley James Cl RG29 .. 72 C2
Mann Rd RG28 .... 86 B2
Manningford Cl SO23 .... 176 A2
Manor Bridge Ct SP9 .... 78 C4
Manor Cl Abbotts Ann SP10 105 D2
  Alton GU34 .... 140 A3
  Basingstoke RG22 .... 91 D3
  Haslemere GU27 .... 189 E3
  Shipton Bellinger SP9 .. 101 F4

Manor Cl continued
  Tongham GU11 .... 100 B4
  Winchester SO23 ...... 198 A4
Manor Copse SP10 ...... 83 D3
Manor Cotts RG28 .... 87 D3
Manor Cres GU27 ...... 189 E3
Manor Ct GU13 .... 75 D2
Manor Farm Bsns Ctr
  GU10 .... 100 B3
Manor Farm Cl GU12 ...... 77 D1
Manor Farm Cotts SO21 .. 131 D1
Manor Farm La SO51 .... 193 F1
Manor Field Schs RG22 .. 91 F4
Manor Fields
  Liphook GU30 .... 188 A2
  Seale GU10 .... 100 C2
Manor Gdns GU10 ...... 122 A3
Manor Ho The GU15 ...... 36 A3
Manor House Farm SO24 . 180 B2
Manor House Flats GU10 .. 100 B3
Manor La Old Basing RG24 .. 70 A3
  Thatcham RG18 .... 2 B3
Manor Lea GU27 .... 189 E3
Manor Park Cotts
  8 Alton GU34 .... 139 F2
  Alton, Wilsom GU34 ...... 140 A2
Manor Park Ctr,
  Farnborough Coll of Tech
  GU11 .... 76 C1
Manor Park Dr
  Wokingham RG40 ...... 16 B3
  Yateley GU46 .... 34 B3
Manor Park Ind Est GU12 .. 77 D1
Manor Pl RG14 .... 1 A3
Manor Rd Aldershot GU9 .. 99 F4
  Alton GU34 .... 140 A3
  Andover SP10 .... 82 C1
  Ash GU10 .... 100 B4
  East Tytherley SP5 ...... 191 F4
  Farnborough GU16 ...... 56 A2
  Farnham GU9 .... 99 E2
  Sherborne St John RG26 .. 47 F2
  Tongham GU10 .... 100 B4
Manor Rise SP10 .... 105 F2
Manor Schs SO24 .... 55 E3
Manor View RG7 .... 8 B4
Manor Wlk GU14 .... 76 C1
Manorside Cl GU12 ...... 100 B4
Manse La RG26 .... 27 D3
Mansell Dr RG14 .... 5 D3
Mansfield Rd RG23 ...... 68 C1
Mansion House St 10 RG14 .. 1 C2
Maple Cl Alton GU34 ...... 139 F3
  Ash GU12 .... 77 E4
  Blackwater GU17 ...... 35 D3
  Middle Wallop SO20 .... 126 A2
  New Alresford SO24 ...... 179 E2
Maple Cres
  Basingstoke RG22 .... 69 D4
  Ludgershall SP11 ...... 57 D1
  Newbury RG14 .... 1 C2
Maple Ct RG23 .... 68 A2
Maple Dr SO23 .... 176 A4
Maple Gdns GU17, GU46 .. 34 A3
Maple Gr RG26 .... 26 C4
Maple Leaf Cl GU14 ...... 55 E2
Maple Leaf Dr GU35 ...... 164 B2
Maple Ridge Special Sch
  RG24 .... 69 D4
Maple Terr 5 SP9 ...... 79 D4
Maple Way GU35 ...... 165 F3
Maple Wlk Aldershot GU10 100 A4
  Andover SP11 .... 105 E3
Maplehurst Chase RG22 .. 91 D3
March Cl SP10 .... 83 D1
Marchant Rd SP11 ...... 105 F4
Marchants Hill Activity Ctr
  GU26 .... 167 D4
Marconi Rd RG14 .... 1 C2
Mareth Cl GU11 .... 76 C1
Margaret Rd RG22 ...... 68 B2
Margha Rd SP9 .... 78 C3
Marigold Cl RG22 ...... 91 D4
Mariners Ct RG26 .... 27 D3
Mariners Dr GU16 .... 56 A3
Marino Way RG40 .... 15 F3
Mark La 17 RG21 .... 69 D2
Mark Way Special Sch The
  SP10 .... 106 B4
Markall Cl SO24 .... 201 E3
Markel Rd SO23 .... 198 A4
Market Pl Basingstoke RG21 69 D2
  11 Newbury RG14 .... 1 C2
Market St Alton GU34 .... 139 F2
  Newbury RG14 .... 1 C1
  Winchester SO23 ...... 198 A4

Markham Ct GU16 .... 36 A3
Markson Rd SO21 .... 153 E2
Marl's La RG24 .... 48 A3
Marlborough Cl GU13 .... 75 E4
Marlborough Cty Inf Sch GU12 .... 77 D4
Marlborough Gdns RG23 .... 67 D1
Marlborough Rise GU15 .... 36 A3
Marlborough St SP10 .... 106 A4
Marlborough Trad Mews RG24 .... 48 C1
Marlborough View GU14 .... 55 E4
Marley Combe Rd GU27 .... 189 E2
Marley Hanger GU27 .... 189 F2
Marley La GU27 .... 189 E2
Marlowe Cl RG24 .... 69 E4
Marlowes The RG14 .... 5 A3
Marnel Schs RG24 .... 48 B1
Marrowbrook Cl GU14 .... 55 F2
Marrowbrook La GU14 .... 55 F2
Mars Ho 12 RG26 .... 9 E1
Marsden Ct RG28 .... 87 E3
Marsh Cl GU35 .... 164 C2
Marsh La Bentley GU10 .... 120 B3
Eversley GU46 .... 33 E4
Newbury RG14 .... 1 C2
Marshall Cl GU14 .... 55 E4
Marshall Gdns RG21 .... 69 D4
Marshall Rd GU15 .... 35 E3
Marshall Sq SP11 .... 83 E1
Marshalls GU9 .... 121 F4
Marshalls Ct RG14 .... 1 A3
Marshcourt RG21 .... 69 F4
Marston Dr
Farnborough GU14 .... 55 F4
Newbury RG14 .... 2 A3
Marston Rd GU9 .... 98 B1
Martin Cl Basingstoke RG24 .... 69 E3
North Tidworth SP9 .... 79 D3
Martin Way Andover SP10 .... 83 D1
Camberley GU16 .... 36 B1
Martingale Ct 8 GU11 .... 76 B1
Martins Cl Alton GU34 .... 140 A3
Blackwater GU47 .... 35 D2
Martins Fields SO21 .... 197 E1
Martins La SO20 .... 129 E2
Martins Wood RG24 .... 48 C2
Mary La
Newton Valence GU34 .... 183 D4
North Waltham RG25 .... 89 F1
Mary Rose Ct RG22 .... 68 C2
Maryland RG40 .... 16 B4
Maskell Way GU14 .... 55 D2
Mason Ct RG20 .... 4 B1
Mason Pl GU17 .... 34 B4
Mason Rd GU14 .... 55 E3
Mason Way GU11, GU12 .... 99 F4
Mathew Terr GU11 .... 77 D1
Mathews-Cl GU14 .... 77 E4
Mathias Wlk RG22 .... 91 E4
Matilda Dr RG22 .... 91 D4
Matilda Pl 3 SO23 .... 198 A4
Matthew Rd GU10, GU9 .... 99 E4
Matthews Rd GU15 .... 36 A4
Matthews Way RG23 .... 67 E1
Mattock Way RG24 .... 48 C2
Maultway Cl GU15 .... 36 C4
Maultway Cres GU16 .... 36 C4
Maultway N GU15 .... 36 C4
Maultway The GU15 .... 36 C4
Mavins Rd GU10 .... 122 A4
Maw Cl RG22 .... 91 F4
May Cl Headley GU35 .... 165 E2
Old Basing RG21 .... 70 B3
Sandhurst GU17 .... 35 D4
May Cres GU12 .... 77 E1
May Pl RG21 .... 69 D2
May St RG21 .... 68 C3
May Tree Cl SO22 .... 197 F2
May Tree Rd SP10 .... 82 B1
May's La RG7 .... 10 C4
Maybrook RG24 .... 48 C2
Maybury Cl GU16 .... 56 A4
Mayfair Dr RG14 .... 1 B1
Mayfair Ho 9 RG24 .... 69 D3
Mayfield GU10 .... 121 E2
Mayfield Ave Ind Pk SP11 .... 81 F1
Mayfield Cl Farnham GU11 .... 99 F3
Shipton Bellinger SP9 .... 101 E4
Mayfield Cl GU46 .... 33 D4
Mayfield Cty Schs GU14 .... 55 F3
Mayfield Rd Camberley GU47 .... 35 F1
Farnborough GU14 .... 55 E3
Mayfield Ridge RG22 .... 91 E3
Mayflower Cl RG24 .... 48 C1
Mayflower Dr GU46 .... 33 F4
Mayflower Rd GU35 .... 164 B1
Mayhill Cty Jun Sch RG29 .... 72 C1

Mayors La RG14 .... 1 C1
Maywood Dr GU15 .... 36 C4
Mc Carthy Way RG40 .... 16 B4
McCartney Wlk RG21 .... 91 E4
McFauld Way RG28 .... 86 B2
Mckay Cl GU11 .... 77 D2
Mckernan Ct GU46 .... 34 B4
McNaughton Cl GU14 .... 55 D2
Mead Cl SP10 .... 105 F4
Mead Hatchgate RG27 .... 51 D1
Mead Hedges SP10 .... 105 F3
Mead Hedges Footpath SP10 .... 105 F4
Mead La GU9 .... 98 C1
Mead Rd Andover SP10 .... 105 F4
Hindhead GU26 .... 167 E2
Winchester SO23 .... 197 F2
Mead The
Farnborough GU14 .... 55 F2
Liphook GU30 .... 187 F3
Liss GU33 .... 207 F2
Old Basing RG24 .... 70 A3
Meade Rd SP11 .... 52 B3
Meadham La RG26 .... 44 C2
Meadow Bank GU9 .... 98 C1
Meadow Cl Ash GU14 .... 56 B1
Blackwater GU17 .... 35 D2
Liphook GU30 .... 188 A2
New Alresford SO24 .... 179 E3
Meadow Ct
Farnborough GU14 .... 55 E2
10 Fleet GU13 .... 53 F1
Meadow Dr SP11 .... 127 F4
Meadow End GU30 .... 188 A3
Meadow Vale GU27 .... 189 F3
Meadow Rd
Basingstoke RG21 .... 69 D1
Farnborough GU14 .... 55 F1
Meadow Rise RG25 .... 89 F1
Meadow Special Sch GU35 .... 165 D2
Meadow Vale GU27 .... 189 F3
Meadow View
Bordon GU35 .... 164 C2
Fleet GU13 .... 74 C3
Micheldever SO21 .... 133 D2
Ropley SO24 .... 158 A1
Whitchurch RG28 .... 86 A3
Meadow Way
Aldershot GU12 .... 77 E2
Blackwater GU47 .... 35 D3
Farnham GU10 .... 121 E2
Liphook GU30 .... 188 A3
Winchester SO22 .... 197 E2
Meadow Wlk Fleet GU13 .... 74 B4
1 Liss GU33 .... 207 F2
Meadowbank RG20 .... 3 F4
Meadowland
Chineham RG24 .... 48 C2
Kings Worthy SO23 .... 174 A4
Meadowridge RG22 .... 91 E3
Meadows The Ash GU12 .... 77 F1
Churt GU10 .... 144 B1
Sandhurst GU15 .... 35 E3
Sherfield on Loddon RG7 .... 29 E1
Meads The GU27 .... 189 E3
Meadsview Ct 4 GU14 .... 55 F2
Meadway Camberley GU15 .... 36 B1
Haslemere GU27 .... 189 E3
Mede Cl RG25 .... 88 A4
Medina Cl 14 SP10 .... 83 E1
Medina Gdns RG23 .... 67 D1
Medlar Dr GU17 .... 35 E2
Medonte Cl GU13 .... 75 D4
Medstead CE Prim Sch GU34 .... 159 F3
Medstead & Four Marks Sta GU34 .... 160 A2
Medstead Rd GU34 .... 139 D1
Medway Ave RG23 .... 67 D1
Medway Cl RG18 .... 2 C3
Medway Ct
10 Andover SP10 .... 83 E1
13 Basingstoke RG21 .... 69 E3
Medway Dr GU14 .... 55 E4
Meerut Rd SP9 .... 78 C3
Meitner Cl RG24 .... 28 C2
Meldrum Cl RG14 .... 5 D3
Melford Gdns RG22 .... 68 A1
Meliot Rise SP10 .... 83 D2
Melksham Ho 1 SP9 .... 78 C3
Mellersh Cl GU13 .... 74 C2
Melrose Ave GU14 .... 55 D2
Melrose Cl GU35 .... 164 B1
Melrose Wlk RG21 .... 69 D4
Melville Ave GU15 .... 36 B1
Membury Cl RG14 .... 56 C4
Memorial Bglws RG25 .... 87 D3
Memorial Rd RG29 .... 72 A4
Mendip Cl RG21 .... 68 A2
Mendip Rd GU11 .... 55 E4
Menin Way GU11 .... 99 D1

Meon Cl Farnborough GU14 .... 55 D3
Tadley RG26 .... 9 F1
Meon Rd RG21 .... 67 D1
Meon Wlk RG21 .... 69 E3
Mercer Cl RG21 .... 68 A4
Merchants Pl 9 SO23 .... 198 A4
Mercia Ave SP10 .... 82 B2
Mercury Cl GU35 .... 164 C2
Mercury Ho 7 RG7 .... 9 F1
Merepond La GU34 .... 204 C2
Meriden Ct 10 SO23 .... 176 A1
Merivale GU13 .... 74 B4
Merlin Ct GU15 .... 36 A1
Merlin Rd GU34 .... 160 A1
Merlin Way GU14 .... 55 D2
Merlins Cl GU9 .... 99 D1
Merriatt Cl RG21 .... 69 D1
Merrileas Gdns RG22 .... 91 D4
Merron Cl GU46 .... 34 A3
Merrydown La RG24 .... 49 D1
Merryfield RG24 .... 48 C2
Merrywood Pk GU10 .... 36 B2
Merryworth Cl GU12 .... 77 E1
Mersey Ct 50 SP10 .... 83 E1
Mersey Way RG18 .... 2 C3
Merton Rd RG21 .... 69 D3
Merton Schs RG24 .... 69 D4
Meryon Rd SO24 .... 179 E2
Mesh Rd SO51 .... 193 D1
Methuen Rd GU33 .... 186 B2
Meudon Ave GU14 .... 55 F2
Meudon Rd GU14 .... 55 F2
Mews La SO22 .... 197 F4
Mews The Andover SP10 .... 106 A3
Bramley RG26 .... 29 D1
Farley Castle RG2 .... 15 D4
Meyrick Dr RG14 .... 5 A3
Michaelmas Cl GU47 .... 34 A2
Michaelmas Dro SP11 .... 81 D1
Micheldever Sta SO21 .... 111 D1
Midas Ho 17 RG7 .... 9 F1
Middle Ave GU10 .... 122 A4
Middle Bourne La GU9 .... 122 A4
Middle Brook St SO23 .... 198 A4
Middle Church La GU9 .... 98 C1
Middle Cl Camberley GU16 .... 36 C3
Newbury RG14 .... 5 A3
Middle Gordon Rd GU16 .... 36 A3
Middle Head RG27 .... 51 D1
Middle Hill GU12 .... 76 C2
Middle Meadow GU33 .... 208 A2
Middle Old Pk GU9 .... 98 B2
Middle Rd SO22 .... 197 F4
Middle Wallop Airfield SO20 .... 126 A1
Middlefield GU11 .... 121 F4
Middlefield Cl GU10 .... 121 F4
Middlemead RG27 .... 51 D1
Middlemoor Rd GU16 .... 56 B4
Middleton Ct RG14 .... 2 B3
Middleton Gdns
Basingstoke RG21 .... 69 D4
Farnborough GU13 .... 55 E3
Middleton Rd
Camberley GU15 .... 36 B4
Middle Winterslow SP5 .... 168 A3
Middleway The
Andover SP11 .... 107 E3
Longparish SP11 .... 107 E3
Midhurst Rd
Haslemere GU27 .... 189 F3
Liphook GU30 .... 188 A1
Midlane Cl RG21 .... 69 D1
Mike Hawthorn Dr GU9 .... 99 D2
Milbeck Cl GU16 .... 56 C3
Milden Gdns GU16 .... 56 C3
Mildmay Ct Odiham RG29 .... 72 C2
12 Winchester SO23 .... 198 A4
Mildmay St SO22 .... 197 E3
Mildmay Terr RG27 .... 52 B3
Miles Rd GU12 .... 77 F2
Milkingpen La RG24 .... 70 A3
Mill Chase Com Sch GU35 .... 164 C2
Mill Chase Rd GU35 .... 164 C2
Mill Ct Haslemere GU27 .... 189 E3
Sherfield on Loddon RG7 .... 29 F1
Mill Cnr GU13 .... 54 B2
Mill Copse Rd GU27 .... 189 F2
Mill Hill SO24 .... 179 E3
Mill Hill Ave SP9 .... 78 C4
Mill La Alton GU34 .... 140 A2
Bishop's Sutton SO24 .... 180 A3
Ecchinswell RG20 .... 23 F2
Fair Oak Green RG26 .... 29 E2
Frensham GU10 .... 143 F4
Hawkley GU34 .... 184 C1

Mill La continued
Headley GU35 .... 165 D3
Kings Worthy SO21 .... 176 B3
Longparish SP11 .... 108 B3
Middle Winterslow SP5 .... 168 A4
North Warnborough RG29 .... 72 A3
Rotherwick RG27 .... 50 B3
Sandhurst GU17 .... 34 A4
Sherfield on Loddon RG26 .... 29 E2
Steep Marsh SO22 .... 206 C1
Yateley GU46 .... 34 A3
Mill Lane Ind Est GU34 .... 140 A2
Mill Rd GU33 .... 208 A3
Mill Reef Cl RG19 .... 2 B2
Mill Rise SO51 .... 192 B1
Mill Stream GU9 .... 99 D3
Mill View RG29 .... 71 F1
Mill Ward SO23 .... 198 A3
Millard Ct RG22 .... 68 C4
Millbridge Rd GU16 .... 33 F4
Millbrook Cl GU33 .... 208 A2
Millbrook Ho RG25 .... 88 A4
Millers Cl GU12 .... 196 C2
Millers Rd RG26 .... 26 C4
Millers Yd SO21 .... 131 E2
Millgate Cl GU9 .... 99 D2
Millgreen La RG19 .... 7 E1
Millmere GU46 .... 34 A4
Mills Ho GU12 .... 77 D1
Millstream Cl SP10 .... 105 F3
Millstream The GU27 .... 189 E3
Millway Cl SP10 .... 105 F4
Millway Rd SP10 .... 105 F4
Milner Pl SO22 .... 197 F3
Milnthorpe La SO22 .... 197 F4
Milsons The SO20 .... 149 F1
Milton Ave SP10 .... 82 B1
Milton Cl RG21 .... 69 F4
Milton Grange GU12 .... 77 F3
Milverton Rd SO22 .... 197 F4
Mimosa Cl GU35 .... 165 D3
Mimosa Ct SP10 .... 105 F3
Minchens La RG26 .... 28 C2
Minden Cl RG24 .... 48 C1
Minden Way SO22 .... 197 E3
Minehurst Rd GU16 .... 56 B2
Minerva Ho 9 RG26 .... 9 E1
Ministry Rd RG14 .... 6 C3
Minley Cl GU14 .... 55 E4
Minley Gr GU13 .... 54 A2
Minley Rd
Farnborough GU13 .... 54 C4
Fleet GU13 .... 54 C4
Hawley GU13 .... 54 C4
Minstead Cl Tadley RG26 .... 26 C3
Winchester SO22 .... 175 E2
Minstead Dr GU46 .... 34 A3
Minster Ct Camberley GU15 .... 36 A4
Camberley, York Town GU17 .... 35 E2
Minster La 27 SO23 .... 198 A4
Mint Rd GU33 .... 208 A3
Minter Ct RG26 .... 9 F1
Mistletoe Rd GU46 .... 34 A2
Mitchell Ave RG27 .... 52 B3
Mitchell Bldgs GU46 .... 33 F3
Mitchell Cl SP10 .... 82 B1
Mitchell Gdns RG21 .... 91 E4
Mitford Rd SO24 .... 179 E2
Moat Cl RG26 .... 28 C2
Moffatts Cl GU46 .... 34 C4
Mole Cl GU15 .... 35 D2
Momford Rd SO22 .... 197 D2
Monachus La RG27 .... 52 B4
Monarch Cl RG22 .... 91 D3
Mongers Piece RG24 .... 49 D2
Monier Williams Rd SP11 .... 108 A2
Moniton Trad Est RG22 .... 68 A2
Monk Sherborne Rd RG26 .... 47 D3
Monk Sherborne Rd RG26 .... 46 C4
Monk's La RG14 .... 4 C1
Monk's Wlk GU10 .... 122 B4
Monks Cl Farnborough GU16 .... 56 A2
North Tidworth SP9 .... 78 C4
Monks Rd SO23 .... 176 A1
Monks Rise GU13 .... 53 E1
Monks' Well GU10 .... 99 E1
Monkshanger GU9 .... 99 E1
Monkswood Cl
Newbury RG14 .... 5 E4
Tadley RG26 .... 26 C4
Monkton La GU10 .... 99 E3
Monkton Pk GU9 .... 99 E2
Monktons La RG7 .... 12 A3
Monmouth Sq SO22 .... 197 D3
Mons Cl GU12 .... 56 A2
Montacute Cl GU16 .... 56 A2
Montague Cl GU15 .... 35 F3
Montague Pl RG21 .... 69 D2
Montague Terr RG14 .... 5 F4
Monteagle La GU46 .... 33 F3

Montgomery Cl GU46 .... 34 C4
Montgomery Ho 5 SP9 .... 78 C4
Montgomery Rd
Farnborough GU14 .... 55 E2
Newbury RG14 .... 5 E4
Montrose Cl Bordon GU35 .... 164 C1
Camberley GU15 .... 36 B1
Fleet GU13 .... 75 D4
Montserrat Pl RG24 .... 48 A1
Montserrat Rd RG24 .... 48 B1
Monument Chase GU35 .... 164 B1
Monument Cl RG14 .... 5 E4
Monxton Rd Amport SP11 .... 103 E1
Andover SP10 .... 105 D4
Grateley SP11 .... 103 E1
Moody's Hill SP5 .... 190 B1
Moons Hill Farnham GU10 .... 122 A1
Frensham GU9 .... 122 A1
Moor Cl Bordon GU35 .... 164 A2
Wokingham RG40 .... 16 B4
Moor Court La SO21 .... 174 A2
Moor La RG14 .... 1 B2
Moor Park La GU9 .... 99 F2
Moor Park Way GU9 .... 99 F2
Moor Rd Bordon GU33 .... 186 B1
Camberley GU16 .... 56 B4
Farnborough GU14 .... 55 F4
Linchmere GU27 .... 189 D3
Moor View RG24 .... 70 A4
Moorcroft Cl SO21 .... 131 E2
Moorcroft Gdns RG22 .... 68 A2
Moore Cl Andover SP10 .... 83 D1
Fleet GU13 .... 75 D3
Moore Rd GU13 .... 75 D3
Moorfield GU27 .... 189 E3
Moorhams Ave RG22 .... 91 D3
Moorings The
10 Basingstoke RG21 .... 69 E3
Grayshott GU26 .... 167 E2
Moorlands Cl
Fleet GU13 .... 75 D3
Hindhead GU26 .... 167 E2
Moorlands Pl GU17 .... 35 F2
Moorlands Rd GU15 .... 35 F2
Moors Ct RG40 .... 16 B4
Moors The GU10 .... 100 B4
Moorside Cl GU15 .... 35 F1
Moorside Rd SO23 .... 176 B1
Moot Cl SP10 .... 83 D2
Moray Ave GU15 .... 35 D4
More House Sch GU10 .... 122 A1
Moreland Cl GU34 .... 140 A1
Morestead Rd
Chilcomb SO21 .... 198 C2
Winchester SO21 .... 198 A3
Winchester SO21 .... 198 C2
Moreton Cl Churt GU10 .... 144 B1
Fleet GU13 .... 74 C2
Morgaston Rd RG24, RG26 .... 47 F4
Morland Rd GU12 .... 100 A3
Morley Cl GU46 .... 33 F3
Morley Rd
Basingstoke RG24 .... 69 D1
Farnham GU10, GU9 .... 99 D1
Mornington Ave RG40 .... 16 B4
Mornington Cl
Andover SP10, SP11 .... 106 A3
Baughurst RG26 .... 9 E1
Mornington Dr SO22 .... 175 E1
Mornington Rd GU35 .... 164 A1
Morris Rd GU14 .... 77 D4
Morris St RG27 .... 71 F4
Morse Rd RG21 .... 68 C2
Mortimer Cl
Hartley Wintney RG27 .... 52 A2
Kings Worthy SO23 .... 176 A3
Mortimer Gdns RG26 .... 27 D4
Mortimer La
2 Basingstoke RG21 .... 69 D3
West End Green RG26 .... 29 D4
Mortimer Sta RG7 .... 12 B3
Morton Cl GU14 .... 56 B1
Morval Cl GU14 .... 55 E2
Morval Rd GU46 .... 34 B3
Moscrop Ct 8 RG21 .... 69 D3
Moselle Cl GU14 .... 55 E4
Moss Cl GU33 .... 208 A1
Moss Rd SO23 .... 198 A4
Mosshill Ho RG26 .... 27 D4
Mottisfont Abbey Gdns SO51 .... 192 C1
Mottisfont Abbey (NT) SO51 .... 192 C1
Moulsham Copse La GU46 .... 33 F3
Moulsham La GU46 .... 33 F4
Mount Carmel Rd SP11 .... 124 C2
Mount Cl
Highclere RG20 .... 21 E3
Newbury RG14 .... 5 E4
Winchester SO22 .... 175 F1
Mount Hermon Rd SP11 .... 124 C2

Mount Pleasant
  Amport SP11 .... 104 A3
  Farnham GU9 .... 98 C1
  Hartley Wintney RG27 .... 52 B3
  Kings Worthy SO23 .... 176 B3
  Laverstoke RG28 .... 87 D3
  Tadley RG26 .... 26 C4
Mount Pleasant Dr RG26 ...... 26 C4
Mount Pleasant Rd
  Aldershot GU12 .... 77 D1
  Alton GU34 .... 139 F1
  Lindford GU35 .... 164 C3
Mount The Fleet GU13 .... 54 A1
  Headley GU35 .... 165 F3
Mount View GU11 .... 76 C1
Mount View Rd SO22 .... 197 D2
Mountbatten CI RG14 .... 2 A3
Mountbatten Ct
  14 Aldershot GU11 .... 76 C1
  Andover SP10 .... 83 E1
  Winchester SO22 .... 175 F2
Mountbatten Pl SO23 .... 176 B4
Mounter's La GU34 .... 139 E1
Mountsom's La GU34 .... 161 F2
Mourne CI RG22 .... 68 A2
Mowatt Rd GU26 .... 167 D1
Mozart CI RG22 .... 91 F4
Mud La RG2 .... 15 E1
Mulberries The GU9 .... 99 E2
Mulberry CI Ash GU11 .... 77 F2
  Sandhurst GU15 .... 35 D4
Mulberry Ct GU34 .... 160 B2
Mulberry Ho 3
  SP10, SP11 .... 106 A4
Mulberry Mead RG28 .... 86 B3
Mulfords Hill RG26 .... 26 C4
Mulgrave Rd GU15 .... 36 B1
Mull CI RG23 .... 67 D1
Mullins CI RG21 .... 69 D4
Mulroy Dr GU15 .... 36 C3
Munnings CI RG21 .... 69 E2
Munnings CI SP10 .... 82 C1
Munnings Dr GU14 .... 35 E3
Murray CI SP10 .... 105 F3
Murray Rd GU14 .... 55 E2
Murray's Rd GU14 .... 77 D3
Murrell Green Bsns Pk RG27 51 F2
Murrell Green Rd
  Hartley Wintney RG27 .... 51 F3
  Hook RG27 .... 51 F3
Murrell Rd GU12 .... 77 F2
Murrells La GU47 .... 35 F2
Mus of Army Flying SO20 126 A2
Muscott CI SP9 .... 101 E4
Museum of the Iron Age
  SP10 .... 106 A4
Musgrave Ct RG22 .... 91 E4
Musgrove Gdns 17 GU34 .. 139 F2
Musket Copse RG24 .... 70 A3
Muss La SO20 .... 172 A2
Myland CI RG21 .... 69 E4
Mylen Bsns Cntr SP10 .... 105 F4
Mylen Rd SP10 .... 82 C1
Myrtle Dr GU47 .... 35 D3
Mytchett Cty Fst Sch GU14 56 B2
Mytchett Heath GU16 .... 56 C2
Mytchett Lake Rd GU16 .... 56 C1
Mytchett Place Rd GU16 ...... 56 C1
Mytchett Rd GU16 .... 56 B2

Naafi Rdbt GU11 .... 76 C1
Nadder Rd SP9 .... 78 C3
Naini Tal Rd SP9 .... 78 C3
Nairn CI GU16 .... 36 B1
Napier CI Ash GU11 .... 77 E4
  North Tidworth SP9 .... 79 D3
Napier La GU12 .... 77 F2
Napier Wlk SP10 .... 83 E1
Napoleon Ave GU14 .... 55 F3
Napoleon Dr RG23 .... 68 B4
Naseby Rise RG14 .... 2 A3
Nash CI Basingstoke RG21 .. 69 E4
  Farnborough GU14 .... 55 E2
Nash Grove La RG40 .... 16 B4
Nash Meadows RG25, RG29 95 D2
Nateley Rd RG27 .... 71 F1
National Dairy Mus RG7 .. 14 A1
Nations Hill SO23 .... 176 B3
Naylors The RG7 .... 14 A3
Neath Rd RG21 .... 69 E3
Neelem Ct 5 GU16 .... 56 A1
Nelson CI Aldershot GU12 .. 77 D1
  Farnham GU9 .... 99 D4
  Stockbridge SO20 .... 149 F1
Nelson St GU11 .... 76 C1
Nelson Way GU47 .... 35 E2
Nelson Wlk SP10 .... 83 E1
Nene Ct 47 SP10 .... 83 E1
Nepaul Rd SP9 .... 78 C4

Neptune Rd GU35 .... 164 C1
Nestor CI SP10 .... 82 C1
Nether Vell-Mead GU13 ...... 74 C2
Nethercliffe Sch SO22 ...... 175 F1
Netherfield CI GU34 .... 139 F2
Netherhouse Ct GU13 .... 74 B3
Netherhouse Moor GU13 .... 74 B3
Netley St GU14 .... 77 D4
Nettlebeds La
  Bighton SO24 .... 158 A1
  Old Alresford SO24 .... 158 A1
Neuvic Way RG28 .... 86 B2
Nevada CI GU14 .... 55 D2
Neville CI Andover SP10 .. 106 A3
  Basingstoke RG21 .... 69 D1
Neville Duke Rd GU14 .... 55 E4
New Barn CI GU13 .... 74 B4
New Barn Cotts SO21 .... 152 C1
New Barn Farm SO24 .... 181 D1
New Barn La Alton GU34 .. 139 F1
  Wherwell SP11 .... 128 C4
New Bldgs SP11 .... 58 B4
New Cotts Bighton SO24 .. 158 B1
  South Warnborough RG29 .. 95 D2
  Wonston SO21 .... 131 E2
New Dawn CI GU14 .... 55 D2
New Farm Rd
  East Stratton SO21 .... 134 A2
  New Alresford SO24 .... 179 D2
New Greenham Pk RG14 .. 6 C3
New House La SP11 .... 81 D4
New La SO20 .... 172 A2
New Market Sq 18 RG21 .. 69 D3
New Mill La RG27 .... 15 E1
New Mill Rd RG40 .... 15 E2
New North Dr RG24 .... 49 F4
New Odiham Rd
  Alton GU34 .... 139 E3
  Shalden GU34 .... 139 E3
New Paddock CI GU34 ...... 140 B3
New Rd Basingstoke RG21 .. 69 D2
  Blackwater GU15 .... 35 E2
  Bordon GU35 .... 164 B1
  Eversley GU46 .... 33 E4
  Fleet GU13 .... 75 D3
  Greenham RG19 .... 6 A4
  Hartley Wintney RG27 ...... 52 B3
  Hook RG27 .... 72 A4
  Linchmere GU27 .... 189 E3
  Littleton SO22 .... 175 D3
  Micheldever SO21 .... 111 D1
  Newbury RG14 .... 6 A4
  North Warnborough RG29 .. 72 B2
  Over Wallop SO20 .... 147 E4
  Pamber End RG26 .... 27 E2
  Sandhurst GU17 .... 34 C4
  Stratfield Mortimer RG7 .. 12 A4
  Tadley RG26 .... 26 C4
  Tongham GU10 .... 100 B3
New Rd Cotts GU34 .... 184 C4
New St Andover SP10 ...... 83 D1
  Basingstoke RG22 .... 69 D2
  Stockbridge SO20 .... 149 F2
  Stratfield Saye RG26 ...... 29 F4
New The GU34 .... 77 F1
New Villas RG20 .... 3 F2
Newall Rd SP10, SP11 .. 105 D4
Newark Rd GU47 .... 34 B1
Newbold Rd RG14 .... 1 A3
Newburgh St SO23 .... 197 F4
Newbury Coll RG14 .... 1 B2
Newbury District Hospl
  RG14 .... 1 B1
Newbury L Ctr RG14 ...... 2 B2
Newbury Rd Andover SP10 .. 83 D3
  Enham Alamein SP10 .... 83 D3
  Kingsclere RG20 .... 24 A2
  Knights Enham SP10 .... 83 D3
  Tangley SP10, SP11 .... 83 D3
  Whitchurch RG28 .... 86 B4
Newbury St RG28 .... 86 B3
Newbury Sta RG14 .... 1 C1
Newchurch Rd RG26 .... 9 F1
Newcomb CI SP10 .... 106 A3
Newcome Pl GU11 .... 100 A4
Newcome Rd GU9 .... 99 E3
Newfield Ave GU14 .... 55 E3
Newfield Rd Ash GU12 .. 77 F3
  Liss GU33 .... 208 A3
Newlands CI GU46 .... 34 A3
Newlands Dr GU14 .... 55 E3
Newlands Prim Sch GU47 .. 34 A3
Newlands Rd GU17 .... 35 F1
Newman La GU34 .... 140 A3
Newmans Ct GU10, GU9 .. 98 C4
Newnham La
  Newnham RG27 .... 70 C4
  Old Basing RG29 .... 70 C4
Newnham Pk RG29 .... 71 F4
Newnham Rd Hook RG27 .. 71 F4
  Newnham RG27 .... 71 F4

Newport CI RG14 .... 1 C2
Newport Jun Sch GU12 .. 77 D1
Newport Rd Aldershot GU12 77 D1
  Newbury RG14 .... 1 C2
Newton RG26 .... 9 F1
Newton La GU34 .... 183 F4
Newton Rd GU16 .... 56 A3
Newton Tony CE Prim Sch
  SP4 .... 123 D3
Newton Way GU10 .... 100 B4
Newtown RG26 .... 26 C4
Newtown CI SP10 .... 105 F4
Newtown Rd Liphook GU30 188 A2
  Newbury RG14 .... 5 F4
  Sandhurst GU17 .... 34 C4
Nicholson Pl SO24 .... 179 D3
Nickel CI SO23 .... 198 A4
Nicola Ct GU12 .... 77 D1
Nicotiana Ct GU13 .... 74 C2
Nightingale CI
  Farnborough GU14 .... 55 D3
  Winchester SO22 .... 197 E3
Nightingale Dr GU16 ...... 56 C2
Nightingale Gdns
  Hook RG27 .... 51 D1
  Sandhurst GU46 .... 34 C4
  Sherborne St John RG22 .. 68 B4
Nightingale La RG7 .... 12 A3
Nightingale Rd GU35 ...... 164 C1
Nightingale Rise RG25 .... 88 A4
Nightingales The RG14 .. 5 F4
Nightjar CI GU9 .... 98 A4
Nine Acres GU32 .... 207 D1
Nine Mile Ride RG40 ...... 16 B3
Nine Mile Ride Prim Sch
  RG40 .... 16 B3
Norden CI RG21 .... 69 D3
Norman CI GU35 .... 164 C2
Norman Court La SP11 .. 105 F2
Norman Ct GU9 .... 99 D1
Norman Gate Special Sch
  SP10 .... 83 E1
Norman Rd SO23 .... 197 F3
Normandy Mews 10 GU34 139 F2
Normandy St GU34 .... 140 A2
Normans SO22 .... 197 F3
Normanton Rd RG21 ...... 69 D4
Normay Rise RG14 .... 5 D3
Norn Hill RG21 .... 69 E4
Norn Hill CI RG21 .... 69 E3
Norris CI GU35 .... 164 A1
Norris Hill Rd GU13 ...... 75 E4
Norris Ho RG25 .... 88 A4
North Acre SP11 .... 108 B3
North Ave GU9 .... 99 D4
North Camp Sta GU12 .. 77 E4
North CI Aldershot GU12 .. 77 E1
  Farnborough GU14 .... 55 F4
  Bordon SO22 .... 175 D3
North End Farm Cotts
  SO24 .... 201 E4
North Farm Rd GU14 ...... 55 E4
North Farnborough Inf Sch
  GU14 .... 56 A3
North Foreland Lodge RG24 49 F3
North Fryerne GU46 ...... 34 A4
North Gate Rd GU14 ...... 56 A1
North Hampshire Hospl The
  RG22 .... 68 C4
North Hill CI SO22 .... 175 F1
North Hill Ct SO22 .... 175 F1
North La Aldershot GU12 .. 77 D1
  West Tytherley SP5 .... 169 D1
North Mall 13 GU13 ...... 53 F1
North Par GU35 .... 164 B3
North Rd Ash GU12 .... 77 E2
  Farnborough GU14 .... 77 D4
  Kings Worthy SO23 .... 176 A4
North Row RG26 .... 28 C2
North Side GU12 .... 100 B4
North St
  Bishop's Sutton SO24 .. 180 B3
  Kingsclere RG20 .... 24 B1
North View SO22 .... 197 F4
North View Gdns 14 RG14 .. 1 C2
North View Rd RG26 ...... 27 D4
North Walls SO23 .... 198 A4
North Waltham Prim Sch
  RG25 .... 89 F1
North Warnborough St
  RG29 .... 72 A2
North Way SP11 .... 83 F1
Northanger CI GU34 ...... 139 F2
Northaw Sch SP5 .... 168 C1
Northbrook SO21 .... 132 C2
Northbrook Ave SO23 .. 198 B4
Northcote CI 11 SO23 .. 198 B4
Northbrook Rd GU14 ...... 99 F4
Northcote Rd Ash GU12 .. 77 F4
  Farnborough GU14 .... 55 E3
Northcroft Ct RG29 ...... 95 D2

Northcroft La RG14 ...... 1 B2
Northcroft Terr RG14 ... 1 B2
Northern Ave
  Andover SP10 .... 83 D1
  Newbury RG14 .... 1 C3
Northfield CI
  Aldershot GU12 .... 77 D1
  Fleet GU13 .... 75 E3
Northfield Rd
  Fleet GU13 .... 75 E3
  Sherfield on Loddon RG7 .. 29 F1
  Thatcham RG18 .... 2 C2
Northfields La GU34 ...... 161 E4
Northgate La RG25 .... 92 A1
Northgate Way RG22 ..... 91 D3
Northington Corner GU11 134 A2
Northington Rd SO21 ..... 177 F4
Northlands Dr SO23 ...... 176 A1
Northmead GU14 .... 55 F2
Northside La SO24 .... 180 C3
Northumberland Rd GU35 164 B1
Northway RG14 .... 1 C1
Northwood Dr RG14 ..... 2 A2
Norton CI RG14 .... 5 D3
Norton Cotts SO21 ...... 131 E4
Norton Rd RG7 .... 14 A2
Norton Ride RG21 ...... 69 F4
Norwich Ave GU16 ...... 36 B2
Norwich CI RG22 .... 91 D4
Novello CI RG22 .... 91 E4
Nuffield Rd RG40 ...... 15 F4
Nuns Rd SO23 .... 176 A1
Nursery CI Camberley GU16 . 56 B4
  Chineham RG24 .... 49 D2
  Fleet GU13 .... 75 E4
  Hook RG27 .... 51 D1
Nursery Field GU33 .... 207 F2
Nursery Gdns SO22 .... 197 E4
Nursery Rd Alton GU34 .. 140 A2
  New Alresford SO24 .... 179 E3
Nursery Terr RG29 .... 72 B2
Nutbane La SP11 ...... 81 F4
Nutbeam La RG7 ...... 14 B3
Nutbourne GU9 .... 99 E4
Nutchers Dro SO20 ... 172 A2
Nutcombe La GU27 ... 189 E4
Nutfield CI GU15 ..... 36 A4
Nuthatch CI GU9 ..... 98 A4
Nutley CI Bordon GU35 .. 164 B1
  Yateley GU47 .... 34 A3
Nutmeg Ct GU14 ...... 55 D3
Nutshell La GU11 ..... 99 D3
Nutter's La RG7 ...... 14 C4

O'Connor Rd GU14 .... 77 E4
O'Gorman Rd GU14 .... 55 F1
Oak Bank SP10 .... 106 A3
Oak CI Basingstoke RG21 .. 69 E3
  Baughurst RG26 .... 26 A4
  Middle Wallop SO20 .... 126 A2
  North Tidworth SP9 .... 79 D4
  Oakley RG23 .... 67 D1
  Overton RG25 .... 88 A4
Oak Cotts GU27 .... 189 E3
Oak Cott Farnborough GU14 .. 56 B1
  Farnham GU10 .... 98 C1
Oak Dr RG14 .... 1 B1
Oak Farm CI GU15 .... 35 D3
Oak Farm Com Sch GU14 .. 55 E3
Oak Grove Cres GU47 .. 35 E3
Oak Hanger CI RG27 .. 51 D1
Oak Ho 3 GU34 ...... 55 F4
Oak Lodge GU35 ...... 164 B1
Oak Rd GU14 .... 56 A2
Oak Tree CI
  Aldershot GU12 .... 100 B4
  Ash GU16 .... 56 B4
  Chilbolton SO20 ...... 129 D2
  Headley GU35 .... 165 E2
  Tadley RG26 .... 9 F1
Oak Tree Dr GU33 .... 208 A2
Oak Tree La GU27 .... 189 D3
Oak Tree View GU9 .. 99 E3
Oak Tree Way RG27 .. 51 D1
Oakdene GU34 .... 139 F3
Oaken Copse GU13 .. 75 D2
Oaken Copse Cres GU14 .. 55 F4
Oaken Gr RG14 ...... 5 D4
Oakfield Rd
  Blackwater GU15 ..... 35 E2
  Pamber Heath RG26 .. 10 B1
Oakfields GU17 ...... 35 F3
Oakfields Ct RG20 ... 23 E2
Oakgreen Par GU34 .. 160 B2
Oakhanger Rd GU35 .. 164 A3
Oakhill Rd GU35 ..... 165 F3
Oakhurst GU26 .... 167 D2
Oakland Ave GU9 .... 99 E4
Oakland Rd RG28 .... 86 B3
Oakland Terr RG28 .. 52 B3

Oaklands
  Hartley Wintney RG27 ... 52 B3
  South Wonston SO21 ... 153 E2
  Yateley GU47 .... 34 A3
Oaklands Way RG23 ... 68 B4
Oaklea GU12 .... 77 F3
Oaklea Dr RG27 ...... 15 E1
Oaklea Gdns RG26 ... 29 D1
Oaklea Ho GU26 ..... 167 D2
Oakley CE Jun Sch RG23 .. 67 E1
Oakley Dr GU13 ..... 75 D4
Oakley Inf Sch RG23 .. 67 D1
Oakley La RG23 ..... 67 D1
Oakley Pl 15 Fleet GU13 .. 53 F1
  Hartley Wintney RG27 .. 52 B3
Oakley Rd Bordon GU35 .. 164 B3
  Camberley GU15 ...... 35 F2
  Hannington RG26 .... 44 C1
  Mottisfont SO51 ..... 192 C2
  Newbury RG14 .... 2 A2
Oakmead RG26 ...... 28 C2
Oakridge Ctr RG21 ... 69 E4
Oakridge Rd RG21 ... 69 D4
Oakridge Schs RG24 .. 69 D4
Oakridge Towers RG21 .. 69 E4
Oaks The Andover SP10 .. 105 F4
  Camberley GU17 ..... 35 E2
  Farnborough GU14 ... 55 D2
  Fleet GU13 .... 53 E1
  Tadley RG26 .... 26 C4
  Yateley GU46 .... 34 A3
Oaktree Rd GU35 ... 164 B1
Oaktrees Ash GU12 .. 77 E1
Oakway Farnham GU9 .. 98 C3
Oakway Dr GU16 ... 36 B1
Oakwood Chineham RG24 .. 48 C2
  Fleet GU13 .... 75 D2
Oakwood Inf Sch RG27 .. 52 B3
Oast House Cres GU9 .. 99 D3
Oast La GU9 .... 99 D3
Oasthouse Dr GU13 .. 54 B2
Oban CI RG23 ...... 67 D1
Obelisk Way GU15 .. 36 A3
Oberursel Way GU11 .. 76 B1
Observer CI GU13 ... 74 C2
Ochil CI RG22 ...... 68 A2
Ockham Hall GU35 .. 142 A1
Octavia Hill SO22 ... 197 E3
Octavian CI RG22 ... 91 D4
Oddfellows Rd RG14 .. 1 B1
Odette Gdns RG27 ... 10 A1
Odiham Cottage Hospl
  RG29 .... 72 C1
Odiham Rd Ewshot GU14 .. 98 B4
  Farnham GU12 ...... 98 B4
  Heckfield RG7 ...... 14 A1
  Odiham RG29 .... 73 D4
  Winchfield RG29 .... 73 D4
Odon CI SP9 .... 79 E3
Officers Row RG7 ... 29 D1
Oglander Rd SO23 .. 176 A1
Olaf CI SP10 .... 83 D2
Old Acre Rd GU34 .. 139 F1
Old Barn CI RG25 .. 89 F1
Old Barn La GU10 .. 144 C1
Old Basing Inf Sch RG24 .. 70 A3
Old Basing Mall 22 RG21 .. 69 D3
Old Bath Rd RG14 .. 1 B2
Old Bisley Rd GU16 .. 36 C2
Old Brick Kiln Trad Est The
  RG26 .... 46 C4
Old Brickfield Rd GU9 .. 99 F4
Old Chapel La GU11 .. 77 F1
Old Church La GU10 .. 122 A4
Old Common Rd RG21 .. 69 F2
Old Compton La GU9 .. 99 E1
Old Cove Rd GU13 .. 54 A2
Old Ct RG29 .... 72 C1
Old Dean Rd GU16 .. 36 A4
Old Down CI RG22 .. 68 A1
Old Down La GU32 .. 205 D1
Old Down Rd SP10 .. 82 C1
Old Farnham La
  Bentley GU9 .... 97 F1
  Farnham GU9 .... 122 A4
Old Forge Gdns SO20 .. 170 A4
Old Frensham Rd
  Farnham GU9 .... 122 B2
  Frensham GU9 ...... 122 B2
Old Gdns SO22 ..... 175 F1
Old Green La GU15 .. 36 A4
Old Guildford Rd GU14 .. 56 C3
Old Heath Way GU11 .. 99 D4
Old Hill The SP11 .. 128 C4
Old Hillside Rd SO22 .. 175 E1

Old Kempshott La RG23 ...... 68 A2
Old Kennels CI SO22 .... 197 D2
Old Kennels La SO22 .... 197 D2
Old Kiln GU9 .... 98 C1
Old Kiln CI GU10 .... 144 B1
Old Kiln La GU10 .... 144 B1
Old La Aldershot GU9 .... 99 F4
  Ashford Hill RG7 .... 8 B1
  Frensham GU10 .... 143 F3
  Hamstead Marshall RG20 ...... 3 E4
  Kintbury RG20 .... 3 E4
Old Litten La GU32 .... 206 B2
Old London Rd SO20 .... 150 A2
Old Micheldever Rd SP11 ... 107 D3
Old Newtown Rd RG14 .... 1 B1
Old Odiham Rd Alton GU34 ... 139 F3
  Shalden GU34 .... 139 F3
Old Orchard The GU9 .... 121 F4
Old Palace Farm SO20 ...... 172 A1
Old Park CI GU10 .... 98 C3
Old Park Farm GU35 .... 142 B1
Old Park La GU9, GU10 ...... 98 C2
Old Park Rd SO24 .... 180 C1
Old Pasture Rd GU16 .... 36 B2
Old Pond CI GU15 .... 36 A1
Old Portsmouth Rd GU15 ...... 36 C3
Old Potbridge Rd RG27 ...... 52 A1
Old Quarry The GU27 .... 189 E2
Old Reading Rd RG21 .... 69 E3
Old Rectory Dr GU12 .... 77 F1
Old Rectory Gdns
  Farnborough GU14 .... 56 A2
  Kings Worthy SO21 .... 176 B3
Old Salisbury Rd SP10 .... 105 D2
Old School CI Ash GU12 ...... 77 F2
  Fleet GU13 .... 54 A1
  Hartley Wintney RG27 .... 52 B3
Old School La GU46 .... 34 A3
Old School Rd Hook RG27 ... 71 F4
  Liss GU33 .... 207 F2
Old Station App SO23 .... 198 A4
Old Station Rd SO21 .... 177 F3
Old Station Way GU35 ...... 164 A3
Old Stockbridge Rd
  Middle Wallop SO20 .... 125 E3
  Over Wallop SO20 .... 125 E3
Old Stoke Rd
  South Wonston SO21 .... 154 A4
  Wonston SO21 .... 154 A4
Old Vicarage La SO20 .... 172 A2
Old Vyne La RG26 .... 26 B1
Old Welmore GU46 .... 34 B3
Old Winton Rd SP10 .... 106 A3
Old Worting Rd RG22 .... 68 B2
Oldberg Gdns RG22 .... 91 F4
Oldbury CI GU16 .... 56 B4
Oldcorne Hollow GU46 ...... 33 F3
Olde Farm Dr GU46 .... 34 C3
Oldfield View RG27 .... 52 B3
Oldwood Chase GU14 .... 55 D2
Oliver Rise GU34 .... 139 F2
Oliver's Battery Cres SO22 197 D2
Oliver's Battery Gdns SO22 197 D2
Oliver's Battery Rd N SO22 197 D3
Oliver's Battery Rd S SO22 197 D2
Oliver's La RG26 .... 29 D2
Oliver's Wlk RG21 .... 69 F4
Olivers CI RG26 .... 29 D1
Omega Pk GU34 .... 140 A2
Omni Bsns Ctr GU34 .... 140 A2
Onslow CI RG24 .... 48 C1
Openfields GU35 .... 165 E3
Orange Gr SP11 .... 124 C3
Orange La SO20 .... 125 E1
Orbit CI RG40 .... 16 B3
Orchard CI Ash GU12 .... 77 F3
  Farnborough, Cove Green
  GU14 .... 55 F2
  Farnham GU9 .... 99 F3
  Linchmere GU27 .... 189 F3
  New Alresford SO24 .... 179 E2
  Newbury RG14 .... 2 A3
  South Wonston SO21 ...... 153 E2
Orchard Cotts SP11 .... 124 C3
Orchard Ct GU10 .... 97 E3
Orchard End GU9 .... 121 E2
Orchard Gate GU46 .... 34 C4
Orchard Gdns GU12 .... 100 A4
Orchard Ho Alton GU34 .... 140 A2
  Tongham GU10 .... 100 B4
Orchard La GU34 .... 140 A2
Orchard Rd Andover SP10 ... 82 C1
  Basingstoke RG22 .... 68 B2
  Farnham GU11 .... 99 F3
  Mortimer RG7 .... 1 F1
  South Wonston SO21 .... 153 E2
Orchard Terr GU34 .... 140 A2

Orchard The
  Kingsclere RG20 .... 24 B1
  Overton RG25 .... 88 A4
  Tadley RG26 .... 27 D4
Orchard Way GU12 .... 100 A4
Orchard Wlk GU21 .... 175 E1
Orchardene RG14 .... 1 C2
Orchid Ct SP10 .... 105 E3
Ordnance Rd
  Aldershot GU12 .... 77 D2
  North Tidworth SP9 .... 78 C3
Ordnance Rdbt GU11 .... 76 C1
Oregon Wlk RG40 .... 16 B4
Oriel Hill GU16 .... 36 A2
Orient Dr SO22 .... 175 E2
Orkney CI RG24 .... 48 B1
Orpheus Ho **4** RG26 ...... 9 E1
Orts Rd RG14 .... 1 C1
Orwell CI GU14 .... 55 E3
Osborn Rd GU9 .... 99 D2
Osborn Way RG29 .... 72 A4
Osborne CI Alton GU34 ..... 139 E2
  Camberley GU16 .... 56 B4
Osborne Ct GU12 .... 77 D4
Osborne Dr GU13 .... 75 D4
Osborne Rd Andover SP10 106 A4
  Farnborough GU14 .... 77 D4
Osbourne CI RG21 .... 69 D4
Osier Ho RG26 .... 26 C4
Osler CI RG26 .... 28 C2
Osnaburgh Hill GU15 .... 35 F3
Osprey Rd RG22 .... 67 F1
Otterbourne Cres RG26 ..... 26 C3
Our Lady of Providence
  Convent Sch GU34 .... 140 A3
Ouse Ct **49** SP10 .... 83 E1
Oval Rd SO51 .... 192 A1
Oval The Andover SP10 ..... 83 E2
  Liss GU33 .... 207 F2
Overbridge Sq RG14 .... 2 B1
Overdale PI GU35 .... 164 B1
Overdale Rise GU15 .... 36 B2
Overdale Wlk GU35 .... 164 B1
Overlord CI GU15 .... 36 A4
Overton CE Prim Sch RG25 65 D1
Overton CI GU11 .... 100 A3
Overton Ho RG25 .... 88 A4
Overton Rd SO21 .... 111 E2
Overton Sta RG25 .... 65 D1
Owen Rd RG14 .... 1 C3
Owen's Rd SO22 .... 175 F1
Owlsmoor Rd GU15 .... 35 D4
Ox Dro SP11 .... 84 A1
Ox Drove Rise SP11 .... 84 A2
Oxenden Ct GU12 .... 100 B4
Oxenden Rd Ash GU11 ..... 100 B4
  Tongham GU10 .... 100 B4
Oxford Rd
  Farnborough GU14 .... 56 A1
  Newbury RG14 .... 1 B3
  Wonston SO21 .... 131 E2
Oxford St RG14 .... 1 B2
Oyster Ct RG24 .... 91 D4

Pack La Basingstoke RG22 ... 67 E1
  Oakley RG23 .... 67 E1
Pack Way GU10 .... 122 B4
Packenham Rd RG22 .... 68 C2
Paddington Ho **13** RG21 ... 69 D3
Paddock CI Camberley GU15 36 C3
  South Wonston SO21 ...... 153 F2
Paddock Ct RG27 .... 52 B3
Paddock Field SO20 .... 129 D3
Paddock Rd
  Basingstoke RG22 .... 68 B2
  Newbury RG14 .... 5 E4
Paddock The
  Farnham GU10 .... 121 E2
  Grayshott GU26 .... 166 C2
  Hartley Wintney RG27 ...... 52 B4
  Haslemere GU27 .... 189 F4
  Headley GU35 .... 165 E3
  Kings Worthy SO23 .... 176 B3
  Kingsclere RG20 .... 24 B1
  Newbury RG14 .... 2 A1
Paddock Way
  Liphook GU30 .... 188 A3
  New Alresford SO24 .... 179 E2
Paddockfields RG24 .... 70 A4
Padwick CI RG24 .... 69 D2
Padworth Rd RG7 .... 11 D4
Pages Yd RG28 .... 92 B2
Paget CI
  Camberley GU16 .... 36 C4
  North Tidworth SP9 .... 78 B4
Paice La GU34 .... 159 F2
Paices Hill RG26 .... 9 D4
Painters Field SO23 .... 197 F2
Painters Pightle RG27 .... 50 C1
Palace CI SO20 .... 171 F1
Palace Gate RG29 .... 72 B2

Pale La Fleet RG27 .... 53 D1
  Hartley Wintney RG27 .... 53 E2
  Winchfield RG27 .... 53 D1
Palestine Rd SP11 .... 124 B3
Palm Hall CI SO23 .... 198 B4
Palmer CI RG21 .... 69 E4
Palmer Dr SP10 .... 106 B4
Palmerston CI GU14 .... 55 D2
Palmerston Ct **2** SO22 ... 197 F3
Pamber Heath Rd RG26 ..... 10 B1
Pamber Rd RG26 .... 10 C1
Pan's Gdns GU15 .... 36 B2
Pankridge St GU9 .... 97 E4
Pannells GU10 .... 122 A3
Pantile Dr RG27 .... 51 E1
Pantings La RG20 .... 21 E3
Paper Mill La GU34 .... 140 A2
Papermakers RG25 .... 88 A4
Parade The Ash GU11 .... 77 F2
  Basingstoke RG21 .... 69 E3
  Tadley RG26 .... 9 F1
Parchment St GU34 .... 198 A4
Pardown RG22 .... 90 A4
Parish CI Ash GU12 .... 77 F1
  Farnham GU10, GU9 .... 98 C3
Parish Rd GU11 .... 77 D4
Park Ave Camberley GU15 ... 36 A2
  Old Basing RG24 .... 70 A3
  Winchester SO23 .... 198 B4
Park CI Binsted GU10 .... 120 C1
  Kingsley GU35 .... 142 B1
  Oakley RG22 .... 67 D1
  Winchester SO23 .... 176 A1
Park Close Rd GU34 .... 140 A3
Park Corner Rd RG27 .... 52 B4
Park Ct Farnham GU9 .... 99 D2
  1 Winchester SO23 .... 176 A1
Park Dro SO20 .... 125 F2
Park End RG14 .... 1 C2
Park Farm End Est GU15 ... 36 A1
Park Gdns RG21 .... 69 E2
Park Hill GU13 .... 74 C3
Park Ho **8** SO23 .... 198 A4
Park House Mews SP9 ..... 101 F2
Park House Sch RG14 .... 5 E3
Park La Arborfield RG40 ..... 15 F3
  Camberley GU15 .... 36 A3
  Hamstead Marshall RG20 ... 3 F4
  Kings Worthy SO21 .... 176 B3
  Lower Froyle GU34 .... 119 E3
  Newbury RG14 .... 1 C2
  Old Basing RG24 .... 70 A3
  Quarley SP11 .... 103 D2
  Ropley SO24 .... 181 D2
  Silchester RG7 .... 12 A1
Park PI GU13 .... 74 C3
Park Prewett Hospl RG22 ... 68 B4
Park Prim Sch GU10 .... 100 A4
Park Rd Aldershot GU11 .... 100 A4
  Camberley GU15 .... 36 A2
  Farnborough GU14 .... 77 E4
  Farnham GU9 .... 99 D2
  Sandhurst GU17 .... 35 D4
  South Tidworth SP9 .... 78 C3
  Winchester SO22, SO23 ... 175 F1
Park Row GU9 .... 98 C2
Park St Bordon GU35 ...... 164 B2
  Camberley GU15 .... 36 A2
  Newbury RG14 .... 1 C2
Park Terr RG14 .... 1 C2
Park View
  Beech RG7 .... 13 D3
  Lockerley SO21 .... 181 F3
Park View Schs RG21 .... 68 B1
Park Way RG14 .... 1 C2
Parkfields GU46 .... 34 A3
Parkhill CI GU17 .... 35 D2
Parkhill Rd GU47 .... 35 D2
Parkhouse Cnr SP9 .... 101 F2
Parkhouse Cross SP9 ...... 101 F2
Parkhouse Rd SP9 .... 101 F4
Parkhurst Fields GU10 .... 144 B1
Parkland Gr GU9 .... 99 E4
Parkside GU9 .... 99 F4
Parkside Farm SO24 .... 181 D1
Parkside La SO24 .... 181 D1
Parkside Rd RG21 .... 69 E2
Parkside Dr GU15 .... 36 A2
Parkstone Rd SO24 .... 181 D1
Parkview CI SP10 .... 82 C1
Parkway GU15 .... 36 A3
Parkwood CI RG24 .... 48 C2
Parliament PI SO22 .... 197 E2
Parmiter Ho **48** SO23 ... 198 A4
Parnell Ct SP11 .... 124 B3
Parnholt Rd SO51 .... 194 C2
Parsonage CI GU34 .... 161 F2
Parsonage Farm Inf Sch
  GU14 .... 55 D3
Parsonage Way GU16 .... 36 B1

Parsons CI Arborfield RG40 ... 15 F4
  Fleet GU13 .... 74 C3
Parsons Down Schs RG19 ... 2 C2
Parsons Field GU17 .... 34 C4
Parsons La GU26 .... 167 D3
Part La RG7 .... 14 B3
Partridge Ave GU46 .... 33 F3
Partridge CI
  Barton Stacey SO21 .... 130 B4
  Camberley GU15 .... 36 B1
  Ewshot GU9 .... 98 A4
Partridge Down SO22 ...... 197 D2
Partridge Gn GU34 .... 139 F3
Paschal Rd GU15 .... 36 B4
Passfield Ent Ctr GU30 .... 187 D4
Passfield Mill Bsns Pk
  GU30 .... 165 D1
Passfield Rd GU30 .... 165 E1
Pastures The
  Cheriton SO24 .... 201 E3
  Kings Worthy SO23 .... 176 C4
Paternoster Ho **51** SO23 . 198 A4
Paternoster Row **20** SO23 198 A4
Paterson CI RG22 .... 91 E4
Paterson Rd GU33 .... 186 B1
Pathfinders The GU14 ...... 55 D2
Patrick's CI GU33 .... 208 A2
Patrick's Copse Rd GU33 ... 208 A2
Patten Ave GU47 .... 34 C3
Pattinson Cres SP11 .... 105 D4
Paul CI GU10 .... 99 E4
Paul's Fld GU46 .... 33 F3
Paulet PI Old Basing RG24 ... 70 A3
  Winchester SO22 .... 197 F3
Pavilion Rd GU11 .... 76 B1
Pavilions End The GU16 ..... 36 A2
Paviors GU9 .... 99 D2
Pawley CI GU10 .... 100 A4
Pax Hill GU34 .... 119 F2
Paxton CI RG22 .... 91 D4
Paynes CI
  Broughton SO20 .... 170 A4
  Headley, Nr Greenham
  RG19 .... 5 E2
Paynes Hay Rd SO51 ...... 194 B1
Paynes La SO20 .... 170 A4
Paynesdown Rd RG19 .... 2 C2
Peabody Rd GU12 .... 77 D4
Peach Gr SP11 .... 124 C3
Peacock PI **5** SO23 ...... 198 B4
Peake CI RG21 .... 69 F4
Peakfield GU10 .... 144 A4
Pear Tree CI GU35 .... 164 C2
Pear Tree Ct GU16 .... 36 A3
Pear Tree La
  Farnham GU10 .... 121 E2
  Newbury RG14 .... 2 A3
Pear Tree Rd GU35 .... 164 C2
Pearl Ho SP10 .... 57 D1
Pearman Dr SP10 .... 106 B4
Pearmoor Ct GU13 .... 53 F1
Peddlars Gr GU46 .... 34 B3
Peel Ave GU16 .... 56 C4
Peel Ct Farnborough GU14 ... 77 D4
  Hartley Wintney RG27 ...... 52 B3
Peel Gdns RG20 .... 24 B2
Pegasus Ave GU14 .... 77 C1
Pegasus CI
  Linchmere GU27 .... 189 D3
  Thatcham RG19 .... 2 C2
Pegasus Ct
  Farnborough GU16 .... 56 B1
  4 Fleet GU13 .... 53 F1
  Whitchurch RG28 .... 86 B3
Pegasus Rd GU14 .... 55 E4
Pelham CI Bordon GU35 ... 164 B1
  Old Basing RG24 .... 70 A3
Pelham PI GU10 .... 121 F2
Pelican La RG14 .... 1 C2
Pelican Rd RG26 .... 10 B4
Pelton Rd RG22 .... 68 C3
Pembroke Bwy GU15 .... 36 A3
Pembroke Ct SP10 .... 106 A4
Pembroke Rd
  Basingstoke RG23 .... 68 A3
  Newbury RG14 .... 1 C2
Pembury PI GU10 .... 77 D1
Pemerton Rd
  Basingstoke RG21 .... 69 E4
  Winchester SO22 .... 175 E2
Pen CI SP10 .... 106 B4
Pendennis CI RG23 .... 68 A3
Pendle Gn SO51 .... 191 F1
Penfold Croft GU11 .... 99 E2
Pengilly Rd GU9 .... 99 E4
Peninsula Rd SO22 .... 197 F4
Peninsula Sq **25** SO22 ... 197 F4
Penn Rd RG14 .... 1 A3
Penn's Yd GU9 .... 98 C1

Pennefather's Rd GU11 ...... 76 B
Pennine CI RG21 .... 68 A3
Pennine Way
  Basingstoke RG23 .... 68 A3
  Farnborough GU14 .... 55 E4
Pennings Rd SP9 .... 78 C4
Penns Wood GU14 .... 56 A1
Penny La SO20 .... 150 A1
Penny's Hatch RG20 .... 24 C2
Penrhyn CI GU12 .... 76 C1
Penrith Rd RG21 .... 69 D2
Penrose CI RG14 .... 1 B3
Penrose Way GU34 .... 160 A1
Penryn Dr GU35 .... 166 A2
Penshurst Rise GU16 .... 56 B4
Pentangle The RG14 .... 1 C1
Pentland CI RG23 .... 68 A2
Pentland PI GU14 .... 55 E4
Penton La SP11 .... 81 F1
Penton PI **8** SO23 ...... 198 A1
Penwith Dr GU27 .... 189 E1
Penwood Hts RG20 .... 21 F1
Penwood Rd RG14 .... 5 D2
Perham Cres SP11 .... 57 D3
Perins CI SO24 .... 179 D2
Perins Com Sch SO24 ..... 179 E1
Periwinkle CI GU35 .... 165 D1
Perowne St GU11 .... 76 B3
Perring Ave GU14 .... 55 E4
Perry Dr GU13 .... 53 E1
Perry Way GU35 .... 165 E2
Pershore Rd RG24 .... 48 A3
Perth CI SP9 .... 79 E4
Peshawar CI SP9 .... 78 B4
Peter Symonds' Coll
  SO22 .... 175 F3
Peters CI SP9 .... 101 F4
Petersfield RG22 .... 90 A4
Petersfield CI RG24 .... 49 D2
Petersfield Ho **8** SP9 ...... 78 C1
Petersfield Rd
  Bordon GU35 .... 186 A3
  Cheriton SO24 .... 201 E2
  East Tisted SO24 .... 182 B3
  Greatham GU33 .... 186 A3
  Ropley SO24 .... 181 E2
  Winchester SO21, SO23 ... 198 B4
Petrel Croft RG23 .... 90 C4
Petty's Brook Rd RG24 ...... 49 D2
Petunia CI RG22 .... 91 D4
Petworth CI
  Basingstoke RG22 .... 91 D3
  Camberley GU16 .... 56 B4
Petworth Ct GU15 .... 36 B2
Pevensey Way GU16 .... 56 C4
Peveral Way RG22 .... 68 B2
Peveril Wlk RG22 .... 68 B2
Pewsey Ho **4** RG22 .... 78 C3
Pheaben's Field RG26 .... 28 C2
Pheasant CI
  Barton Stacey SO21 .... 130 C4
  Basingstoke RG23 .... 90 C4
  North Tidworth SP9 .... 79 D3
Pheasant Copse GU13 .... 53 F1
Pheasant La RG20 .... 6 B2
Pheby Rd RG22 .... 91 E3
Pheonix CI RG27 .... 52 A2
Pheonix Terr RG27 .... 52 A2
Philips Ho GU26 .... 166 C2
Phillips CI GU35 .... 165 E3
Phillips Cres GU35 .... 165 E3
Phoenix CI
  15 Aldershot GU11 ..... 76 C1
  Kingsclere RG20 .... 24 B1
Phoenix Park Terr RG24 .... 69 D3
Phoenix Wlk RG14 .... 5 D3
Pickaxe La GU34 .... 118 A3
Picket Twenty SP11 .... 106 C4
Picketts Hill GU35 .... 143 D1
Pickford St GU12 .... 77 D4
Picton Rd SP10 .... 106 A3
Pierrefondes Ave GU14 ...... 55 F3
Pierrepont Sch GU17 .... 122 B1
Pigeon CI RG26 .... 29 D1
Pigeons Farm Rd RG19 ...... 6 B4
Pike St RG14 .... 1 C2
Pilcot Rd GU13 .... 74 B3
Pilgrims CI GU10 .... 121 F4
Pilgrims Gate SO22 .... 175 F1
Pilgrims Sch The
  SO23 .... 198 A4
Pilgrims Way
  Andover SP10 .... 83 E1
  Headley GU35 .... 165 E3
Pilgrims Way City
  Prim Sch The GU10 ...... 121 F4
Pimpernel Way RG21 .... 69 F4
Pinchington La RG14 .... 5 F4
Pindar PI RG21 .... 2 B3
Pine Ave GU15 .... 36 B3
Pine Bank GU26 .... 167 E2

Pine Cl
Middle Wallop SO20 126 A2
Sandhurst GU47 35 E4
South Wonston SO21 153 F2
Winchester SO21, SO22 197 D2
Pine Cotts GU33 208 A4
Pine Dr Blackwater GU17 35 E2
Mortimer RG7 11 E3
Wokingham RG40 16 C4
Pine Gr GU10 122 B3
Pine Grove GU13 75 D3
Pine Mount Rd GU15 36 A2
Pine Rd GU34 160 B2
Pine Ridge RG14 2 A3
Pine Ridge Dr GU10 122 A3
Pine View GU35 166 A3
Pine View Cl GU9 99 F3
Pine Wlk Andover SP10 105 E3
Liss GU33 208 A3
Pinehill Rd GU35 164 B1
Pinehill Rise GU17 35 D4
Pinehurst RG26 26 C4
Pinehurst Ave GU14 55 F1
Pinehurst Cotts GU14 55 F1
Pines Rd Fleet GU13 53 F1
Liphook GU30 187 E2
Pines The Andover SP10 105 F4
Camberley GU15 36 B4
Pinetree Ho 6 SP9 79 D4
Pineview GU14 55 F2
Pinewood Cl Baughurst RG26 9 D1
Sandhurst GU47 34 B4
Pinewood Cres GU14 55 D3
Pinewood Ct 1 GU13 54 A1
Pinewood Hill GU13 54 A1
Pinewood Inf Sch GU14 55 D4
Pinewood Pk GU14 55 D4
Pinkerton Rd RG22 68 B1
Pinks La RG26 9 E1
Pinnell Cl RG22 91 D3
Pipers Croft GU13 75 D2
Pipers Patch 1 GU14 55 F2
Pipit Cl RG19 2 C2
Pipsons Cl GU46 34 A3
Pirbright Rd GU16 56 A2
Pitcairn Cl RG24 48 B1
Pitfield La RG7 12 A2
Pitfold Ave GU27 189 D3
Pitfold Cl GU27 189 E3
Pither Rd RG29 95 E4
Pitman Cl RG22 68 A1
Pitt Hall Cotts RG26 45 F3
Pitt Rdbt SO22 197 D3
Pitt Way GU14 55 E3
Pittard Rd RG22 68 C2
Pitter Cl SO22 175 D3
Pitts La SP10 106 A3
Place Ct GU11 100 A4
Plantation Rd
Andover SP10 105 F4
Hill Brow GU33 208 A1
South Tidworth SP9 78 C3
Tadley RG7 9 E1
Plantation Row GU15 35 F3
Plantation The RG24 49 E4
Plantation Way GU35 186 A4
Plassey Rd SP9 78 C4
Pleasant Hill RG26 26 C4
Plough Gdns SO20 170 A3
Plough La RG27 31 F3
Plough Rd GU46 34 B4
Plough Way SO22 197 E2
Plover Cl Andover SP10 83 D1
Basingstoke RG22 68 A1
Plover La RG27 15 E1
Plovers Down SO22 197 D2
Plovers Way GU34 140 A3
Plumer Rd GU33 186 B2
Plumpton Rd RG14 2 A1
Plumpton Way GU34 139 F1
Poachers Field RG29 95 D2
Pococks La GU33 206 C4
Poets Way SO22 197 E4
Poland La RG29 72 C3
Polden Cl GU14 55 E4
Polecat Cnr RG24 70 A1
Police Hos GU35 164 B1
Polkerris Way GU13 75 E2
Pollards The GU10 120 A2
Pollen's Almhouses SP10 106 A4
Polmear Cl GU13 75 E2
Pond Cl Newbury RG14 5 D4
Overton RG25 88 A3
Pond Croft GU46 34 B3
Pond La Churt GU10 144 A2
Headley GU10 144 A2
Pond Rd Bramley RG26 29 D1
Headley GU35 165 F2
Pondtail Cl GU13 75 E4
Pondtail Gdns GU13 75 E4
Pondtail Rd GU13 75 E4
Pool Rd Aldershot GU10 100 A4
Hartley Wintney RG27 52 B4
Poors Farm Rd RG24 70 C4
Popes Hill RG20 24 B1
Popham La RG25 112 C4
Poplar Cl Baughurst RG26 26 A4
Mytchett GU16 56 C2
Sherfield on Loddon RG26 29 E1
Poplar Cotts GU16 56 B3
Poplar Path SO20 126 A2
Poplar Pl RG14 1 C3
Poplar Wlk GU9 99 D4
Poplars Cl GU14 55 D3
Poppy Fields RG24 70 A4
Poppyhills Rd GU15 36 B4
Porchester Rd RG14 1 C1
Porchester Sq 16 RG21 69 D3
Port La SO21 196 C1
Portacre Rise RG22 68 C2
Portal Cl SP10 105 D4
Portal Rd SO23 198 A3
Portchester Cl SP10 82 B2
Porter Cl RG29 95 E4
Porter End RG14 5 F4
Porter Rd RG21 68 C1
Porters Cl Andover SP10 82 B1
Dummer RG22 90 B1
Portesbery Hill Dr GU15 36 A4
Portesbery Rd GU15 36 B3
Portesbery Sch GU15 36 A3
Portiswood Cl RG26 27 D4
Portland Dr GU13 75 D2
Portland Gr SP10 106 A4
Portland Sq 5 GU33 207 F2
Portsmouth Cres RG22 68 B1
Portsmouth Ho 10 SP9 78 C3
Portsmouth Rd
Bramshott GU26 167 D1
Camberley GU15 36 B2
Grayshott GU26 167 D1
Haslemere GU26 167 D1
Liphook GU30 187 F1
Portsmouth Way RG21 68 B1
Portsmouth Wlk RG22 68 B1
Portway Baughurst RG26 9 E1
Riseley RG7 14 A1
Portway Cl SP10 105 E4
Portway Cty Inf Sch SP10 105 E4
Portway Ind Est SP10 82 A1
Portway Jun Sch SP10 105 E4
Portway Pl RG22 68 A3
Post Office La RG22 90 B1
Posting House Mews RG14 1 B2
Pot La RG24 70 C4
Potbridge Rd RG27 72 C4
Potley Hill Prim Sch GU47 34 C3
Potley Hill Rd GU17, GU46 34 B3
Potter's Cross SP9 101 F2
Potter's Wlk 11 RG21 69 D3
Potteries La GU14 56 B2
Potteries The GU14 55 D3
Potters Cres GU12 77 F1
Potters Field GU33 208 A2
Potters Gate GU9 98 C1
Potters Gate CE Prim Sch
GU9 98 C1
Potters Ind Pk GU13 75 E3
Potters La RG26 29 F2
Pottery Ct GU9 121 E3
Pottery La GU10 121 E3
Poultons Cl RG25 88 A4
Poultons Rd RG25 88 A4
Pound Cl
Bramley RG26 28 C2
Headley GU35 165 E3
Over Wallop SO20 125 E1
Upper Wield SO24 137 D1
Yateley GU17, GU46 34 B3
Pound Gate GU34 140 A3
Pound Hill SO24 179 E3
Pound La
Burghclere RG20 22 B3
Newbury RG14 1 A2
Thatcham RG19 2 C2
Pound Meadow
Sherfield on Loddon RG24 49 F4
Whitchurch RG28 86 B3
Pound Rd
3 Aldershot GU12 77 D1
Kings Worthy SO23 176 B4
Over Wallop SO20 125 E1
Overton RG25 88 A4
Pound St RG14 1 B1
Poveys Mead RG20 24 C1
Poyle Rd GU10 100 C4
Poynings Cres RG24 69 E1
Poynters Cl SP10 82 C1
Poyntz Rd RG25 88 A4
Pragnells Cotts SP5 169 D1
Prentice Cl GU14 55 F4
Prescelly Cl RG22 68 A2
Preston Candover
CE Prim Sch RG25 136 A4
Preston Pl RG14 2 A2
Pretoria Cl GU33 186 B1
Pretoria Rd SP11 57 D1
Preymead Ind Est GU9 99 F4
Priestley Way GU11 76 A1
Priestly Rd
Basingstoke RG22 68 C4
Sherborne St John RG23 68 C4
Primrose Ct SP11 105 E3
Primrose Dr RG27 52 B4
Primrose Gdns
Basingstoke RG22 91 D3
Farnborough GU14 55 E2
Primrose La GU33 208 B2
Primrose Wlk 3 Fleet GU13 53 F1
Yateley GU46 33 F3
Primula Rd GU35 164 C2
Prince Albert Gdns 17
SP10 106 A4
Prince Charles Cres GU16 56 A4
Prince Cl SP10 83 E1
Prince Hold Rd RG19 2 C2
Prince of Wales Wlk GU15 36 A3
Prince's Ave GU11 77 D3
Prince's Bldgs 10 SO23 198 A4
Prince's Mead Sch SO22 197 F3
Princes Cl GU35 164 B1
Princes' Cres RG22 68 C2
Princes Ct 15 SP9 78 C4
Princes Mead GU14 55 F2
Princes Pl SO22 197 F3
Princes Way GU11 76 C1
Princess Ct 7 SO23 198 A4
Princess Dr GU34 139 E2
Princess Marina Dr RG27 15 E4
Princess Way GU15 36 A3
Prinstead Cl 7 SO23 198 A3
Prior Croft Cl GU15, GU16 36 C2
Prior End GU15 36 C3
Prior Heath Inf Sch GU15 36 C3
Prior Place Cross Roads
GU15 36 C2
Prior Rd GU15 36 C3
Prior's La GU17 34 C3
Priors Barton SO23 197 F3
Priors Cl Farnborough GU14 55 F4
Kingsclere RG20 24 B1
Priors Ct GU12 77 E1
Priors Dean Rd SO22 175 E2
Priors Keep GU13 75 D4
Priors Rd RG26 9 F1
Priors Row RG29 72 B2
Priors Way SO22 197 D2
Priors Way The SO24 182 A1
Priors Wood GU27 189 E3
Priory Cl GU13 74 B4
Priory Croft GU10 122 A4
Priory Ct GU17 35 E3
Priory Gdns RG24 70 A4
Priory La Frensham GU10 144 B4
Hartley Wintney RG27 52 B2
Priory Prim Sch The RG26 27 D1
Priory Rd RG14 1 C1
Priory St GU14 56 A2
Privet La SP11 80 C3
Privet Rd GU35 165 D3
Privett Cl RG24 70 A4
Privett Rd GU32 205 F1
Prospect Ave GU14 55 F3
Prospect Cott GU12 77 F2
Prospect Hill GU35 165 E4
Prospect Pl RG14 1 C1
Prospect Rd Ash GU11 77 F3
Farnborough GU14 55 F3
Farnham GU10 121 E2
New Alresford SO24 179 E2
Providence Pl 3 GU9 99 D1
Pruetts La GU33 207 F1
Puckridge Hill Rd GU11 76 B3
Pudding La SO23 176 A3
Puffers Way RG14 1 B1
Pug's Hole SP5 191 D3
Punsholt La SO24 203 F3
Purbrook Rd RG26 26 C4
Purcell Cl RG22 68 C1
Purley Way GU16 56 B4
Purmerend Cl GU14 55 D3
Puttenham Rd
Chineham RG24 49 D2
Seale GU11 100 C2
Puttock Cl GU27 189 D3
Pyestock Cres GU14 55 D2
Pyle Hill RG14 1 C1
Pyotts Copse RG24 49 D1
Pyotts Ct RG24 49 D1
Pyotts Hill Chineham RG24 49 D1
Old Basing RG24 70 A4

Quadrant The GU12 77 F2
Quantock Cl RG22 68 A2
Quarry La GU46 34 B3
Quarry Rd SO23 198 B4
Quarters Rd GU14 56 A1
Quebec Gdns GU47 35 D2
Queen Anne's Wlk 7 RG21 69 D3
Queen Elizabeth Dr GU11 76 B1
Queen Mary Ave
Basingstoke RG21 69 D3
Camberley GU15 35 F3
Queen Mary Cl GU13 53 F2
Queen Mary's Coll RG21 69 D2
Queen St GU12 77 D1
Queen Victoria Cross Roads
GU15 35 F3
Queen Victoria Ct GU14 55 F3
Queen's Ave Aldershot GU11 76 C3
Farnborough GU11 76 C3
Queen's Cl GU11 76 C4
Queen's Ct GU12 77 D4
Queen's Par RG24 69 D2
Queen's Rd
Basingstoke RG22 68 C3
Newbury RG14 1 C1
Winchester SO22 197 E4
Queen's Rdbt GU11 76 C4
Queen's St RG22 68 C3
Queens Ave SP10 106 A4
Queens Cotts SP11 61 F1
Queens Ct RG14 1 C1
Queens Keep GU15 36 A3
Queens La GU9 98 C4
Queens Mead SO22 197 E3
Queens Rd Aldershot GU11 76 B1
Alton GU34 139 F2
Bordon GU30 187 D2
Camberley GU17 35 F2
Farnborough GU12 77 D4
Farnham GU9 99 D3
Fleet GU13 75 D4
Kingsclere RG20 24 C1
North Warnborough RG29 72 B2
Whitchurch RG28 86 B2
Queensberry Pl GU15 35 D2
Queensfield RG25 90 B1
Queensmead GU14 55 F2
Queensway Andover SP10 83 E1
Camberley GU14 56 C4
Queenwood Rd SO20 170 A3
Queenwood Rise SO20 170 A3
Quennells Hill GU10 121 E3
Quetta Pk GU13 75 D1
Quilter Rd RG22 68 B1
Quince Tree Way RG27 51 D1
Quinneys GU16 56 A1

R.E.M.E. Mus RG40 15 F4
Race Course Rd RG14 1 C1
Race Course Sta RG14 2 A1
Racedown Cotts SP11 102 C3
Raceview Bsns Ctr RG14 1 C1
Rack Cl SP10 106 A4
Rack Close Rd GU34 139 F2
Rack & Manger Cotts SO21 174 A4
Rackfield GU27 189 D4
Rackstraw Rd GU47 35 D4
Radcliffe Cl GU16 56 C4
Radford Cl GU9 99 E3
Radford Gdns RG21 68 C1
Radical Ride RG40 16 B4
Raeburn Cl SO24 201 E3
Raeburn Way GU15 35 D3
Raghill RG26 10 A3
Raglan Cl Aldershot GU12 77 D1
Camberley GU16 56 C4
Raglan Ct RG22 91 E4
Ragmore La GU32 205 F3
Railway Cotts GU34 204 B3
Railway Rd Bordon GU33 186 B2
Newbury RG14 1 C1
Rainbow Cl RG24 70 B3
Rainham Cl RG25 90 C4
Rake Bsns Pk GU33 208 C2
Rake CE Prim Sch GU33 208 C3
Rake Rd GU33 208 A2
Rakemakers GU34 140 B4
Ramillis Cl GU12 77 E4
Ramparts The SP10 105 F3
Rampton Rd RG28 86 B2
Ramptons La RG26 10 C3
Ramptons Meadow RG26 27 D4
Ramridge Ho SP11 81 E2
Ramsay Rd SO23 176 B4
Ramsdell Cl RG26 26 C4
Ramsdell Rd
Baughurst RG26 25 E1
Pamber End RG26 27 D1
Ramsey Cl GU15 36 C4
Ramsholt Cl RG25 89 F1
Rances Way SO22 197 F3
Randell Cl GU14 35 E1
Randolph Dr GU14 55 D2
Range Rd RG40 16 C4
Range Ride GU15 35 E4
Range View GU47 35 E4
Rank The Fyfield SP11 80 C1
Hurstbourne Tarrant SP11 60 C4
Penton Grafton SP11 81 E1
Rankine Cl GU9 99 F3
Rankine Rd RG21 69 E4
Rapallo Cl GU14 56 A2
Raphael Cl RG21 69 E2
Rapley Cl GU15 36 B4
Ratcliffe Rd GU14 55 E4
Rathbone Rd SP11 108 B1
Ravel Cl RG22 68 C1
Ravelin Cl GU10 97 E3
Raven Cl
North Tidworth SP9 78 C3
5 Yateley GU46 33 F3
Raven Rd RG27 51 D1
Raven Sq GU34 139 F3
Ravens Wood Dr GU15 36 C3
Ravenscote Jun Sch GU15 36 C2
Ravenscroft RG27 51 D1
Ravensworth Rd RG7 11 E3
Rawdon Rise GU15 36 C3
Rawlings Rd RG29 72 A4
Rawlinson Rd GU17 35 F3
Rayleigh Rd RG21 69 D3
Read's Field GU34 160 A1
Reading Rd
Basingstoke RG24 48 B1
Blackwater GU17 34 B3
Chineham RG24 48 C1
Eversley GU17 34 B3
Farley Hill RG40 15 E2
Farnborough GU16 56 A1
Hook RG27 51 D3
Mattingley RG27 51 D3
Sherfield on Loddon RG24 49 E4
Yateley GU46 34 B3
Reading Rd N GU13 53 F1
Reading Rd S GU13 75 D3
Rebecca Cl GU13 74 C2
Recreation Rd
Andover SP10 106 A4
Farnham GU10 121 E2
Odiham RG29 72 B1
Rectory Cl Newbury RG14 1 B1
Sandhurst GU17 34 B4
Tadley RG26 27 D3
Rectory Cotts RG25 92 A4
Rectory Hill
West Dean SP5 190 B2
West Tytherley SP5 169 A1
Rectory La Bentley GU10 120 A2
Bramshott GU30 188 A4
Broughton SO20 170 A4
Itchen Abbas SO21 178 A4
Kingsclere RG26 45 D4
Rectory Pl SP11 81 E1
Rectory Rd
Farnborough GU16 56 A2
Hook RG27 72 A4
Oakley RG23 66 C1
Padworth RG7 10 B4
Reculver Way SP10 82 B2
Red Hill
Ashmansworth RG20 41 D4
Mattingley RG27 31 F1
Medstead GU34 160 A3
Red La Aldermaston RG26 10 A3
Bradley RG25 115 E2
Headley GU35 165 F4
West Tytherley SP5 191 D4
Red Lion La
15 Basingstoke RG24 69 D2
Farnham GU9 98 C1
Overton RG25 88 A4
Red Oaks GU10 121 D2
Red Post La
Abbotts Ann SP11 104 C4
Monxton SP11 104 C4
Penton Grafton SP11 104 C4
Red Rice Rd SP10 105 E1
Redan Gdns 1 GU14 77 D1
Redan Hill Est GU12 77 D1
Redan Rd GU12 77 D1
Redbridge Dr SP10 105 F3
Redbridge La
Old Basing RG24 69 F3
Ropley SO24 182 A2
Redcrest Gdns GU15 36 B3
Rede Ct 4 GU14 56 A1
Redenham Dro SP11 81 D4
Redfield Ct RG14 2 A2
Redfields Cl GU13 74 C1
Redfields Pk GU13 74 C1

Redgrave Ct GU12 .... 77 E1
Redhearne Fields GU10 .... 144 B1
Redhouse Mews GU30 ...... 188 A1
Redlands La GU10 .... 97 F4
Redlane Hill RG7 .... 10 A3
Redon Way SP10 .... 82 C1
Redvers Buller Rd GU12 .... 77 D4
Redwood La GU34 .... 160 A4
Redwoods Way GU13 .... 75 D3
Reed Cl GU12 .... 77 D3
Reed Wlk RG14 .... 2 A2
Reeds La Liss GU33 .... 208 B3
Rake GU33 .... 208 B3
Reeds Rd The
  Frensham GU10 .... 122 B2
  Tilford GU10 .... 122 B2
Rees Rd SO21 .... 153 E1
Reeves Rd GU12 .... 77 D1
Regent Cl GU13 .... 75 D4
Regent Ct Fleet GU13 .... 74 C4
  17 Winchester SO23 ...... 176 A1
Regent St GU13 .... 75 D4
Regent Way GU16 .... 36 C1
Regents Ct Andover SP10 .... 83 F1
  Newbury RG14 .... 1 B2
Regents Pl GU15 .... 35 D4
Regiment Cl GU14 .... 55 D2
Regnum Dr RG14 .... 1 C3
Reith Way SP10 .... 82 A1
Rembrandt Cl RG21 .... 69 E2
Remembrance Gdns RG24 .. 48 C1
Remembrance Rd RG14 .... 1 B1
Renoir Cl RG25 .... 69 E2
Renown Way RG24 .... 48 C2
Restormel Ct RG22 .... 68 A3
Reubens Cres RG26 .... 26 C4
Revelstoke Ave GU14 .... 55 F3
Rewlands Dr SO22 .... 197 F1
Rex Ct GU27 .... 189 E3
Reynards Cl RG26 .... 26 C4
Reynolds Cl RG24 .... 69 F2
Reynolds Ct SP10 .... 82 C1
Reynolds Gn GU47 .... 35 D3
Reynolds Ho RG21 .... 68 B1
Reyntiens View RG29 .... 72 C1
Rhine Banks GU14 .... 55 D3
Rhodes Sq SP10 .... 83 E2
Rhododendron Rd GU14 ...... 56 C4
Ribble Cl **31** SP10 .... 83 E1
Ribble Pl GU14 .... 55 E4
Ribble Way **14** RG21 .... 69 E3
Richard Aldworth
  Com Sch The RG22 .... 68 B1
Richard Cl GU13 .... 74 C4
Richard Moss Ho **6** SO23 .. 198 A4
Richards Cl GU11 .... 77 F3
Richborough Dr SP10 .... 82 B2
Richmond Cl Bordon GU35 164 B1
  Camberley GU15 .... 36 B1
  Farnborough GU14 .... 55 D2
  Fleet GU13 .... 74 C3
Richmond Ho GU47 .... 35 E4
Richmond Rd
  Basingstoke RG21 .... 69 D3
  Sandhurst GU47 .... 35 E4
Riddings La RG7 .... 8 A1
Rideway Cl GU15 .... 35 F2
Ridge Cl RG22 .... 91 E3
Ridge La Hook RG27 .... 50 C1
  Newnham RG27 .... 50 C1
Ridgemoor Cl GU26 .... 167 E3
Ridges View SP10 .... 83 E4
Ridgeway SO22 .... 197 E3
Ridgeway Par GU13 .... 75 D3
Ridgeway Sch GU10 .... 122 A4
Ridgeway The GU34 .... 139 F1
Ridgway Hill Rd GU9 .... 122 A4
Ridgway Rd GU9 .... 122 A4
Ridings The
  Camberley GU15 .... 36 C2
  Liss GU33 .... 208 A2
Ridley Cl GU13 .... 74 C4
Ridleys Piece RG29 .... 95 D2
Rifle Way GU14 .... 55 D2
Riley La RG24 .... 70 A4
Rimbault Cl GU11 .... 77 D4
Rimes's La RG26 .... 26 B3
Ringlet Way **3** SO23 .... 198 A4
Ringshall Gdns RG26 .... 28 C2
Ringway Ctr The RG23 .... 68 C4
Ringway E RG21 .... 69 E3
Ringway N RG21 .... 69 D4
Ringway S RG21 .... 69 E2
Ringway W RG22 .... 68 C3
Ringwood Rd
  Blackwater GU17 .... 35 D3
  Farnborough GU14 .... 56 A4
Ripon Rd GU46 .... 34 B1

Ripplesmore Cl
  GU17, GU46 .... 34 C4
Rise The RG27 .... 15 F1
River Cl GU34 .... 160 A1
River Ho **50** SP10 .... 83 E1
River La GU10 .... 121 E4
River Rd GU46 .... 33 F4
River Row Cotts GU10 .... 121 E4
River View GU12 .... 128 C2
River View Cotts GU34 ...... 140 A2
River Way SP10 .... 83 E1
River Wlk RG14 .... 2 A2
Riverdale GU9 .... 121 E4
Riverhead SO24 .... 180 B2
Rivermead Ho GU47 .... 34 B4
Rivermead Rd GU47 .... 35 F1
Rivermede GU35 .... 164 C2
Rivers Cl GU14 .... 56 B1
Riverside Cl
  Farnborough GU14 .... 55 E3
  Liss GU33 .... 207 F2
  Old Basing RG24 .... 70 A4
  Overton RG25 .... 88 A4
Riverside Ct GU9 .... 99 D2
Riverside Gn SO20 .... 172 A2
Riverside Ho **24** SO23 .... 198 A4
Riverside Ind Pk GU9 .... 99 D2
Riverside Rd GU35 .... 165 E1
Riverside Way GU15 .... 35 F2
Riverwey Ind Est GU34 ...... 140 A2
Robert May's Sch RG29 .... 72 B2
Robert Mays Rd RG29 .... 72 B1
Robert Sandilands
  Cty Prim Sch RG14 .... 1 B2
Robert Way GU16 .... 56 B2
Roberts Cl SO23 .... 154 A1
Roberts Rd Aldershot GU12 .. 77 D1
  Barton Stacey SO21 .... 130 C4
  Bordon GU33 .... 186 B1
  Camberley GU15 .... 35 F3
  Sandhurst GU17 .... 35 F3
Robertsfield RG19 .... 2 B2
Robertson Rd SO24 .... 179 E2
Robertson Way GU11 .... 77 E1
Robin Cl Ash GU11 .... 77 F3
  Basingstoke RG22 .... 91 D4
Robin Hill Dr GU16 .... 36 C2
Robin Hood Cl GU14 .... 55 F4
Robin La
  Bishop's Green RG19 .... 6 B2
  Sandhurst GU17 .... 34 C4
Robin Way SP11 .... 83 D1
Robin's Bow GU15 .... 35 F2
Robins Grove Cr GU46 .... 33 F3
Robinson Way GU35 .... 164 C1
Rochester Cl GU12 .... 91 D4
Rochester Gr GU13 .... 75 D4
Rochford Rd RG21 .... 69 D2
Rock Gdns GU11 .... 76 B1
Rock La GU10 .... 121 F3
Rockbourne Rd SO22 .... 175 E2
Rockdale Dr GU26 .... 167 D2
Rockdale Ho GU26 .... 167 D2
Rockery The GU14 .... 55 F2
Rockfield Way GU15 .... 35 D4
Rockingham Rd RG14 .... 1 B1
Rockmoor La SN8 .... 18 B1
Rockpit Cotts GU33 .... 208 A2
Rodfield La SO24 .... 200 B3
Roding Cl **1** RG21 .... 69 E3
Rodney Cl SP10 .... 83 E1
Roe Downs Rd GU34 .... 160 A3
Roebuts Cl RG14 .... 5 E4
Roedeer Copse GU27 .... 189 E3
Roentgen Rd RG24 .... 69 F4
Roke La RG29 .... 96 A4
Rokeby Cl RG14 .... 5 F4
Rokes Pl GU46 .... 33 F3
Roman Cl
  Basingstoke RG23 .... 68 A3
  Stockbridge SO20 .... 149 E2
Roman Way
  Barton Stacey SO21 .... 130 C4
  Basingstoke RG23 .... 68 A3
  Farnham GU9 .... 99 E2
  Knights Enham SP10 .... 83 D2
  Thatcham RG18 .... 2 C2
Roman Way Prim Sch
  SP10 .... 83 D2
Romano Ct RG14 .... 1 C1
Romans Bsns Pk GU9 .... 99 D2
Romans Field RG7 .... 10 C1
Romans Gate RG26 .... 10 B1
Romans Ind Pk GU9 .... 99 D2
Romans's Rd **1** SO23 .... 198 A3
Romayne Cl GU14 .... 55 F3
Romley Ct GU9 .... 99 D1

Romsey Cl
  Aldershot GU10 .... 100 A3
  Basingstoke RG24 .... 48 A1
  Blackwater GU17 .... 35 D3
Romsey Rd
  Broughton SO20 .... 170 A3
  King's Somborne SO20 .... 171 F1
  Nether Wallop SO20 .... 147 F3
  Wherwell SP11 .... 128 B3
  Winchester SO22, SO23 ... 197 E3
Ronald Bowker Ct **1** SO22 197 F4
Rook La SO21 .... 133 D2
Rookery Cotts SP5 .... 190 B2
Rookery Ct RG40 .... 15 F3
Rookery La SO20 .... 170 B3
Rookery The RG28 .... 86 B3
Rooks Down Rd SO22 .... 197 E3
Rooksbury Rd SP10 .... 105 F3
Rooksdown Ave RG22 .... 68 B4
Rooksdown La RG26 .... 47 E1
Rookwood Cl GU14 .... 6 C1
Rookwood GU34 .... 139 F3
Rookwood Cl RG27 .... 51 D1
Rookwood La GU34 .... 159 E1
Rookwood Sch SP11 .... 105 F4
Room Cotts SO20 .... 129 D3
Ropley CE Prim Sch SO24 . 181 E2
Ropley Cl RG26 .... 26 C4
Ropley Rd GU34 .... 183 D2
Rorkes Drift GU14 .... 56 C2
Rosary Gdns GU47 .... 34 A3
Rose Cl RG22 .... 91 D4
Rose Cotts GU12 .... 77 F1
Rose La GU12 .... 55 E2
Rose Hodson Pl RG23 .... 68 B4
Rose Wlk GU13 .... 53 F1
Rosebank Cl RG26 .... 26 C4
Rosebay Gdns RG27 .... 51 E1
Roseberry Cl RG23 .... 91 D3
Rosebery Rd SO24 .... 179 E3
Rosedale GU17 .... 34 C4
Roseherne Gdns RG23 .... 53 F1
Rosedene La GU15 .... 35 D4
Rosehip Way RG14 .... 69 F4
Rosemary Ave GU12 .... 77 F4
Rosemary Cl GU14 .... 55 D2
Rosemary Gdns GU47 .... 35 D3
Rosemary La
  Blackwater GU17 .... 35 D3
  Farnham GU10 .... 121 E2
Rosemary Terr RG14 .... 1 B1
Rosetree Cotts GU34 .... 140 A2
Rosewane Ct **28** SO23 .... 176 A1
Rosewood Cl GU14 .... 56 C2
Rosewood Ct **4** SP9 .... 79 D4
Rosewood Rd GU35 .... 165 D3
Ross Cl RG21 .... 69 D1
Ross Terr RG14 .... 1 B1
Rossini Cl RG22 .... 91 F4
Rossmore Gdns GU11 .... 76 B1
Rothay Ct **16** RG24 .... 69 E3
Rother Cl GU47 .... 35 D4
Rother Ho GU33 .... 207 F2
Rother Rd GU14 .... 55 E4
Rotherbank Farm La GU33 208 A3
Rotherwick Cl GU12 .... 77 D4
Rotherwick La RG27 .... 50 B4
Rotherwick Rd RG26 .... 26 C4
Rotten Green Rd GU13 .... 53 F3
Rotten Hill RG25 .... 87 F3
Rotunda Est The **18** GU11 .. 76 C1
Round End RG14 .... 5 D3
Roundabouts The GU33 .... 208 A3
Roundaway La SP11 .... 58 C2
Roundhouse Rise **4** SO23 . 198 A4
Roundmead Rd RG24 .... 69 D2
Roundway GU15 .... 105 F4
Rounton Rd GU13 .... 75 D3
Rowan Chase GU10 .... 121 F3
Rowan Cl Camberley GU16 .. 36 B4
  Fleet GU13 .... 54 B1
  South Wonston SO21 ...... 153 F2
  Tadley RG26 .... 27 D4
Rowan Ct **8** SP9 .... 78 C4
Rowan Dale GU13 .... 74 C3
Rowan Dr RG14 .... 1 C3
Rowan Rd RG26 .... 27 D4
Rowan Tree Cl GU33 .... 208 A2
Rowans The Andover SP10 . 82 C1
  Grayshott GU26 .... 167 D1
Rowanside Cl GU35 .... 166 A2
Rowanwood RG40 .... 15 F3
Rowcroft Cl GU12 .... 77 F3
Rowcroft Rd RG42 .... 15 E4
Rowdell Cotts SO24 .... 181 E3
Rowhill Ave GU11 .... 99 E4
Rowhill Cres GU11 .... 99 E4
Rowhills GU11 .... 99 E4
Rowhills Cl GU11 .... 99 E4
Rowland's Cl RG7 .... 11 D3

Rowledge CE Prim Sch
  GU10 .... 121 E2
Rowlings Rd SO22 .... 175 E2
Rowlplats GU25 .... 164 B1
Royal Cl RG22 .... 91 D3
Royal Greenjackets Mus
  The SO22 .... 197 F4
Royal Hampshire County
  Hospl SO22 .... 197 E4
Royal Hampshire Regiment
  Mus SO22 .... 197 F4
Royal Military Academy
  Hospl GU17 .... 35 F4
Royal Naval Sch GU26 .... 167 F1
Royal Par GU26 .... 167 E2
Royale Cl GU10 .... 100 A4
Royce Cl SP10 .... 82 A1
Roycroft La RG40 .... 16 B4
Roydon Cl SO22 .... 197 F3
Rozeldene GU26 .... 167 E2
Rozelle Cl SO22 .... 175 D3
Rubens Cl RG21 .... 69 E2
Rucstall Prim Sch RG21 ...... 69 E2
Rudd Hall Rise GU15 .... 36 A2
Ruffield Cl SO22 .... 175 E1
Rufford Cl GU13 .... 75 D3
Runfold-St George GU9 ...... 99 F3
Runnymede Ct **1** GU14 ...... 55 F4
Runwick La GU9 .... 98 A1
Rupert Rd RG14 .... 5 E4
Rural Life Ctr GU9 .... 122 B2
Rushden Way GU9 .... 99 D4
Rushmoor Cl GU13 .... 75 D4
Rushmoor Ct GU12 .... 77 D4
Rushmoor Ind Sch GU16 .... 56 A1
Rushmoor Rd GU11 .... 76 A2
Ruskin Cl RG21 .... 69 F2
Russel Rd RG21 .... 69 D2
Russell Cl Blackwater GU17 . 35 D3
  Hindhead GU26 .... 167 E2
Russell Rd Newbury RG14 .... 1 B1
  Winchester SO23 .... 176 A1
Russet Cl
  New Alresford SO24 .... 179 E2
  Tongham GU11 .... 100 B4
Russet Gdns GU15 .... 36 A2
Russet Glade GU11 .... 99 E4
Russett Rd GU34 .... 140 A2
Russetts Dr GU13 .... 75 D4
Rustic Glen GU13 .... 74 C3
Ruth Cl GU14 .... 55 D3
Rutherford Rd RG21 .... 69 E4
Rutland Cl GU11 .... 76 C2
Ryan Mount GU17 .... 34 C4
Rydal Cl Bordon GU35 .... 164 B3
  Farnborough GU14 .... 55 D2
Rydal Dr Fleet GU13 .... 74 C3
  Thatcham RG19 .... 2 C2
Ryde Cl GU46 .... 33 F3
Ryde Croft GU13 .... 74 C2
Rydeck Rd GU13 .... 75 D3
Ryecroft Gdns GU47 .... 35 E2
Ryeland Cl GU13 .... 54 B3
Ryelaw Rd GU13 .... 75 D3
Ryle Rd GU10 .... 121 F4
Ryon Cl SP10 .... 83 D2
Ryves Ave GU46 .... 33 F3

Sabre Cl **3** GU11 .... 76 B1
Saddleback Rd GU15 .... 36 B4
Saddleback Way GU13 .... 54 A2
Saddlers Cl SO21 .... 131 E2
Saddlers Ct RG14 .... 1 B2
Saddlers Scarp GU26 .... 166 C2
Saddlewood GU15 .... 36 A2
Saffron Cl Chineham RG24 .. 49 D2
  Newbury RG14 .... 1 B2
Saffron Ct GU14 .... 55 D2
Sages La GU34 .... 204 B3
Sainfoin La RG25 .... 90 A4
Sainsbury Cl SP10 .... 105 F3
St Albans Rdbt GU12 .... 77 D4
St Andrew's Cl **5** GU11 ..... 99 D1
St Andrew's Inf Sch GU10 .. 98 C1
St Andrew's Rd RG22 .... 68 B2
St Andrew's Way GU16 .... 56 B4
St Andrews Rd
  Bordon GU35 .... 164 A1
  North Tidworth SP9 .... 78 C3
St Ann's Cl SP11 .... 105 F4
St Anne's RC Prim Sch
  RG22 .... 68 B2
St Annes Cl SO22 .... 197 E2
St Aubins Cl GU34 .... 160 A1
St Augustine's Cl GU12 ...... 77 D1
St Austins GU26 .... 167 D2
St Barbara's Cl RG27 .... 29 D1
St Bartholomews Sch RG14 .. 1 B1

St Bede CE Prim Sch SO23 198 A4
St Bede's Ct **20** SO23 .... 176 A1
St Bede's RC Prim Sch
  RG24 .... 48 A1
St Benedict's Convent Sch
  SP11 .... 82 A2
St Benedicts Cl GU11 .... 76 C3
St Bernadette RC Prim Sch
  GU14 .... 55 F3
St Catherine's Hill RG7 .... 11 E3
St Catherine's Prep Sch
  GU15 .... 36 A2
St Catherine's Rd SO23 ..... 198 A3
St Catherines Rd GU14 .... 56 C4
St Catherines Way SO23 ... 198 B3
St Christopher's Gn GU27 . 189 F3
St Christopher's Rd GU27 . 189 F3
St Christophers Cl
  Basingstoke RG22 .... 68 B2
  Haslemere GU27 .... 189 F3
St Christophers Pl GU14 ..... 55 F2
St Christophers Rd GU14 .... 55 F2
St Clement St **2** SO23 .... 198 A4
St Clements Ct GU14 .... 55 F4
St Cross Cl **4** SO22 .... 197 F3
St Cross Mede SO22 .... 197 F2
St Cross Rd Camberley GU16 56 C4
  Crondall GU10 .... 97 E3
  Farnham GU11 .... 99 D2
  Winchester SO22 .... 197 F3
St David's Cl
  Farnborough GU14 .... 55 E4
  Farnham GU9 .... 99 E4
St David's Rd
  Basingstoke RG22 .... 68 C2
  Newbury RG14 .... 1 B1
St Davids Cl RG29 .... 72 B1
St Donats Pl RG14 .... 1 C1
St Edmunds Sch GU26 ...... 167 D2
St Faith Cl GU34 .... 160 A1
St Faith's CE Prim Sch
  SO22 .... 197 F3
St Faith's Rd SO22 .... 197 F3
St Gabriel's Sch
  Sandleford Priory RG14 ...... 5 F3
St George's Cl GU9 .... 99 F3
St George's Rd
  Aldershot GU12 .... 76 C3
  Farnham GU9 .... 99 D1
St George's Rd E GU11 .... 76 C1
St George's St SO23 .... 198 A4
St Georges Ave RG14 .... 1 B1
St Georges Ind Est GU17 ... 35 F2
St Georges Mews GU9 .... 99 D2
St Georges Rd
  Farnham GU9 .... 99 F3
  North Tidworth SP9 .... 78 C3
St Georges Yd GU9 .... 99 D1
St Giles Cl SO23 .... 198 A4
St Gregory's RC Fst Sch
  GU15 .... 35 F3
St Helens Cres GU17 .... 34 C4
St Hubert Rd SP10 .... 105 F4
St James' Ave GU9 .... 99 D2
St James Cl Farnham GU9 ... 99 D2
  Fleet GU13 .... 74 C4
St James' La SO22 .... 197 F4
St James Rd Fleet GU13 ...... 74 C4
  Wokingham RG40 .... 16 B4
St James' Terr
  Farnham GU9 .... 99 D2
  Winchester SO22 .... 197 F4
St John the Baptist
  RC Prim Sch SP10 .... 105 E4
St John the Evangelist
  CE Inf Sch RG14 .... 1 B1
St John's CE Prim Sch
  RG21 .... 69 D2
St John's Cotts RG27 .... 71 F4
St John's Ct
  Farnborough GU14 .... 55 D3
  10 Fleet GU13 .... 74 C4
St John's Hospital (N) **21**
  SO23 .... 198 A4
St John's Hospital (S) **32**
  SO23 .... 198 A4
St John's Inf Sch RG7 .... 11 F3
St John's Piece RG26 .... 90 A4
St John's Rd Andover SP10 106 A4
  Farnborough GU14 .... 55 D3
  Farnham GU10 .... 121 F4
  Mortimer RG7 .... 11 F3
  Newbury RG14 .... 1 B1
  Oakley RG23 .... 67 E1
  Sandhurst GU46 .... 34 C4
  Winchester SO23 .... 198 A4
St John's St SO23 .... 198 A4
St John's Wlk **21** RG21 ..... 69 D3
St Johns CE Inf Sch GU10 144 B1
St Johns Cl RG27 .... 51 D3
St Johns Gr GU10 .... 121 F4

St Johns Rd RG27 .... 52 B3
St Joseph's Cres RG24 .... 48 C1
St Joseph's RC Prim Sch
  RG14 .... 1 C2
St Joseph's Rd GU12 .... 76 C1
St Josephs Ct RG14 .... 1 C2
St Josephs RC GM Prim Sch
  GU9 .... 99 F4
St Just Cl SP4 .... 123 D3
St Lawrence CE Prim Sch
  GU34 .... 139 F2
St Lawrence Rd GU34 .... 139 F2
St Leger Ct RG14 .... 1 B2
St Leonard's Ave RG24 .... 49 D2
St Leonard's Rd SO23 .... 198 B3
St Lucia Pk GU35 .... 164 C3
St Margarets SP11 .... 81 F4
St Mark's CE Prim Sch
  Basingstoke RG22 .... 91 D3
  Farnborough GU12 .... 77 D4
St Marks Cl GU14 .... 56 A1
St Marks Pl GU9 .... 98 C4
St Martin Cl SO23 .... 198 A4
St Martin's CE Prim Sch
  RG20 .... 20 C4
St Martins Ind Est SO23 .... 198 A4
St Mary Bourne
  Cty Prim Sch SP11 .... 61 F1
St Mary Magdalen
  Almshouses 35 SO23 .... 198 A4
St Mary St SO22 .... 197 E3
St Mary's Almshouses
  RG14 .... 1 B1
St Mary's Ave RG26 .... 29 D1
St Mary's CE Inf Sch GU10 144 A4
St Mary's CE Jun Sch RG24 70 A3
St Mary's Cl
  Kings Worthy SO21 .... 176 B3
  Old Basing RG24 .... 70 A3
St Mary's Coll SO23 .... 198 A3
St Mary's Ct
  Basingstoke RG21 .... 69 E3
  Bramley RG7 .... 29 D1
  4 Newbury RG14 .... 1 C2
St Mary's Meadow SP11 .... 105 D2
St Mary's Pl
  Farnham GU9 .... 99 D2
  Newbury RG14 .... 1 C2
St Mary's Rd Ash GU12 .... 77 F3
  Camberley GU15 .... 36 A3
  Hartley Wintney RG27 .... 52 B3
  Kingsclere RG20 .... 24 B1
  Liss SO23 .... 207 F2
  Mortimer RG7 .... 11 F3
  Newbury RG14 .... 1 C2
St Marys CE Jun Sch RG7 .... 12 A3
St Marys Cl GU17 .... 35 D4
St Matthew's CE Prim Sch
  GU33 .... 186 A4
St Matthews Rd SO22 .... 175 E1
St Michael's CE Inf Sch
  GU9 .... 99 F4
St Michael's CE Jun Sch
  GU10 .... 100 A4
St Michael's CE Prim Sch
  GU46 .... 34 B4
St Michael's Cl RG25 .... 89 F1
St Michael's Gdns 20 SO22 197 F4
St Michael's Hall GU9 .... 99 F4
St Michael's Pass SO23 .... 198 A3
St Michael's Rd
  Aldershot GU12 .... 76 C1
  Basingstoke RG22 .... 68 B2
  Farnborough GU14 .... 55 F3
  Newbury RG14 .... 1 B1
  Sandhurst GU47 .... 34 B4
  Winchester SO22 .... 197 F3
St Michaels Ave SP9 .... 78 C3
St Michaels Cl Fleet GU13 .... 75 D4
  South Tidworth SP9 .... 78 C3
St Michaels Rd GU15 .... 35 F3
St Michaels Sch RG26 .... 21 E3
St Neot's Rd RG27 .... 32 B4
St Neot's Sch RG27 .... 32 B4
St Nicholas CE Jun Sch RG14 1 C1
St Nicholas Cl SP11 .... 57 D1
St Nicholas Ct RG22 .... 68 B2
St Nicholas Rd RG14 .... 1 B1
St Nicholas Rise SO23 .... 176 A3
St Patrick's La Liss GU33 .... 208 B3
  Rake GU33 .... 208 B3
St Patrick's CE Prim Sch
  GU16 .... 56 A2
St Patrick's Rd RG22 .... 68 C2
St Patricks Ave SP9 .... 78 C3
St Paul's CE Inf Sch GU10 100 C4
St Paul's Hill SO22 .... 197 F4
St Paul's Hospl SO22 .... 197 F4
St Paul's Rd RG22 .... 68 C2
St Pauls Pl 11 SO22 .... 197 F4
St Peter St SO23 .... 198 A4

St Peter's CE Jun Sch
  Farnborough GU14 .... 56 A2
  Yateley GU46 .... 34 B3
St Peter's CE Prim Sch
  GU10 .... 121 F3
St Peter's Gdns
  Farnham GU10 .... 121 E3
  Yateley GU47 .... 34 A3
St Peter's Rd RG22 .... 68 B2
St Peter's Way GU16 .... 56 B4
St Peters Ct
  Headley, Nr Greenham RG19 7 D1
  Tadley RG26 .... 26 C4
St Peters Mead GU12 .... 77 F1
St Peters Pk GU11 .... 99 E4
St Philips Cl 4 GU31 .... 54 A1
St Polycarp's RC Prim Sch
  GU9 .... 99 D1
St Richards Rd RG14 .... 1 C3
St Stephen's Rd SO22 .... 175 E1
St Stephens Cl GU27 .... 189 E3
St Swithun St SO23 .... 198 A4
St Swithun's Sch SO23 .... 198 B4
St Thomas' Cl RG21 .... 69 D4
St Thomas Cl SO22 .... 82 C2
St Thomas' Pas 2 SO22 .... 197 F4
St Thomas St 4 SO23 .... 198 A4
Salamanca Pk GU11 .... 76 B1
Salcombe Rd RG14 .... 1 B1
Salcot Rd SO23 .... 176 A1
Salerno Cl GU11 .... 76 C1
Salerno Rd SP9 .... 79 E3
Sales Ct 5 GU11 .... 76 C1
Salesian Coll
  Farnborough GU16 .... 56 A1
  Farnborough GU12 .... 77 D4
Salesian View GU12 .... 77 E4
Salisbury Cl Alton GU34 .... 140 A1
  Odiham RG29 .... 72 B1
Salisbury Gdns RG22 .... 68 B2
Salisbury Gr GU16 .... 56 C2
Salisbury Rd GU16 .... 56 C2
Salisbury Row 17 SP9 .... 78 C4
Salisbury SO20 .... 147 E4
Salisbury Rd
  Abbotts Ann SP10 .... 105 D2
  Andover SP10 .... 105 F3
  Ash GU12 .... 77 F1
  Blackwater GU17 .... 35 D3
  Broughton SO20 .... 169 F4
  Farnborough GU14 .... 56 A2
  New Alresford SO24 .... 179 E3
  Over Wallop SP11 .... 124 C3
  Shipton Bellinger SP9 .... 101 F3
  Upper Clatford SP11 .... 105 F3
Salisbury Terr GU16 .... 56 C2
Salmond Rd SP10, SP11 .... 105 D4
Salmons Rd RG29 .... 72 B1
Salters Acres SO22 .... 175 E2
Salters Heath Rd RG26 .... 47 D4
Salters La SO22 .... 175 D1
Saltmarsh Cl GU15 .... 56 B1
Samarkand Cl GU15 .... 36 C2
Sampson Bsns Pk GU17 .... 35 F2
Sampson's Almshouses 11
  GU9 .... 98 C1
Samuel Cody Ho GU12 .... 77 F4
Samuel Cody Sch GU14 .... 76 C4
San Carlos App GU14 .... 77 D1
Sand Hill GU14 .... 55 F4
Sand Hill La GU14 .... 55 F4
Sandbanks Dr RG22 .... 91 D4
Sandford Cl RG21 .... 24 C1
Sandford Rd GU11 .... 76 B1
Sandford Rd
  Aldershot GU11 .... 76 B1
  Farnham GU9 .... 98 C4
  Tadley RG26 .... 26 C4
Sandheath Rd GU26 .... 167 D4
Sandhurst La GU47 .... 34 C3
Sandhurst Rd
  Wokingham RG40 .... 16 C4
  Yateley GU46 .... 34 B4
Sandhurst Royal Military
  Acad GU17 .... 35 F4
Sandhurst Sch GU47 .... 35 D4
Sandhurst Sta GU47 .... 34 C4
Sandleford Hospl RG14 .... 5 F4
Sandleford Rise RG14 .... 5 F4
Sandown Cl Alton GU34 .... 140 A1
  Blackwater GU17 .... 35 D3
Sandown Cres GU9 .... 99 F4
Sandown Dr GU15 .... 36 A1
Sandown Way RG22 .... 2 A1
Sandpiper Way RG22 .... 90 C4
Sandpit Cotts GU13 .... 75 D1
Sandpit Hill RG26 .... 5 D2
Sandpit La RG7 .... 14 C3
Sandringham Cl
  Alton GU34 .... 139 E2
  Farnborough GU11 .... 76 C4
Sandringham Ct RG22 .... 68 B2

Sandringham Ho 5 SP10 .... 83 D2
Sandringham Inf Sch GU14 56 B4
Sandringham Way GU16 .... 56 B4
Sandrock Hill Rd GU10 .... 121 F3
Sands Cl GU11 .... 100 A1
Sands Rd Farnham GU10 .... 100 A1
  Seale GU10 .... 100 A1
Sands The GU35 .... 164 A1
Sandy Cross GU10 .... 100 B2
Sandy Hill Rd GU9 .... 98 C4
Sandy La Bramshott GU27 189 D4
  Camberley GU15 .... 36 B3
  Farnborough GU14 .... 55 D4
  Fleet GU13 .... 75 D4
  Frensham GU9 .... 144 C3
  Frensham GU10 .... 144 C3
  Hartley Wintney RG27 .... 52 B3
  Haslemere GU27 .... 167 E1
  Rake GU33 .... 208 C2
  Tadley RG26 .... 27 D4
Sandys Cl RG23 .... 68 C2
Sandys Rd RG23 .... 68 C2
Sandys Road Rdbt RG22 .... 68 C2
Sangro Rd SP9 .... 79 E3
Sankey La GU13 .... 54 B2
Santina Cl GU11 .... 99 D4
Saor Mews SP10 .... 105 F4
Sapley La RG25 .... 88 A4
Sarah Way GU14 .... 55 F2
Sarisbury Cl RG26 .... 26 C4
Sarson Cl SP11 .... 104 A3
Sarson La Amport SP11 .... 104 A4
  Thruxton SP11 .... 104 A4
Sarum Cl
  Over Wallop SO20 .... 147 E4
  Shipton Bellinger SP9 .... 101 E4
  Winchester SO22 .... 197 E4
Sarum Hill RG21 .... 69 D2
Sarum Rd Tadley RG26 .... 9 F1
  Winchester SO22 .... 197 D4
Sarum Ho 16 RG26 .... 9 E1
Saturn Cl GU11 .... 99 D4
Saunton Gdns GU14 .... 55 F3
Savernake Ho 2 SP9 .... 78 C3
Saville Cres GU35 .... 164 B2
Saville Gdns GU14 .... 36 C2
Savoy Cl SP10 .... 106 A4
Savoy Gr SP17 .... 35 D2
Sawyer Cl SO22 .... 175 D1
Saxon Croft GU11 .... 99 D1
Saxon Ct 1 SP10 .... 83 D2
Saxon Leas SP5 .... 168 A3
Saxon Mews 9 GU34 .... 139 F2
Saxon Rd GU11 .... 176 A1
Saxon Way RG14 .... 69 F4
Saxon Wood Sch RG22 .... 68 A4
Saxony Way GU17 .... 34 A2
Sayers Cl Camberley GU14 .... 56 B4
  Newbury RG14 .... 1 C2
Scamblers Mead SP11 .... 81 F2
Scarlatti Rd RG22 .... 91 F4
Scarlet Oaks GU16 .... 36 B2
Scarlett's Rd GU11 .... 76 C2
School Cl SP11 .... 38 B3
School Fields GU35 .... 142 A1
School Hill Farnham GU9 .... 121 E3
  Seale GU10 .... 100 C2
School La Bentley GU10 .... 120 A3
  Bishop's Sutton SO24 .... 180 A2
  Broughton SO20 .... 170 A4
  Ewshot GU9 .... 98 A4
  Farnham GU10 .... 122 A3
  Itchen Abbas SO21 .... 177 F4
  Kings Worthy SO23 .... 176 A3
  3 Liss GU33 .... 207 F2
  Michelmersh SO51 .... 193 E1
  Middle Wallop SO20 .... 147 F4
  Riseley RG7 .... 14 B2
  Ropley SO24 .... 181 E2
  Silchester RG7 .... 10 C1
  Yateley GU46 .... 33 F3
Schubert Rd RG22 .... 91 F4
Scotland Cl GU12 .... 77 F3
Scotland Farm Rd GU12 .... 77 F3
Scotland Hill GU46 .... 34 C4
Scotland La GU27 .... 189 E3
Scotlands Cl GU27 .... 189 F3
Scotlands Dr GU27 .... 189 F3
Scotney Rd RG21 .... 69 D4
Scott Cl Andover SP10 .... 83 F1
  King's Somborne SO20 .... 172 A1
Scott's Ct GU14 .... 55 F4
Scrubbs La SO24 .... 180 A2
Scures Rd RG27 .... 50 C1
Seagull Cl RG23 .... 90 C4

Seal Rd 8 RG21 .... 69 D3
Searle Cl GU9 .... 122 A4
Searle La Hook RG27 .... 51 D2
  Hook RG27 .... 51 E1
Searles Cl SO24 .... 179 E3
Seaton Rd GU15 .... 35 F3
Sebastopol Rd GU11 .... 76 C1
Second St E RG14 .... 6 C3
Second St W RG19 .... 6 B2
Sedgefield Rd RG14 .... 6 A4
Sedgemoor GU14 .... 55 F4
Seebys Oak GU17 .... 35 E3
Sefton Rd 12 GU11 .... 76 C1
Sek Kong Cl SO20 .... 126 A2
Selborne Ave GU10 .... 100 A3
Selborne Cl
  Blackwater GU17 .... 35 D3
  Hook RG27 .... 51 D1
Selborne Pl SO22 .... 197 E3
Selborne Rd Alton GU34 .... 162 B3
  East Worldham GU34 .... 162 B3
  Selborne GU34 .... 162 B3
Selborne Way GU35 .... 164 A1
Selborne Wlk RG26 .... 26 C4
Selbourne CE Prim Sch
  GU34 .... 184 B4
Selbourne Gdns GU10 .... 121 F4
Selby Wlk RG24 .... 48 A1
Selby Cl SO22 .... 197 D2
Selwyn Dr GU46 .... 33 F3
Sepen Meade GU13 .... 74 C2
Seremban Cl SO20 .... 126 A3
Sermon Rd SO22 .... 175 D1
Seton Dr RG27 .... 71 F4
Sett The GU46 .... 33 F3
Seventh St RG14 .... 6 B3
Severals The RG26 .... 47 F2
Severn Cl Sandhurst GU15 .... 35 D4
  Thatcham RG18 .... 2 C3
Severn Ct 52 SP10 .... 83 E1
Severn Gdns RG22, RG23 .... 67 D1
Severn Rd GU14 .... 55 E3
Seville Cl RG26 .... 26 C4
Seville Cres SP10 .... 83 E1
Seymour Cl Fleet GU13 .... 54 A1
  Odiham RG29 .... 72 C2
Seymour Dr GU15 .... 36 C4
Seymour P RG29 .... 72 C2
Seymour Rd
  Basingstoke RG22 .... 68 B1
  Headley GU35 .... 166 A2
Shackleton Sq SP10 .... 83 E1
Shady Nook GU9 .... 98 C3
Shaftesbury Ct
  Bordon GU35 .... 164 B1
  Farnborough GU11 .... 77 D4
Shaftesbury Mount GU47 .... 35 D2
Shakespeare Ave SP10 .... 82 B1
Shakespeare Gdns GU14 .... 55 D3
Shakespeare Rd RG21 .... 69 E4
Shalbourne Rise GU15 .... 36 A3
Shalden La GU34 .... 138 C4
Shalden Rd GU12 .... 100 A4
Shamrock Cl GU16 .... 56 A4
Shanklin Ct GU12 .... 77 D1
Shannon Ct 53 SP10 .... 83 E1
Shapley Heath RG27 .... 52 A1
Shapley Hill RG27 .... 52 B1
Shap Cl SP10 .... 105 E4
Shaw cum Donnington
  Parochial Prim Sch RG14 .... 1 B3
Shaw Farm Rd RG14 .... 1 C3
Shaw Hill RG14 .... 1 C3
Shaw Ho SP11 .... 81 D3
Shaw House Comp Sch
  RG14 .... 1 C3
Shaw La RG26 .... 26 B4
Shaw Mill RG14 .... 1 C3
Shaw Pightle RG27 .... 50 C1
Shaw Rd RG14 .... 1 C3
Sheddon Pl SO21 .... 174 B1
Sheep Dro SP20 .... 147 E2
Sheep Fair SP10, SP11 .... 106 B4
Sheep Fair Cl SP10 .... 106 B4
Sheep Ho GU10 .... 122 A4
Sheephatch La GU9 .... 122 C3
Sheepwash RG14 .... 5 F1
Sheepwash La RG26 .... 46 B4
Sheerlands Rd RG40 .... 15 E3
Sheffield Cl GU14 .... 55 E2
Shefford Lodge 7 RG14 .... 1 C1
Sheldon's La RG27 .... 51 D1
Sheldon's Rd RG27 .... 51 D1
Shell La GU34 .... 183 D1
Shelley Cl Basingstoke RG24 .... 69 E4
  Fleet GU13 .... 75 D4
  Itchen Abbas SO21 .... 177 F3
  Winchester SO21, SO22 .... 197 E4

Shelley Ct GU15 .... 36 A3
Shelleys La GU34 .... 140 C1
Shelly Rise GU14 .... 55 E3
Shenstone Cl RG40 .... 16 C4
Shepherds Cl SO22 .... 197 D2
Shepherds Ct GU9 .... 122 A4
Shepherds Down SO24 .... 179 E2
Shepherds Rd SO23 .... 198 B4
Shepherds Rise SP11 .... 38 B3
Shepherds Row SP11 .... 106 B4
Shepherds Spring La SP10 .... 83 D1
Shepherds Spring Schs
  SP10 .... 83 D2
Shepherds Way GU30 .... 188 A2
Shepherds Wlk GU14 .... 55 E4
Sheppard Almshouses
  SP11 .... 104 A3
Sheppard Cl RG28 .... 86 B2
Sheppard Rd RG21 .... 69 D1
Sheppard Sq SP10 .... 83 E1
Sheraton Ave RG22 .... 91 D4
Sheraton Cl GU17 .... 35 E2
Sherborne Rd
  Basingstoke RG24 .... 69 D4
  Farnborough GU11 .... 77 D4
Sherborne St John
  CE Prim Sch RG26 .... 47 F2
Sherbrooke Cl SO23 .... 176 B4
Sherfield Rd RG26 .... 29 D1
Sheridan Cl SO22 .... 197 E3
Sheridan Cres RG26 .... 9 E1
Sheridan Ct Camberley GU16 56 A4
  Newbury RG14 .... 2 A2
Sheridan Rd GU16 .... 56 A4
Sherlock Lea GU17, GU46 .... 33 E4
Sherrard Mead RG14 .... 1 C3
Sherrington Way RG22 .... 68 C1
Sherwin Cres GU16 .... 56 A4
Sherwood Cl
  Basingstoke RG22 .... 91 E3
  Liss GU33 .... 208 A4
Sherwood Terr GU34 .... 140 A2
Shetland Rd RG24 .... 48 B1
Shetland Way GU13 .... 54 A2
Ship Alley GU14 .... 56 A4
Ship La GU16 .... 56 A3
Shipley Ct GU30 .... 188 A2
Shipton Bellinger
  Cty Prim Sch SP9 .... 101 E4
Shipton Way RG22 .... 68 B1
Shire Ave GU13 .... 54 B2
Shire Ct 2 GU11 .... 76 B1
Shires Way GU46 .... 34 B4
Shoddesden La
  Kimpton SP11 .... 80 B3
  Ludgershall SP11 .... 57 D1
Shoe La GU11 .... 76 C3
Shooters Way RG24 .... 69 E3
Shop La RG14 .... 1 B3
Short Dale Rd GU11 .... 100 A3
Short La SP10 .... 82 A1
Short St Aldershot GU11 .... 76 C1
  Ludgershall SP11 .... 57 D1
Shortheath Crest GU10 .... 121 E3
Shortheath Rd GU9 .... 121 F3
Shotter's La GU34 .... 183 F3
Shotterfield Terr GU33 .... 207 F2
Shottermill Cty Fst Sch
  GU27 .... 189 E4
Shottermill Cty Jun Sch
  GU27 .... 189 E4
Shottermill Rd GU27 .... 189 E3
Shrave The GU34 .... 160 C3
Shrewsbury Terr RG14 .... 1 B1
Shrivenham Cl GU47 .... 35 D4
Shrubbery The GU14 .... 55 D2
Shrubbs La GU10 .... 121 E2
Shyshack La Baughurst RG26 9 E1
  Tadley RG26 .... 9 E1
Sian Cl GU13 .... 75 D3
Sibelius Cl RG22 .... 91 F4
Sickle Rd GU27 .... 189 F3
Sickles SO23 .... 142 A1
Sidbury Circular Rd SP9 .... 78 B4
Sidbury Hill Ave SP9 .... 78 C4
Sidings The GU12 .... 77 D2
Sidlaw Cl RG22 .... 68 A2
Sidlaws Rd GU14 .... 55 D3
Sidmouth Rd SP10 .... 106 A4
Silchester CE Prim Sch RG7 .... 10 C1
Silchester Cl SP10 .... 82 C1
Silchester Rd Bramley RG26 .... 28 B2
  Pamber End RG26 .... 27 F2
  Silchester RG26 .... 10 B1
  Pamber Heath RG26 .... 10 B1
Silk Mill La RG25 .... 87 F4
Silkweavers Rd SP10 .... 106 A4

Silver Birch Cl Fleet GU13 .... 74 C3
Liss GU33 .... 208 A2
Silver Birch Rd SP10 .... 82 C1
Silver Hill Sandhurst GU17 ... 35 E4
Winchester SO23 .... 198 A4
Silver La RG7 .... 10 C4
Silver Park Cl GU13 .... 75 D3
Silverdale GU13 .... 75 D3
Silverdale Rd RG26 .... 9 F1
Silverglades GU46 .... 34 A2
Silverwood Dr GU15 .... 36 C4
Silvester Cl RG21 .... 69 E4
Silvester Way GU13 .... 74 C3
Silwood Cl SO22 .... 175 E1
Simmondstone La GU10 .. 144 A1
Simmons Wlk **20**
RG21, RG24 .... 69 E3
Simms Farm La RG7 .... 11 E2
Simonds Ct **5** SO23 .... 176 A1
Simons Cl GU14 .... 48 C1
Simons Rd PG24 .... 48 C1
Sine Cl GU14 .... 55 F4
Sinhurst Rd GU17 .... 35 F2
Sixth St RG14 .... 6 B3
Skates La RG26 .... 27 D3
Skew Rd Amport SP11 .... 103 D2
Quarley SP11 .... 103 D2
Skinners Green La RG14 .... 4 C4
Skippetts La E RG21 .... 69 E1
Skippetts La W RG21 .... 69 D1
Skippons Cl RG14 .... 5 D3
Skylings RG14 .... 2 A2
Slade Hill Gdns RG20 .... 4 B1
Sleeper's Hill Ho SO22 ...... 197 E3
Sleeper's Hill Rd SO22 .... 197 E3
Sleepers Delle Gdns SO22 197 F3
Sleepers Hill SO22 .... 197 E3
Slessor Cl SP10 .... 105 D4
Slim Cl GU12 .... 77 E4
Slim Rd GU47 .... 35 F4
Smallfield Dr RG27 .... 51 E1
Smallridge RG14 .... 5 D2
Smannell & Enham
CE Prim Sch SP10 .... 83 F4
Smannell Rd
Knights Enham SP10 .... 83 E2
Smannell Rd SP10 .... 83 E2
Smay Down La RG40 .... 17 D2
Smeaton Rd SP10 .... 82 A1
Smithfield La GU35 .... 143 F1
Smiths Mead RG25 .... 89 F1
Smithy Cl GU34 .... 140 B4
Smithy La GU35 .... 143 E1
Smugglers La SO24 .... 182 A1
Smugglers' Way GU12 ...... 100 B1
Snailing La GU33 .... 207 F4
Snailslynch GU9 .... 99 D1
Snipe La
Bishop's Green RG20 .... 6 B1
Linchmere RG27 .... 189 F1
Snoddington Rd SP11 .... 80 A1
Snode Hill GU34 .... 139 D2
Snowdon Rd GU14 .... 55 E4
Snowdrop Cl RG22 .... 91 D4
Snowdrop Wlk **2** GU13 ... 53 F1
Soame's La SO24 .... 181 F1
Sobers Sq SP10 .... 83 E1
Society of St Pius X
St Michael's Sch RG20 ...... 22 B3
Soke Hill SO24 .... 159 F1
Soke Rd Aldermaston RG26 . 10 B2
Silchester RG26 .... 10 B2
Soke The SO24 .... 179 E3
Solarton Rd GU14 .... 55 F2
Solby's Rd RG21 .... 69 D3
Soldridge Rd GU34 .... 159 F2
Solent Dr RG22 .... 91 D4
Somborne Park Rd SO20 .. 172 B4
Somers Cl SO22 .... 197 E3
Somerset Ave GU35 .... 164 B2
Somerset Ct **11** GU14 ...... 56 A1
Somerset Rd GU14 .... 56 A1
Somerville Cres GU47 .... 34 B3
Somerville Ct SP11 .... 83 E1
Somerville Rd SO23 .... 176 B4
Somme Rd SP9 .... 79 E4
Sonnige Cl GU47 .... 35 D4
Sonning Cl RG22 .... 90 C4
Soper Gr RG21 .... 69 D3
Sopwith Cl SO20 .... 172 A1
Sopwith Pk SP10 .... 82 A1
Sorrel Cl Farnborough GU14 55 D3
Newbury RG14 .... 2 A3
Sorrell's Ct RG14 .... 2 A2
Sotherington La GU34 .... 185 E3
South Atlantic Dr GU14 ...... 77 D2
South Ave GU9 .... 99 D3
South Cl SO24 .... 179 D3

South Dr Littleton SO22 ..... 175 D2
Sherfield on Loddon RG24 .... 49 E4
South Tidworth SP9 .... 78 C2
South End Rd SP10 .... 106 A3
South Farnborough Inf Sch
GU11 .... 77 D4
South Farnborough Jun Sch
GU14 .... 56 A1
South Farnham Sch GU9 .... 99 D1
South Gr GU33 .... 54 B2
South Ham Rd RG22 .... 68 C2
South Hill RG25 .... 94 B3
South Hurst GU35 .... 164 B1
South La GU11 .... 77 F1
South Mall **18** GU13 .... 53 F1
South Rd Broughton SO20 . 170 B3
Kingsclere RG20 .... 24 C1
Liphook GU30 .... 188 A1
New Alresford SO24 .... 179 D3
South Ridge RG29 .... 72 C1
South Side GU10 .... 100 B4
South St Andover SP10 ...... 106 A4
Ash GU11 .... 77 F2
Farnborough GU14 .... 56 B1
Farnham GU9 .... 99 D1
Ropley SO24 .... 181 E2
South Town Rd GU34 .... 159 F3
South View SO22 .... 197 F4
South View Cl SO21 .... 131 E2
South View Cotts
Bentley GU10 .... 120 A2
Hook RG29 .... 72 A4
South View Gdns
Andover SP10 .... 106 A4
16 Newbury RG14 .... 1 C2
South View Rd SO22 .... 197 D2
South View Schs RG21 .... 69 E4
South View Terr SP10 .... 85 D4
South Way SP11 .... 83 F1
South Wlk GU11 .... 77 D1
South Wonston Prim Sch
SO21 .... 153 E2
Southampton Cl GU15 .... 35 D3
Southampton Ho **8** SP9 ... 78 C3
Southampton St GU11 .... 76 C4
Southbrook Cotts SO21 ..... 133 D2
Southbrook Pl SO21 .... 133 D2
Southby Dr GU14 .... 54 A1
Southcote Dr GU15 .... 36 C3
Southdown Rd Tadley RG26 26 C4
Thatcham RG19 .... 29 D2
Southend Rd **1** RG21 .... 69 D3
Southern Haye RG27 .... 52 B3
Southern Rd
Basingstoke RG21 .... 69 D2
Bordon GU35 .... 164 B3
Camberley GU15 .... 36 A3
Southern Way
Farnborough GU14 .... 55 E2
Farnham GU9 .... 99 D1
Southgate St SO23 .... 197 F4
Southgate Villas SO23 ...... 197 F4
Southington La RG25 .... 87 F4
Southlands RG26 .... 48 C2
Southlands Cl GU12 .... 77 F1
Southlands Rd GU12 .... 77 F1
Southlea RG25 .... 92 A4
Southmead Rd GU9 .... 99 F4
Southrope Gn RG25 .... 116 B4
Southside Cotts SO20 .... 149 F2
Southside Rd SP11 .... 108 A3
Southview Cotts GU10 ...... 122 A1
Southview Rd GU35 .... 165 F3
Southview Rise GU34 .... 139 F3
Southwark Cl GU34 .... 34 A3
Southway GU15 .... 35 F2
Southwell Park Rd GU15 ..... 36 A3
Southwick Cl SO22 .... 175 E2
Southwood Cres The GU14 . 55 D2
Southwood Inf Sch GU14 ... 55 D2
Southwood La GU14 .... 55 D2
Southwood Rd
Farnborough GU14 .... 55 E2
Hawley GU46 .... 34 B1
Shalden GU34 .... 139 D4
Sovereign Cl **11** GU13 ..... 53 F1
Sovereign Dr GU15 .... 36 C4
Sowcroft La GU34 .... 118 A3
Spain La Bentworth RG25 .. 115 F2
Bradley RG25 .... 115 F2
Lasham RG25 .... 115 F2
Sparkford Cl SO22 .... 197 E3
Sparkford Rd SO22 .... 197 F3
Sparrowhawk Cl GU10 .... 98 A4
Sparsholt CE Prim Sch
SO21 .... 174 B2
Sparsholt Coll Hampshire
SO21 .... 174 A2
Sparsholt Rd SO21 .... 196 B2
Sparvell Way GU15 .... 36 A3
Sparvells GU46 .... 33 E4

Spats La GU35 .... 165 E4
Speen Hill Cl RG14 .... 1 B2
Speen La RG14 .... 1 A2
Speen Lodge Ct RG14 .... 1 B2
Speen Pl RG14 .... 1 B2
Speenhamland Ct **3** RG14 .. 1 C2
Speenhamland Cty Prim Sch
RG14 .... 1 B2
Spencer Cl Camberley GU14 56 B3
Fleet GU13 .... 75 E3
Four Marks GU34 .... 160 A2
Pamber Heath RG26 .... 10 B1
Spencer Ct GU35 .... 164 B1
Spencer Rd RG14 .... 5 D3
Spenser Cl GU34 .... 140 A3
Sperrin Cl RG22 .... 68 A2
Spey Ct **48** SP10 .... 83 E1
Spicer Cl **4** SO22 .... 197 F4
Spicers GU34 .... 140 A2
Spiers Cl RG24 .... 49 D1
Spiers Cl RG26 .... 27 D4
Spiers La SO24 .... 135 F2
Spindle Ho **2** SP10 .... 106 A4
Spinney The Fleet GU13 ...... 74 B4
Grayshott GU26 .... 166 C2
Hook RG27 .... 51 D1
Wokingham RG40 .... 16 B4
Yateley GU46 .... 34 A4
Spitalfields Rd GU34 .... 139 F2
Spitalhatch GU34 .... 140 A2
Spitfire End **7** SO23 .... 198 B4
Spitfire Link SO23 .... 198 B4
Spitfire Rdbt SO23 .... 198 B4
Spoil La GU12 .... 100 B4
Spounder Cl GU9 .... 99 E4
Sprat's Hatch La
Dogmersfield RG27 .... 73 F4
Winchfield RG29 .... 73 F4
Spray Leaze SP11 .... 57 D1
Spreents La RG25 .... 88 A4
Spring Gl RG26 .... 47 F2
Spring Gdns
Camberley GU15 .... 36 C3
Farnborough GU14 .... 55 F4
New Alresford SO24 .... 179 E2
Spring Hill La SP11 .... 61 F1
Spring La Aldermaston RG7 . 10 A4
Burghclere RG20 .... 22 B3
Mortimer RG7 .... 11 F3
Swallowfield RG7 .... 13 F2
Spring La W GU9 .... 98 C3
Spring Mews SP10 .... 83 D1
Spring Way SO24 .... 179 E2
Spring Woods GU13 .... 74 C4
Springcross Ave GU17 .... 35 D2
Springdale RG40 .... 16 B4
Springfarm Rd GU27 .... 189 E3
Springfield **2** Liss GU33 .. 207 F2
Oakley RG23 .... 67 E1
Springfield Ave RG27 .... 52 B4
Springfield Cl SP10 .... 106 B4
Springfield La GU13 .... 53 F1
Springfield Rd Ash GU12 ..... 77 F3
Camberley GU15 .... 36 C3
Pamber Heath RG26 .... 10 B1
Springlakes Est GU12 .... 77 E2
Springmead Ct GU27 .... 189 D3
Springs The RG26 .... 29 D4
Springvale Ave SO23 .... 176 A3
Springvale Rd SO23 .... 176 A4
Springwell La RG27 .... 52 C4
Spruce Ave GU35 .... 164 A2
Spruce Cl Andover SP10 .... 105 E4
South Wonston SO21 .... 153 F3
Spruce Way GU13 .... 54 B1
Spurs Ct **11** GU11 .... 76 B1
Spybush La SO24 .... 135 E1
Square Dr GU27 .... 189 F1
Square The Farnham GU9 .. 121 E2
Grayshott GU26 .... 167 D2
Liphook GU30 .... 187 F2
Nether Wallop SO20 .... 148 A3
Upper Froyle GU34 .... 119 D1
Winchester SO23 .... 198 A4
Wonston SO21 .... 131 E2
Squarefield Gdns RG27 .... 51 E1
Squirrel Cl GU17, GU46 .... 34 C4
Squirrel Cl GU35 .... 165 D3
Stable Cl RG27 .... 50 C1
Stable Cl RG14 .... 1 C3
Stable La GU35 .... 164 B3
Stable View GU46 .... 34 A4
Stables Rd SP9 .... 78 C2
Stables The RG26 .... 28 C1
Stacey's Ind Est RG26 .... 9 F1
Staddlestones Cotts SP11 .. 82 A2
Staff College Rd
Camberley GU15 .... 35 F3
Sandhurst GU15 .... 35 F3
Staff Rd Aldershot GU12 ..... 77 D1
Michelmersh SO51 .... 193 D1
Stag Hill GU22 .... 68 B1

Stainers La SO21 .... 153 E2
Stake La GU14 .... 55 F2
Stamford Ave GU15 .... 36 B1
Stanbury Cl SP11 .... 103 F4
Stanbury Rd Fyfield SP11 .... 80 B1
Thruxton SP11 .... 80 B1
Stancomb Broad La GU34 . 159 E1
Stancombe La GU34 .... 159 E1
Standford Hill GU35 .... 165 D1
Standford La GU35 .... 165 D2
Standing Hill SP5 .... 190 C4
Stanfield RG26 .... 26 C4
Stanford Rd RG22 .... 91 E4
Stanham Cl SO21 .... 153 E1
Stanhope Rd GU15 .... 35 E2
Stanley Dr GU14 .... 55 D2
Stanley Rd RG14 .... 1 C1
Stanmore Gdns RG7 .... 11 E3
Stanmore La SO22 .... 197 E3
Stanmore Prim Sch SO22 . 197 F3
Stanton Dr GU13 .... 74 C4
Staple Gdns SO23 .... 197 F4
Stapleton Cl RG14 .... 5 D3
Stapley La SO24 .... 181 E1
Star Hill Churt GU10 .... 144 A1
Hartley Wintney RG27 .... 32 C1
Star Hill Dr GU10 .... 144 A2
Star La GU12 .... 77 E1
Star Post Rd GU15 .... 36 B4
Starling Cl RG22 .... 90 C4
Starting Gates RG14 .... 2 A1
Statham Sq SP10 .... 83 E2
Station App Andover SP10 . 105 F4
Ash GU12 .... 77 F1
Grateley SP11 .... 124 C4
Haslemere GU27 .... 189 F3
Medstead GU34 .... 160 A2
New Alresford SO24 .... 179 E3
Station Cl SO21 .... 177 F3
Station Hill
Farnham GU9 .... 99 D1
Itchen Abbas SO21 .... 177 F3
Overton RG25 .... 65 D1
Ropley SO24 .... 180 C3
Winchester SO21, SO23 ... 197 F4
Station Ind Est GU13 .... 54 A2
Station Rd
Aldershot GU11 .... 76 C1
Alton GU34 .... 140 A2
Bentley GU10 .... 120 A2
Binsted GU10 .... 120 A2
Bordon GU35 .... 164 B3
Camberley GU16 .... 56 A4
Chilbolton SO20 .... 128 C2
Cliddesden RG25 .... 92 A4
Farnborough GU14 .... 55 F2
Grateley SO20 .... 125 D4
Hook RG29 .... 72 A4
Liphook GU30 .... 188 A1
Liss GU33 .... 207 F2
New Alresford SO24 .... 179 E3
Newbury RG14 .... 1 C1
Newbury, Speen RG14 .... 1 A3
Oakley RG23 .... 66 C1
Over Wallop SO20 .... 125 E1
Overton RG25 .... 65 D1
South Tidworth SP9 .... 78 C3
Stratfield Mortimer RG7 ...... 12 B3
Whitchurch RG28 .... 86 B3
Woolton Hill RG20 .... 4 C1
Station Rd E GU12 .... 77 F4
Station Rd W GU12 .... 77 F4
Station Terr SO24 .... 181 D3
Station View GU12 .... 77 F4
Stavedown Rd SO21 .... 153 E2
Steele's Rd GU11 .... 76 C2
Steeple Dr GU34 .... 139 F2
Steepways GU26 .... 166 C3
Stenbury Dr RG25 .... 136 A4
Step Terr SO22 .... 197 F4
Stephen's Cl RG7 .... 11 E3
Stephen's Rd RG7 .... 11 E3
Stephendale Rd GU9 .... 99 D2
Stephens Firs RG7 .... 11 E3
Stephens Rd RG26 .... 27 D4
Stephenson Cl SP10 .... 82 B1
Stephenson Rd
Arborfield RG40 .... 15 F4
Basingstoke RG23 .... 68 C3
Sterling Rd SP10 .... 82 B1
Stevens Dro SO20 .... 171 E3
Stevens Gn SP11 .... 62 A1
Stevens Hill GU46 .... 34 B3
Steventon Rd SP11 .... 108 B1
Steventon Rd RG25 .... 89 F1
Stewards Rise GU10 .... 121 E4
Stewart Rd RG24 .... 49 F4
Stile Gdns GU27 .... 189 E3
Stiles Dr SP10 .... 106 B4
Stillions Cl GU34 .... 140 A2

Stilwell Cl GU46 .... 34 B1
Stirling Cl Camberley GU15 .. 36 B1
Farnborough GU14 .... 55 F1
Stirling Est RG14 .... 1 C1
Stoatley Hollow GU27 .... 189 F3
Stoatley Rise GU27 .... 189 F3
Stockbridge Cl RG24 .... 49 D1
Stockbridge Dr GU11 .... 100 A4
Stockbridge Prim Sch
SO20 .... 149 F4
Stockbridge Rd
Goodworth Clatford SP11 . 127 D2
King's Somborne SO20 ..... 172 A4
Upper Clatford SP11 .... 127 D1
Wherwell SP11 .... 127 D2
Winchester
SO21, SO22, SO23 .... 175 E1
Wonston SO21 .... 131 E2
Stockbridge Way GU46 .... 34 A3
Stocker Cl RG21 .... 69 D2
Stockers Ave SO22 .... 175 E1
Stockton Ave GU13 .... 53 F2
Stockton House Sch GU13 .. 53 F2
Stockton Pk GU13 .... 53 F2
Stockwood Rise GU16 .... 36 B3
Stockwood Way GU9 .... 99 E4
Stodham La GU33 .... 207 F1
Stoke Charity Rd
SO21, SO23 .... 154 A1
Stoke Gate SP11 .... 61 E1
Stoke Hill SP11 .... 61 D3
Stoke Hills GU9 .... 99 D1
Stoke Ho RG26 .... 26 C4
Stoke Rd SP11 .... 61 D1
Stoke Rd Stoke SP11 .... 61 D1
Winchester SO23 .... 176 A1
Stoken La
Hartley Wintney RG27 .... 51 F4
Mattingley RG27 .... 51 F4
Stone Cl Andover SP10 ...... 105 F1
Middle Winterslow SP5 ..... 168 A1
Stone Copse RG14 .... 2 B4
Stone St GU10 .... 100 A4
Stonedene Cl GU35 .... 165 F1
Stonehill Pk GU35 .... 165 F2
Stonehills RG26 .... 89 D3
Stonehouse Rd GU30 .... 188 A2
Stonemasons Rise GU15 ..... 36 B3
Stoneleigh Ct GU16 .... 36 B3
Stoney Bottom GU26 .... 167 D2
Stoney La GU46 .... 34 A2
Stoney La Cold Ash RG19 ..... 2 B4
Medstead GU34 .... 160 A2
Newbury RG14 .... 2 B4
Stoneycroft **18** GU11 .... 76 B1
Stoneyfields GU9 .... 99 E3
Stony La GU32 .... 205 F3
Stookes Way GU46 .... 33 F2
Stour Rd RG23 .... 67 D3
Stourhead Cl
Andover SP10, SP11 .... 105 F4
Farnborough GU14 .... 56 A2
Stovold's Way GU9 .... 99 E4
Stratfield Ave RG26 .... 26 C4
Stratfield Ct GU15 .... 27 D4
Stratfield Ho **16** RG14 .... 1 C1
Stratfield Saye Ho RG26 .... 30 B1
Stratfield Saye Rd
Bramley RG26 .... 29 D3
Fair Oak Green RG26 .... 29 D3
Stratford Ct
Farnborough GU14 .... 56 A2
Farnham GU9 .... 99 D1
9 Winchester SO23 .... 176 A1
Stratford Rd GU12 .... 77 E4
Strathfield Rd SP10 .... 106 A3
Strathmore Ct GU15 .... 36 A3
Stratton La SO21 .... 134 A2
Stratton Lo SO21 .... 134 A2
Stratton Rd
Basingstoke RG21 .... 68 C1
Winchester SO23 .... 198 B4
Stratton Wlk GU14 .... 56 A1
Strauss Rd RG22 .... 91 E4
Stravinsky Rd RG22 .... 91 F4
Strawberry Fields RG26 ...... 28 C2
Strawberry Hill RG14 .... 1 B2
Stream Farm Cl GU10 .... 122 A4
Stream Valley Rd GU10 ..... 122 A3
Streamside GU33 .... 75 D4
Street End RG27 .... 53 D2
Street The Aldermaston RG26 .. 9 F4
Binsted GU34 .... 141 F4
Bramley RG26 .... 28 B2
Crookham Village GU13 ...... 74 B3
Farnham GU10 .... 121 E3
Frensham GU10 .... 144 A4

Street The continued
Frensham, Dockenfield
GU35 .... 143 E3
Long Sutton RG29 .... 95 E2
North Warnborough RG29 .. 72 B2
Old Basing RG24 .... 70 A4
Rotherwick RG27 .... 50 C3
Swallowfield RG7 .... 14 A3
Tongham GU11 .... 100 B3
Streetway Rd SP11 .... 124 C4
Strokins Rd RG20 .... 24 B2
Stroller Cl RG19 .... 3 C2
Stroud Cl Chineham RG24 .. 48 C1
Pamber Heath RG26 ...... 10 B1
Stroud La GU13 .... 74 B3
Stroudley Rd RG24 .... 69 E4
Stuart Cl GU14 .... 55 F3
Stuart Cres SO22 .... 197 F3
Stuart Ct 2 SP10 .... 83 D2
Stuart Rd RG14 .... 5 D3
Stubbington Ave GU35 .... 164 B1
Stubbs Ct SP10 .... 82 C1
Stubbs Folly GU17 .... 35 D4
Stubbs Ind Site GU12 ...... 77 E3
Stubbs Moor Rd GU14 .... 55 E3
Stubbs Rd RG21 .... 69 E1
Studland Ind Est RG20 .... 3 F2
Stukeley Rd RG21 .... 69 D2
Sturdee Cl GU16 .... 36 B1
Sturt Ave GU27 .... 189 E3
Sturt Rd Camberley GU16 .. 56 B3
Farnham GU9 .... 98 C4
Mytchett GU14 .... 56 B3
Stymies GU35 .... 164 A1
Suffolk Rd SP10 .... 105 F4
Sullivan Cl GU14 .... 55 F2
Sullivan Rd
Basingstoke RG22 .... 68 C1
Camberley GU15 .... 39 E3
Summer Down La RG23 .... 66 C2
Summerdown Cotts RG25 .. 66 C2
Summerfield La GU12 .... 121 F1
Summerfields RG24 .... 49 D2
Summerhouse Ct GU26 .... 167 D2
Summersfield GU33 .... 207 F2
Summit Ave GU14 .... 55 D2
Sumner Ct GU11 .... 99 D2
Sumner Rd GU9 .... 99 D2
Sun Brow GU27 .... 189 F3
Sun Hill Cres SO24 .... 179 E2
Sun Hill Cty Schs SO24 .... 179 E3
Sun La SO24 .... 179 E2
Sun Ray Est GU46 .... 34 B4
Sunbury Cl GU35 .... 164 C2
Sunflower Cl RG22 .... 91 D4
Sunley Cl RG14 .... 5 D3
Sunny Hill Rd GU11 ...... 76 A1
Sunny Mead RG22 .... 90 A4
Sunny View Cl 5 GU12 .. 77 D1
Sunnybank SP11 .... 104 C3
Sunnybank Mews GU12 .... 77 F2
Sunnybank Rd GU14 ...... 55 D3
Sunnydell La GU10 ...... 121 F3
Sunnydown Rd SO22 ...... 197 D2
Sunnyside Fleet GU13 .... 53 F1
Kingsley GU35 .... 142 B1
Newbury RG14 .... 1 B3
Sunnyside Cl SP10 .... 82 C1
Sunnyside Cotts RG20 .... 24 B1
Sunnyside Rd GU35 ...... 166 A2
Sunvale Ave GU27 ...... 189 D3
Sunvale Cl GU27 .... 189 D3
Surrey Ave GU15 .... 35 F2
Surrey Inst of Art &
Design The GU9 .... 98 C1
Sussex Gdns GU13 .... 54 B2
Sussex St SO23 .... 197 F4
Sutcliffe Sq SP10 .... 83 E2
Sutherland Cl GU35 ...... 164 B1
Sutherland Ct SP10 ...... 83 D1
Sutherlands RG14 .... 5 E4
Sutton Field GU35 .... 164 B1
Sutton Gdns SO23 .... 198 A4
Sutton Rd Basingstoke RG24 69 D4
Camberley GU16 .... 36 C4
Newbury RG14 .... 1 A3
Suttonwood La SO24 ...... 180 C4
Swains Cl RG26 .... 26 C4
Swaledale RG26 .... 26 C4
Swale Rd GU14 .... 55 E3
Swaledale Gdns GU13 .... 54 A2
Swallow Cl Alton GU34 .. 140 A3
Basingstoke RG22 .... 90 C4
North Tidworth SP9 ...... 78 C3
Yateley GU46 .... 33 F3
Swallowfield Pk RG7 ...... 14 B4
Swallowfield Rd RG7 ...... 14 B4
Swallowfields SP10 ...... 83 D1
Swan Ct 5 Andover SP10 .. 106 A4
Newbury RG14 .... 1 B2
Swan Ho GU46 .... 34 C4

Swan La Sandhurst GU46 .... 34 C4
Winchester SO23 .... 197 F4
Swan Mews RG29 .... 72 B2
Swan St RG20 .... 24 B1
Swan Way GU13 .... 74 B4
Swanmore Cl SO22 ...... 175 E2
Swansdown Wlk RG19 .... 2 C2
Swanwick Wlk RG26 .... 26 C4
Swedish Hos RG26 .... 27 D4
Sweetzer's Piece RG7 .... 11 E3
Swelling Hill
Four Marks SO24 .... 182 A3
Ropley SO24 .... 182 A3
Swift Cl Andover SP10 .... 83 D1
Winchester SO22 .... 197 E3
Swift Rd GU9 .... 99 D1
Swift's Cl GU10 .... 99 F1
Swindon Ho 9 SP9 ...... 78 C4
Swing Swang La RG21 .... 69 F4
Swingate Rd GU10 ...... 122 A4
Swiss Cl GU10 .... 121 F2
Switchback La
Farnham GU10 .... 121 E2
Farnham GU10 .... 121 E2
Sycamore Cl
Camberley GU16 .... 36 B1
North Tidworth SP9 ...... 79 D3
Sandhurst GU17 .... 34 C4
Sycamore Cr GU13 .... 74 C3
Sycamore Cres SO20 .... 126 A2
Sycamore Dr Ash GU12 .. 77 F4
Camberley GU16 .... 36 B1
Farnham GU10 .... 121 E3
Kings Worthy SO23 ...... 176 A4
Sycamore Ho RG14 ...... 49 D2
Sycamore Rd GU14 ...... 56 A1
Sycamore Rise RG14 ...... 2 A3
Sycamore Way RG21 ...... 68 B4
Sycamore Wlk GU11 .... 105 E3
Sycamores The
Blackwater GU17 .... 34 C3
Farnborough GU16 ...... 56 A2
Sydings The RG14 .... 1 A3
Sydney Cl SP9 .... 79 E4
Sydney Rd GU35 .... 164 B2
Sydney Villas GU12 ...... 77 F4
Syers Cl GU33 .... 207 F2
Syers Rd GU33 .... 207 F2
Sylvan Way GU13 .... 74 C3
Sylvaner Ct RG21 .... 69 D3
Sylvester Cl RG14 .... 1 B3
Sylvia Cl RG21 .... 69 D2
Symonds St SO23 .... 198 A4
Sympson Rd RG7 .... 10 A1
Syon Pl GU14 .... 56 A1

Tadley Common Rd RG7 .. 10 A1
Tadley Hill RG26 .... 27 D4
Tadley Prim Sch RG26 .... 27 D3
Tadpole La GU13 .... 75 D1
Taiping Rd SO20 .... 126 A3
Talavera Schs GU11 ...... 76 C2
Talbot Cl Mytchett GU14 .. 56 C2
Newbury RG14 .... 1 B3
Talbot Rd GU10 .... 121 F4
Talgarth Dr GU14 .... 56 A1
Tallis Gdns RG21 .... 68 C1
Tallywater Hill GU32 .... 205 E2
Tamar Dr RG23 .... 67 D1
Tamarisk Cl RG22 .... 91 E3
Tamworth Dr GU13 ...... 54 A2
Tangier Ct 6 GU11 ...... 76 B1
Tanglewood RG40 .... 16 C4
Tangway RG24 .... 48 C2
Tanhouse La GU34 .... 139 F2
Tank Rd GU47 .... 35 E3
Tanner Ct RG14 .... 1 C2
Tanner St 20 SO23 ...... 198 A4
Tanners Way RG23 .... 67 D1
Taplin's Farm La RG27 .... 52 C2
Taplings Cl SO22 .... 175 E2
Taplings Rd SO22 .... 175 E2
Tarbat Ct GU15 .... 35 D4
Tarn Cl GU14 .... 55 E1
Tarn La RG14 .... 5 E4
Tarn Rd GU26 .... 167 E2
Tarragon Cl GU14 .... 55 D2
Tarrant Gdns RG27 .... 52 B2
Taskers Dr SP10 .... 105 E2
Tasmania Cl RG24 .... 48 B1
Tate Sq SP10 .... 83 E2
Taverner Cl RG24 .... 69 E4
Tavistock Gdns GU14 .... 55 F4
Tavistock Inf Sch GU13 .. 74 B4
Tavistock Rd GU13 ...... 74 B4
Tawny Gr GU34 .... 160 A1
Tay Cl GU14 .... 55 E3
Taylors Cl GU35 .... 164 C3
Taylors Cnr SO23 .... 176 A3
Taylors La RG25 .... 164 C3
Teal Cres RG22 .... 90 C4

Tedder Cl SP10 .... 105 D4
Tees Cl GU14 .... 55 E3
Teg Down Meads SO22 .. 175 E1
Tegg Down Rd SO24 .... 180 C2
Tekels Ave GU15 .... 36 A2
Tekels Cl GU15 .... 36 B2
Tekels Way GU16 .... 36 B2
Telecoma Cl GU15 ...... 166 A2
Telegraph La GU34 ...... 160 B1
Telford Gate SP10 .... 82 A1
Telford Rd RG21 .... 68 C4
Templar Cl GU47 .... 34 C4
Temple Rd GU33 .... 208 A3
Temple Towers RG21 .... 69 D3
Temple's Cl GU12 ...... 100 A1
Ten Acre Wlk GU10 ...... 122 C2
Tenby Rd GU14 .... 56 C4
Tennyson Way RG23 ...... 68 C1
Terra Cotta Ct GU9 ...... 121 E3
Terrace The
Camberley GU15 .... 35 F3
Chawton GU34 .... 161 E4
Terrys Cotts RG29 .... 72 A2
Tesimond Dr GU46 .... 33 F3
Test Ct 37 SP10 .... 83 E1
Test Mews RG28 .... 86 B2
Test Rd RG28 .... 86 B2
Test Rise SO20 .... 129 D2
Test Valley Sch The SO20 .. 149 E1
Test Way RG21 .... 69 E3
Testbourne GM Com Sch
RG28 .... 86 A2
Tewkesbury Cl RG24 .... 48 A1
Texas Dr SO22 .... 197 D2
Thackham's La RG7 ...... 52 A3
Thames Cl GU14 .... 55 E3
Thames Ct
56 Andover SP10 .... 83 E1
7 Basingstoke RG23 .... 69 E3
Thames Rd RG18 .... 2 C3
Theal Cl GU15 .... 35 D4
Thibet Rd GU47 .... 35 D4
Third St RG41 .... 16 B4
Thirlmere Cl Bordon GU35 164 B3
Farnborough GU14 ...... 55 E2
Thirlmere Cres GU13 .... 74 C3
Thistledown GU15 .... 82 C1
Thomas La RG40 .... 16 B4
Thomas Merriman Ct 1
RG14 .... 1 C1
Thomas Rd SP11 .... 108 B1
Thorlands GU27 .... 189 F4
Thorn Cl GU10 .... 121 E2
Thorn Cres GU34 .... 160 A1
Thorn Ct GU34 .... 160 A1
Thorn Dr GU34 .... 160 A1
Thorn La GU34 .... 160 B1
Thorn Rd GU10 .... 121 F3
Thornburn Chase GU15 .. 35 E3
Thorneley Rd RG20 ...... 24 B1
Thornfield RG19 .... 7 D2
Thornfield Gn GU47 ...... 35 E2
Thornford Rd
Greenham RG19 .... 7 D3
Headley, Nr Greenham RG19 7 F2
Thornhill Rd GU12 .... 77 D2
Thornhill Rdbt GU24 .... 49 D1
Thornhill Way RG24 .... 49 D2
Thornton Cl RG26 .... 29 D1
Thornton End GU34 .... 140 B3
Thornyhurst Rd GU16 .... 56 C2
Thorold Rd GU10 .... 99 D2
Thorpe Gdns GU34 ...... 139 F2
Threadgill Way SP9 ...... 101 E4
Threadneedle Ho 4 SP10 106 A4
Three Acre Rd RG14 ...... 5 E4
Three Horse Shoes La
GU34 .... 203 F1
Three Stiles Rd GU9 .... 98 B1
Three Ways GU35 .... 143 D3
Threshers Cnr GU15 .... 54 B2
Throakmead GU10 ...... 120 A1
Throgmorton Rd GU46 .. 33 F3
Thrush Cl RG23 .... 67 F1
Thruxton Airfield Rd SP11 103 D4
Thuillier Rd SP11 .... 108 B1
Thumwood RG24 .... 48 C2
Thundery Hill GU10 .... 100 B2
Thurbans Rd GU10 ...... 121 F4
Thurmond Cres SO22 .... 197 E3
Thurmond Rd SO22 ...... 197 E3
Thurstons GU34 .... 141 F4
Thyme Ct RG24 .... 49 D3
Thyme Cl GU14 .... 55 D3
Tid's Meadow SP11 ...... 57 F4
Tiberius Cl RG22 .... 68 B4
Tiberius Rd SP10 .... 108 B1
Tiberus Rd SP10 .... 83 D2
Tiberus Cl RG21 .... 68 B4
Tichborne Cl GU47 ...... 35 D3
Tichborne Down SO24 .. 179 E2
Tichborne Pl GU10 ...... 100 A4

Tichbourne Cl GU15 ...... 36 B2
Tickenor Dr RG40 .... 16 B4
Tidbury Cotts SP11 ...... 109 D1
Tidworth Rd SP4 .... 101 D4
Tigwells Field RG29 ...... 95 D2
Tilbury's Cl GU35 .... 164 B2
Tile Barn Cl GU14 .... 55 F3
Tile Barn Row RG20 ...... 4 B1
Tilford Rd
Beacon Hill GU26 ...... 167 D3
Farnham GU10 .... 122 B3
Tilford GU9 .... 122 B3
Tilling Cotts GU34 ...... 141 D1
Tilney Cl GU34 .... 139 F2
Timber Bank GU14 ...... 56 C3
Timber Cl 8 GU9 .... 98 C1
Timbercroft GU34 ...... 160 A1
Timberlake Rd RG21 .... 69 D3
Timbermill Ct GU27 .... 189 E3
Timor Cl RG24 .... 48 A1
Tindal Cl GU47 .... 34 A3
Tinley Gdns RG29 .... 72 C2
Tintagel Cl
Basingstoke RG22 ...... 68 B3
Knights Enham SP10 .... 83 D2
Tintagel Dr GU16 .... 36 B1
Tintagel Rd RG40 .... 16 C4
Tintern Cl RG23 .... 68 C4
Tippet Gdns RG22 ...... 91 F4
Titan Ho 10 RG26 .... 9 E1
Titchfield Cl RG26 ...... 27 D4
Tithelands La SP10 ...... 202 C2
Tittymouse La SP11 ...... 81 E1
Tiverton Rd RG23 .... 68 A3
Tiverton Way GU13 ...... 36 B1
Toad La GU17 .... 35 E2
Tobago Cl RG24 .... 48 A1
Tobruk Cl SP10 .... 83 D4
Tobruk Rd SP9 .... 77 F2
Tockington Ct GU17 .... 34 A3
Todmore GU33 .... 185 F2
Toledo Grove SP10 ...... 83 E1
Tollgate Cl RG23 .... 67 D2
Tollgate Rd SP10 .... 82 C1
Tollgate The 20 SO23 .. 176 A1
Tollway RG24 .... 49 D2
Tolpuddle Way GU47 .... 34 B3
Tomlins Ave GU16 ...... 36 B1
Tomlins Cl RG26 .... 26 C4
Tomlinscote Sch GU16 .. 36 C1
Tomlinscote Way GU16 .. 36 C1
Tomlison Dr RG40 ...... 16 C4
Tongham Meadows GU10 100 B4
Tongham Rd
Aldershot GU12 .... 100 A4
Farnham GU10 .... 100 A3
Farnham, Runfold GU12 .. 100 A2
Tope Cres RG22 .... 15 E4
Tope Rd RG2 .... 15 E4
Topiary The
Farnborough GU14 ...... 55 E2
Old Basing RG24 .... 70 A4
Toplady Pl GU9 .... 99 D4
Tor Rd GU9 .... 98 B1
Torrington Cl GU34 .... 165 D3
Totland Cl GU14 .... 55 F3
Tottenham Cl RG26 ...... 28 C2
Totters La RG27 .... 51 F1
Tournai Cl GU11 .... 77 E4
Tovey Ct SP10 .... 83 E1
Tovey Pl SO23 .... 176 B4
Tower Cl Charlton SP10 .. 82 B2
Liphook GU30 .... 187 F2
Tower Ct 6 SO22 .... 197 F4
Tower Hill GU14 .... 55 F2
Tower Hill Prim Sch GU14 .. 55 E2
Tower Rd Hindhead GU26 .. 167 E2
Liphook GU30 .... 187 F2
Tower St Alton GU34 .... 139 F1
Winchester SO23 .... 197 F4
Town Centre West Junction
RG23 .... 68 C2
Town Cl SO24 .... 181 E3
Town Hall Ct RG28 ...... 86 B3
Town Mill RG25 .... 88 A4
Town Mill La RG28 ...... 86 B3
Town Mills RG14 .... 1 B2
Town Sq GU16 .... 36 A3
Townsend Cl RG24 ...... 68 C2
Townside GU15 .... 36 A3
Trafalgar Cl GU9 .... 99 D1
Trafalgar St
Stockbridge SO20 ...... 149 F2
Winchester SO23 .... 197 F4
Trafalgar Way
Camberley GU47 .... 35 E2
Stockbridge SO20 ...... 149 F1
Trafford Rd GU16 .... 56 A4
Trajan Wlk SP11 .... 83 D2
Travis La GU17 .... 35 D4

Treble Cl SO22 .... 197 D2
Trebor Ave GU9 .... 99 D1
Tredenham Cl GU14 ...... 77 D4
Tree Tops Ave GU16 .... 36 C4
Treeside Dr GU9 .... 99 E4
Trefoil Cl RG22 .... 52 B4
Tregenna Ho GU30 ...... 187 F3
Tregolls Dr GU16 .... 56 A2
Trellis Dr RG24 .... 70 A4
Trenchard Pk GU35 .... 164 B2
Trenchard Rd SP11 ...... 105 D4
Trent Cl GU14 .... 55 E3
Trent Cres RG18 .... 2 C3
Trent Ct 54 SP10 .... 83 E1
Trent Way 8 RG21 ...... 69 E3
Trenton Cl GU16 .... 36 C1
Tresham Cres GU46 ...... 33 F3
Triangle The RG14 .... 1 B2
Trilakes Fishery & Ctry Pk
GU46 .... 34 B4
Trimmer's Almshouses 8
GU9 .... 98 C1
Trimmers Cl GU9 .... 99 D4
Trimmers Field GU9 .... 99 E1
Trimmers Wood GU26 .. 167 E3
Trinidad Cl RG24 .... 48 A1
Trinity Fields GU9 ...... 98 C3
Trinity Hill Farnham GU9 .. 98 C3
Medstead GU34 .... 159 F4
Trinity Rd SO24 .... 137 F1
Trinity Rise SP11 .... 81 F2
Trooper Bottom GU32 .. 206 A2
Trout Rd GU27 .... 189 E3
Trout Wlk RG14 .... 1 C2
Trowbridge Ho 13 SP9 .. 78 C4
Trowe's La Beech Hill RG7 .. 13 D2
Swallowfield RG7 ...... 14 A3
Trueman Sp SP10 .... 83 E2
Trunk Rd GU14 .... 74 A4
Trussell Cl SO22 .... 175 E2
Trussell Cres SO22 ...... 175 E2
Trust Cl RG27 .... 50 C1
Tubb's La RG26 .... 47 D4
Tubbs La RG20 .... 21 E3
Tudor Cl GU26 .... 167 D1
Tudor Ct Ash GU11 .... 77 D1
3 Knights Enham SP10 .. 83 D2
Tudor Dr GU46 .... 34 A2
Tudor Hall GU15 .... 36 B3
Tudor Rd RG14 .... 1 C1
Tudor Way Fleet GU13 .. 75 D2
Kings Worthy SO23 .... 176 A4
Tulip Cl RG22 .... 91 D4
Tulls La GU35 .... 165 D1
Tunball La SP11 .... 37 E4
Tunbridge Cres GU30 .. 187 F3
Tunbridge La
Bramshott GU30 .... 187 F3
Liphook GU30 .... 187 F3
Tunnel La RG29 .... 72 A2
Tunworth Ct RG26 ...... 27 D4
Tunworth Mews RG26 .. 27 D4
Tunworth Rd RG25 ...... 70 C1
Turbary Gdns RG26 ...... 9 F1
Turf Hill Rd GU15 .... 36 B4
Turk Cl SP10 .... 83 D2
Turk St GU34 .... 139 F2
Turk's La RG7 .... 11 E2
Turner Cl RG21 .... 69 F2
Turner Ct SP10 .... 82 C1
Turner Pl GU17 .... 35 D3
Turner's Green La RG27 .. 53 E3
Turnhill Ct SP10 .... 83 D4
Turnpike Ind Est RG14 .. 2 A3
Turnpike Rd Newbury RG14 .. 2 B2
Thatcham RG18, RG14 .. 2 B2
Turnpike Sch The RG14 .. 2 A2
Turnpike Way RG22 ...... 67 D1
Turnstone End 3 GU46 .. 33 F3
Tuscam Way GU15 ...... 35 E2
Tweed Cl GU14 .... 55 E3
Tweedsmuir Cl
Basingstoke RG23 ...... 68 A2
Farnborough GU14 ...... 55 D2
Twelve Acres Cres GU14 .. 55 E3
Tweseldown Inf Sch GU13 .. 75 D2
Tweseldown Rd GU10 .. 75 D2
Twisell Thorne GU13 .... 74 C2
Two Gate La RG25 ...... 88 A4
Two Gate Meadow RG25 .. 88 A4
Two Rivers Way RG14 .... 2 B2
Twoways Ct GU35 ...... 164 B1
Twyford Ct 15 SO23 .... 176 A1
Twyford La GU10 .... 121 F3
Tydehams RG14 .... 5 E4
Tyfield RG26 .... 47 F2
Tylney La RG27 .... 50 B1
Tylston Meadow GU30 .. 187 F3

Tyndalls Est GU26 .... 167 E2
Tyne Cl GU14 .... 55 E3
Tyne Ct **58** SP10 .... 83 E1
Tyne Way RG18 .... 2 C3
Tytherley Rd SP5 .... 168 B3

Ullswater Ave GU14 .... 55 E2
Ullswater Cl Bordon GU35 164 B3
  Farnham GU9 .... 98 C3
  Thatcham RG19 .... 2 C2
Ullswater Ct GU11 .... 77 E3
Ullswater Gr SO24 .... 179 E2
Underhill La GU9 .... 121 F4
Underwood Ave GU14 .... 77 E1
Underwood Rd GU27 .... 189 E4
Union La RG20 .... 24 B3
Union Rd GU9 .... 99 E3
Union Rise GU33 .... 186 B1
Union St Aldershot GU11 .... 76 C1
  Andover SP10 .... 106 A4
  Farnborough GU14 .... 55 D2
  Winchester SO23 .... 198 A4
Union Terr GU11 .... 76 C1
Up St Dummer RG25 .... 113 E4
  North Waltham RG25 .... 89 F1
Upfallow RG24 .... 70 A4
Uphill Rd SO22 .... 175 E3
Upland La GU33 .... 207 D4
Upland Rd GU16 .... 36 A4
Uplands Cl GU46 .... 34 C4
Uplands Cty Prim Sch
  GU46 .... 34 C4
Uplands La GU34 .... 160 A1
Uplands Rd Farnham GU9 ... 99 E1
  Winchester SO22 .... 175 F2
Upnor Cl SP9 .... 79 E4
Upper Bourne La GU10 ..... 121 F3
Upper Bourne Vale GU10 .. 121 F3
Upper Brook St SO23 .... 198 A4
Upper Charles St GU15 ...... 36 A3
Upper Chestnut Dr RG21 .... 68 C2
Upper Chobham Rd GU15 ... 36 C4
Upper Church La GU9 .... 98 C1
Upper College Ride GU15 ... 36 B4
Upper Dro SP10 .... 82 B1
Upper Elms Rd GU11 .... 76 C1
Upper Farm Rd RG22 .... 90 A4
Upper Gordon Rd GU15 ...... 36 A3
Upper Grove Rd GU34 .... 139 F1
Upper Hale Rd GU9 .... 98 B1
Upper High St SO23 .... 197 F4
Upper Lanham La SO24 .... 158 B4
Upper Mount GU21 .... 207 F2
Upper Neatham Mill La
  GU34 .... 140 B3
Upper Old Park La GU9 ...... 98 C4
Upper Park Rd GU15 .... 36 B3
Upper Raymond Almshouses
  RG14 .... 1 B1
Upper Sherborne Rd RG21 . 69 D4
Upper Soldridge Rd GU34 . 159 F1
Upper South View GU9 .... 99 D2
Upper St Michael's Rd GU9 . 99 F4
Upper Union St GU11 .... 76 C1
Upper Union Terr GU11 .... 76 C1
Upper Verran Rd GU15 .... 36 A2
Upper Way GU10 .... 121 F4
Upper Weybourne La GU9 ... 99 E4
Upron Field Cl RG22 .... 91 D4
Upton Cl GU16 .... 56 A2
Upton Cres RG21 .... 69 D4
Upton Grey Cl SO22 .... 175 E2
Upton Grey Rd RG27 .... 71 F1
Urchfont Ho **1** SP9 .... 79 D3

Vale Cl GU10, GU9 .... 122 A2
Vale Rd Ash GU12 .... 77 F3
  Camberley GU14 .... 35 F2
  Winchester SO23 .... 198 B3
Vale The RG22 .... 67 D1
Vale View Dr RG7 .... 13 D3
Vale Way SO23 .... 154 A1
Vale Wood Dr GU10 .... 122 A2
Vale Wood La GU26 .... 167 D2
Valencia Way SP10 .... 83 D1
Valentine Wood Ind Est
  RG26 .... 10 B2
Valley Ct The **4** SO22 .... 197 E3
Valley La GU10 .... 122 A4
Valley Mead SP11 .... 105 C2
Valley Rd Camberley GU16 .. 56 C4
  Littleton SO22 .... 175 D3
  Newbury RG14 .... 5 E4
Valley Rise SP11 .... 105 F2
Valley Side GU30 .... 207 F3
Valley The SO22 .... 197 E3
Valley View GU46 .... 34 C4
Valley Way RG26 .... 10 B1

Valmeade Cl RG27 .... 51 D1
Valon Rd RG2 .... 15 E4
Valroy Cl GU15 .... 36 A3
Van Dyck Cl RG21 .... 69 F2
Vanburgh Gdns RG22 .... 91 D4
Vanners La RG20 .... 4 A3
Varna Rd GU35 .... 164 C2
Varney Cl GU14 .... 55 E3
Vaughans GU34 .... 140 A2
Vectis Cl GU34 .... 160 A1
Velmead Cl GU13 .... 75 D4
Velmead Jun Sch GU13 ...... 75 D4
Velmead Rd GU13 .... 75 D4
Venice Ct SP10 .... 83 E2
Venison Terr SO20 .... 170 A4
Venning Rd RG2 .... 15 E4
Ventnor Terr GU12 .... 77 D1
Venture Rdbt RG21 .... 69 E1
Verdi Cl RG22 .... 91 E4
Verge Wlk GU11 .... 99 F4
Verity Sq SP10 .... 83 E2
Verlynch Cotts SO20 .... 149 F4
Vermont Woods RG40 .... 16 B4
Verne The GU13 .... 75 D3
Verner Cl GU35 .... 165 E2
Vesey Cl GU14 .... 55 F3
Vespasian Rd SP10 .... 83 D2
Vetch Fields RG27 .... 51 F1
Viables La RG21 .... 69 D1
Viables Rdbt RG21 .... 68 C1
Vian Pl SO23 .... 175 F2
Vicarage Cl GU10 .... 122 A4
Vicarage Gdns Fleet GU13 . 74 C2
  Grayshott GU26 .... 167 D2
Vicarage Hill Alton GU34 .. 139 F2
  Hartley Wintney RG27 .... 52 B3
Vicarage La Farnham GU9 ... 98 C1
  Farnham GU10 .... 122 A4
  Farnham, Upper Hale GU9 . 99 D4
  Haslemere GU27 .... 189 E3
  Mattingley RG27 .... 31 D1
  Ropley SO24 .... 181 D2
  Yateley GU47 .... 34 A4
Vicarage Rd Alton GU34 ... 139 F1
  Blackwater GU47 .... 35 E2
  Yateley GU46 .... 34 A4
Vickers Bsns Ctr RG22 .... 68 C4
Victoria Ave GU15 .... 35 F3
Victoria Cotts RG20 .... 20 C4
Victoria Ct Andover SP11 . 105 F4
  11 Fleet GU13 .... 53 F1
Victoria Dr GU15 .... 35 D2
Victoria Gdns
  9 Fleet GU13 .... 53 F1
  Newbury RG14 .... 1 C2
Victoria Hill Rd GU13 .... 53 F1
Victoria Pl RG21 .... 68 A2
Victoria Rd Aldershot GU11 . 76 C1
  Alton GU34 .... 139 F2
  Farnborough GU14 .... 55 F2
  Farnham GU11 .... 99 D1
  Fleet GU13 .... 53 F1
  Mortimer RG7 .... 11 F3
  Winchester SO23 .... 175 F1
Victoria Rd E GU34 .... 140 A2
Victoria Rd W GU34 .... 139 F2
Victory Rdbt RG21 .... 69 D3
Vidlers Farm RG26 .... 47 F2
Vienna Ct GU14 .... 55 F3
Vigo La GU47 .... 34 A3
Vigo Rd SP10 .... 83 E1
Vigo Schs SP10 .... 83 E1
Viking Way SP10 .... 83 D2
Villa Pl RG7 .... 14 A3
Village St Bentworth GU34 138 A3
  Chilbolton SO20 .... 129 D3
Village The
  Finchampstead RG40 .... 16 B2
  Litchfield RG28 .... 86 B2
Village Way GU46 .... 34 A4
Villiers Way RG14 .... 5 D3
Villiers Wlk RG14 .... 5 D3
Vindomis Cl GU34 .... 140 B4
Vine Cl Farnborough GU11 .. 76 C3
  Farnham GU10 .... 121 F2
Vine Ct RG14 .... 1 C1
Vine House Cl GU14 .... 56 C2
Vine La GU9 .... 121 F3
Vine St GU11 .... 76 C1
Vine Tree Cl RG18 .... 27 D4
Vine Way GU10 .... 121 F3
Vinns La RG25 .... 92 B4
Vinson Rd GU33 .... 208 A2
Violet Cl RG22 .... 91 D4
Violet La RG26 .... 26 A3

Virginia Gdns GU14 .... 56 A1
Viscounts Ct SP10 .... 83 F1
Vivaldi Cl RG22 .... 91 F4
Vivian Cl GU13 .... 75 D3
Vivian Rd RG22 .... 69 E4
Vo-tec Ctr RG14 .... 2 B1
Vockins Cl **2** SP9 .... 78 C4
Vulcan Cl GU46 .... 34 C4
Vulcan Ct GU17, GU46 .... 34 C4
Vulcan Ho **6** RG26 .... 9 E1
Vulcan Way GU46 .... 34 C4
Vyne Cl GU34 .... 139 F2
Vyne Meadow RG26 .... 47 F2
Vyne Rd Basingstoke RG21 . 69 D3
  Sherborne St John RG24 .. 48 A3
Vyne Sec Sch The RG21 .... 69 D4

Wade Rd RG24 .... 49 F4
Wadwick Bottom SP11 .... 62 A3
Waggoners Way GU26 ...... 166 C2
Waggoners Wells RG26 .... 166 C1
Wagner Cl RG22 .... 91 F4
Wakeford Cl RG26 .... 10 B1
Wakeford Ct RG26 .... 10 B1
Wakefords Copse GU13 ...... 75 D2
Wakefords Pk GU13 .... 75 D2
Wakes Cotts GU34 .... 184 C4
Walburton Ho RG27 .... 52 B3
Waldegrave Pl RG14 .... 1 C2
Waldorf Hts GU17 .... 35 D2
Wales St SO23 .... 198 A4
Walk The RG24 .... 49 F4
Walker's Ridge GU15 .... 36 B3
Wall La RG7 .... 11 D1
Walldown Rd GU35 .... 164 C1
Walled Meadow SP10 .... 106 A4
Wallins Copse RG24 .... 48 C2
Wallis Cl RG22 .... 68 B3
Wallis Dr RG14 .... 2 B3
Wallis Rd RG21, RG24 .... 69 D2
Wallop Dro SO20 .... 147 E2
Wallop Prim Sch SO20 ..... 147 F4
Wallop Rd Grateley SO20 . 125 D4
  Over Wallop SO20 .... 125 D2
Walmer Cl GU16 .... 56 C4
Walnut Cl Aldershot GU9 ... 99 F4
  Alton GU34 .... 139 F3
  Yateley GU17, GU47 .... 34 A2
Walnut Tree Cl SO21 .... 153 E2
Walnut Tree Gr SP11 .... 80 C1
Walnut Tree Rd SP10 .... 105 F4
Walpole Gdns RG27 .... 52 B4
Walpole Rd SO22 .... 197 E3
Walsh Meml CE Schs GU12 . 77 F1
Waltham Ct RG27 .... 88 A4
Waltham La
  North Waltham RG25 .... 88 B3
  Overton RG25 .... 88 B3
Waltham Rd RG25 .... 88 A4
Walton Cl GU13 .... 75 D4
Walton Rd SO22 .... 197 E3
Walton Way RG14 .... 2 A2
Walworth Ent Ctr SP10 ...... 83 E1
Walworth Ind Est SP10 ...... 83 E1
Walworth Rd
  Andover SP10 .... 83 E1
  Picket Piece SP11 .... 84 B2
Wandle Cl GU12 .... 77 F1
Wandsdyke Cl GU16 .... 56 B4
Wantage Rd GU15 .... 35 D4
Warblington Cl RG26 .... 27 D4
Warbrook La RG27 .... 32 C4
Ward Cl SP10 .... 83 D1
Warehouse Rd RG14 .... 6 B3
Wargrove Dr GU17 .... 35 D4
Warminster Ho **11** SP9 .... 78 C4
Warner Cl **11** SO23 .... 176 A1
Warren Cl Bordon GU35 ... 164 A1
  Fleet GU13 .... 75 D4
  Hartley Wintney RG27 .... 52 B3
  Sandhurst GU17 .... 34 C4
  Wokingham RG40 .... 16 B3
Warren Rd
  Bordon GU33 .... 186 B1
  Liss GU33 .... 208 A4
  Newbury RG14 .... 5 D3
  Winchester SO23 .... 198 B4
Warren Rise GU15 .... 36 B2
Warren The
  Aldershot GU11 .... 76 B1
  Farnham GU9 .... 99 E4
  Tadley RG26 .... 26 C4
Warren Way RG24 .... 68 B2
Warrington Mews GU11 ..... 99 F4
Warton Rd RG21 .... 69 E3

Warwick Cl
  Aldershot GU10 .... 100 A4
  Camberley GU15 .... 36 C2
  Whitchurch RG28 .... 86 B3
  13 Winchester SO23 ..... 176 A1
Warwick Ct **14** SO23 .... 176 A1
Warwick Dr RG14 .... 1 C1
Warwick Rd Ash GU12 .... 77 F4
  Basingstoke RG22 .... 68 B3
Wash Brook RG27 .... 51 D1
Wash Water RG20 .... 4 C2
Washbury Ho RG14 .... 5 E4
Washford Cl GU35 .... 164 C2
Washford La Bordon GU35 164 C2
  Lindford GU35 .... 164 C2
Washington Gdns RG40 ..... 16 C4
Wasing La RG7 .... 9 F3
Watch La RG25 .... 64 A1
Watchetts Cty Mid Sch
  GU17 .... 35 F1
Watchetts Dr GU15 .... 36 A1
Watchetts Lake Cl GU16 .... 36 A2
Watchetts Rd GU47 .... 35 F2
Watchmoor Pk GU47 .... 35 F2
Watchmoor Rd GU15 .... 35 F2
Watchmoor Trad Est GU15 . 35 F2
Water Cl SO23 .... 198 A4
Water End La RG24 .... 71 D4
Water La Andover SP11 ..... 105 F2
  Bishop's Sutton SO24 ..... 180 A2
  Farnborough GU14 .... 55 A4
  Farnham GU9 .... 99 E2
  Greenham RG19 .... 6 A4
Upper Clatford SP10 .... 105 F2
Water Lea RG19 .... 6 A4
Water Rede GU13 .... 74 C2
Water Ridges RG22 .... 90 A4
Watercress Meadow SO24 179 D2
Waterfront Bsns Pk GU13 .. 54 A2
Waterhouse Mead GU15 ..... 35 D4
Wateridge Rd RG24 .... 69 E4
Waterloo Ave RG23 .... 68 B4
Waterloo Cl GU15 .... 35 D4
Waterloo Ct Andover SP10 106 A4
  Whitchurch RG28 .... 86 B3
Waterloo Rd GU12 .... 77 D1
Waterloo Terr SP11 .... 105 E2
Watermills Ct SP11 .... 105 F1
Waterside GU30 .... 187 E4
Waterside Ct GU35 .... 164 C2
  Fleet GU13 .... 54 A2
  Newbury RG14 .... 2 A2
Waterside News GU13 .... 54 A2
Watersmeet **22** SO23 ...... 198 A4
Watery La Andover SP10 ..... 83 D1
  Crookham Village GU13 .... 74 C2
  Hamstead Marshall RG20 ... 3 E3
  Kintbury RG20 .... 3 B4
Watkins Cl RG40 .... 16 B4
Watley La SO21 .... 174 B2
Watling End RG22 .... 91 D4
Watson Acre SP11 .... 105 F4
Watson Way RG22 .... 68 B3
Watt Cl SP10 .... 82 B1
Watts Rd GU14 .... 55 E3
Wavell Cl RG23 .... 68 C1
Wavell Rd SP9 .... 78 B4
Wavell Sch The GU11 .... 76 C4
Wavell Way SO22 .... 197 E3
Waverley Abbey
  GU10, GU9 .... 122 C4
Waverley Ave
  Basingstoke RG22 .... 69 D1
  Fleet GU13 .... 54 A1
Waverley Cl
  Camberley GU15 .... 36 B2
  Farnham GU11 .... 99 D1
  Odiham RG29 .... 113 F2
Waverley Dr Ash GU12 .... 77 F3
  Camberley GU15 .... 36 B2
  South Wonston SO21 ...... 153 F2
Waverley Gdns GU12 .... 77 F3
Waverley La GU9 .... 99 E1
Waverley Rd
  Farnborough GU14 .... 56 A2
  Wokingham RG40 .... 16 B4
Wayman Rd GU14 .... 55 D4
Waynflete La GU9 .... 98 B1
Waynflete Pl SO22 .... 197 E3
Ways End GU15 .... 36 B2
Waysend Ho GU15 .... 36 A2
Wayside Cotts GU10 .... 144 B2
Wayside Rd GU33 .... 68 A3
Weale Ct RG21 .... 69 D3
Weatherby Gdns RG27 .... 52 B3
Weathermore La GU34 ...... 160 B1
Weaver's Wlk RG14 .... 1 C2
Weavers Cl SP10 .... 106 A4
Weavers Gdns GU10 .... 121 E4

Webb Cl RG24 .... 48 C2
Webbs Farm Cl RG28 .... 86 B2
Webster Rd SO22 .... 175 D1
Wedman's La RG27 .... 50 C3
Wedman's Pl RG27 .... 50 C3
Wedmore Cl SO22 .... 197 D2
Weeke Manor Cl SO22 ...... 175 E1
Weeke Prim Sch SO22 .... 175 E1
Weir Ave GU14 .... 55 F2
Weir Cl GU14 .... 55 F2
Weir Corts GU34 .... 42 C4
Weir Rd RG27 .... 52 A2
Weir The RG28 .... 86 B2
Weirs The **14** SO23 .... 198 A3
Welbeck Cl GU14 .... 55 E2
Weldon Cl GU13 .... 75 D3
Well Cl Camberley GU15 ..... 35 F2
  North Waltham RG25 .... 89 F1
  Wooton St Lawrence RG23 . 67 F4
Well House La
  Bramshill RG27 .... 14 C2
  Kings Worthy SO22 .... 175 F3
Well La Long Sutton GU34 . 119 D4
  Lower Froyle GU34 .... 119 D4
Well Meadow RG14 .... 1 C3
Well Rd GU10 .... 97 E3
Well St RG20 .... 22 C3
Wella Rd RG23 .... 68 C1
Wellburn Cl GU17, GU47 .... 34 C4
Weller Dr Arborfield RG40 ... 15 F3
  Camberley GU15 .... 36 A2
Wellesley Cl GU12 .... 77 E4
Wellesley Cl SP10 .... 106 A3
Wellesley Gate **16** GU9 .... 99 D4
Wellesley Gdn GU9 .... 99 D4
Wellesley Rd
  Aldershot GU11 .... 76 B1
  Andover SP10 .... 106 A3
  Frensham GU10 .... 144 C3
Wellhouse Rd GU34 .... 138 C1
Wellington Ave
  Aldershot GU11 .... 76 B1
  Bordon GU35 .... 164 B1
  Fleet GU13 .... 54 A1
Wellington Cl
  Newbury RG14 .... 2 A3
  Sandhurst GU17 .... 35 D4
Wellington Cotts RG20 .... 3 F1
Wellington Cres RG26 .... 9 F1
Wellington Ctr The **10**
  GU12 .... 76 C1
Wellington Ctry Pk RG7 ..... 14 B1
Wellington Gdns **18** GU11 . 76 B1
Wellington La GU9 .... 99 D4
Wellington Rd
  Andover SP10 .... 82 C1
  North Tidworth SP9 .... 79 D3
  Sandhurst GU47 .... 35 D4
Wellington St GU11 .... 76 C1
Wellington Terr
  Basingstoke RG22 .... 68 B4
  Sandhurst GU15 .... 35 D4
Wellmans Meadow RG20 ... 24 B2
Wells Cotts GU10 .... 121 F4
Wells's La RG28 .... 86 A2
Wellspring Ho RG23 .... 68 B1
Wellurn Ct SP10 .... 106 A4
Welsh La RG7 .... 13 F1
Welshman's Rd RG26 .... 10 C3
Wendan Rd RG14 .... 5 E4
Wensley Dr GU33 .... 54 A2
Wentworth Cl Ash GU12 .... 77 F4
  Farnham GU9 .... 99 E3
  Yateley GU46 .... 34 A3
Wentworth Cres GU12 .... 77 F3
Wentworth Ct RG14 .... 1 C1
Wentworth Gdns GU34 .... 139 F2
Wentworth Grange SO22 . 197 F3
Wentworth Lodge RG14 .... 1 B1
Wesley Rd SO23 .... 176 B4
Wesley Wlk **17** RG21 .... 69 D3
Wessex Ave RG29 .... 72 B1
Wessex Cl RG21 .... 69 D2
Wessex Cres RG29 .... 72 B1
Wessex Dr Odiham RG29 .... 72 B1
  Winchester SO22 .... 175 F1
Wessex Gdns SP10 .... 105 F4
Wessex Mews SO20 .... 149 F2
Wessex Rd SP10 .... 99 D1
West Ave GU9 .... 99 D3
West Cl GU9 .... 99 D4
West Cotts GU26 .... 167 D3
West End Rd RG26 .... 9 F1
West End Rd SO22 .... 197 F4
West End Gr GU9 .... 98 C3
West End Inf Sch GU11 ...... 76 B3
West End La SO24 .... 159 D2
West End Terr SO22 .... 197 F4
West Field Rd SO23 .... 154 B3
West Fryerne GU47 .... 34 A4
West Gn GU46 .... 99 D1

West Green Ho RG27 .... 51 F3
West Green Rd RG27 .... 52 A3
West Ham Cl RG22 .... 68 B2
West Ham Est RG23 .... 68 C2
West Ham La
  Basingstoke RG22 .... 68 B3
  Basingstoke, Worting RG22 68 A2
West Ham Pk RG22 .... 68 B3
West Ham Rdbt RG22 .... 68 B2
West Hayes SO22 .... 197 E4
West Heath Rd GU14 .... 55 C2
West Hill Dr SO22 .... 197 F4
West Hill Pk SO22 .... 197 E4
West Hill Rd N SO21 .... 153 F3
West Hill Rd S SO21 .... 153 F2
West Mills RG14 .... 1 B2
West Mills Yd RG14 .... 1 B2
West Pk SP11 .... 81 D3
West Portway SP10 .... 82 B1
West Rd
  Barton Stacey SO21 .... 130 B4
  Camberley GU15 .... 36 A3
  Farnborough GU14 .... 55 F4
West Ring GU10 .... 100 C4
West St Andover SP10 .... 106 A4
  Burghclere RG20 .... 22 B2
  Farnham GU9 .... 98 C1
  New Alresford SO24 .... 179 E3
  Newbury RG14 .... 1 B2
  Odiham RG29 .... 72 B1
  Tadley RG26 .... 27 D4
West Tytherley CE Prim Sch
  SP5 .... 191 D4
West View GU35 .... 164 A1
West View Dr SO20 .... 129 D2
West View Rd GU35 .... 166 A2
West Way SP10 .... 83 E1
Westbourne Rd GU47 .... 35 E4
Westbourne Terr 2 RG14 ... 1 C2
Westbrook Cl RG23 .... 90 A4
Westbrook Ct RG22 .... 68 A2
Westbrook Wlk 7 GU34 .... 139 F2
Westbrooke Cl 15 SP10 ... 106 A4
Westbrooke Rd GU34 .... 139 F2
Westburn Fields GU34 ...... 119 F2
Westbury Ave GU13 .... 75 E4
Westbury Cl GU13 .... 75 E4
Westbury Gdns GU13 .... 75 E4
Westbury Ho 5 SP9 .... 78 C3
Westdeane Ct RG21 .... 68 C2
Westerdale Dr GU16 .... 36 C2
Western Ave
  Andover SP10 .... 106 A4
  Newbury RG14 .... 1 B2
Western CE Prim Sch
  SO22 .... 197 E4
Western Cross RG29 .... 72 B1
Western End RG14 .... 1 B1
Western La RG29 .... 72 B2
Western Rd Aldershot GU11 76 B1
  Andover SP10 .... 106 A4
  Bordon GU35 .... 164 B3
  Liss GU33 .... 207 F2
  Winchester SO22 .... 197 F4
Western Way RG22 .... 68 B2
Westfield Cl RG26 .... 27 D4
Westfield Cres RG18 .... 2 C2
Westfield Ct 9 GU13 .... 54 A1
Westfield Dro SO24 .... 201 D1
Westfield Rd
  Basingstoke RG21 .... 69 E2
  Camberley GU17, GU47 ... 35 F1
  Littleton SO22 .... 175 D3
  Thatcham RG18 .... 2 C3
Westfield Way RG14 .... 1 B1
Westfields Schs GU46 .... 33 F3
Westgate Cl RG23 .... 68 A3
Westgate Ct RG14 .... 1 B1
Westgate Rd RG14 .... 1 B1
Westgate Sec Sch SO22 .... 175 F1
Westglade GU14 .... 55 D2
Westland RG18 .... 2 C2
Westlands Rd RG14 .... 5 F4
Westley Cl SO22 .... 175 E1
Westley Cotts SO21 .... 174 A2
Westley La SO21 .... 174 B2
Westlyn Rd RG26 .... 10 B1
Westmarch Bsns Ctr SP10 . 83 D1
Westmead
  Farnborough GU14 .... 55 F2
  2 Farnham GU9 .... 98 C1
Westmead Dr RG14 .... 5 E4
Westminster Cl
  Basingstoke RG22 .... 91 D4
  Fleet GU13 .... 54 A1
Westminster Gate SO22 .... 197 D3
Westminster Ho 5 RG21 ... 69 D3
Westmorland Dr GU15 .... 36 C2
Weston Cl RG29 .... 94 A3
Weston Colley SO21 .... 132 B2
Weston Down Rd SO21 ..... 132 C3

Weston Ho RG26 .... 29 E1
Weston La SP5 .... 168 A3
Westover Farm SP11 .... 128 A3
Westover Rd GU13 .... 54 B1
Westray Cl RG21 .... 69 E4
Westside Cl RG21 .... 68 B2
Westview Rd SO22 .... 175 D1
Westwood RG14 .... 2 A1
Westwood Rd RG14 .... 6 A4
Westwood View SO24 .... 201 F1
Wetherby Gdns
  Charlton SP10 .... 82 C1
  10 Farnborough GU16 ...... 56 A1
Wetherby Ho GU15 .... 36 A4
Wey Cl Ash GU12 .... 77 F1
  Camberley GU47 .... 35 F3
Wey Hill GU27 .... 189 F3
Wey Lodge Cl GU30 .... 188 A2
Weybank Cl GU9 .... 99 D2
Weybourne Cty Inf Sch
  GU9 .... 99 E3
Weybourne Rd
  Aldershot GU9 .... 99 E3
  Farnham GU9 .... 99 E3
Weybridge Mead GU47 .... 34 B4
Weybrook Ct RG26 .... 47 E2
Weydon Hill Cl GU9 .... 121 F4
Weydon Hill Rd GU9 .... 121 F4
Weydon La GU9 .... 121 F4
Weydon Mill La GU9 .... 98 C1
Weydon Sch GU9 .... 121 E4
Weydown Cl GU27 .... 189 F4
Weydown Ind Est GU27 .... 189 F4
Weydown Rd GU27 .... 189 F4
Weyford Schs GU35 .... 164 C2
Weyhill 5 SP11 .... 81 E1
Weyhill Rd Andover SP10 . 105 E4
  Penton Grafton SP11 .... 81 F1
Weyland Cl GU34 .... 188 A3
Weyside GU11 .... 99 D1
Weysprings GU27 .... 189 F3
Weysprings Cl 3 RG21 ...... 69 E3
Weywood Cl GU9 .... 99 E4
Weywood La GU9 .... 99 E4
Wharf Hill SO23 .... 198 A3
Wharf Mill 2 SO23 .... 198 A3
Wharf Rd Ash GU12 .... 77 F2
  Camberley GU16 .... 56 C3
  Newbury RG14 .... 1 C2
Wharf St RG14 .... 1 C2
Wharf The Newbury RG14 .... 1 C2
  Odiham RG29 .... 72 C2
Wharf Way GU14 .... 54 B3
Wharfenden Way GU14 .... 56 B3
Wheatland Cl SO22 .... 197 E3
Wheatlands La RG14 .... 4 C3
Wheatley La GU34 .... 142 A3
Wheatleys Cl RG25 .... 89 D2
Wheatsheaf La RG14 .... 1 C2
Wheeler Cl RG28 .... 88 B2
Wheeler Hill RG27 .... 51 E1
Wheelwrights La GU26 .... 166 C2
Wherwell Cty Prim Sch
  SP11 .... 128 A4
Whetstone Rd GU14 .... 55 D2
Whin Holt GU13 .... 75 D3
Whinchat Cl RG27 .... 52 B4
Whins Cl GU47 .... 35 F2
Whins Dr GU15 .... 35 F2
Whistler Cl RG21 .... 69 E2
Whistler Gr GU15 .... 35 D3
Whistlers La RG26 .... 10 C1
Whitchurch CE Prim Sch
  RG28 .... 88 B2
Whitchurch Cl GU11 .... 100 A3
Whitchurch Silk Mill RG28 86 B2
Whitchurch Sta RG28 .... 86 B3
White Acres Rd GU16 .... 56 B2
White Ave GU33 .... 186 B1
White Cottage Cl GU9 .... 99 D3
White Farm La SN8 .... 18 A3
White Hart Ho GU15 .... 35 E2
White Hart Ind Est GU15 ... 35 E2
White Hart La
  Basingstoke RG21 .... 69 E2
  Charter Alley RG26 .... 46 C4
White Hart Par GU47 .... 35 E2
White Hill
  Burghclere RG20 .... 22 A1
  Ecchinswell RG20 .... 23 E2
  Kingsclere RG20 .... 44 A3
  Long Sutton RG29 .... 96 A1
White Horse Crossroads
  GU32 .... 205 F3
White Horse La RG40 .... 16 A3
White House Cl RG22 .... 68 A4
White House Gdns GU46 ... 34 A4
White House The SP9 .... 78 C3
White House Wlk GU9 .... 99 D4

White La Greywell RG25 ..... 71 E1
  Hannington RG26 .... 66 B3
  Mapledurwell RG25 .... 71 E1
White Lion Way GU46 .... 34 A4
White Oak Way GU10 .... 105 E2
White Post La GU9 .... 121 F2
White Rd GU15 .... 35 E3
White Rose La GU10 .... 121 F4
White Swan Cl SO21 .... 132 B3
Whitebeam Gdns GU14 ...... 55 D2
Whitebines GU9 .... 99 D1
Whitedown GU34 .... 139 F1
Whitedown Cotts 1 GU34 139 F2
Whitedown La GU34 .... 139 E1
Whitedown Rd RG26 .... 26 B4
Whitedown Special Sch
  GU34 .... 139 F1
Whitehall Dr RG22 .... 15 E4
Whitehall Rd SO20 .... 172 C4
Whitehead Cl RG21 .... 69 F4
Whitehill Cl GU15 .... 36 A4
Whitehill La
  Bishop's Sutton SO24 ..... 179 F2
  New Alresford SO24 .... 179 F2
Whitehill Pk GU35 .... 186 C4
Whitehill Rd GU35 .... 164 C1
Whites Cl RG27 .... 50 C1
Whites Rd GU16 .... 56 B1
Whiteshoot SO20 .... 170 A3
Whiteshute La SO23 .... 197 F3
Whitestones RG22 .... 91 E3
Whitethorn Cl GU12 .... 77 F1
Whitewater CE Prim Sch
  RG27 .... 50 C3
Whitewater Rd RG29 .... 72 B2
Whitewater Rise RG27 .... 51 E1
Whiteways End GU10 .... 100 A2
Whitewood RG24 .... 48 C2
Whitlet Cl GU14 .... 98 C1
Whitley Rd GU46 .... 34 A2
Whitmoor Vale Rd
  Beacon Hill GU26 .... 166 C3
  Grayshott GU26 .... 166 C3
Whitmore Cl GU17 .... 35 D4
Whitmore Gn GU9 .... 99 E3
Whitmore Way GU26 .... 166 B3
Whitmore Vale Rd
  Grayshott GU26 .... 166 C2
  Headley GU26 .... 166 B4
Whitney Rd RG21 .... 69 F4
Whittle Cl RG40 .... 16 B4
Whittle Cres GU14 .... 55 E4
Whittle Rd SP10 .... 82 A1
Whittle Rdbt GU11 .... 55 D1
Whynot La SP10 .... 105 F4
Whyte Ave GU11 .... 100 A4
Wick Hill La RG40 .... 16 C3
Wicket Hill GU10 .... 121 F3
Wickham Cl Alton GU34 ... 139 E1
  Fleet GU13 .... 74 C3
  Tadley RG26 .... 26 C4
Wickham Pl GU13 .... 74 C3
Wickham Rd
  Camberley GU15 .... 36 B4
  Fleet GU13 .... 74 C3
Wicklow Cl RG23 .... 68 A2
Widgeons GU34 .... 139 F3
Widmore Rd RG22 .... 68 B1
Wield Grange SO24 .... 136 C1
Wield Industries SO24 ..... 137 D2
Wield Rd RG14 .... 159 E4
Wights Wlk RG22 .... 91 D4
Wigmore Rd RG26 .... 9 E1
Wilberforce Cl 2 SO22 ..... 197 E3
Wild Briar RG40 .... 16 B4
Wild Herons RG27 .... 51 E1
Wilderness Rd GU16 .... 36 B1
Wildern Cl GU15 .... 36 A2
Wildern SP11 .... 59 F1
Wildmoor La
  Church End RG24 .... 49 E3
  Sherfield on Loddon RG24 49 F4
Wildwood Dr RG26 .... 9 D1
Wildwood Gdns GU46 .... 34 A2
Will Hall Cl GU34 .... 139 E2
Willems Ave GU11 .... 76 B1
William Cobbett Cty Jun Sch
  GU9 .... 99 E3
William Farthing Cl
  GU11 .... 76 C1
William Hitchcock Ho 5
  GU14 .... 55 F4
William Way GU34 .... 140 A3
Williams Way GU13 .... 54 B1
Willian Pl GU26 .... 167 E3
Willington Cl GU15 .... 35 F3
Willis La GU34 .... 160 C1
Wills Mus The RG21 .... 69 D2
Wills Waye SO23 .... 176 B3
Willoughby Cl GU34 .... 139 F2
Willoughby Way RG22 .... 68 B3

Willow Cl Bordon GU35 .... 164 C2
  Liphook GU30 .... 188 A2
  Mytchett GU16 .... 56 B2
  Newbury RG14 .... 1 B1
Willow Cres GU14 .... 55 F4
Willow Ct Ash GU12 .... 77 F4
  Camberley GU15 .... 36 A1
Willow Gdns GU30 .... 188 A2
Willow Gr SP11 .... 105 F4
Willow Ho RG24 .... 49 D2
Willow La GU17 .... 35 D2
Willow Mews 3 SP9 .... 79 D4
Willow Pk GU12 .... 77 E1
Willow Rd
  Bishop's Green RG20 .... 6 B1
  Liss GU33 .... 208 A2
  Tadley RG26 .... 26 C4
Willow Way
  Aldershot GU12 .... 100 B4
  Basingstoke RG22 .... 68 B4
  Farnham GU9 .... 99 D3
  Middle Wallop SO20 ...... 126 A2
  Sherfield on Loddon RG26 29 E1
Willowdale RG40 .... 16 B4
Willowford GU46 .... 34 A3
Willowmead Cl RG14 .... 5 D3
Willows End GU46 .... 34 C4
Willows The Andover SP10 105 F3
  Farnham GU12 .... 100 A2
  North Warnborough RG29 72 B2
Wilmot Way
  Basingstoke RG22 .... 68 B3
  Camberley GU16 .... 36 B2
Wilmot Wlk RG14 .... 5 D3
Wilsom Rd GU34 .... 140 A2
Wilson Cl Alton GU34 .... 140 A2
  Middle Wallop SO20 ...... 126 A2
Wilson Ho 6 SP9 .... 78 C4
Wilson Rd Aldershot GU12 . 77 D1
  Farnborough GU14 .... 55 F3
Wilton Cl RG23 .... 68 C2
Wilton Pl RG23 .... 68 C2
Wilton Rd GU47 .... 35 F2
Wilton Terr SP9 .... 101 F4
Wimborne Ho GU14 .... 56 A1
Wimbushes RG40 .... 16 A3
Wincanton Cl GU34 .... 140 A1
Winchcombe Cl GU13 .... 75 D4
Winchcombe Cty Schs RG14 1 C2
Winchcombe Rd
  2 Basingstoke RG24 ...... 69 D2
  Newbury RG14 .... 1 C1
Winchester Coll (New Hall)
  SO23 .... 198 A3
Winchester College SO22 . 197 F3
Winchester Gdns SP10 .... 106 A3
Winchester Hill SO21 .... 131 E2
Winchester Ho 9 SP9 .... 78 C3
Winchester Rd
  Alton GU34 .... 161 E4
  Andover SP10 .... 106 A2
  Ash GU12 .... 77 F2
  Basingstoke RG22 .... 91 D4
  Chawton GU34 .... 161 E4
  Four Marks GU34 .... 160 B2
  Frensham GU10 .... 144 C4
  Goodworth Clatford SP10 106 A2
  King's Somborne SO20 ... 172 A2
  Kingsclere RG20 .... 44 B4
  Micheldever SO21 .... 133 D1
  New Alresford SO24 .... 179 D3
  Upper Clatford SP10, SP11 106 A2
  Wherwell SP11 .... 106 A2
  Whitchurch RG28 .... 86 B2
Winchester Road Rdbt
  RG23 .... 68 C2
Winchester Sch of Art
  SO23 .... 198 A4
Winchester St
  18 Andover SP11 .... 106 A4
  12 Basingstoke RG24 ..... 69 D2
  Chilbolton SO20 .... 129 D3
  Farnborough GU12 .... 77 D4
  Overton RG25 .... 88 A4
  Whitchurch RG28 .... 86 B2
Winchester Sta SO22 .... 197 F4
Winchester Way GU15 .... 35 D3
Winchfield Ct RG27 .... 53 D1
Winchfield Gdns RG26 ...... 27 D4
Winchfield Hurst RG27 ...... 52 C1
Winchfield Sta RG27 .... 52 B1
Windermere Ave RG22 ...... 68 A1
Windermere Cl GU14 .... 55 E2
Windermere Ct GU12 .... 77 E2
Windermere Gdns SO24 .. 179 E2
Windermere Rd GU35 ...... 164 B3
Windermere Way
  Farnham GU9 .... 98 C3
  Thatcham RG19 .... 2 C2

Winding Wood Dr GU16 ..... 36 C2
Windmill Cnr RG7 .... 11 F3
Windmill Ct
  4 Aldershot GU12 .... 77 D1
  Mortimer RG26 .... 11 F3
Windmill Dr GU35 .... 165 F3
Windmill Fields
  East Worldham GU34 ...... 141 D1
  Four Marks GU34 .... 160 B2
Windmill Hill GU34 .... 140 A1
  Hurstbourne Tarrant SP11 60 B4
Windmill Rd
  Aldershot GU14 .... 77 D1
  Mortimer RG7 .... 11 F3
Windrush Cl 16 RG21 .... 69 E3
Windrush Hts GU46 .... 34 C4
Windsor Cl GU34 .... 139 E2
Windsor Cres GU9 .... 98 C3
Windsor Ct Camberley GU12 36 A2
  7 Fleet GU13 .... 54 A1
Windsor Gdns Ash GU12 ... 77 D1
  Basingstoke RG22 .... 91 D3
Windsor Ho 18 SO23 .... 198 A4
Windsor Pk GU34 .... 159 F1
Windsor Rd Andover SP10 . 105 F4
  Farnborough GU16 .... 56 A1
  Lindford GU35 .... 164 C3
  Medstead GU34 .... 160 A2
  New Alresford SO24 .... 179 E2
Windsor Ride
  Sandhurst GU17 .... 35 F4
  Wokingham RG40 .... 16 C4
Windsor Rise RG14 .... 6 A4
Windsor Way
  Aldershot GU11 .... 76 C1
  Camberley GU14 .... 56 B4
Windsor Wlk GU35 .... 164 C3
Wingate Cl GU11 .... 76 B1
Wings Cl GU9 .... 98 C4
Wings Rd GU9 .... 98 C3
Winklebury Ctr RG21 .... 68 B3
Winklebury Schs RG22 ...... 68 B3
Winklebury Way RG23 .... 68 B3
Winkworth La RG26 .... 10 A1
Winkworth Pl GU9 .... 98 C2
Winnall End 9 SO23 .... 198 A3
Winnall Cl SO23 .... 176 B1
Winnall Manor Rd SO23 .. 198 A4
Winnall Prim Sch SO23 ... 198 A4
Winnall Trad Est SO23 .... 198 B4
Winnall Valley Rd SO23 ... 198 B4
Winslade La RG25 .... 115 E4
Winslade Rd SO22 .... 175 E2
Winston Ave RG26 .... 27 D3
Winston Cl GU16 .... 56 B3
Winston Rise GU34 .... 160 A2
Winston Way RG10 .... 2 B2
Winston Wlk GU10 .... 122 A3
Winterbourne Ho RG22 ..... 68 B1
Winterbourne Wlk GU14 .... 56 B4
Winterdyne Mews SP10 .... 106 A4
Winterthur Way RG21 .... 69 D3
Winterton Dr RG14 .... 1 A3
Winton Chase SP10 .... 106 B4
Winton Cl SP9 .... 78 C2
Winton Cres GU46 .... 34 A3
Winton Hill SO20 .... 150 A2
Winton Rd
  24 Aldershot GU11 .... 76 C1
  Farnham GU9 .... 99 D2
  Winton Sch SP10 .... 106 B4
Winton Sq RG21, RG25 ..... 69 D2
Wiremead La Amport SP11 103 F4
  Thruxton SP11 .... 103 F4
Wishanger La GU10 .... 143 F1
Wishmoor Cl GU15 .... 36 B4
Wishmoor Rd GU15 .... 36 B4
Wisley Gdns GU14 .... 55 D1
Wisley Rd SP10 .... 105 F4
Wistaria Cl SP10 .... 105 F4
Wistaria La GU46 .... 34 A3
Wistaria Dr GU35 .... 164 B1
Wistaria Mews GU34 .... 140 B3
Witan Cl SP10 .... 83 D2
Wither Rise RG23 .... 67 D1
Witherslack Cl GU35 .... 166 A2
Withes The GU10 .... 97 E3
Withies The SP11 .... 108 A3
Witt Rd SP5 .... 168 A3
Wittcomb Terr GU35 .... 164 B1
Wittmead Rd GU16 .... 56 B2
Wolfe Hill SO24 .... 179 E2
Wivelrod Rd GU34 .... 138 B1
Woburn Ave GU16 .... 56 A2
Woburn Cl GU16 .... 36 C1
Woburn Gdns RG22 .... 68 B2
Wolds The RG23 .... 68 A2

Wolf's La GU34 .... 161 F4
Wolfe CI SO22 .... 197 E3
Wolfe Rd GU12 .... 77 D1
Wolfmere La GU33 .... 186 A1
Wolseley Rd GU11 .... 76 C1
Wolverdene Special Sch
  SP10 .... 106 A4
Wolversdene CI SP10 ...... 106 B4
Wolversdene Gdns SP10 ... 106 B4
Wolversdene Rd SP10 ...... 106 B4
Wolverton La RG26 .... 25 E1
Wolverton Rd
  Ashford Hill RG26 .... 25 F3
  Baughurst RG26 .... 25 F3
Wolvesey Terr **3** SO23 ... 198 A3
Wonston CI SO21 .... 131 E2
Wonston La SO51 .... 131 E1
Wood CI RG21, RG22 .... 91 D3
Wood La Beech Hill RG7 ...... 13 E3
  Bramdean SO24 .... 202 C3
  Farnborough GU14 .... 55 F2
  Fleet GU13 .... 54 B1
  Seale GU12 .... 100 C3
Wood Moor RG40 .... 16 B1
Wood Rd Beacon Hill GU26 167 D3
  Camberley GU15 .... 35 F1
  Farnham GU9 .... 99 D4
Wood St GU12 .... 77 F3
Woodbarn The GU9 .... 99 D1
Woodbine CI GU17 .... 35 D4
Woodbine La RG14 .... 5 E1
Woodbourne GU9 .... 99 E4
Woodbourne CI Liss GU33 208 A2
  Yateley GU47 .... 34 A3
Woodbridge Dr GU15 .... 36 A4
Woodbridge Rd GU46 .... 34 C3
Woodbury Rd RG22 .... 91 D3
Woodcock CI SP9 .... 78 C3
Woodcot Gdns GU14 .... 55 D2
Woodcote Cotts SO24 ...... 202 B2
Woodcote Gn GU13 .... 74 B4
Woodcote Rd SN8 .... 18 A4
Woodcott Ho RG26 .... 26 C4
Woodcott Terr GU10 .... 100 A4
Woodcut Rd GU10 .... 121 E3
Woodend Camberley GU15 .. 36 C4
  Farnborough GU16 .... 56 A2
Woodfield GU35 .... 142 A1
Woodfield Cotts GU32 ...... 206 A2
Woodfield Dr SO22 .... 197 D3
Woodgarston Dr RG22 .... 91 D3
Woodgate GU13 .... 54 B2
Woodgreen Rd SO22 .... 175 E2

Woodhouse La RG7 .... 8 B1
Woodland Dr Bramley RG26 . 29 D1
  Farnham GU10 .... 121 F3
Woodland Rise GU13 .... 74 C3
Woodlands Andover SP10 .. 106 B4
  Chineham RG24 .... 49 D2
  Farnham GU10 .... 100 A2
  Fleet GU13 .... 53 F1
  Highclere RG20 .... 21 F4
  Overton RG25 .... 88 A4
  Yateley GU46 .... 34 A2
Woodlands Ave GU9 .... 99 E4
Woodlands Bsns Village
  RG21 .... 69 E3
Woodlands CI Ash GU12 .... 77 F3
  Farnborough GU47 .... 35 E1
Woodlands Ct **18** SO23 ... 176 A1
Woodlands La
  Haslemere GU27 .... 189 E4
  Liss GU33 .... 208 A2
Woodlands Rd
  Baughurst RG26 .... 9 D1
  Camberley GU15 .... 35 F3
  Farnborough GU14 .... 55 D3
Woodlands The
  Bordon GU35 .... 186 B4
  Kings Worthy SO23 .... 176 B3
Woodlands Way SP10 ...... 106 B4
Woodlands Wlk GU47 .... 35 E1
Woodlane CI SO24 .... 202 B3
Woodlea CI SO22 .... 175 F1
Woodlea Prim Sch GU35 .. 164 B1
Woodleigh GU13 .... 75 D4
Woodleys RG20 .... 23 E2
Woodman CI SO21 .... 174 B1
Woodman La SO21 .... 174 B1
Woodmanfield RG25 .... 94 B3
Woodmere Croft RG23 ...... 90 C4
Woodpecker CI
  Basingstoke RG23 .... 90 C4
  Bordon GU35 .... 164 B1
  Ewshot GU9 .... 98 A4
Woodpecker Dr SO22 ...... 175 E1
Woodpeckers **1** SP10 ... 106 A4
Woodroffe Dr RG22 .... 68 B1
Woodruff CI GU35 .... 186 B4
Woods La RG25 .... 91 F4
Woodside Blackwater GU17 . 35 D2
  Farnborough GU14 .... 55 F4
  Hawley GU15 .... 35 D2
  Newbury RG14 .... 5 D4
  Sandhurst GU17 .... 35 E4
Woodside CI Bordon GU35 164 B2
  Mortimer RG7 .... 11 F3
  Wokingham RG40 .... 16 B4
Woodside Cres GU35 ...... 164 B2

Woodside Gdns
  Chineham RG24 .... 49 D2
  Fleet GU13 .... 54 B1
Woodside La GU34 .... 161 D2
Woodside Pk GU35 .... 164 B2
Woodside Rd
  Farnborough GU11 .... 76 B4
  Farnham GU9 .... 99 E4
Woodstock Mead RG22 ...... 91 D3
Woodstocks GU16 .... 56 A3
Woodville CI
  Blackwater GU46 .... 34 C3
  Chineham RG24 .... 48 C1
Woodville Rise RG24 .... 48 C1
Woodway GU17 .... 35 F3
Wool Gr SP10 .... 106 B4
Wooland Ct GU13 .... 74 C2
Wooldridge Cres RG29 ...... 95 E4
Woolfield La GU34 .... 205 D2
Woolford CI **1** SO22 ...... 197 E3
Woolford Way RG22 .... 68 B3
Woollards Rd GU12 .... 77 F2
Woolley Sq SP10 .... 83 E2
Woolmead Ct GU9 .... 99 D2
Woolmead Rd GU9 .... 99 D2
Woolmead The GU9 .... 99 D2
Woolmead Wlk GU9 .... 99 D2
Woolmer Hill Rd GU27 .... 189 D4
Woolmer Hill Sch GU27 ... 189 D4
Woolmer La GU30 .... 188 A4
Woolmer Rd GU33 .... 186 A2
Woolmer St GU33 .... 186 A2
Woolmer Trad Est GU35 .. 164 B2
Woolmer View GU26 ...... 167 D2
Woolton Hill CE Schs RG20 21 D4
  Wonder Lodge Gdns RG20 .. 4 B1
Wootey Schs GU34 .... 139 F3
Wooteys Way GU34 .... 139 F3
Worcester Ave RG25 .... 91 D4
Worcester CI GU14 .... 55 F4
Wordsworth Ave GU46 ...... 33 F2
Wordsworth CI
  Basingstoke RG21 .... 69 E4
  Winchester SO22 .... 197 E4
Worldham Hill GU34 .... 141 D1
Worrell Sq SP10 .... 83 E2
Worsley Rd GU14 .... 56 B4
Worthy La SO23 .... 175 F1
Worthy Rd SO23 .... 176 A1
Worting Inf Sch RG22 ...... 68 A2
Worting Jun Sch RG22 ...... 68 A2
Worting Rd
  Basingstoke RG23 .... 68 A2
Basingstoke
  RG21, RG22, RG23 .... 68 C2
Worting Road Rdbt RG22 ... 68 B2

Wote St RG21 .... 69 D2
Wouldham CI SP9 .... 79 E4
Wrecclesham Hill GU10 ... 121 E3
Wrecclesham Rd GU10 ..... 121 E4
Wrekin CI RG21, RG22, RG23 68 A2
Wren CI Alton GU34 .... 140 A3
  Winchester SO22 .... 197 E3
  Yateley GU46 .... 33 F3
Wren Ct GU12 .... 77 F2
Wren Way GU14 .... 55 E4
Wrights CI SO21 .... 153 E2
Wrights Way SO21 .... 153 E2
Wychwood CI GU12 .... 77 E1
Wychwood Pl GU16 .... 36 C4
Wyck La Binsted GU34 .... 141 F3
  Binsted, Wyck GU34 ...... 141 D2
  East Worldham GU34 ..... 141 D2
Wye Ct **55** SP10 .... 83 E1
Wykeham Ct RG29 .... 95 E4
Wykeham Dr
  RG21, RG22, RG23 .... 68 A2
Wykeham Ho GU12 .... 77 D4
Wykeham Ind Est The
  SO23 .... 176 B2
Wykeham Pl SO22 .... 197 E3
Wykeham Rd GU9 .... 99 D2
Wykwood GU30 .... 188 A2
Wyld Green La GU33 ...... 208 A3
Wylye Rd SP9 .... 78 C4
Wymering Ct GU14 .... 56 A2
Wyndham CI GU17 .... 34 A4
Wyndham Rd
  Andover SP10 .... 105 F3
  Newbury RG14 .... 2 A3
Wyndham St GU12 .... 77 D1
Wynfields GU16 .... 56 B2
Wynne Gdns GU13 .... 75 D3

Yarnhams CI GU34 .... 160 A1
Yateley Common (Ctry Pk)
  GU46 .... 34 B2
Yateley Inds GU17 .... 34 A4
Yateley Inf Sch GU46 .... 34 A3
Yateley Manor Prep Sch
  GU46 .... 34 A3
Yateley Rd GU47 .... 34 B4
Yateley Sch GU46 .... 34 A3
Yates Copse RG14 .... 2 B3
Yatesbury CI GU10 .... 121 E4
Yellowhammers GU34 ..... 139 F3
Yeomans GU46 .... 33 E4
Yeomans CI Ash GU10 .... 100 B4
  Farnborough GU14 .... 55 F3
Yeomans La
  Burghclere RG14 .... 5 F1
  Liphook GU30 .... 187 F2

Yeomans Pl GU35 .... 165 E3
Yeomans Way GU15 .... 36 B3
Yeosfield RG7 .... 7 B4
Yeovil CI GU14 .... 56 A1
Yeovil Rd GU14 .... 56 B1
Yetminster Rd GU16 .... 56 A1
Yew CI RG20 .... 24 C1
Yew Gate RG14 .... 1 B3
Yew Tree CI Bramley RG26 .. 29 D1
  Farnborough GU14 .... 55 D2
  Goodworth Clatford SP11 106 A1
  Oakley RG22 .... 90 A4
Yew Tree La
  North Waltham RG25 ...... 89 F1
  West Tytherley SP5 .... 169 D2
Yew Tree Pl GU33 .... 208 A2
Yew Tree Wlk GU16 .... 36 B1
Yolland CI GU9 .... 99 D4
York CI Basingstoke RG22 ... 91 D4
  Bordon GU35 .... 164 B1
  Newbury RG14 .... 1 C1
York Cres GU11 .... 76 B1
York Ct **4** SP10 .... 83 D2
York Ho **17** Aldershot GU11 . 76 B1
  Basingstoke RG23 .... 68 C3
  32 Winchester SO23 ... 176 A1
York La RG27 .... 52 B3
York Mews GU34 .... 140 A2
York Pl GU15 .... 36 A4
York Rd Aldershot GU14 .... 76 B1
  Ash GU12 .... 77 F2
  Farnborough GU14 .... 56 A1
  Farnham GU9 .... 99 D1
  Newbury RG14 .... 1 C1
York Terrace La GU15 .... 35 F3
York Town Ind Est GU15 ... 35 F2
York Way GU17 .... 34 C4
Yorktown Rd GU15 .... 35 E4
Yorkwood GU33 .... 207 F2
Youlden CI GU15 .... 36 C3
Youlden Dr GU16 .... 36 C3
Young Cres RG19 .... 6 A4
Young's Ind Est RG26 .... 9 E2
Youngs Dr GU12 .... 77 E1
Youngs Paddock SP5 ...... 168 A3
Youngs Rd GU34 .... 139 F2

Zephyr Ho **13** RG26 .... 9 E1
Zinnia CI RG22 .... 91 D4
Zion Rd SP11 .... 124 B3
Zodiac Ho **14** RG26 .... 9 E1
Zouch Ave SP9 .... 78 C4
Zouch CI SP9 .... 78 C4
Zouch Farm Rd SP9 .... 78 C4
Zouch Mkt SP9 .... 78 B4
Zouch Prim Sch SP9 .... 78 B4

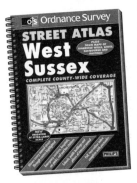

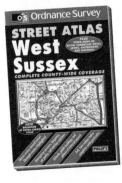

All Street Atlases contain Ordnance Survey mapping and provide the perfect solution for the driver who needs comprehensive, detailed regional mapping in a choice of compact and easy-to-use formats. They are indispensable and are ideal for use in the car, the home or the office.

The series is available from all good bookshops or by mail order direct from the publisher. Before placing your order, please check by telephone that the complete range of titles are available. Payment can be made in the following ways:

By phone Phone your order through on our special Credit Card Hotline on 01933 443863 (Fax: 01933 443849). Speak to our customer service team during office hours (9am to 5pm) or leave a message on the answering machine, quoting your full credit card number plus expiry date and your full name and address.

By post Simply fill out the order form (you may photocopy it) and send it to: **Philip's Direct, 27 Sanders Road, Wellingborough, Northants** NN8 4NL.

COLOUR EDITIONS				
	HARDBACK	SPIRAL	POCKET	
	Quantity @ £10.99 each	Quantity @ £8.99 each	Quantity @ £4.99 each	£ Total
BERKSHIRE	☐ 0 540 06170 0	☐ 0 540 06172 7	☐ 0 540 06173 5	➤
	Quantity @ £10.99 each	Quantity @ £8.99 each	Quantity @ £3.99 each	£ Total
MERSEYSIDE	☐ 0 540 06480 7	☐ 0 540 06481 5	☐ 0 540 06482 3	➤
	Quantity @ £12.99 each	Quantity @ £8.99 each	Quantity @ £4.99 each	£ Total
SURREY	☐ 0 540 06435 1	☐ 0 540 06436 X	☐ 0 540 06438 6	➤
	Quantity @ £12.99 each	Quantity @ £9.99 each	Quantity @ £4.99 each	£ Total
BUCKINGHAMSHIRE	☐ 0 540 07466 7	☐ 0 540 07467 5	☐ 0 540 07468 3	➤
DURHAM	☐ 0 540 06365 7	☐ 0 540 06366 5	☐ 0 540 06367 3	➤
HERTFORDSHIRE	☐ 0 540 06174 3	☐ 0 540 06175 1	☐ 0 540 06176 X	➤
EAST KENT	☐ 0 540 07483 7	☐ 0 540 07276 1	☐ 0 540 07287 7	➤
WEST KENT	☐ 0 540 07366 0	☐ 0 540 07367 9	☐ 0 540 07369 5	➤
GREATER MANCHESTER	☐ 0 540 06485 8	☐ 0 540 06486 6	☐ 0 540 06487 4	➤
EAST SUSSEX	☐ 0 540 07306 7	☐ 0 540 07307 5	☐ 0 540 07312 1	➤
WEST SUSSEX	☐ 0 540 07319 9	☐ 0 540 07323 7	☐ 0 540 07327 X	➤
TYNE AND WEAR	☐ 0 540 06370 3	☐ 0 540 06371 1	☐ 0 540 06372 X	➤
SOUTH YORKSHIRE	☐ 0 540 06330 4	☐ 0 540 06331 2	☐ 0 540 06332 0	➤
WEST YORKSHIRE	☐ 0 540 06329 0	☐ 0 540 06327 4	☐ 0 540 06328 2	➤
	Quantity @ £12.99 each	Quantity @ £9.99 each	Quantity @ £5.99 each	£ Total
NORTH HAMPSHIRE	☐ 0 540 07471 3	☐ 0 540 07472 1	☐ 0 540 07473 X	➤

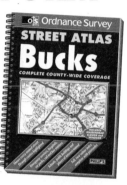

COLOUR EDITIONS

	HARDBACK	SPIRAL	POCKET	£ Total
	Quantity @ £12.99 each	Quantity @ £9.99 each	Quantity @ £5.99 each	
SOUTH HAMPSHIRE	☐ 0 540 07476 4	☐ 0 540 07477 2	☐ 0 540 07478 0	➤ ☐
	Quantity @ £14.99 each	Quantity @ £9.99 each	Quantity @ £4.99 each	£ Total
LANCASHIRE	☐ 0 540 06440 8	☐ 0 540 06441 6	☐ 0 540 06443 2	➤ ☐

BLACK AND WHITE EDITIONS

	HARDBACK	SOFTBACK	POCKET	£ Total
	Quantity @ £12.99 each	Quantity @ £9.99 each	Quantity @ £4.99 each	
BRISTOL AND AVON	☐ 0 540 06140 9	☐ 0 540 06141 7	☐ 0 540 06142 5	➤ ☐
CARDIFF, SWANSEA GLAMORGAN	☐ 0 540 06186 7	☐ 0 540 06187 5	☐ 0 540 06207 3	➤ ☐
CHESHIRE	☐ 0 540 06143 3	☐ 0 540 06144 1	☐ 0 540 06145 X	➤ ☐
DERBYSHIRE	☐ 0 540 06137 9	☐ 0 540 06138 7	☐ 0 540 06139 5	➤ ☐
EDINBURGH & East Central Scotland	☐ 0 540 06180 8	☐ 0 540 06181 6	☐ 0 540 06182 4	➤ ☐
EAST ESSEX	☐ 0 540 05848 3	☐ 0 540 05866 1	☐ 0 540 05850 5	➤ ☐
WEST ESSEX	☐ 0 540 05849 1	☐ 0 540 05867 X	☐ 0 540 05851 3	➤ ☐
GLASGOW & West Central Scotland	☐ 0 540 06183 2	☐ 0 540 06184 0	☐ 0 540 06185 9	➤ ☐
NOTTINGHAMSHIRE	☐ 0 540 05858 0	☐ 0 540 05859 9	☐ 0 540 05860 2	➤ ☐
OXFORDSHIRE	☐ 0 540 05986 2	☐ 0 540 05987 0	☐ 0 540 05988 9	➤ ☐
STAFFORDSHIRE	☐ 0 540 06134 4	☐ 0 540 06135 2	☐ 0 540 06136 0	➤ ☐
	Quantity @ £10.99 each	Quantity @ £8.99 each	Quantity @ £4.99 each	£ Total
WARWICKSHIRE	☐ 0 540 05642 1	—	—	➤ ☐

Post to: Philip's Direct, 27 Sanders Road, Wellingborough, Northants, NN8 4NL

◆ Free postage and packing

◆ All available titles will normally be dispatched within 5 working days of receipt of order but please allow up to 28 days for delivery

◆ Please tick this box if you do not wish your name to be used by other carefully selected organisations that may wish to send you information about other products and services

Registered Office: 25 Victoria Street, London SW1H 0EX.

Registered in England number: 3396524

I enclose a cheque / postal order, for a **total** of ☐

made payable to *Reed Book Services,* or please debit my

☐ Access ☐ American Express ☐ Visa ☐ Diners

account by ☐

Account no ☐☐☐☐ ☐☐☐☐ ☐☐☐☐ ☐☐☐☐

Expiry date ☐☐ ☐☐

Signature..

Name..

Address..

....

....

....POSTCODE

ISBN 978-0-483-45762-1
PIBN 11291949

This book is a reproduction of an important historical work. Forgotten Books uses
state-of-the-art technology to digitally reconstruct the work, preserving the original format
whilst repairing imperfections present in the aged copy. In rare cases, an imperfection in
the original, such as a blemish or missing page, may be replicated in our edition. We do,
however, repair the vast majority of imperfections successfully; any imperfections that
remain are intentionally left to preserve the state of such historical works.